# ILLICIT ANTIQUITIES

The One World Archaeology (OWA) series stems from conferences organized by the World Archaeological Congress (WAC), an international non-profit making organization, which provides a forum of debate for anyone who is genuinely interested in or has a concern for the past. All editors and contributors to the OWA series waive any fees that they might normally receive from a publisher. Instead, all royalties from the series are received by the World Archaeological Congress Charitable Company to help the wider work of the World Archaeological Congress. The sale of OWA volumes provides the means for less advantaged colleagues to attend World Archaeological Congress conferences, thereby enabling them to contribute to the development of the academic debate surrounding the study of the past.

The World Archaeological Congress would like to take this opportunity to thank all editors and contributors for helping the development of world archaeology in this way.

D1141576

ONE WORLD ARCHAEOLOGY

Series Editor: (Volumes 1–37): Peter J. Ucko
Academic Series Editors (Volume 38 onwards): Martin Hall and Julian Thomas
Executive Series Editor (Volume 38 onwards): Peter Stone

1. *What is an Animal?*, T. Ingold (ed.)
2. *The Walking Larder: Patterns of domestication, pastoralism and predation*, J. Clutton-Brock
3. *Domination and Resistance*, D. Miller, M.J. Rowlands and C. Tilley (eds)
4. *State and Society: The emergence and development of social hierarchy and political centralization*, J. Gledhill, B. Bender and M.T. Larsen (eds)
5. *Who Needs the Past? Indigenous values and archaeology*, R. Layton (ed.)
6. *The Meaning of Things: Material culture and symbolic expression*, I. Hodder (ed.)
7. *Animals into Art*, H. Morphy (ed.)
8. *Conflict in the Archaeology of Living Traditions*, R. Layton (ed.)
9. *Archaeological Heritage Management in the Modern World*, H.F. Cleere (ed.)
10. *Archaeological Approaches to Cultural Identity*, S.J. Shennan (ed.)
11. *Centre and Periphery: Comparative studies in archaeology*, T.C. Champion (ed.)
12. *The Politics of the Past*, P. Gathercole and D. Lowenthal (eds)
13. *Foraging and Farming: The evolution of plant exploitation*, D.R. Harris and G.C. Hillman (eds)
14. *What's New? A closer look at the process of innovation*, S.E. van der Leeuw and R. Torrence (eds)
15. *Hunters of the Recent Past*, L.B. Davis and B.O.K. Reeves (eds)
16. *Signifying Animals: Human meaning in the natural world*, R.G. Willis (ed.)
17. *The Excluded Past: Archaeology in education*, P.G. Stone and R. MacKenzie (eds)
18. *From the Baltic to the Black Sea: Studies in medieval archaeology*, D. Austin and L. Alcock (eds)
19. *The Origins of Human Behaviour*, R.A. Foley (ed.)
20. *The Archaeology of Africa: Food, metals and towns*, T. Shaw, P. Sinclair, B. Andah and A. Okpoko (eds)
21. *Archaeology and the Information Age: A global perspective*, P. Reilly and S. Rahtz (eds)
22. *Tropical Archaeobotany: Applications and developments*, J.G. Hather (ed.)
23. *Sacred, Sites, Sacred Places*, D.L. Carmichael, J. Hubert, B. Reeves and A. Schanche (eds)
24. *Social Construction of the Past: Representation as power*, G.C. Bond and A. Gilliam (eds)
25. *The Presented Past: Heritage, museums and education*, P.G. Stone and B.L. Molyneaux (eds)
26. *Time, Process and Structural Transformation in Archaeology*, S.E. van der Leeuw and J. McGlade (eds)
27. *Archaeology and Language I: Theoretical and methodological orientations*, R. Blench and M. Spriggs (eds)
28. *Early Human Behaviour in the Global Context*, M. Petraglia and R. Korisettar (eds)
29. *Archaeology and Language II: Archaeological data and linguistic hypotheses*, R. Blench and M. Spriggs (eds)
30. *Archaeology and Anthropology of Landscape: Shaping your landscape*, P.J. Ucko and R. Layton (eds)
31. *The Prehistory of Food: Appetites for Change*, C. Gosden and J.G. Hather (eds)
32. *Historical Archaeology: Back from the edge*, P.P.A. Funari, M. Hall and S. Jones (eds)
33. *Cultural Resource Management in Contemporary Society: Perspectives on managing and presenting the past*, F.P. MacManamon and A. Hatton (eds)
34. *Archaeology and Language III: Artefacts, languages and texts*, R. Blench and M. Spriggs (eds)
35. *Archaeology and Language IV: Language change and cultural transformation*, R. Blench and M. Spriggs (eds)
36. *The Constructed Past: Experimental archaeology, education and the public*, P.G. Stone and P. Planel (eds)
37. *Time and Archaeology*, T. Murray (ed.)
38. *The Archaeology of Difference: Negotiating cross-cultural engagements in Oceania*, R. Torrence and A. Clarke (eds)
39. *The Archaeology of Drylands: Living at the margin*, G. Barker and D. Gilbertson (eds)
40. *Madness, Disability & Social Exclusion: The archaeology & anthropology of 'difference'*, J. Hubert (ed.)
41. *Destruction and Conservation of Cultural Property*, R.L. Layton, P.G. Stone and J. Thomas (eds)
42. *Illicit Antiquities: The theft of culture and the extinction of archaeology*, N. Brodie and K. Walker Tubb (eds)

# ILLICIT ANTIQUITIES
## The theft of culture and the extinction of archaeology

Edited by

Neil Brodie and Kathryn Walker Tubb

London and New York

First published 2002 by Routledge
2 Park Square, Milton Park, Abingdon, Oxfordshire OX14 4RN

Simultaneously published in the USA and Canada
by Routledge
711 Third Avenue, New York, NY 10017

*Routledge is an imprint of the Taylor & Francis Group*

First issued in paperback 2011

Typeset in Bembo by
Florence Production Ltd, Stoodleigh, Devon

*British Library Cataloguing in Publication Data*
A catalogue record for this book is available from the
British Library

*Library of Congress Cataloging in Publication Data*
Illicit antiquities: the theft of culture and the extinction of
archaeology/edited by Neil Brodie and Kathryn Walker Tubb.
     p. cm. – (One world archaeology; 42)
   Papers given at a session of the WAC4 held in Cape Town,
South Africa. Includes bibliographical references and index.
     1. Antiquities—Collection and preservation—Congresses.
2. Antiquities—Collection and preservation—Moral and ethical
aspects—Congresses.   3. Historical sites—Conservation and
restoration—Congresses.   4. Historic sites—Conservation and
restoration—moral and ethical aspects—Congresses.   5.
Cultural property—Protection—Congresses.   6. Cultural
property—Protection (International law)—Congresses.
7. Archaeological thefts—Congresses.
I. Brodie, Neil.   II. Tubb, Kathryn Walker.   III. Series.
CC135.I36 2001
363.6'9—dc21  2001019938

ISBN 978-0-415-23388-0 (hbk)
ISBN 978-0-415-51077-6 (pbk)

# Contents

List of illustrations                                                    vii
List of contributors                                                      ix
Series editors' foreword                                                   x
Preface and acknowledgements                                              xi

Introduction                                                               1
Neil Brodie

1   Greek vases for sale: some statistical evidence                       23
    Vinnie Nørskov

2   Walking a fine line: promoting the past without selling it            38
    Paula Lazrus

3   The concept of cultural protection in times of armed conflict: from
    the crusades to the new millennium                                    43
    Patrick J. Boylan

4   Law and the underwater cultural heritage: a question of
    balancing interests                                                  109
    Sarah Dromgoole

5   Negotiating the future of the underwater cultural heritage           137
    Patrick J. O'Keefe

6   Perceptions of marine artefact conservation and their relationship
    to destruction and theft                                             162
    Amanda Sutherland

7   Metal detecting in Britain: catastrophe or compromise?               179
    Peter V. Addyman and Neil Brodie

8   Britannia waives the rules? The licensing of archaeological material
    for export from the UK                                               185
    Neil Brodie

9    *Mexico's archaeological heritage: a convergence and confrontation of interests*     205
     Enrique Nalda

10   *What's going on around the corner? Illegal trade of art and antiquities in Argentina*     228
     Daniel Schávelzon

11   *Looting graves/buying and selling artefacts: facing reality in the US*     235
     Hester A. Davis

12   *Reducing incentives for illicit trade in antiquities: the US implementation of the 1970 UNESCO Convention*     241
     Susan Keech McIntosh

13   *The rape of Mali's only resource*     250
     Téréba Togola

14   *Dealing with the dealers and tomb robbers: the realities of the archaeology of the Ghor es-Safi in Jordan*     257
     Konstantinos D. Politis

15   *Plunder of cultural and art treasures – the Indian experience*     268
     S.K. Pachauri

16   *Point, counterpoint*     280
     Kathryn Walker Tubb

     *Index*     301

# Illustrations

## FIGURES

1.1 Total number of vases offered for sale, 1954–98     25

1.2 Number of vases offered for sale 1954–98 related to the
number of catalogues used in the analysis     26

1.3 Percentage of vases offered on the market more than once,
1963–98     26

1.4 Provenance of vases offered on the market, 1954–98     27

1.5 Provenance of vases offered on the market, 1989–98     28

1.6 Distribution of five selected groups of vases, 1954–98
(total numbers)     29

1.7 Distribution of five selected groups of vases, 1954–98
(percentage)     30

1.8 Relationship between the number of Attic black-figure
and Attic red-figure vases, 1954–98     31

1.9 The acquisitions of eight museums compared with the
number of vases offered for sale on the market, divided
into gifts and purchases     32

1.10 Acquisitions of Ashmolean Museum of Art and Archaeology,
1945–94     33

8.1 Export licensing requirements for archaeological material
not of UK origin and not of limited interest     195

9.1 Looters' trench in one of the buildings of Plaza Yaxná in
Kohunlich     216

9.2 Looters' trench in one of the buildings of a site in the south
of Quintana Roo, Mexico     218

9.3 Monochrome ceramic left by looters next to a Maya tomb
in a site in the south of Quintana Roo     219

9.4 Teotihuacán. Entrance leading to the Pyramid of the Sun,
lined up with stores selling souvenirs to the tourists     220

9.5 Teotihuacán. Entrance leading to the Quetzalpapalotl palace,
lined with stores selling souvenirs to the tourists     221

9.6    Entrance to the site of Tulum, lined with stores selling
       souvenirs to tourists                                           222
9.7    Photo of Tulum taken towards its entrance                      222
11.1   A 'pothunter' in north-east Arkansas uses a metal probe to
       locate more, 1970                                              236
11.2   A 'pothunter' at work in north-east Arkansas, 1970             237
11.3   A headpot from the late prehistoric Bradley site in north-east
       Arkansas                                                       238
12.1   At least 200 looters dug at this site near Thial between
       September 1989 and April 1990                                  244
12.2   Hired by an antiquities dealer from Mopti, looters hack
       away at ancient settlements 35 miles north-west of Jenne       247
14.1   Bulldozed remains of the medieval and Byzantine buildings
       of the ancient city of Zoar                                    259
14.2   The cemetery of an-Naq' showing looted graves                  260
14.3   Villagers looting an-Naq'                                      260
14.4   Bracelets and glass vessels cushioned in a shell-suit jacket
       during looting                                                 261
14.5   Looted small finds offered for sale through the author's
       car window                                                     261
14.6   Aerial photograph showing the cemetery of an-Naq' in
       1992 before the onset of large-scale looting                   265
14.7   Aerial photograph showing the cemetery of an-Naq' in
       1999. The largely undisturbed surface of 1992 is pockmarked
       by looted graves                                               266

## TABLES

8.1    Total value in thousands of pounds of exports of cultural
       material                                                       191
8.2    Licences granted for archaeological material of UK origin.
       The bar indicates the introduction of the EC licence in
       1993                                                           193
8.3    Number of lots for sale by auction requiring a licence for
       export                                                         196
8.4    Total number of cultural objects (in the UK for less than
       50 years) licensed for export                                  196
8.5    Value in thousands of pounds of cultural material licensed
       (DCMS) and exported (DTI)                                      198
8.6    Annual value of exports from the UK to the US of SITC
       category 896.50                                                199

# Contributors

*Peter V. Addyman*, York Archaeological Trust, Cromwell House, 13 Ogleforth, York, YO1 7FG, UK.

*Patrick J. Boylan*, Department of Arts Policy and Management, City University, Frobisher Crescent, London EC2, UK.

*Neil Brodie*, McDonald Institute for Archaeological Research, Downing Street, Cambridge, CB2 3ER, UK.

*Hester A. Davis*, Arkansas Archaeological Survey, Box 1249, Fayetteville, AR 72702, USA.

*Sarah Dromgoole*, Faculty of Law, University of Leicester, LE1 7RH, UK.

*Paula Lazrus*, Social Sciences, New School University, New York, NY 10003, USA.

*Susan Keech McIntosh*, Department of Anthropology, Rice University, 6100 Main Street, Houston, Texas 77005–1892, USA.

*Enrique Nalda*, Instituto Nacional de Antropologia e Historia Mexico, Cordoba 45, Colonia Roma, Mexico D.F.

*Vinnie Nørskov*, Department of Classical Archaeology, University of Aarhus, DK-8000, Aarhus, Denmark.

*Patrick J. O'Keefe*, 6 Villa des Entrepreneurs, 75015 Paris, France.

*S.K. Pachauri*, Ministry of Home Affairs, Vigyan Bhawan Annexe, New Delhi 110 011, India.

*Konstantinos D. Politis*, Department of Medieval and Later Antiquities, British Museum, Great Russell Street, London WC1B 3DG, UK.

*Daniel Schávelzon*, Centro de Arqueologia Urbana, Universidad de Buenos Aires, Ciudad Universitaria, 1428 Buenos Aires, Argentina.

*Amanda Sutherland*, Devon and Cornwall Constabulary Headquarters, Middlemoor, Exeter, EX4 7HQ, UK.

*Téréba Togola*, Directeur National des Arts et de la Culture, BP 91, Bamako, Mali.

*Kathryn Walker Tubb*, Institute of Archaeology, 31–34 Gordon Square, London, WC1H 0PY, UK.

# Foreword

One World Archaeology is dedicated to exploring new themes, theories and applications in archaeology from around the world. The series of edited volumes began with contributions that were either part of the inaugural meeting of the World Archaeological Congress in Southampton, UK in 1986 or were commissioned specifically immediately after the meeting – frequently from participants who were inspired to make their own contributions. Since then the World Archaeological Congress has held three further major international congresses in Barquisimeto, Venezuela (1990), New Delhi, India (1994), and Cape Town, South Africa (1999) and a series of more specialized 'inter-congresses' focusing on *Archaeological ethics and the treatment of the dead* (Vermillion, US, 1989), *Urban origins in Africa* (Mombassa, Kenya, 1993), and *The destruction and restoration of cultural heritage* (Brač, Croatia, 1998). In each case these meetings have attracted a wealth of original and often inspiring work from many countries.

The result has been a set of richly varied volumes that are at the cutting edge of (frequently multidisciplinary) new work. They aim to provide a breadth of perspective that charts the many and varied directions that contemporary archaeology is taking.

As series editors we should like to thank all editors and contributors for their hard work in producing these books. We should also like to express our thanks to Peter Ucko, inspiration behind both the World Archaeological Congress and the One World Archaeology series. Without him none of this would have happened.

Martin Hall, Cape Town, South Africa
Peter Stone, Newcastle, UK
Julian Thomas, Manchester, UK
June 2000

# Preface and acknowledgements

The seeds of this volume were first sown at the 1998 WAC Inter-congress on the Destruction and Conservation of Cultural Heritage, which was held in Brač, Croatia. Interest generated by two papers given by the editors which examined the trade in illicit antiquities (and subsequently combined for publication: Tubb and Brodie 2001) resulted in the decision to devote an entire session to the subject at WAC-4 held in Cape Town, South Africa.

This session, entitled 'Illicit Antiquities: Destruction and Response', was intended to expose the current status of the various threats posed to the international archaeological heritage and to attempt to understand the many facets of the looting–trade continuum. At the same time, it addressed concerns raised about the legitimacy of trying to prevent poor local inhabitants from exploiting archaeology to ameliorate the economic hardship of their lives.

The core of this book consists of the papers given at the session. It has been augmented by further contributions solicited by the editors to incorporate areas such as the protection of the underwater heritage, heritage under threat in areas of conflict and the role of contemporary collecting, and it includes more examples from nations around the globe. Representation is still far from comprehensive since no country's cultural heritage is free from the depredations of thieves and looters.

It is clear that protective responses continue to be inadequate. The pace of public and professional education and the conversion of sites into longer-term resources are easily being outstripped by the destruction of the world's archaeology. Knowledge of past cultures is being extinguished and solutions must be sought if anything is to be salvaged. It is hoped that readers will direct their ingenuity and energies to such endeavours.

At the concluding plenary session of the Congress the following resolution was moved and agreed:

> Believing that the world's cultural heritage cannot sustain the losses resulting from illicit excavation and export of archaeological material.

Taking into consideration the resolution adopted by the Pan-African Congress of Prehistory and Related Studies in June 1995 at Harare, Zimbabwe; the resolution adopted by the UK Standing Conference on Portable Antiquities on 13 November 1997; the resolution adopted at the Annual Meeting of the European Association of Archaeologists on 26 September 1998 at Gothenburg, Sweden; resolution no. 4 adopted by the 19th Assembly of ICOM on 16 October in Melbourne, Australia; and resolution no. 5 adopted by the participants at the international conference 'Art, Antiquity and the Law: Preserving our Global Cultural Heritage' on 1 November 1998 at Rutgers University in New Brunswick, New Jersey, USA.

Recognizing that international cooperation is essential for the protection of the world's cultural heritage.

World Archaeological Congress 4 held in Cape Town, South Africa on Thursday 14th January 1999 urges all nations that have not already done so to become party to the relevant international conventions, including the Hague Convention for the Protection of Cultural Property in the event of Armed Conflict, 1954.

UNESCO Convention on the Means of Prohibiting and Preventing the Illegal Import, Export and Transfer of Ownership of Cultural Property, 1970

UNIDROIT Convention on Stolen or Illegally Exported Cultural Objects, 1995.

Finally, the editors are extremely grateful to all the contributors to this volume and would also like to thank the McDonald Institute, University of Cambridge, for making possible the attendance of Neil Brodie, Dino Politis, Téréba Togola and Peter Addyman and the Institute of Archaeology, UCL, for making possible the attendance of Kathryn Walker Tubb. Neil Brodie acknowledges the continued enthusiasm of Colin Renfrew, Jenny Doole, Peter Watson and Chris Scarre, and Kathryn Walker Tubb would like to thank Peter Ucko, Suzanne Ryder, Harriet Harrison and Jonathan Tubb for all their support. Manuel Arroyo-Kalin translated into English the original Spanish texts of Chapters 9 and 10.

## REFERENCE

Tubb, K.W. and N.J. Brodie. 2001. The antiquities trade in the United Kingdom. In *Destruction and Conservation of Cultural Property*. R.L. Layton, P.G. Stone and J. Thomas (eds). London: Routledge.

# Introduction

## NEIL BRODIE

## INTRODUCTION

This is a book about the recent plunder of archaeological sites and cultural institutions, much of which is thought to be commercially motivated. Concerns raised by this plunder during the late 1960s led to the drafting of the Convention on the Means of Prohibiting and Preventing the Illicit Import, Export and Transfer of Ownership of Cultural Property, which was adopted by UNESCO in 1970 (Coggins 1969; Meyer 1973), but since then the situation has grown out of all control (Leyten 1995; Tubb 1995; Schmidt and McIntosh 1996; Vitelli 1996a; O'Keefe 1997; Messenger 1999; Brodie et al. 2000; Renfrew 2000). This seems to be for two reasons. First, the means of destruction have become much more powerful. For millennia, the tools of the tomb robbing trade consisted of little more than simple digging implements and probing rods, but they have been joined over the past couple of decades by bulldozers and mechanical diggers, dynamite, metal detectors, power saws and drills and, underwater, propwash deflectors. Second, improving technology has also opened up areas which had until recently been out of reach, as all-terrain vehicles probe deep into the desert, helicopters hover over the jungle and, on the deep seabed, remotely operated submersibles nose out long-lost wrecks. Access to sites has also been made easier by the falling cost of international travel and the erosion of political barriers. This new combination of destructive power and easy communication has proved disastrous for the world's archaeological and cultural heritage, and it seems that no site or museum around the world is now safe from the attentions of archaeological bandits – the nighthawks, tombaroli or huaqueros – who have been joined by treasure salvors, militiamen and common thieves.

But this calamity is not purely a technological phenomenon, detached from any socio-cultural matrix. Stolen material needs a market, and in this instance it is provided by private and institutional collectors who regard archaeological or ethnographic objects as works of art, investment opportunities, or even as fashionable decorations. There is a global aspect to the problem too, an imbalance, as the market – museums, collectors and salerooms – is concentrated in the countries of Europe and North America, which have been called the 'demand' countries. Those countries whose cultural heritage is under serious threat of plunder – the so-called 'source' countries – are found largely in the developing world, although as chapters in this volume by Addyman and Brodie (Chapters 7 and 8), Schávelzon (Chapter 10) and Davis (Chapter 11) make clear, the archaeology and culture of demand countries themselves are not immune.

## ILLICIT ANTIQUITIES

Archaeological objects which have been torn from monuments, stolen from museums or illegally excavated and/or exported have been christened 'illicit antiquities'. This is not a legal term, but has been coined by archaeologists to highlight a unique characteristic of the trade in such material, which is that although in most countries of the world (with important exceptions such as the US and the UK) archaeological heritage has been taken into public ownership, so that its unlicensed excavation or export is illegal, its ultimate sale in a country other than that of its origin may not be. Thus the antiquities are illicit inasmuch as the method of their original acquisition was; it says nothing of the legality or otherwise of their subsequent trade.

An illicit antiquity may change hands several times before being bought by an institutional or private collector and details of its illicit origin are lost or erased in the process. Ultimately it is sold without provenance – without indication of ownership history or find spot. However, once published in an academic paper or exhibition catalogue, or even sale catalogue, it acquires a new, respectable pedigree as an object of scholarly interest or of esteem (Gill and Chippindale 1993), and its illicit origin is quietly forgotten. Illicit material is, in effect, 'laundered' by sale or publication in Europe or North America. This was the case in 1997, for example, when two Attic kylikes stolen from the Corinth Museum in 1990 were offered for sale in a major New York auction house described as the property of an American private collector.

Although stolen, most illicit antiquities, particularly those which have been clandestinely excavated, evade detection because they were not registered on any museum or excavation inventory prior to their theft and disposal. The Corinth kylikes had been inventoried and were identifiable, and were, in consequence, recovered. Most material is not. Even when a piece is recognized to be from a country which claims ownership, it will not be treated as stolen unless the country in question can prove that it was exported after the date of the relevant national patrimony law. Obviously, if an antiquity has been secretly excavated and smuggled, the date of its export is unlikely to be revealed. For example, there is the case of the Roman statue of the 'Weary Herakles'. The upper half of this statue surfaced in the US in the early 1980s and is currently in the joint ownership of the Boston Museum

of Fine Arts and an American private collector. The lower half was excavated near the Turkish town of Antalya in 1980. However, despite this fact,
the American owners of the top half insist that there is no evidence to show
that it was stolen as it may have been removed from Turkey many years –
centuries even – before the relevant 1906 patrimony law. Without evidence
to prove otherwise, the Turkish government has not pressed its case.

The situation is further clouded by what has been called a 'loophole' in
international law (Ellis 1995: 223). Many antiquities and other cultural objects
are sold in civil law countries of continental Europe, whose property law
differs from that of US and UK common law in that title to a stolen object
can be obtained by means of a 'good faith' purchase. Thus, even if it can
be demonstrated unequivocally that an antiquity was taken illegally from its
country of origin, if it was subsequently bought in good faith in a country
such as Switzerland it will no longer be regarded in law as stolen.

Illicit antiquities move erratically across many national borders and juris-
dictions. This allows them to be easily laundered, but it also facilitates the
entry on to the market of fakes. Without a verifiable provenance, objects
that are faked – completely or in part – can easily be passed off as genuine,
and it is left to the connoisseur or scientific test to determine their authenticity, and both have in the past been proved fallible. There are now many
fakes in private and institutional collections around the world (Muscarella
2000), their true number will probably never be known, although it has been
estimated that nearly 80 per cent of the terracotta statuettes which have left
Mali since the 1980s may be forgeries (Brent 2001: 27). While the fakes
remain undetected, perhaps even unsuspected, the effect on scholarship can
hardly be guessed at.

Not all antiquities appearing on the market are illicit, however. Dealers
are keen to stress that large quantities of antiquities moved out of their countries of origin during the 'grand tour', or in colonial times, and that
documentary proof of original provenance is long lost. They are right and
this is the crux: in the absence of provenance, how can licit material be
distinguished from illicit? 'From an old European collection' is a common
enough auction appellation, but one that might hide an old family heirloom
or a recently looted (or fake) piece. Who is to know? The only cautious
response is to regard all unprovenanced material as looted.

## THE EXTINCTION OF ARCHAEOLOGY

Archaeological extinction may seem an incongruous concept. After all, how
can something already dead become extinct? But if archaeology is viewed as a
resource, at a time when both natural and cultural resources have become
commodities to be bought and sold, the relevance of the association becomes
clear. For many people in the developing world, the sale of looted archaeological or cultural material can help supplement a meagre income, so much so

that looting in these areas has been termed subsistence digging (Matsuda, 1998: 91), it is the same spectre of poverty that is seen behind illegal timber extraction and animal poaching. But these depredations share more than a cause – left unchecked they are unsustainable. The resource is exhausted or becomes extinct. Even government-sponsored – albeit environmentally unsuited – development can be detrimental to the archaeological record, as described by Nalda in Chapter 9.

Thus there are very real links between economic underdevelopment and the degradation of natural and archaeological environments, and the fundamental problem is that of rural poverty. It is estimated that 65 per cent of the developing world's population live in rural areas and depend upon immediately available resources to meet their daily needs (Elliot 2000: 102). While, presumably, most easily accessible archaeological sites are in rural areas, this is an economic and demographic reality that cannot be ignored. Since the failure of 1960s' modernization policies, it has become clear that underdevelopment is a global problem, caused as much by unrestrained market forces as by poorly developed economic infrastructures. As such, a global response is necessary, with more ethical investment and trade practices put in place to support economic developments of a type which are sustainable in local environments and of benefit to local populations. If, in the developed world, deforestation and species – and even archaeological – extinction are high on the agenda, in developing countries improved standards of living are higher still, and any equitable resolution of the trade in illicit antiquities and of the plunder of archaeological sites must take this into account. Matsuda's point about subsistence digging was well made, and until rural poverty is eradicated it will no doubt continue.

## SHIPWRECKS

Looting on land is well documented but this book brings to general archaeological attention the problems caused by treasure salving of deep-water wrecks, which is a relatively recent phenomenon. The development of scuba gear during the 1950s first allowed the exploration and excavation of wrecks lying in shallow coastal waters, perhaps down to a depth of about 50 m, but it also allowed their plunder. Although treasure hunting in these waters is a lottery (most wrecks do not contain treasure and many archaeologically significant examples can be damaged or destroyed during a futile search (Conlin and Lubkemann 1999: 64)), damage has been widespread in some areas and most wrecks lying in territorial waters now enjoy some degree of legal protection.

Those in deeper water remained safe from human interference until the 1980s when, in 1985, the recovery of gold and porcelain from the wreck of the Dutch East Indiaman *Geldermalson* and gold and silver bullion from the Spanish galleon *Nuestra Señora de Atocha*, both lying just outside territorial waters, showed that there were fortunes waiting to be made on the international seabed. In the same year, the *Titanic* was discovered in 3600 m of water, and a new prospect of deep-water recovery opened up. By 1987, a remotely operated submersible had been instrumental in the removal of over $1 million worth of gold bars from the wreck of the *Central America*, which had sunk in 1857 in 2,400 m of water 420 km off the coast of South Carolina. The deepest wreck currently known is that of the Japanese submarine *I-52*, sunk in 1944 while carrying a load of gold bullion to Germany, and presently 5,400 m down (Delgado 1996; Johnston 1997). The sudden 'appearance' of deep-water wrecks grabbed the attention of governments, archaeologists and treasure hunters, and Dromgoole (Chapter 4) and O'Keefe (Chapter 5) discuss the competing claims to access, jurisdiction and ownership, and their possible resolution by means of the UNESCO Draft Convention on the Protection of the Underwater Cultural Heritage.

Archaeological participation in treasure salving expeditions can be in contravention of professional ethics which hold that archaeological sites should be preserved *in situ*, excavated material should be carefully conserved for future study, and that recovered artefacts should not be sold, even if the sale is intended to fund further research (Elia 1992). Thus, future collaborations between salvors and archaeologists seem unlikely unless an excavation is properly conducted and recorded, the material recovered is properly conserved, and, crucially, the excavated assemblage is preserved intact (Johnston 1993: 59; Delgado 1996: 43). Salvage operations are now typically investor-funded and the returns have not to date been reliable – they are high-risk investments. Salvors themselves may make more money from investors than treasure. A more secure, albeit longer-term, strategy would be to conserve excavated ships for public presentation, a strategy that would not require the break up and sale of any recovered assemblage (Throckmorton 1990: 183; Johnston, 1993: 59). Only under these circumstances might it be possible to envisage future cooperation between salvors and archaeologists.

The anaerobic conditions of deep-water wrecks have favoured good preservation and Sutherland (Chapter 6) discusses the technical and ethical issues that conservators face when confronted with recovered material. It is in everybody's interest to avoid disasters such as that of the *De Braak*, a British warship that sank off the coast of Delaware in 1798. It was raised by cranes in 1986, artefacts spilling out as it rose, but ownership – and the responsibility for conservation – has now reverted to Delaware, and to the public purse (Johnston 1993: 57; *US News* 1999). It is clear that for any collaboration between salvors and archaeologists to succeed, a budget must make good allowance for the proper conservation and curation of the ship, its fittings and all its accoutrements, which is not a primary concern for a treasure hunter interested only in a valuable cargo.

## LOOTING DURING WARTIME

In the past, war has perhaps been the greatest enemy of cultural heritage, and this is recognized in Boylan's (Chapter 3) account of the long series of international agreements and conventions which have been drafted in consequence. There are three ways in which war might have a damaging impact. First, there is what the military would call collateral damage – accidental damage caused to a cultural monument or institution, or archaeological site, during an attack on a legitimate military target. Second, there is the age-old practice of taking booty – the forcible removal of cultural material for profit or purposes of aggrandizement. Finally, there is the deliberate destruction of religious or other culturally important structures or artefacts for the purpose of erasing the material symbols of an ethnic or religious group – what would today be referred to as 'cultural cleansing'. Perhaps all destruction during wartime comes out of a confluence of all three causes, but in some recent conflicts looting for saleable material has certainly been to the fore and has exacerbated an already disastrous situation. Two in particular are well documented: Afghanistan and Cambodia.

After the Soviet withdrawal from Kabul, Afghanistan in 1992, the various mujahideen factions began fighting among themselves for control of the city. The National Museum was repeatedly hit by rocket or artillery fire and it was also badly looted. By 1996, more than 70 per cent of the museum's collections were missing, with only the less valuable pieces left behind, a sure sign that the plunder was commercially motivated and not carried out for reasons of cultural cleansing (Dupree 1996). Once aware of the commercial potential of Afghanistan's archaeological remains, local militia commanders also began to sponsor illegal excavations of archaeological sites and used the money gained from the sale of artefacts to pay soldiers or buy munitions (Lee 2000a).

However, not all of the damage in Afghanistan can be attributed to the search for saleable material. In 1996, the fundamentalist Taliban took over in Kabul and issued an edict banning all forms of figurative representation, but also decreed that ancient cultural objects were exempt and to be protected. Nevertheless, in 1997, a Taliban commander besieging Bamiyan threatened to destroy the two monumental Buddhas for which the town is famous (Dupree 1998). The central government again warned against such vandalism, but in 1998 the head of the smaller of the two Buddhas was blown off in a deliberate act of iconoclasm (Lee 2000a). This prompted the issue of a new law decree in July 1999, which outlawed the excavation of historic sites (Lee 2000b), but in March 2001 the Taliban leader ordered that all religious 'idols' were to be destroyed, and the larger of the two Bamiyan Buddhas was subsequently blown up with high explosive.

In Cambodia, military factions have engaged in the plunder of Khmer temples and monuments. It is reported that Angkor Wat alone used to have 1000 Buddha statues but that only 18 now survive (Rooney 2001: 45). Many were vandalized during the Khmer Rouge regime (1975–79) but since then they have been looted and sold. In 1999, more than twenty tons of archaeological material were found hidden in the headquarters of the last Khmer Rouge commander, and not long afterwards the temple of Banteay Chmar was attacked and stripped of its famous bas-reliefs by renegade units of the regular army. Material from Cambodia is smuggled into Thailand and sold in the River City area of Bangkok for export abroad (Rooney 2001: 48), although the Banteay Chmar reliefs were intercepted on the Thai side of the border and in March 2000 were displayed at the National Museum of Thailand prior to their return to Cambodia (Bahn 2000: 753).

It is clear from these two conflicts that when central authority breaks down the existence of an international market intensifies the looting as material is sought out and sold, with the proceeds helping to keep soldiers in the field. In May 1999, Pakistani customs seized six boxes of archaeological material at Peshawar Airport. Much of it had been smuggled out of Afghanistan. The boxes were bound for London, Dubai and Frankfurt, and two were addressed to a London art-shipping agency (which denied any knowledge of the consignment (Levy and Scott-Clark 1999)). Nevertheless, in January 2000, material from Afghanistan was openly on sale in central London at an outlet only a few hundred metres away from the British Museum. The publication by ICOM in 1993 of their first edition of *Looting in Angkor* led to the recovery of six Cambodian pieces, two of which had been sold at Sotheby's London and one at Sotheby's New York (ICOM 1993: 10–11). One of the pieces sold in London was found in the Honolulu Academy of Arts, while a further piece was in the possession of the Metropolitan Museum of Art, New York. Both have now been returned to Cambodia. However, the occasional recovery or return cannot disguise the fact that in wartime the money pumped into the market by Western collectors not only fuels archaeological destruction, but also helps underwrite and thus prolong the conflict.

But not all wilful cultural destruction during times of civil disturbance or war is commercially driven. The fighting in former Yugoslavia has seen massive destruction of religious and other buildings and monuments. It is estimated that in Bosnia more than 12,000 mosques, together with 300 Catholic and 100 Orthodox churches, were destroyed during the fighting (Chapman 1994; Dodds 1998), and since the NATO bombing of Serbia in 1999, mosques and Orthodox churches in Kosovo have also been damaged or destroyed (*Art Newspaper* 2000: 6). In 1993, the sixteenth-century bridge over the River Neretva at Mostar, a long-time symbol of a multi-ethnic state, was deliberately blown apart by a Bosnian-Croat tank. It is a measure of the importance that might be attached to such architectural symbols that the Muslim community of Mostar is hoping to restore the bridge at a cost of $5 million, using the original stones (Dodds 1998: 53).

The 1954 Hague Convention was drafted with World Wars I and II in mind, but most recent conflicts have taken the form of civil wars or guerrilla actions. With this in mind, the 1999 Second Protocol to the Convention was adopted for what Boylan (Chapter 3) terms 'dirty' armed conflicts. Yet although the former Yugoslav states are all parties to the 1954 Hague Convention, the destruction proceeded nevertheless (Clément 1996: 159). During the Serbian bombing of Dubrovnik in 1991–92, houses protected under the terms of the Hague Convention seem to have been deliberately targeted (Burnham 1998: 153). In conflicts such as this, when cultural obliteration is a primary war aim, it is difficult to see how international protective legislation can be effective.

## THE TERMINOLOGIES OF CULTURE

From a legal perspective, Merryman (1996) has identified three competing images of the international debate over cultural, including archaeological, material. First, there is his nationalist image, the discourse of source nations which stresses the relationship between cultural objects and a national heritage, and which expects such objects to remain in their country of origin. Second, there is his internationalist image, which maintains that cultural heritage is international and that objects should be free to circulate. Finally, there is his object/context image of archaeologists and ethnographers, which places primary emphasis on the information or meaning held trapped in the relationship between an object and its context.

Through an archaeological lens, however, these images refract into alternative discourses, with different concepts requiring different terminologies. Merryman's nationalist and internationalist images are in fact manifestations of an object-centred discourse of ownership, while archaeologists and ethnographers are but part of a larger (perhaps Western) academic discourse which values knowledge over property.

Collectors, dealers, politicians and lawyers are largely (though not exclusively) focused on issues of ownership (as is Merryman). This is quite clearly seen in the use of the term 'cultural property' to describe the material under consideration. The concept of private property as enshrined in the common law of the UK and US is very much a European (ultimately English) one, and implies rights of uninterrupted ownership – rights of an owner to exploit, alienate and exclude (Prott and O'Keefe 1992: 310), unencumbered by any greater, public, interest. Conceptions of property in other cultural traditions differ and might recognize rights in an object other than those of the owner, or deny alienability. Differences between common law and civil law are discussed by Dromgoole (Chapter 4). Nevertheless, in common law the concept of exclusive, private ownership is a powerful one, as, since the end of the seventeenth century at least, it has been thought fundamental to the constitution of liberal society (Macfarlane 1998: 104), and appeals made to the rights of a private owner are guaranteed a sympathetic ear. It might be argued against this that the public interest vested in academic enquiry is sufficient to outweigh the right of an individual to exclusive ownership, a sentiment that has been expressed by Sax (1999) in his wider analysis of cultural material.

In contrast to dealers and politicians, as Merryman correctly points out, many (though not all) archaeologists subscribe to an ideal of knowledge, and the information-rich relationship between object and context. A forthright statement of this position has been made by Vitelli:

> Frankly, my major concern has never been with who owns or possesses an archaeological object, where the object resides, or, for that matter, whether an object was traded licitly or illicitly. My real concern is with information, which, for archaeological objects derives from their original context.
>
> (Vitelli 1996b: 109).

Vitelli is making two points. First, she is expressing dissatisfaction with current object-centred concepts of property, as they are applied to archaeology, and to debates over ownership that pervade the non-archaeological literature. But Vitelli is also questioning the very nature of the enquiry, she is stressing the importance of intangible relationships, the archaeological context where information resides, and downplaying the role of artefacts, of the material objects themselves.

The archaeological ideal is based on the concept of an archaeological site as an entity with emergent properties, an entity whose whole (artefacts in context) is greater than the sum of its parts (artefacts out of context). But although it is usual for archaeologists to talk about an artefact and its context, as fields of study multiply it is becoming increasingly difficult to choose what is context and what is object. For example, to an archaeologist interested in identifying ancient foodstuffs, a pot might become context and its contents the object. Similarly, for a student of ancient textiles, the fragment preserved in copper salts on the surface of a corroded bronze blade might be the object and the blade its context. An ancient coin might provide the context which dates the soil showing traces of human alteration. Thus the terms 'object' and 'context' are relative and are decided within the frame of a particular research project. It makes no sense to talk of objects as a single category of entities with distinctive properties that set them apart from another entity, the context. An archaeological site is composed of a web of relationships which are destroyed when antiquities – the so-called objects – are removed.

Thus the debate over archaeological material appears often to be a polemical one, fought between two extreme camps, and neutral observers – sometimes self-styled moderators – despair of the zealots with whom they are forced to deal. But the extremism is more apparent than real, as arguments which are developed within incompatible frames of reference can easily be misunderstood, and what seems sometimes to be an uncompromising rebuttal is due simply to a different understanding of the issues involved.

It has been proposed that the less ideologically loaded term 'cultural heritage' should be substituted for 'cultural property', the word 'heritage' being chosen to express better the idea of a cultural object as something to be shared and conserved, not something to be bought and sold, used in exclusion and, even, possibly, consumed (Prott and O'Keefe 1992: 311). This change in terminology has already occurred in some areas. The term 'cultural property' was first used in the 1954 Hague Convention and next in the 1970 UNESCO Convention, but by 1972 it had been replaced in the UNESCO Convention on the Protection of the World's Cultural and Natural Heritage (ibid.: 318–19), and now also in the UNESCO Draft Convention on the Protection of Underwater Cultural Heritage. The 1995 UNIDROIT Convention on Stolen and Illegally Exported Objects avoids the use of either term. The shift in terminology is also clearly demonstrated in the edited volume *The Ethics of Collecting Cultural Property* (Messenger 1999). The first edition of this book was published in 1989 when the term 'cultural property' was included in its title, but by the time of the epilogue to the second, 1999, edition, the editor preferred to use the term 'cultural heritage', noting that even this might be objectionable to some (presumably those who partake of Merryman's internationalist image), but that it had the advantage of not ascribing symbolic qualities of cultural or political dominance to material remains (ibid.: 254).

Nevertheless, the discourse of ownership is the dominant one, and archaeologists are forced to enter the debate over cultural material on, quite literally, disadvantageous terms. There are huge quantities of decontextualized antiquities in circulation that can only be talked of as objects, as they are in this chapter, and which are categorized on the basis of monetary value. Political solutions and legal arguments are also framed using such terms, despite the suggested alternative of 'heritage'. The reasons for this are political and historical. Political because national governments and rich institutions and individuals – Merryman's nationalist and internationalist images – together form a powerful constituency, but also historical because in the past archaeologists too have subscribed (some still do) to the ideals of object and ownership. The development of an archaeological methodology with its associated terminology is an ongoing process, and will continue to be so, but outside the discipline this is not generally understood.

Thus, sometimes it is suggested that the sale of duplicate objects – small pots perhaps – from an archaeological site might go some way towards satisfying the demand of the market, and so reduce looting. To a neutral observer this sounds a perfectly reasonable suggestion. A representative sample can be kept back for the purposes of archaeological research while the remainder can enter circulation. Archaeologists appear extreme and unreasonable when they oppose such a scheme, but their opposition is rational within their own understanding of the material in question. At the end of the day who is to decide which pot is the duplicate? Is each one to be scientifically characterized by all available techniques? If a representative sample is to be kept back 'just in case', how many? In fact, the truth is that there is no such thing as a duplicate pot. Indices of diversity and standardization can throw light upon the organization of ceramic manufacture, and such indices cannot be derived from a single pot.

For example, at Myrtos, on the south coast of Crete, a small site which had been destroyed sometime during the Early Minoan period (early Bronze Age) was excavated in 1967–68, and some 700 pottery vessels were recovered, some only partially preserved, but including 350 vessels which were complete and had been in use at the time of the site's destruction (Warren 1972). This material recently formed the basis of a large-scale project of stylistic and scientific analysis which, according to the investigators, provided them with '. . . a unique opportunity to begin to investigate the significance of ceramic variation within and between Early Minoan communities, and to broaden the range of issues concerning Early Minoan society which ceramics can be used to address' (Whitelaw *et al.* 1997: 267). This would not have been possible if all 'duplicates' had been released on to the market once the excavation had been published. Thus, archaeologists are not being extreme or unreasonable when they oppose proposals which advocate the break-up of excavation assemblages, but they are merely being realistic. A large set of ostensibly similar pots is a valuable resource to be carefully curated, not one to be thoughtlessly scattered on the winds of a contrary market.

The misunderstandings that arise out of this clash of terminologies can only be addressed by archaeologists adopting a more positive or proactive stance towards public education, and better explaining what archaeology is and what archaeologists do.

## WHAT IS ARCHAEOLOGY?

If the discourse of ownership is currently dominant it is due in part to the failure of archaeologists to make their own voices heard through active engagement with the public that provides the ultimate sanction for their activities. Lazrus (Chapter 2) and Nalda (Chapter 9) discuss this failure in some depth and it is clear that it is to some degree institutional. University departments continue to privilege exploration over conservation or presentation: '. . . it is . . . sexier to hire a specialist in Oldowan technology or Inka urbanism than in the impact of tourism on the archaeological record' says Fagan (1996: 240) and this is also true of research funds which are channeled into fieldwork (termed 'primary research') rather than what are considered to be secondary activities of archaeological resource management and public education. The result is a surfeit of (unemployable) specialists in ancient cultures while the needs of the general public for an accessible archaeology are not met (ibid.: 241); and if the success of television programmes devoted to archaeology – whether fringe or mainstream – is anything to go by, the public is certainly hungry for such fare.

Public enthusiasm for archaeology in demand countries is often sparked by the perceived romance of treasure hunting, and the challenge for archaeologists is to redirect this enthusiasm, without dimming it, towards a more nuanced understanding of the past (Dromgoole, Chapter 4; McManamon

1994: 63; see papers in Stone and Molyneux 1994). In the US, the challenge is being met by the Society for American Archaeology, which established a Public Education Committee in 1990 to offer consultation on media projects and travelling displays of archaeological education resources, while the American Institute of Archaeology continues publication of its popular – and successful – magazine *Archaeology*. In the UK, the CBA publishes *British Archaeology* and there is the long-running independent *Current Archaeology*, and though public education seems to be more a concern of museum archaeologists than of fieldworkers (Schadla-Hall 1999: 150), this is not to overlook the success of model sites constructed for purposes of experimentation, education and public presentation (Stone and Planel 1999a: 4; see also papers in Stone and Planel 1999b). Although subject to commercial constraints, it seems desirable that museums and sites should seek to engage rather than entertain the public, and to challenge their preconceptions rather than pander to their stereotypes and prejudices, otherwise the damaging stereotype of archaeology as treasure hunting will only be reinforced.

## PUBLIC PARTICIPATION

Although many modern archaeological techniques require specialist skills or instrumentation, there is still a role for active public participation and employment in fieldwork, particularly in the so-called source countries. This has been shown on several occasions to be an effective strategy for dealing with looting. In Agua Blanca, Ecuador, local *huaqueros* were trained in archaeological techniques (Howell 1996: 50) and at Sipán, Peru, *huaqueros* were also employed on the excavation. In the UK, the technical expertise of metal detectorists is increasingly called upon. There are two reasons for the success of these experiments. First, the perception often held by locals that (outsider) archaeologists are interested only in stealing their patrimony is exploded, and the true nature of archaeological concerns are revealed and accepted as valid. The archaeology is seen as something to be understood and curated rather than consumed. Second, the work is legal, probably less hazardous than tomb robbing at night and remuneration is guaranteed (Seeden 1994: 96). Interpretations, too, can benefit from the multiple perspectives which are engendered through such cooperations.

An ideal scenario seems to have been realized by the inhabitants of La Conga, a Peruvian village close to the archaeological site of Kuntur Wasi in the northern Andes (Onuki 1999). The villagers first organized themselves in 1972 to guard Kuntur Wasi and received the support of the National Cultural Institute (NCI) at Lima. In 1988, the NCI invited an archaeological team from Tokyo University to begin excavating the site, and in 1989, three tombs were discovered and found to contain gold, which normally should have been removed to Lima. However, in this case the NCI gave special dispensation for the finds to remain in the village, but in 1990, more tombs were discovered and it became clear that a museum would have to be built. In 1991, a travelling exhibition of the excavation finds visited Japan to raise funds and in 1994, the museum was opened – the first Peruvian museum built with the explicit participation of the local community. In 1996, a small library was added and the museum has now become a cultural centre where villagers can meet to watch videos and television, or give and attend lectures. The excavations at Kuntur Wasi continue and the site itself has remained free of damage.

Kuntur Wasi is an exemplary case, but the development and maintenance of such a centre is not without pitfalls. It may be politically untenable if the 'version' of the past presented differs radically from that of the dominant group, and any tourist attraction is irresistible for commercial interests wishing to 'develop' it further. The vicissitudes that such centres may face are discussed by Ucko (1994). The Kuntur Wasi museum seems to be successful as it is situated at the conjunction of a proactive local community, a sympathetic government and a foreign archaeological mission sensitive to local opinion. Crucially, perhaps, the initiative was indigenous and not imposed. The villagers now appear on television and visit towns and cities in northern Peru to talk about their experience, so that their innovative strategy might be copied.

Matsuda (1998: 93) has recently pointed to an apparent hypocrisy whereby subsistence diggers are treated as criminals and denigrated by archaeologists who profit culturally and financially from the same resource base. While it is clear that many archaeologists would not regard subsistence diggers as the real looters, collectors are the real looters says Elia (Elia 1996: 61), it is also true that archaeologists working in developing countries have an intellectual and economic obligation to the people who host their research. How this obligation can be met within current institutional and financial structures is problematical, but suggests that the war against archaeological looting must be fought in the committee room as much as in the field or the market-place.

## CULTURAL TOURISM

It is well established that archaeological sites and museums can act as the mainspring of tourist developments, with the economic benefits that accrue. In Turkey, an archaeological museum was founded in Bodrum in 1959 at a time when the town received almost no tourists, but by 1990 it was the second most popular museum in Turkey and the population of the town had tripled. In the Cypriot town of Kyrenia the number of visitors doubled in the three years following the opening of a museum to display a fourth-century BC shipwreck (Throckmorton 1990: 180). The several museums and monuments along the Kenyan coast in 1989 attracted 167,000 foreign visitors, and continue to have a beneficial effect on the entire regional economy (Wilson and Omar 1996: 241). At Chiclayo, Peru, the nearest big town to the archaeological site of Sipán, a spectacularly rich (and partly looted) Moche site in Peru, in the ten years following the plunder and then excavation of the site the number of tourists grew from 'a handful' to between 40,000 and 70,000 a year (Watson 1999: 16).

The long-term benefits to a depressed economy of cultural tourism have rarely been quantified, although it has been estimated that at Sipán, after careful excavation, the subsequent display of both artefacts and site now generates something in the region of $14 million a year in tourist revenue, a far cry from the $250,000 the looters are thought to have earned for their initial finds (ibid.: 16). The Swedish Tourist Board has estimated that every year the salvaged seventeenth-century AD battleship *Vasa* attracts several hundred million dollars into the Swedish economy (Throckmorton 1990: 181). This is the economic reality that underlies the observation by several contributors to this volume (Nalda, Chapter 9; Togola, Chapter 13; Politis, Chapter 14) that the curation and imaginative display of archaeological material in local museums, and the development of archaeological sites for public presentation, can create a resource which will help to attract tourists, and that sustainable employment will then follow.

It is essential that the income derived from tourist support be used for the benefit of communities in the immediate vicinity of sites, and not be siphoned off by a central, and perhaps distant, government or by outside commercial concerns. Where possible, local people should be employed and the development of the necessary infrastructure should be under local guidance and meet local needs or aspirations. As shown in the case of Kuntur Wasi, excavated material needs to be curated and displayed in museums close by and not removed to a 'national' museum in a far-off capital city.

But tourism of course brings along its own set of problems. Too many tourists can cause the physical erosion of a site and even the deterioration of museum exhibits if environmental control systems are overloaded. (Nalda Chapter 9; Périer-D'Ieteren 1998; Merhav and Killebrew 1998: 15). The list of the world's 100 most endangered sites published in 1996 included such famous sites as Angkor Wat, Teotihuacan, Petra, Mesa Verde and Pompeii (Burnham 1998: 150), all physically decaying despite the huge numbers of tourists they attract. Until recently at Pompeii, with two million visitors per year, only 40 per cent of the site was open to the public because of its poor state of repair. In 1997, the Italian Government moved to rectify the situation by declaring the site an autonomous area so that in future any tourist revenue will be retained for conservation and further research at the site (ibid.: 151). Again, this illustrates the point that money from entrance fees must be used directly to maintain the fabric of the site or monument, and not to support a centralized bureaucracy.

Commercial development can also trivialize the local or traditional significance of a site and even the experience of curation in a museum can be viewed as foreign or alienating for material which is considered to be still sacred or otherwise important for the social well-being of a community (Ucko

1994: 260; jegede 1996: 129–30). For this reason alone, the primary audience for any display should be considered to be the local population, and all
parts of this population (including minority groups) should be consulted about
possible presentations.

In 1999, ICOMOS adopted a new Cultural Tourism Charter to replace
the earlier, 1976, version, and which was thought necessary on account of the
growth of international tourism in the intervening period, as well as changing
attitudes to site conservation. While the original, 1976, Charter emphasized
the negative effects of tourism, the 1999 Charter stresses the need to make
heritage sites (broadly interpreted) more accessible to the visitor. In its introduction it states:

> Tourism should bring benefits to host communities and provide an
> important means and motivation for them to care for and maintain
> their heritage and cultural practices. The involvement and co-
> operation of local and/or indigenous community representatives,
> conservationists, tourism operators, property owners, policy makers,
> those preparing national development plans and site managers is
> necessary to achieve a sustainable tourist industry and enhance the
> protection of heritage resources for future generations.
>
> (ICOMOS 1999: 2)

This might often require imaginative legislation but again there is a need for
reorientation of archaeological concerns, as already discussed, away from the
academic ethic of research and peer-reviewed publication and instead towards
one of conservation and presentation. Again, it might be a mistake to consider
archaeology in isolation, something tourists are not prone to do. The original
definition of ecotourism included 'cultural manifestations (both past and present)' and if this has since been played down (Weaver, 1998: 18) it is probably due more to the interests of (non-archaeological) academics whose studies
have focused upon destinations which are popular on account of their wildlife
and scenery. In other countries, archaeology might be the primary attraction,
and even when it is not, in many areas of the developing world a sustainable
strategy of ecotourism might include an archaeological component.

## A FREE TRADE?

Dealers and collectors, who adhere to the liberal ideology of Merryman's
internationalist image, demand a free trade in archaeological and other cultural
material (Bordkey 1996; Marks 1998; Ortiz 1998; White 1998). Suggestions that the trade has a damaging effect on the world's archaeological and
cultural heritage are dismissed, and instead it is claimed that free trade acts
in the common interest: it puts money into the pockets of the poor, it
preserves valuable material for posterity and it promotes a universal appreciation of a diverse range of artistic forms. This claim can be opposed from

the theoretical position that there are social inequalities which are deeply rooted and not so easily overcome, and that the concept of a common interest has no grounding in reality. But, as more case studies are reported and quantifiable data are made available, each of the individual propositions has become more amenable to empirical examination.

First, there is the proposition that the trade is justified on economic grounds. Often, particularly in developing countries, the money derived from illicit digging can supplement a small and uncertain income. Politis (Chapter 14) tells how the cemetery at an-Naq' in Jordan has for years been looted by impoverished locals and this is not unusual, but those who dig are swindled out of the true value of their finds by the middlemen who organize the trade and the dealers who make the final sale. This point is made by Schávelzon (Chapter 10) and Togola (Chapter 13), and other studies suggest that diggers routinely receive less than one per cent of the final sale price of an object (Boylan 1995: 103; Brodie 1998).

Nevertheless, what, in western terms, is a small sum of money might represent a substantial amount to a poor subsistence farmer. But it is a short-term gain. Once removed from their original contexts archaeological and other cultural objects become commodities on the art market, and presumably continue to increase in monetary value, or at least are thought to have done so in recent times. But again, this appreciation, or profit, is lost to the original finder, and to the economy of the country of origin. And again, it is to the long-term benefit of western economies as jobs and income are generated on the back of this expropriated material. Thus, in reality, the original diggers are swindled twice over: first out of the initial monetary value of their find, and then out of its long-term economic potential. Governments who are prepared to allow treasure salvors to operate in their territorial waters in return for a share of any treasure found are cheated in similar fashion, out of a long-term economic resource in return for a one-off, undervalued payment.

The second proposition used to justify free trade is that the market 'rescues' what are euphemistically termed 'chance finds' which are thrown up during the course of industrial or agricultural development projects, or through urban expansion or renewal. Without the market these pieces would simply be discarded and destroyed, but their monetary value guarantees their recovery and their ultimate sale and collection ensures their survival.

Quantitative studies – such as they are – suggest that as a cause of damage to archaeological sites, sometimes commercially motivated looting does indeed rank below agricultural or urban development. A study of 12,725 sites in Andalusia, Spain showed that the greatest cause of damage was surface ploughing, which had affected 24 per cent of sites, while looting was second at 14 per cent (Fernández Cacho & Sanjuán 2000: 18). In the Aegean area of Turkey, a survey of 180 palaeolithic–early bronze age sites showed looting to rank third (at 13 per cent) behind agricultural and urban development. In the Marmara area of the same country, looting again ranked third (at 6 per cent) behind the same two causes (Tay Project 2001). However, caution is needed here as surveys such as these probably underestimate the true scale of looting. This is for two reasons. First, looting may be sporadic and the results not observable at the time of site inspection. Second, not all sites will be targeted by looters. Prehistoric sites of the type registered in the Turkish surveys, for instance, are probably less attractive than the country's many iron age, classical or Roman sites. This latter point was confirmed by a study of Mayan sites in Belize, known by looters to be a good source of saleable material, which showed that 58.6 per cent of 181 sites had been damaged by looting, while only 34.2 per cent had been touched by agricultural, urban or industrial development (Gutchen 1983).

Thus, although development projects are sometimes a major cause of archaeological destruction, it is not always so. Even when it is the case, it is not clear to what extent the destruction is exacerbated or ameliorated by the market and, if the latter, whether, on balance, local episodes of amelioration can justify the greater global mischief caused by the market. In his discussion of the Jordanian site of Zoar, Politis (Chapter 14) provides a rare case study of how the development-led destruction of an archaeological site articulated with the global antiquities market. Clearly, in this particular instance there was a destructive synergy between the market and development that proved disastrous for the local archaeology, but more studies of this type are urgently needed.

The final proposition is that a free trade in archaeological and other cultural material can help to promote a universal appreciation of human creativity and engender mutual respect. For this to be true, however, there would need to be a *fair* exchange of material, while at the present time the exchange is manifestly unfair. Material flows from source countries to demand countries and there is no countervailing flow, no fair exchange. Thus, free trade does not promote international harmony, it merely sustains economic inequality and causes resentment among those whose culture is traded.

Collectors and dealers claim that, although in the first instance they may be acting out of self-interest, their actions ultimately have beneficial consequences, but it is difficult to muster empirical support for this position. A free trade in archaeological and cultural material seems to bestow few, if any, long-term benefits on those who, in the source countries, are its ultimate victims.

## CONVENTIONS AND ETHICS

No country has the resources necessary to protect its archaeology. Even rich nations such as the US and the UK suffer from looting (Addyman and Brodie, Chapter 7; Davis, Chapter 11). It is futile to demand that large countries such as Mali or India should protect their own heritage from depredations fuelled by rich collectors and institutions abroad. Countries such as these are

dependent upon the international community to ensure that their own
domestic laws are not broken, which in practice means enforcement of instruments such as the 1970 UNESCO Convention on the Means of Prohibiting
and Preventing the Illicit Import, Export and Transfer of Ownership of
Cultural Property (McIntosh, Chapter 12; Pachauri, Chapter 15).

McIntosh describes the US implementation of the 1970 UNESCO
Convention, with special reference to the bilateral agreement reached between
the US and Mali within its framework. However, she also emphasizes that
at the time of writing only two of the major market nations (US and France)
had ratified the Convention, although Switzerland is currently drafting implementing legislation and in March 2001 the UK Government announced its
intention to accede. Implementation of the Convention by these latter countries will allow their participation with the US in future multilateral agreements, an eventuality envisaged by the US at the time of its ratification
(Kouroupas 1995).

It could be argued that the main effect of the UNESCO Convention has
been moral rather than material. For a long time museums acted to underwrite the trade, buying material on the open market and accepting as bequests
privately accumulated collections. Nørskov (Chapter 1) demonstrates how the
research interests of individual curators in the past has influenced the composition of museum collections, but also suggests that attitudes are now changing.
In no small part this is due to the introduction of ethical codes which call
for acquisition policies to be adopted in accordance with the principles laid
down in the UNESCO Convention. Section 3.2 of the 1986 ICOM Code
of Professional Ethics for instance states that:

> A museum should not acquire, whether by purchase, gift, bequest
> or exchange, any object unless the governing body and respon-
> sible officer are satisfied that the museum can acquire a valid title
> to the specimen or object in question and that in particular it has
> not been acquired in, or exported from, its country of origin
> and/or any intermediate country in which it may have been legally
> owned (including the museum's own country), in violation of that
> country's laws . . .
>
> So far as excavated material is concerned, in addition to the
> safeguards set out above, the museum should not acquire by
> purchase objects in any case where the governing body or respon-
> sible officer has reasonable cause to believe that their recovery
> involved the recent unscientific or intentional destruction or
> damage of ancient monuments or archaeological sites, or involved
> a failure to disclose the finds to the owner or occupier of the
> land, or to the proper legal or governmental authorities.

Archaeologists too are responding. In 1988, the International Congress for
Classical Archaeology recommended in the Berlin Declaration that archaeologists should not provide expertise or advice to dealers or private collectors.

Principle no. 3 of the 1996 Society for American Archaeology's Principles of Archaeological Ethics warns that archaeologists should be aware that the commercialization of archaeological objects results in the destruction of archaeological sites and of contextual information, and recommends that archaeologists should discourage and avoid activities that enhance the commercial value of an object. The Archaeological Institute of America's 1990 (amended 1997) Code of Ethics also requires that its members do not encourage or participate in the trade in unprovenanced antiquities. In the UK, the British Academy passed a resolution in 1998 affirming its adherence to the principles laid down in the 1970 Convention, and in 1999, the Institute of Archaeology in London became the first university department to adopt an ethical policy based on similar principles (Tubb, Chapter 16). These principles are also guiding the editorial policies of some academic journals such as the *American Journal of Archaeology*.

The 1995 UNIDROIT Convention on Stolen and Illegally Exported Cultural Objects, designed to augment the 1970 UNESCO Convention looks set to be equally influential on the development of codes of due diligence, which are intended to help prevent the inadvertent purchase of illicit cultural material.

Nevertheless, many museums continue to collect or display unprovenanced material in complete contravention of ethical codes, although in so doing they risk public embarrassment and financial loss (Brodie *et al.* 2000: 43–58; McIntosh, Chapter 12).

## CONCLUSION

Gill and Chippindale (1993) have written of the material and intellectual consequences of collecting. By intellectual consequences they mean the 'corruption of reliable knowledge' (ibid.: 269), which is caused by the revaluation and reinterpretation of decontextualized objects in a modern setting. This book focuses more on the material consequences, the damage caused to the material record by irresponsible collecting, and for good reason: it seems that those who benefit from the illicit trade – the dealers and collectors – are in a state of denial. The scale of the trade is often played down and the damage it causes is discounted. For this reason, eye-witness testimony and factual, preferably quantitative, data are invaluable in what is an ongoing debate. While this book was being prepared, the US implementation of the UNESCO Convention was challenged in the US Senate, and in the UK both Parliament and Government carried out enquiries into the trade in illicit material. The Second Protocol to the Hague Convention was adopted and negotiations continued over the UNESCO Draft Convention on the Protection of the Underwater Cultural Heritage. Several of the book's contributors were directly involved in these processes. Thus, as Tubb also makes clear in Chapter 16, this book is not an exercise in academic obscurity, a faint polemic from a distant ivory tower, as its contributors are actively engaged in the political process and its chapters will be instrumental in changing the present reality of archaeological plunder – in stopping the theft before extinction.

## REFERENCES

*Art Newspaper* 2000. Systematic destruction. *Art Newspaper* no. 105 (July–August), 6.

Bahn, P.G. 2000. Khmer artefacts return to Cambodia. *Antiquity* 74, 753–4.

Bordkey, A.K. 1996. The failure of the nationalization of cultural patrimonies. In *Legal Aspects of International Trade in Art*, M. Briat and J.A. Freedberg (eds), 135–40. The Hague: Kluwer Law International.

Boylan, P.J. 1995. Illicit trafficking in antiquities and museum ethics. In *Antiquities Trade or Betrayed: Legal, Ethical and Conservation Issues*, K.W. Tubb (ed.), 94–104. London: Archetype/UKIC.

Brent, M. 2001. Faking African Art. *Archaeology* 54, 27–32.

Brodie, N.J. 1998. Pity the poor middlemen. *Culture Without Context* no. 3, 7–9.

Brodie, N.J., J. Doole and P. Watson 2000. *Stealing History: the Illicit Trade in Cultural Material*. Cambridge: McDonald Institute.

Burnham, B. 1998. Architectural heritage: the paradox of its current state of risk. *International Journal of Cultural Property* 7, 149–65.

Chapman, J. 1994. Destruction of a common heritage: the archaeology of war in Croatia, Bosnia and Hercegovina. *Antiquity* 68, 120–6.

Clément, E. 1996. UNESCO: some specific cases of recovery of cultural property after an armed conflict. In *Legal Aspects of International Trade in Art*, M. Briat and J.A. Freedberg (eds), 157–62. The Hague: Kluwer Law International.

Coggins, C. 1969. Illicit traffic in Pre-Columbian antiquities. *Art Journal* XXIX(1), 94–8.

Conlin, D.L. and S.C. Lubkemann 1999. What's relevant about underwater archaeology . . . and not about treasure hunting. *Archaeology Newsletter*, April: 64, 62.

Delgado, J.P. 1996. Lure of the Deep. *Archaeology* 49(3), 41–7.

Dodds, J.D. 1998. Bridge over the Neretva. *Archaeology* 51(1), 48–53.

Dupree, N.H. 1996. Museum under siege. *Archaeology* 49(2), 42–51.

Dupree, N.H. 1998. The plunder continues. *Archaeology online*. Available HTTP: http://www.archaeology.org/online/features/afghan/update.html (accessed 28 October 1999).

Elia, R.J. 1992. The ethics of collaboration: archaeologists and the Whydah project. *Historical Archaeology* 22: 105–17; reprinted in L.V. Prott and I. Srong (eds) 1999, *Background Materials on the Protection of the Underwater Cultural Heritage*, 107–19. Paris and Portsmouth: UNESCO/Nautical Archaeology Society.

Elia, R.J. 1996. A seductive and troubling work. In *Archaeological Ethics*, K. Vitelli (ed.), 54–62. Walnut Creek: AltaMira.

Elliot, J.A. 2000. *An Introduction to Sustainable Development*. London: Routledge.

Ellis, R. 1995. The antiquities trade: a police perspective. In *Antiquities Trade or Betrayed: Legal, Ethical and Conservation Issues*, K.W. Tubb (ed.), pp. 222–5. London: Archetype/UKIC.

Fagan, B. 1996. The arrogant archaeologist. In *Archaeological Ethics*, K. Vitelli (ed.), 238–42. Walnut Creek: AltaMira.

Fernández Cacho, S. and L.G. Sanjuán 2000. Site looting and illicit trade of archaeological objects in Andalusia, Spain. *Culture Without Context* no. 7, 17–24.

Gill, D. and C. Chippindale 1993. Material and intellectual consequences of esteem for Cycladic figures. *American Journal of Archaeology* 97, 601–59.

Gutchen, M. 1983. The destruction of archaeological resources in Belize, Central America. *Journal of Field Archaeology* 10, 217–28.

Howell, C.L. 1996. Daring to deal with huaqueros. In *Archaeological Ethics*, K. Vitelli (ed.), 238–42. Walnut Creek: AltaMira.

ICOM 1993. *Looting in Angkor*. Paris: ICOM.

ICOMOS 1999. *International Cultural Tourism Charter*. Available HTTP: http://www. icomos.org/tourism/sugaya.html (accessed 24 June 2000).

jegede, d. 1996. Nigerian art as endangered species. In *Plundering Africa's Past*, P.R. Schmidt and R.J. McIntosh (eds), 125–42. London: James Currey.

Johnston, P.F. 1993. Treasure salvage, archaeological ethics and maritime museums. *International Journal of Nautical Archaeology* 22, 53–60.

Johnston, P.F. 1997. Treasure Hunting. In *British Museum Encyclopaedia of Underwater and Maritime Archaeology*, J.P. Delgado (ed.), 424–6. London: British Museum.

Kouroupas, M.P. 1995. US efforts to protect cultural property: implementation of the 1970 UNESCO Convention. In *Antiquities Trade or Betrayed: Legal, Ethical and Conservation Issues*, K.W. Tubb (ed.), 83–93. London: Archetype/UKIC.

Lee, D. 2000a. History and art are being wiped out. *Art Newspaper* no. 101 (March), 31.

Lee, D. 2000b. A small step forward. *Art Newspaper* no. 107 (October), 6.

Levy, A. and C. Scott-Clark 1999. Looters take millions in Afghan treasures. *Sunday Times* 11 July.

Leyten, H. (ed.) 1995. *Illicit Traffic in Cultural Property: Museums Against Pillage*. Amsterdam: Royal Tropical Institute.

McManamon, F.P. 1994. Presenting archaeology to the public in the USA. In *The Presented Past: Heritage, Museums and Education*, P.G. Stone and B.L. Molyneux (eds), 61–81. London: Routledge.

Macfarlane, A. 1998. The mystery of property: inheritance and industrialization in England and Japan. In *Property Relations: Renewing the Anthropological Tradition*, C.M. Hann (ed.), 104–23. Cambridge: Cambridge University Press.

Marks, P. 1998. The ethics of dealing. *International Journal of Cultural Property* 7, 116–27.

Matsuda, D.J. 1998. The ethics of archaeology, subsistence digging, and artefact looting in Latin America: point, muted counterpoint. *International Journal of Cultural Property* 7, 82–97.

Merhav, R. and A. Killebrew 1998. Public exposure: for better and for worse. *Museum International* 50(4), 5–14.

Merryman, J.H. 1996. A licit international trade in cultural objects. In *Legal Aspects of International Trade in Art*, M. Briat and J.A. Freedberg (eds), 3–46. The Hague: Kluwer Law International.

Messenger, P.M. 1999. *The Ethics of Collecting Cultural Property*. Albuquerque: University of New Mexico.

Meyer, K.E. 1973. *The Plundered Past*. London: Readers Union.

Muscarella, O. 2000. *The Lie Became Great: the Forgery of Ancient Near Eastern Cultures*. Groningen: Styx.

O'Keefe, P.J. 1997. *Trade in Antiquities: Reducing Destruction and Theft*. London: Archetype/UNESCO.

Onuki, Y. 1999. Kuntur Wasi: temple, gold, museum . . . and an experiment in community development. *Museum International* 51(4), 42–6.

Ortiz, G. 1998. The cross-border movement of art: can it and should it be stemmed? *Art, Antiquity and Law* III, 53–60.

Périer-D'Ieteren, C. 1998. Tourism and conservation: striking a balance. *Museum International* 50(4), 5–14.

Prott, L.V. and P.J. O'Keefe 1992. 'Cultural heritage' or 'cultural property'? *International Journal of Cultural Property* 1, 307–20.

Renfrew, C. 2000. *Loot, Legitimacy and Ownership: the Ethical Crisis in Archaeology.* London: Duckworth.

Rooney, S. 2001. Tomb raiders. *Times Magazine,* 6 January, 44–8.

Sax, J.L. 1999. *Playing Darts with a Rembrandt.* Ann Arbor: University of Michigan Press.

Schadla-Hall, T. 1999. Public Archaeology. *European Journal of Archaeology* 2, 147–58.

Schmidt, P.R. and R.J. McIntosh 1996. *Plundering Africa's Past.* London: James Currey.

Seeden, H. 1994. Archaeology and the public in Lebanon: developments since 1986. In *The Presented Past: Heritage, Museums and Education,* P.G. Stone and B.L. Molyneux (eds), 95–108. London: Routledge.

Stone, P.G. and B.L. Molyneux (eds) 1994. *The Presented Past: Heritage, Museums and Education.* London: Routledge.

Stone, P.G. and P.G. Planel 1999a. Introduction. In *The Constructed Past: Experimental Archaeology, Education and the Public,* P.G. Stone and P.G. Planel (eds), 1–14. London: Routledge.

Stone, P.G. and P.G. Planel (eds) 1999b. *The Constructed Past: Experimental Archaeology, Education and the Public.* London: Routledge.

Tay Project 2001. Destruction report. Available HTTP: http://tayproject.org/raporeng.html (accessed 18 January 2001).

Throckmorton, P. 1990. The world's worst investment: the economics of treasure hunting with real life comparisons. *Underwater Archaeology Proceedings from the Society for Historical Archaeology, 6–10*; reprinted in L.V. Prott and I. Srong (eds) 1999, *Background Materials on the Protection of the Underwater Cultural Heritage,* 179–83. Paris and Portsmouth: UNESCO/Nautical Archaeology Society.

Tubb, K.W. 1995. *Antiquities Trade or Betrayed: Legal, Ethical and Conservation Issues.* London: Archetype/UKIC.

Ucko, P.J. 1994. Museums and sites: cultures of the past within education – Zimbabwe, some ten years on. In *The Presented Past: Heritage, Museums and Education,* P.G. Stone and B.L. Molyneux (eds), 237–82. London: Routledge.

*US News* 1999. The race for riches. *US News* 10 April.

Vitelli, K.D. (ed.) 1996a. *Archaeological Ethics.* Walnut Creek: AltaMira.

Vitelli, K.D. 1996b. An archaeologist's response to the draft principles to govern a licit international traffic in cultural property. In *Legal Aspects of International Trade in Art,* M. Briat and J.A. Freedberg (eds), 109–12. The Hague: Kluwer Law International.

Warren, P. 1972. *Myrtos: an Early Bronze Age Settlement in Crete.* London: Thames and Hudson.

Watson, P. 1999. The lessons of Sipán: archaeologists and huaqeros. *Culture Without Context* no. 4, 15–20.

Weaver, D.B. 1998. *Ecotourism in the Less Developed World.* New York: CAB International.

White, S. 1998. A collector's odyssey. *International Journal of Cultural Property* 7, 170–6.

Whitelaw, T., P.M. Day, E. Kiriatzi, V. Kilikoglou and D.E. Wilson 1997. Ceramic traditions at EM IIB Myrtos, Fournou Korifi. In *TEXNH Craftsmen, Craftswomen and Craftsmanship in the Aegean Bronze Age II* (Aegaeum 16), R. Laffineur and P.P. Betancourt (eds), 265–74.

Wilson, T.H. and A.L. Omar 1996. Preservation of cultural heritage on the East African coast. In *Plundering Africa's Past,* P.R. Schmidt and R.J. McIntosh (eds), 225–49. London: James Currey.

# 1     *Greek vases for sale: some statistical evidence*

VINNIE NØRSKOV

## INTRODUCTION

In 1993, the market for Greek vases reached a new peak when a Caeretan hydria from the Hirschmann collection was sold for £2.2 million at Sotheby's in London (9.12.1993, lot 35). This hydria is but the latest sign of the entry on to the classical antiquities market of 'investment collecting' (Herchenröder 1994). This new kind of collecting first appeared in the field of antiquities in the 1970s, probably stimulated by the well-known story of the 'One-Million-Dollar Vase': the Euphronios krater acquired in 1972 by the Metropolitan Museum of Art in New York (Meyer 1973: 86–100; Hoving 1993: 307–40). During the 1990s, reports from the antiquities market (as found, for instance, in the magazine *Minerva*) testify to the increased number of record prices over the last ten years and suggest that investment collecting has become more common. This development has been greeted by alarm bells – rung by scholars and others who see a connection between high prices on the art market and the illegal excavation and trade of antiquities.

This is all well known but there have been, surprisingly, few attempts to analyse the actual market situation, perhaps due to a fear of 'contamination' among archaeologists working in related areas. However, in consequence, it is now impossible to research into the modern collecting of antiquities without also considering the source of the objects. This chapter considers the field of Greek vases and approaches the phenomenon from two different angles in order to understand the different mechanisms at work. The aim is to investigate the development of the art market in order to see if certain changes on the market can be detected and explained. This has been done in two ways. First, from the perspective of the seller, through an analysis of the actual market supply, and, second, from that of the buyer, through studies of eight selected collections, of which one is examined in detail.

First, however, the relationship between the market and archaeology must be considered, as this is the premise for the entire work – the idea that the market and its consequences of clandestine excavation and illegal trade cannot be examined as an independent phenomenon but as part of the larger society, which also comprises archaeologists and their field of study. The argument is that several recent changes must have influenced the field of antiquities collecting. Among these changes, three seem to be of major importance: (1) classical archaeology has developed into what has been called the phase of contextual archaeology; (2) ethical behaviour concerning objects offered on the market has changed; and (3) collecting ancient art has become a strategy of investment.

The Euphronios krater in many ways symbolizes these changes in the history of collecting Greek vases. When the Metropolitan bought the vase in 1972, it was claimed that it came from an old collection. A few months later the *New York Times* revealed that European scholars believed the vase to have derived from a recently looted grave in Cerveteri. An Italian *tombarolo* confessed to its discovery. The Metropolitan then stated that it had bought the vase from an intermediary acting for a Lebanese dealer who said that it had been in his family's possession since 1920. Since then, the true origin of the vase has never convincingly been explained, but the fact that a museum had bought a vase with a very dubious provenance and at such a high price shocked the archaeological world. This was just two years after the 1970 UNESCO Convention had been adopted. The following year, in 1973, Karl Meyer published his famous book *The Plundered Past* where several similar stories were brought to light, together with some scary evidence concerning the production of forgeries of Greek vases.

Historically, it is noticeable that new trends and interests in research have often had a direct influence on the development of collecting. This is because collecting involves three 'actors': the dealer, the collector and the specialist. Art is no mere luxury good, and the specialist is an essential part of the triangle because he or she is required to authenticate and evaluate the objects. Many of the finest vase collections were assembled because of a close relationship between a collector and an archaeologist – the latter often being the *primus motor*. Seen in this light, the importance of the interconnection between collecting and research is clear.

The new ethical standards being adopted among classical archaeologists, together with the development of a contextual archaeology, have put the cooperation between the three actors to a difficult test. However, it still exists in the museum environment and will continue to do so as long as the museums acquire on the art market. Many museum curators also have close contacts with collectors, and the museum can be considered the main meeting place of the three actors.

## A LOOK AT THE MARKET

An analysis of the antiquities market would ideally encompass the entire market. However, although the market was, until recently, limited to a small circle of collectors and museums, it does nevertheless comprise a considerable number of objects. For this reason the present study concentrates on Greek vases. Besides coins – which are a special case – Greek vases constitute the largest group of classical antiquities on the market. In addition, they have, in the past, been appreciated for several different reasons and their painted decoration has long made them cherished objects among private collectors.

The development of the market for Greek vases has been studied through a statistical analysis based on 597 auction catalogues and gallery publications from the years 1954–98. Figure 1.1 shows the number of vases appearing on the market during this period, 18,431 in total, with a gently rising, regular curve peaking in the 1980s. Figure 1.2 compares this total number with the number of catalogues used in the analyses. Ideally, the number of catalogues printed each year should be included, but this information is difficult, if not impossible, to obtain. Catalogues published by Christie's and Sotheby's account for about 70 per cent of those consulted. The chart shows a positive correlation between the number of catalogues and the number of vases, but the average number of vases per catalogue has also increased during the last twenty years, which shows clearly that the total number of vases actually on the market increased during the 1980s.

The last period shows a decrease in the number of vases but also of catalogues studied. As the average number of vases in each catalogue remains pretty much the same, it seems that the decrease is not too significant. It should be mentioned, however, that there have been fewer auctions in total since Sotheby's stopped their London sales in 1997.

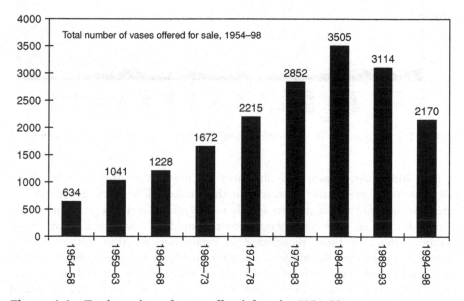

**Figure 1.1** Total number of vases offered for sale, 1954–98

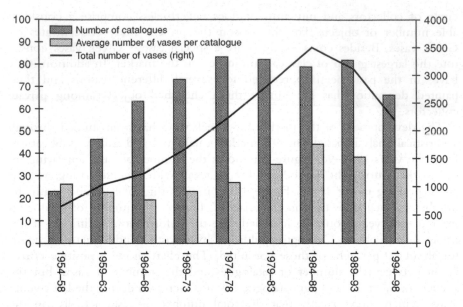

**Figure 1.2**   The number of vases offered for sale 1954–98 related to the number of catalogues used in the analysis

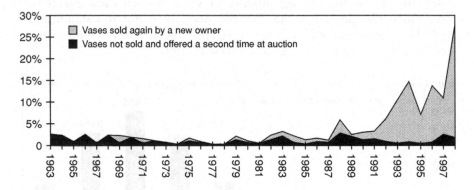

**Figure 1.3**   Percentage of vases offered on the market more than once, 1963–98

The third chart, Figure 1.3, illustrates the percentage of vases offered for sale which had previously appeared on the market. The black group constitute vases not sold at first auction and therefore offered again, a group normally termed bought in. The percentage shown should be considered a minimum – comprising only those recognized in catalogues. Auction houses do not mention in catalogue descriptions whether an object has been offered before but failed to sell. Thus it is often sheer luck when a vase offered up for sale again in this way is recognized, particularly as very few vases were illustrated in early catalogues. The grey group constitutes vases which had been sold in earlier auctions. Clearly, there is a marked increase in this group through time. Interestingly, this information is always given under the heading 'provenance'.

This leads to the next set of charts, which illustrate the provenance of the vases. It must be stressed in this context that the term 'provenance' has nothing to do with archaeological provenance, but that it is the art market term for the modern history of an object. Figure 1.4 shows that from the 1950s onwards, about 80 per cent of the vases offered lacked any information on provenance. By the late 1980s/early 1990s, this figure had fallen to just above 75 per cent, but then there seems to be a further, recent, drop, as the last period (1994–98) shows that only 58 per cent of the vases lacked information on provenance. In Figure 1.5 the last ten years have been singled out, and except for 1995 there is a steady trend downwards. This must be seen as a positive development, and it becomes even clearer, when looking at the next set of charts, which show what types of vases have been offered.

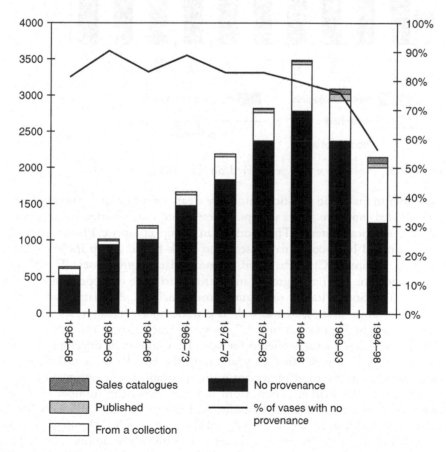

**Figure 1.4** Provenance of vases offered on the market, 1954–98

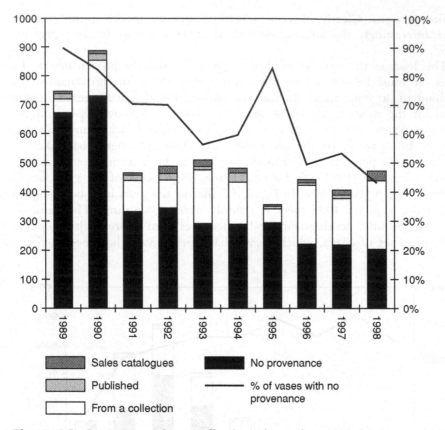

**Figure 1.5**   Provenance of vases offered on the market, 1989–98

In order to make the statistics reasonably clear, a major part of the vases have been divided into five larger groups. These groups are formed using stylistic and chronological criteria. The Corinthian group comprise Protocorinthian, Corinthian and Italo-corinthian vases. The black-figure group includes Attic, Boeotian, Laconian, Chalcidian and Etruscan black-figure vases. The white-ground and Attic red-figure groups are restricted to these two eponymous types of vase. The South Italian red-figure group includes Apulian, Campanian, Paestan, Lucanian and Sicilian as well as generic South Italian vases.

The charts in Figures 1.6 and 1.7 show for each group the number and relative percentage of vases offered for sale. Two important developments are to be stressed: during the first 15 years, until the late 1960s, Corinthian and black-figure were the most important groups, comprising together more than 50 per cent of the market. Then, from the late 1960s, the number of South Italian red-figure vases increased rapidly, and from then until the early 1990s they constituted more than 30 per cent of the total supply. The most reason-able explanation of this increase is that it is a result of clandestine excavations in South Italy and especially in Apulia, as for example illustrated in the trav-

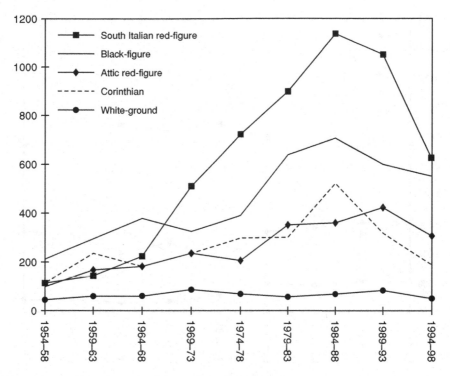

**Figure 1.6**  Distribution of five selected groups of vases, 1954–98 (total numbers)

elling exhibition *Fundort: unbekannt* (Graepler 1993). Comparing this result with Figure 1.1 (which shows that the overall increase of vases on the market was largest in the 1980s), it seems clear that the market growth during this period was fuelled by tomb robbing in Apulia. The only other possible explanation would be that the market was flooded by forgeries, and although there are some scholars who are inclined to prefer this explanation, it still remains unproven (but see Paolucci 1995: VII).

It is interesting to note, however, that the number of South Italian vases on the market has decreased dramatically in the last five years, not only in number but, more importantly, also in percentage. This suggests that there is a real decrease in supply and that it is not only because a smaller number of catalogues has been consulted. This decrease could be a reflection of the intensified and successful work of the Italian police, who recovered quite extensive depots of archaeological objects during the 1990s (Graepler 1993: 56).

Before turning to the museum studies, one curiosity should be mentioned: a striking result of the investigation is that the market has offered more Attic black-figure vases than red-figure vases during the entire period (Figure 1.8), yet the known corpus of Attic vases shows a much larger proportion of red-figure than of black-figure (Boardman 1974: 7). How is this inverted pattern of the market to be understood? Perhaps it is because the antiquities market

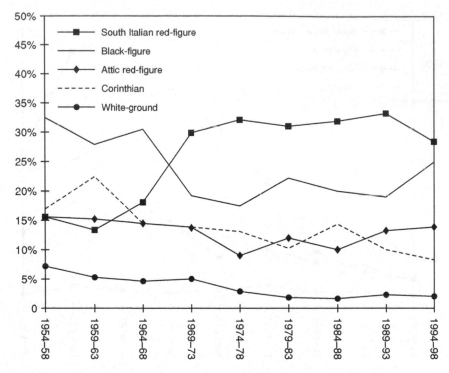

**Figure 1.7** Distribution of five selected groups of vases, 1954–98 (percentage)

is much larger than can be investigated on the basis of auction and gallery catalogues alone. If so, it means that a large number of red-figure vases have been sold on what could be called the 'invisible' market. An aforementioned example is the Euphronios krater in New York.

Such an interpretation has further implications. It might be possible that many of the vases from South Italy are a kind of 'windfall' for the *tombaroli*. Since the early 1980s one of the largest private collections of ancient armour has been formed by a German collector (Graepler 1995: 70–1) and it is possible that tomb robbers in Apulia and elsewhere were not, in fact, primarily looking for vases, but for armour, which had a ready 'buyer'. The existence of such ready purchasers tends to stimulate clandestine excavations, known for instance in Greece in the 1960s when the government encouraged private citizens to buy Cycladic objects – as a means of preventing them from leaving Greece, but thereby of course not preventing the loss of provenance (Gill and Chippindale 1993: 606).

With about 17,000 vases registered in the catalogues, together with the knowledge of the 'invisible' market, it must be concluded that the market for Greek vases has been quite buoyant in the post-war era. Where did all the vases go?

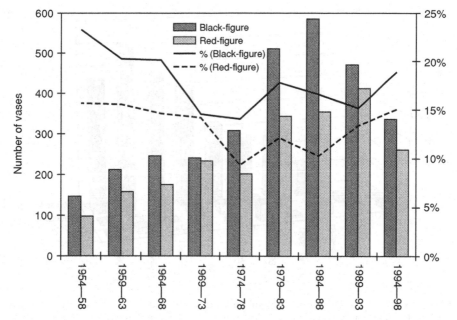

**Figure 1.8** Relationship between the number of Attic black-figure and Attic red-figure vases, 1954–98

## MUSEUM ACQUISITIONS

Eight museums were chosen for study of their vase collections, which had been developed in quite different ways and periods. They comprised five public museums (British Museum in London, The National Museum in Copenhagen, The Metropolitan Museum of Art and Archaeology in New York, Ny Carlsberg Glyptotek in Copenhagen and Antikenmuseum Basel und Sammlung Ludwig in Basle), and three university collections (Ashmolean Museum of Art and Archaeology in Oxford, Antikensammlung in Kiel and Duke University Collection in Durham). For detailed analysis, all acquisitions over the past fifty years, both purchases and gifts, were registered. When the number of vases acquired by these eight museums is compared to the market supply, until 1993, a negative correlation is revealed (Figure 1.9): while the museums acquisitions gradually declined, the market supply increased dramatically. The discrepancy should in fact be larger as few of the vases acquired by the museums were among those registered in the investigation of the supply. Many of the vases bought by museums were offered directly. Again this testifies to the existence of a so-called 'invisible' market, where the most expensive and cherished objects seem to have been traded. The decrease in museum acquisitions was not the result of poor availability.

This analysis shows that the museum curator enters the scene as a very important actor, as the following presentation of the development of the

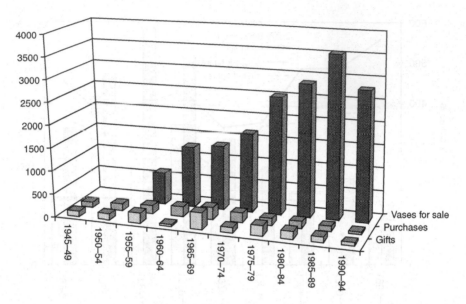

**Figure 1.9**  The acquisitions of eight museums compared with the number of vases offered for sale on the market, divided into gifts and purchases

Ashmolean Museum's collection will demonstrate. Some very distinguished scholars of Greek vases have been involved with the Ashmolean collection over the years and it is an obvious case for examining the relationship between scholar, market and museum.

Figure 1.10 shows vase acquisitions of the Ashmolean Museum between 1945 and 1994 (as registered in the Visitors Report). It includes 1,131 vases and fragments. A total number of acquisitions is not available, however, because several groups of fragments were not specified in the museum registration. These have not been included in the charts but are mostly fragments found during trips by university alumni, a source which has now died out.

The division of the vases into certain groups offers the possibility of identifying collecting trends in different periods. During the first post-war decade, there were many acquisitions and they covered the entire range of Greek vases, although with very few Geometric vases, but this is the normal picture (of purchases as well as of market availability). In the late 1950s the number of acquisitions fell. During this period the curator was a classical archaeologist who has explained that he only bought objects which he found curious and interesting for further research. He was succeeded by a specialist in prehistoric Greece. The chart shows a rise in the acquisitions of Mycenaean and Minoan pottery. What is not obvious from the chart is that earlier acquisitions were gifts, whereas several of those in the 1960s were bought on the market.

In 1965 and 1966 the very tall bars mark the acquisition by the Ashmolean of two large private collections. In 1965 Captain E.G. Spencer-Churchill died

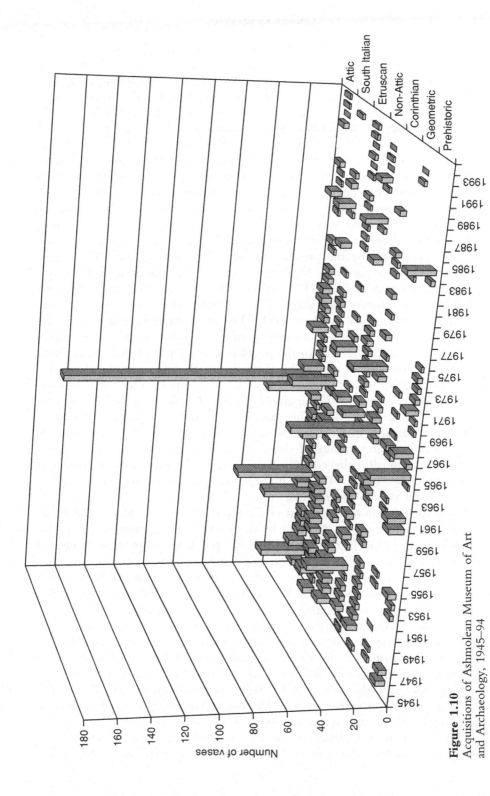

**Figure 1.10**
Acquisitions of Ashmolean Museum of Art
and Archaeology, 1945–94

(Exhibition 1965). He originally wanted to present his vase collection to the museum but, being concerned about death duties, he changed his will, and instead the Ashmolean was given first choice in buying from the collection at a reasonable price – in all forty-four vases were bought. The large number of acquisitions in 1966 were practically all gifts from the collection of Mr and Mrs Beazley – the former being a famous vase scholar and Oxford professor (Beazley 1967). In all, more than 800 objects, including many vases, especially black-glazed, and many vase fragments were presented. In general, however, Beazley had already given the more important, better preserved vases to the museum before this last gift of his remaining collection.

Figure 1.10 shows a significant decline in acquisitions from the middle of the 1970s. The Reports of the Visitors have several comments on the financial cuts which seem to be the main reason for the decline, something that was also confirmed by the present curator. Then, during the 1980s, there were more vase acquisitions. Many vases entered the museum in 1984 as a gift from the private collector Richard Hattatt, who had the idea of creating a collection of different vase shapes – a collection which was dissolved after he had reached his goal (Vickers 1993). The most interesting fact about the 1980s' acquisitions is that – as with his predecessor – the main research interests of the curator are visible in the purchases, namely a preoccupation with shapes and technique. This can be illustrated with two examples. First is a Faliscan oinochoe with a rending similar to one found on a twin oinochoe in a private collection in Washington DC, but decorated by another painter (Vickers 1992: 248, no. 48). This vase, bought in 1986, questions the individuality and artistic 'freedom' of the vase painter. Next, in 1987, the museum bought a calyx-krater of unusual shape – so unusual that one specialist in the field, A.D. Trendall, believed it to be fake until a thermoluminescence test proved otherwise (ibid.: 247, no. 26). This vase clearly documents the influence of metal vessels on ceramics.

These latest acquisitions are best understood as a reaction to the Beazleyan tradition, and indeed the decrease in the number of acquisitions may also partly be understood in that context: if painted vases were mere copies of metal originals, they are a source of information on the now lost but more valuable metal prototypes, but not works of art which, in themselves, would justify the prices paid today (Vickers and Gill 1996). Since the early 1990s the Ashmolean has not bought any vases on the art market.

The imprint made on museum acquisitions by the curator's research interest has been confirmed by the other museum studies, where scholars have also left their fingerprints on the vase collection (Nørskov 1998). This is visible in a large museum like the Metropolitan in New York where Dietrich von Bothmer increased the collection of Attic vases immensely, and also in the university collection in Kiel, where Konrad Schauenburg created a research centre of South Italian pottery (Raeder 1994: 20).

The important role played by curators in building up a collection is an encouraging finding. Acquisitions are based on their deep knowledge of the field, and as long as archaeologists are employed as curators, archaeological concerns over the importance of context should be addressed.

The British Museum and the Ashmolean are the only museums included in this study that have an official acquisitions policy specifically related to this issue (Report of the Trustees 1984: 37; Cook 1991: 534–5; Vickers 1992: 246). Several other museums have similar policies – for example the J. Paul Getty Museum which introduced the so-called 'Getty Rules' in 1995. This was a revised version of an *Acquisitions Policy for Classical Antiquities* published in 1987 (Pinkerton 1987: 25–8); it was an important step because the museum is so wealthy, and many of its purchases in the past have been of dubious provenance. Most museum curators also subscribe to the ethical rules adopted by the International Council of Museums (ICOM) in 1986 (Boylan 1995: 96–8; O'Keefe 1997: 44–5). In nearly all of the eight museums studied, the number of acquisitions fell during the post-war era. This decrease was often caused by cuts in funding, as at Oxford, but from the 1980s onwards there was also an increased awareness of the problems surrounding the purchase of objects with no documented provenance.

Ultimately, it seems that each curator acts individually according to his or her own moral guidelines when choosing whether or not to buy an object without provenance. On the basis of the interviews with curators, there seems now to be a kind of generation shift. Many older scholars work in an art historical tradition which privileges the object per se over knowledge of the find context. For the younger generation, trained in contextual archaeology, knowledge of find context is often crucial.

## CONCLUSION

In some of the literature on collecting, ethics and the trade, a horror picture of irresponsible archaeologists, careless collectors and corrupt dealers is drawn. The reality is, of course, much more complex and such generalizations are hardly constructive, if not indeed destructive. However, during the 1990s, some developments should be seen as the start of a move away from this negative picture, and can be presented as 'positive' conclusions:

- Museum curators are clearly changing their criteria for the acquisition of objects on the art market, stressing the importance of a documented provenance for gifts as well as purchases.
- The percentage of objects with a documented provenance on the market is rising. During the 1990s the proportion of provenanced vases grew and is now above 50 per cent.
- This tendency is probably a result of the demand: a high price for an object seems today to be dependent on a documented history. It is not possible to explore this further here, but it suggests that collectors are also moving in the direction of acquiring only objects of known provenance.

In 1994 Peter Cannon-Brookes suggested that a price difference between provenanced and unprovenanced objects would be a way to regulate the market from inside (Cannon-Brookes 1994: 350). This is already happening. Even if it is going only slowly it seems at least to be going in the right direction.

## NOTE

This paper was presented at the 5th Annual Meeting of EAA in Bournemouth in September 1999. The results are part of a larger investigation into the collecting of Greek vases accepted as Ph.D. thesis at the University of Aarhus in 1999 under the title *Greek Vases in New Contexts, Collecting Greek Vases: an Aspect of Modern Reception of Antiquity*. The thesis is at the moment being revised for full publication.

## BIBLIOGRAPHY

Beazley 1967. *Select Exhibition of Sir John and Lady Beazley Gifts to the Ashmolean Museum 1912–1966*. London: Oxford University Press for Ashmolean Museum.

Boardman, J. 1974. *Athenian Black Figure Vases*. London: Thames and Hudson.

Boylan, P.J. 1995. Illicit trafficking in antiquities and museum ethics. In *Antiquities Trade or Betrayed: Legal, Ethical and Conservation Issues*, K.W. Tubb (ed.), 94–104. London: Archetype/UKIC.

Cannon-Brookes, P. 1994. Antiquities in the market-place: placing a price on documentation. *Antiquity* 68, 349–50.

Cook, B.F. 1991. The archaeologist and the art market: policies and practice. *Antiquity* 65, 533–7.

Exhibition 1965. *Exhibition of Antiquities and Coins Purchased from the Collections of the Late Captain E.G. Spencer-Churchill*. Oxford: Ashmolean Museum.

Gill, D. and C. Chippindale 1993. Material and intellectual consequences of esteem for Cycladic figures. *American Journal of Archaeology* 97, 601–59.

Graepler, D. 1993. *Fundort: unbekannt. Raubgrabungen zerstören das archäologische Erbe*. Heidelberg: Archäologisches Institut.

Graepler, D. 1995. In margine alla mostra itinerante 'Luogo de tinvenimento: sconosclliuto. Scavi clandestini distruggono il patrimonio archeologico'. *Antichità senza provenienza. Atti della tavola rotonda. Bottetino d'arte*, 89–90, 63–75.

Herchenröder, C. 1994. Der Antikensammler – Vom Kenner zum Investor. *Kunst und Antiquitäten* 4, 39–40.

Hoving, T. 1993. *Making the Mummies Dance*. New York: Touchstone Books.

Meyer, K. 1973. *The Plundered Past. The Traffic in Art Treasures*. New York: Atheneum.

Nørskov, V. 1998. Greek vases in new contexts. Collecting Greek vases – an aspect of modern reception of antiquity. Unpublished Ph.D. dissertation, University of Aarhus.

O'Keefe, P.J. 1997. *Trade in Antiquities. Reducing Destruction and Theft*. Paris: Archetype Publications/UNESCO.

Paolucci, A. 1995. Prefazione. *Antichità senza provenienza. Atti della tavola rotonda. Bolletino d'arte* 89–90, VII-VIII.

Pinkerton, L.F. 1987. Due diligence in fine art transactions. *Journal of International Law* 22 (1), 1–29.

Raeder, J. 1994. 150 Jahre Kieler Antikensammlung. In *IÄEAI. Konturen des griechischen Menschenbildes*, B. Schmaltz (ed.), 14–21. Kiel: Antikensammlung Kiel.
Report of the Trustees 1984. *The British Museum. Report of the Trustees 1981–1984.* London: British Museum Publications.
Vickers, M. 1992. Recent acquisitions of Greek and Etruscan antiquities by the Ashmolean Museum, Oxford 1981–1990. *Journal of Hellenic Studies* CXII, 246–8.
Vickers, M. 1993. Richard Hattatt: collector and benefactor. *Ashmolean* 25, 6–9.
Vickers, M.J. and D. Gill 1996. *Artful Crafts.* Oxford: Clarendon Press.
Visitors Reports. *Report of the Visitors* (1901–1977), thereafter *Annual Report of the Visitors of the Ashmolean Museum 1979–1994.*

## 2     *Walking a fine line: promoting the past without selling it*

PAULA LAZRUS

At times, archaeologists find themselves straddling a difficult divide. While conscious of the shared and non-renewable nature of cultural resources, they are also aware that archaeological activities can encourage the destruction of that which they endeavour to preserve. The spectacular character of certain types of discoveries can arouse excitement and interest in archaeological activities, but it can also fuel resentments and jealousies on the part of those who perceive that professionals benefit personally from their discoveries. Archaeologists are well aware that the global patrimony provides a unique foundation for comprehending humanity's myriad different faces, as well as its similarities, but they are not always aware of how others view their activities, or the past itself. Although they may recognize the need to encourage a more involved and educated public, the question can also be asked: which public? For example, local inhabitants see cultural resources differently than governmental agencies and academic departments; tourists, collectors and well-endowed foundations have different expectations than local inhabitants; and citizens in one country may or may not see the benefits of protecting resources in their original context but far from home and so forth.

Professional archaeologists cannot afford to focus their interests solely in the academic sphere because they rely on members of each of the other constituencies cited above for their survival. Permissions and funding for projects are both necessary and the support and interest of those who provide them are essential. Although there is at times a disciplinary aversion to confronting the economics and politics of protecting cultural resources, these issues are only avoided at archaeology's peril. The varying perspectives and attitudes that exist with regard to cultural resources have an impact on the defacement of sites and on the illicit trade in antiquities. The perception that archaeologists must benefit monetarily from finds is as pervasive as it is erroneous. It is likely that all archaeologists must eventually face a member of the public asking what the most precious object they have ever found might be, or what the most valuable item they have ever taken home has been. It is significant that the question asked is rarely whether they have ever taken anything home. While these questions may leave professionals annoyed or bemused, perhaps it has become necessary to consider what these questions have to say about how people view the activities of individual archaeologists and the profession as a whole. Italy's *tombaroli* utilize this attitude when writing articles and books for the general public where they boast of their 'accomplishments' and denounce the activities of archaeologists who are portrayed as bumbling academics, at heart no better than licensed *tombaroli* (Perticarari and Giuntani 1986). New York's art dealers have made similar accusations and have done so in print (Brandt 1990). In general, academics are dismissive of these comments, which they consider to be beneath them. Perhaps it is necessary, however, while recognizing the validity within the academic community of the 'moralistic' stance taken by the profession as 'stewards of the past', to ask what can be done to change this perception, which is not a glamorous or 'popular' image to other people. If archaeologists are to be more successful in combating ill-conceived perceptions of their profession, they must find a way to make their position appealing, valid, even 'sexy', to the public. While problems of image and the communication of what archaeologists do and why are apparently peripheral aspects of the profession, they are ignored at a cost because those distorted perceptions fuel support for the renegade or underdog and thus for the tomb robber or aggressive collector or dealer.

It is useful to consider what sort of archaeological activities have the most impact on the public. Is it the digs themselves, the object/s or monuments brought to light, a survey project, or perhaps the presence of a group of foreigners working during a season in which no self-respecting local would consider going out? Might it be the impact of a museum display, or simply a sensational article in the local or national press? How do fund-raising initiatives or educational activities present the goals of archaeology and archaeologists? Within the discipline it is necessary to consider with greater thoroughness the importance of how archaeologists are perceived by those in the local community. It is imperative to ask how these local communities might be involved with promoting and safeguarding sites. The members of these communities are a crucial link to improved preservation, as is the direct involvement of individuals in archaeology, law enforcement and government. Without this shared understanding and cooperation, all attempts to curb the illicit trade in antiquities and to encourage the preservation of archaeological sites are all but futile. Community involvement and increased global awareness are crucial, but so is a deeper understanding of the impact professionals have in creating and sustaining a positive image of cultural resources. Sometimes, actions taken by archaeologists may result in the further or continued destruction of sites. Occasionally, the mere presence or interest in a site or in a survey area may alert those who live there year round to the fact that there are precious artefacts to be found and thus spur clandestine activity. Interest in potential archaeological research areas may also instigate efforts to remove or otherwise disassemble materials that appear 'worthless' to local inhabitants in order to prevent expected work stoppages or land confiscation. The majority of archaeologists are aware of these issues on an intellectual level; now it is time to work at integrating that knowledge into fund-raising and research strategies. Working towards global education, creating and supporting strong and enforceable legislation and engaging people in the preservation and promotion of our cultural resources are paramount in the quest for change.

How are archaeologists most visible to the public? Globally they are most visible through museum exhibitions, glossy magazines and television programmes. Every calendar, poster, magazine or TV show with 'GOLD' or 'Mysterious Treasures' in the title or emblazoned in bold letters on a cover sends the message: that is what archaeology is about. In truth, this is what patrons pay for; it is what draws the public. The key then is to find ways to fund-raise and to inform while building excitement and interest, but without being dull or selling the wrong image. The Mary Rose Museum in Portsmouth, England is an excellent example of how a collection of everyday items can inspire a sense of wonder, adventure and discovery while being informative and fascinating, even 'glamorous', at the same time. Clearly, much forethought and financial backing were invested in the museum and its displays, but they succeed in making the past live while preserving the integrity of the enterprise. The ideas and principles can certainly be applied to other collections, even those with a limited budget. Balancing events that will draw interest and funding with disciplinary goals is not an easy task, but it merits serious attention and consideration by groups such as the European Association of Archaeologists and the Society for American Archaeology. The way in which the profession promotes itself is crucial and the skills to do so effectively should be an integral part of our undergraduate and graduate curriculum. Conservation efforts must move beyond simply identifying the appropriate technology to utilize on a site or the law to apply in order to protect cultural resources. All efforts to legislate protection are for naught if the people who must enforce and abide by the laws perceive them as ill conceived, non-sustainable, elitist and/or protectionist. Educational efforts must address these issues.

An understanding of different cultural attitudes towards antiquities and the past is an important requirement for the implementation of protective and punitive legislation to be successful and for the creation of solutions for effective site preservation. The modality selected to promote archaeological activities in the popular media is equally important. It is critical to be attentive to the methods selected, since, although the goals may be the preservation and guardianship of cultural resources or the continued investigation of a particular site or research problem, archaeologists themselves are just as often presenting ambiguous images about the profession and the cultural resources. Professionals must be aware that at times their activities may inadvertently put sites at risk, as experienced by the writer in Sardegna (Lazrus 1995). In that instance, while conducting a survey on the island, the author found that the attention given to particular find-spots attracted the interest of local inhabitants engaged in the illicit antiquities trade. They would return to sites where she had stopped to take notes and photographs and to collect surface materials, at several of which they dug deep trenches searching for potentially exotic goods. In one case their trenches resulted in the almost complete excavation of a previously unrecorded bronze age monument; in another, an additional section of a known monument was ruthlessly excavated. In both cases earth removal was so thorough that neither artefacts nor any stratigraphy were left behind, thus destroying any interpretative information that might have elucidated the nature and use of the monuments. Survey is generally perceived by archaeologists as a non-destructive activity and yet, on this occasion, that was not the case.

On the other hand, some local inhabitants were involved in the educational and research aspects of the project. Several of them commented that it was the first time they had understood what existed in their backyard; that is to say, in an area not 5 km from their homes that they traversed regularly. One of these people decided to renew his studies at the university level and enrolled in an archaeology programme.

The contrast in the individual relationships towards antiquities is worth some reflection. The citizens in this example live in a G7 country with a decent standard of living, an accessible public education system, and a highly developed governmental bureaucracy dedicated to the promotion and protection of the country's cultural resources. Those individuals engaged in the illicit trade in antiquities are neither impoverished nor lacking in a basic education – the qualities that are often cited as the motivation for tomb robbing and trafficking in other countries. Tombaroli are average citizens but there are also many educated citizens in Italy who have never visited their country's numerous and well-known archaeological sites in any purposeful or systematic manner. Again in Sardegna, a local merchant at a weekly market wanted information about selling an artefact. This led to a discussion about the worth of the objects in terms of the local inhabitants and their local history. His position was that few knew or cared about the local history which was not taught in the local schools and besides, when one could sell things abroad to museums and collectors, why not make as much money from the artefact as possible? Archaeologists must attempt to understand the perspective of such people and not simply dismiss their views if they are to change how things are presented to the public and make any headway in protecting sites, monuments and artefacts. Local newspaper articles that tout underwater archaeology as the new alternative to sport fishing, now prohibited in many areas of the Mediterranean, is another example. Such an article was published in a Rome edition of an Italian newspaper in the late 1980s or early 1990s, and yet there was no rebuttal from the professional community. Silence in these matters is often the response selected by archaeologists to block or deflect attention from negative publicity, but it can also be perceived by those outside the profession as a form of tacit agreement or approval. There are times when comments might simply add fuel to the fire,

but there are also many situations when taking a strong position to counteract misinformation about archaeological activities should be the imperative.

It is time for archaeologists to take renewed and additional responsibility
for the cultural patrimony they study and seek to preserve for future generations. Progress can only be made by archaeologists becoming increasingly
cognizant of the impact that their work has on those who will be called
upon to sustain, enjoy and preserve the precious information that they bring
to light. They must consider fully their actions as professionals, their public
relations strategies and their interactions with local populations. By assimi-
lating that information, by analysing its impact upon their work and by
examining how it influences others' views of their activities, they should
improve their ability to promote their activities while reducing the ambiguity sometimes apparent in their message. Only with increased attention to
these facets of the profession and greater understanding and attention to the
economic, social and political implications of archaeological activities in local
communities can the archaeologists begin to have some impact on curbing
the illicit traffic in antiquities and the exploitation of sites and communities.

## REFERENCES

Brandt, A. 1990. Room for cynicism. The booming antiquities trade: it is only a
    moral issue, so who cares? *Connoisseur* January, 92–117.
Lazrus, P. 1995. Is field survey always non-destructive? Thoughts on survey and
    looting in Sardegna, *Journal of Field Archaeology* 22, 131–5.
Perticarari, L. and A.M. Giuntani 1986. *I Segreti di un Tombarolo*. Milano: Rusconi.

## 3    The concept of cultural protection in times of armed conflict: from the crusades to the new millennium

PATRICK J. BOYLAN

### EARLY CONCERN WITH THE PROTECTION OF CULTURAL PROPERTY IN TIMES OF WAR

Historically, the fate and treatment of cultural property have often been important issues in both international wars and in many kinds of internal armed conflicts, such as civil, religious and liberation wars. The taking of important movable cultural symbols of invaded and conquered states and peoples as trophies of war (or merely for their economic value), and the defacing or destruction of their monuments as marks of victory, have been important parts of the culture of the waging of war for millennia: see, for example, the general historical reviews of cultural damage and destruction of Treue (1960: 32–40) and of Chamberlin (1983: 139–41).

One of the best known of many thousands of well-recorded examples that could be cited are the famous gilded bronze horses of St Mark's, Venice. The horses of St Mark's (themselves assumed to have been removed from either Rome or Greece to Constantinople, probably in doubtful circumstances, many centuries earlier) were reputedly captured from Constantinople in the sacking of the city by the Venetians following its fall to the Fourth Crusade on 13 April 1204. The Pope of the day, shocked at the earlier occupation and sack of the City of Zara, which had further damaged the already seriously strained relations between Rome and the Orthodox Church, ordered that the holy city of Constantinople, seat of the Eastern Church, should not even be entered by the Crusaders let alone sacked (under threat of excommunication). Despite this, as the Orthodox cleric, Nicetas Choniates, recorded in his account of the Sack of Constantinople:

> Nor can the violation of the Great Church [Hagia Sophia] be listened to with equanimity. For the sacred altar, formed of all kinds of precious materials and admired by the whole world, was broken into bits and distributed among the soldiers, as was all the other sacred wealth of so great and infinite splendor. When the

sacred vases and utensils of unsurpassable art and grace and rare material, and the fine silver, wrought with gold, which encircled the screen of the tribunal and the ambo, of admirable workmanship, and the door and many other ornaments, were to be borne away as booty, mules and saddled horses were led to the very sanctuary of the temple.

(Translation by Munro 1912: 15–16)

The Crusaders' own chronicler, Geoffrey de Villhardouin, reported that after extensive burning of the City and a veritable orgy of looting:

The spoils and booty were collected together, and you must know that all was not brought into the common stock, for not a few kept things back, maugre the excommunication of the Pope. That which was brought to the churches was collected together and divided, in equal parts, between the Franks and the Venetians, according to the sworn covenant. And you must know further that the pilgrims, after the division had been made, paid out of their share fifty thousand marks of silver to the Venetians, and then divided at least one hundred thousand marks between themselves, among their own people.

(Villehardouin 1908: 67)

After being for almost six centuries among the best-known features of Venice, the four horses were in turn seized by France on the orders of Napoleon I and taken to Paris in 1798, only to be returned under the detailed terms of the peace treaty of the Congress of Vienna of 1815 (Treue 1960: 195–8). (During World War II they were again to become a key State target for art looting – this time as part of the 'wants' list of Hitler's art collecting squads.)

However, the destruction, defacing or conversion to a deliberately inappropriate use of monuments of special cultural value to the identity and spiritual values of a conquered people – such as religious buildings and national historic sites – has been widely used throughout history as a sign of conquest and subjugation. Such actions were if anything even more common in non-international strife, such as the internal religious wars in northern and central Europe during the Protestant Reformation of the sixteenth and seventeenth centuries, in which there were enormous losses of both building complexes, such as churches and monasteries, and of cultural objects of religious significance, such as works of art, reliquaries and sacred vessels.

From the Renaissance there was a growing debate about the obligations of belligerents in conflicts towards cultural buildings and objects. In his more general examination of the emergence of concepts of international humanitarian law protection, Nahlik (1988: 203–4) briefly refers to successive discussions on an implied fundamental obligation to respect and protect works of art and religious and other cultural property by the Polish jurist Jacob Przyluski in 1553, and German jurists Justin Gentilis in 1690 and Emer de

Vattel in 1758. In the same study, Nahlik also outlines the important precedent set by the Peace of Westphalia, 1648, otherwise known as the Treaty of Münster, which ended the Thirty Years War, with its explicit provisions for the restitution of looted cultural and other private property, while codifying, probably for the first time, the still applicable distinction in the laws of war between private and civil property which is protected from seizure to looting, and the right of the victorious forces to retain captured military *materiel*, including weapons and military supplies:

> CXIV. That the Records, Writings and Documents, and other Moveables be also restor'd; . . . But they shall be allow'd to carry off with them, and cause to be carry'd off, such as have been brought thither from other parts after the taking of the Places, or have been taken in Battels, with all the Carriages of War, and what belongs thereunto.
>
> (Treaty of Westphalia, 1648)

Much destruction and looting of cultural property took place in the political revolutions of the eighteenth century and more recent times, beginning with the French Revolution, although – alarmed by the scale of iconoclastic devastation of both buildings and collections of the first two years of the revolutionary period – the French Convention soon took urgent legislative action in the *Quatres Instructions Initiales* of 1791 to try to halt such destruction (for which the new word 'vandalisme' was coined) (Boylan 1992).

## THE EARLY NINETEENTH CENTURY

During the Napoleonic Wars the traditional understanding of the rights of booty and prize-taking in war began to be questioned, at least in relation to museum collections. For example, in the 1812 War the British Navy captured a ship, the *Marquis de Somereuils,* the cargo of which included works of art belonging to the Philadelphia Museum of Art, and both the vessel and all its cargo were claimed as war prize in accordance with the usual practice of the day. However, in a subsequent action under British law in the Vice-Admiralty Court, sitting in the colony of Nova Scotia, the Court held that objects of artistic value on the ship are part of the common heritage of all mankind and are hence exempt from the normal law of possession and reward for captured enemy vessels and thus seizure during war. Consequently, the Court ordered that the works of art had to be returned to the Museum and this was done when hostilities ceased (*Stewart's Vice-Admiralty Reports for Nova Scotia, 1803–1813*: 482; cited by Bassiouni, 1983: 288, note 19).

The history of Van Eyck's famous *Adoration of the Mystic Lamb* polyptych altarpiece, commissioned for St Bavon's Church, Ghent, in 1432, is famous in the history of state looting and forced returns. The altarpiece was seized by France in the Napoleonic Wars and was part of the large number of items

(along with the Horses of St Mark's already mentioned) that were returned
to their country of origin under the decisions of the 1815 Congress of Vienna.

However, as in many other areas of the laws or customs of war, the relevant modern international humanitarian law can be traced back to the classic
five volume *Vom Kreige* [On War] of Karl von Clausewitz, published in 1832,
followed by the US of America War Department's General Orders No. 100:
Instructions for the Governance of the Armies of the United States in the
Field, drafted by Francis Lieber (and hence known as the Lieber Code) first
published during the Civil War in April 1863, and which still forms a core
element of US military law.

In Book V Chapter III(B) von Clausewitz stressed the principle of propor-
tionality in relation to the conduct of war, and on the need to restrict the
war effort to genuine military targets and imperatives:

> In this manner, he who undertakes War is brought back again into
> a middle course, in which he acts to a certain extent upon the prin-
> ciple of only applying so much force and aiming at such an object
> in War as is just sufficient for the attainment of the political object.
>
> (von Clausewitz 1968: 374–5)

Cultural property was explicitly protected for the first time in the Lieber
Code drawn up for the US Federal Army. Following a general prohibition
on the seizure or destruction of private property, this continued by stressing
that works of art, scientific collections, libraries and hospitals must be protected
from injury even in fortified places while these were being besieged or
bombarded. If necessary they could be removed (for their own safety) but
they could not be given away or injured. The Code also stressed that the
ultimate ownership of such material after the war was a matter for including
in the terms of the eventual treaty of peace:

> 34. As a general rule, the property belonging to churches, to hospi-
> tals, or other establishments of an exclusively charitable character,
> to establishments of education, or foundations for the promotion
> of knowledge, whether public schools, universities, academies of
> learning or observatories, museums of fine arts, or of a scientific
> character – such property is not to be considered public property
> . . .
>
> 35. Classical works of art, libraries, scientific collections, or precise
> instruments, such as astronomical telescopes, as well as hospitals,
> must be secured against all avoidable injury, even when they are
> contained in fortified places whilst besieged or bombarded.
>
> 36. If such works of art, libraries, collections, or instruments
> belonging to a hostile nation or government can be removed
> without injury, the ruler of the conquered state or nation may
> order them to be seized and removed for the benefit of the said
> nation. The ultimate ownership is to be settled by the ensuing

treaty of peace. In no case shall they be sold or given away, if captured by the armies of the United States, nor shall they ever be privately appropriated, or wantonly destroyed or injured.

(Quoted by Wright 1971: 64–6)

Further, Article 44 of the Lieber Code declared that unauthorized destruction or damage of property was 'prohibited under penalty of death or other severe penalty adequate for the gravity of the offense' (Wright 1971: 69).

The first international codifications of wartime protection for cultural property followed the Lieber Code closely. These were in the Declaration of Brussels, drawn up by the 1874 international conference, and which provided as Article 8:

> The property of parishes (communes), or establishments devoted to religion, charity, education, arts and sciences, although belonging to the State, shall be treated as private property. Every seizure, destruction of, or wilful damage to, such establishments, historical monuments, or works of art or science, shall be prosecuted by the competent authorities.

(Quoted in Merryman 1986: 834)

The Oxford Code of 1880, drawn up at a conference of the Institute of International Law, adopted similar terms in its Articles 34 and 53:

> Art. 34. In the case of bombardment, all necessary steps must be taken to spare, if it can be done, buildings dedicated to religion, art, science and charitable purposes, hospitals and places where the sick are gathered on the condition that they are not being utilised at the time, directly or indirectly, for defence. It is the duty of the besieged to indicate the presence of such buildings by visible signs notified to the assailant beforehand.

> Art. 53. The property of municipalities, and that of institutions devoted to religion, charity, education, art and sciences, cannot be seized. All destruction or wilful damage to institutions of this character, historic monuments, archives, works of art, or science, is formally forbidden, save when urgently demanded by military necessity.

(Oxford Manual 1880)

However, neither Brussels, 1874, nor Oxford, 1880, were formally ratified by sufficient numbers of countries to become official international treaties.

## FROM THE FIRST HAGUE CONVENTION, 1899 TO THE ROERICH PACT, 1935

The first formal international treaty providing some protection for cultural property that actually came into force was that adopted by the first (1899)

Hague Peace Conference. As was stressed in the May 1999 centenary cele-brations held in the Peace Palace in The Hague, this measure not only remains in force a century later (though in practice it has been largely superseded by subsequent international conventions), but its terms are by now considered to be Customary International Law, binding on all states and persons, whether or not they are formal signatories to Hague 1899 as such. The States drafting the Convention in effect adopted the principles of the earlier unratified Brussels/Oxford proposals as Article 56 of the Regulations Respecting the Laws and Customs of War on Land, while the parallel rules governing naval bom-bardment which tried to afford some protection to churches and other impor-tant cultural monuments, including provision for marking such protected buildings with a distinctive flag, were included as Article 27 of the Convention.

A much larger international conference, convened jointly by the US and Russia and attended by 44 sovereign states, was held in 1907, again in The Hague. After much debate and consideration, this finally adopted a series of interrelated treaties relating to the Laws and Customs of War (and incorpo-rating the earlier provisions of the 1899 Hague Conventions). Of the 1907 provisions, the Fourth Hague Convention on the Laws and Customs of War on Land was most directly relevant to cultural protection, although the Ninth Hague Convention Concerning Bombardment by Naval Forces in Time of War carried forward the Hague 1899 prohibition on the shelling from the sea of historic monuments etc.

The Regulations annexed to the Fourth Hague Convention took the attempted protection of cultural monuments and institutions in times of land warfare further than any of the nineteenth-century codes, providing in Articles 25, 27, 28 and 56 respectively that:

> 25. The attack or bombardment, by whatever means, of towns, vil-lages, dwellings, or buildings which are undefended is prohibited.

> 27. In sieges and bombardments all necessary steps must be taken to spare, as far as possible, buildings dedicated to religion, art, science or charitable purposes, historic monuments . . . provided that they are not being used at the time for military purposes. It is the duty of the besieged to indicate the presence of such build-ings or places by distinctive and visible signs, which shall be notified to the enemy before hand.

> 28. The pillage of a town or place, even when taken by assault, is prohibited . . .

> 56. The property of municipalities, that of institutions dedicated to religion, charity and education, the arts and the sciences, even when State property, shall be treated as private property. All seizure of, destruction or wilful damage done to institutions of this char-acter, historic monuments, works of art and science, is forbidden, and should be made the subject of legal proceedings.
>
> (International Committee of the Red Cross 1989: 25, 30)

However, despite the provisions of the Fourth Hague Convention of 1907 there were grave losses of cathedrals, churches, other historic monuments, museums, libraries and collections across the various land battlefields of World War I, leading to much concern and debate about the effectiveness of the existing Laws of War. It was considered that the failures were partly due to claims of 'military necessity' on the part of both attacking and defending forces. The damage was particularly severe across the mainly low-lying battlefields of Flanders and north-eastern France. In this flat countryside any relatively high building, such as a church, cathedral, medieval or later town hall tower or important country house, was almost automatically regarded as a legitimate target under the then current interpretation of 'military necessity'. (The argument used was that if not 'neutralised', such high points could be used by the enemy as observation points for directing shelling or by snipers.)

There was also much concern about the development of new technologies of war. Some of the poisonous gases used extensively for the first time in World War I, such as chlorine and phosgene, are highly corrosive and therefore capable of causing physical damage to many kinds of works of art and other cultural objects themselves (while further threatening the lives and health of non-combatant cultural protection personnel such as civilian library and museum personnel). The war also saw the rapid development of aerial bombardment first from airships and then from increasingly sophisticated and ever larger aircraft.

State-ordered looting and seizure of important works of art and other cultural property was also a major problem in World War I. The Ghent Altarpiece by Van Eyck, coveted and removed to Paris by Napoleon a century earlier, was taken again by the Germans (and was also to be seized again in World War II, this time with the Michelangelo *Madonna and Child* from the nearby Bruges Cathedral), (see, for example, Treue 1960; Chamberlin 1983). The restitution of the Van Eyck, the Dirk Bouts' *Last Supper* from the Church of St Peter in Louvain, and of books and manuscripts from the University of Louvain Library were among a number of specific reparations conditions of the 1919 Treaty of Versailles. These also insisted on the return of important cultural property seized by the Germans from the Franco-Prussian War of 1870 onwards, not just World War I booty. The terms followed the principles established in the Hague Conventions of 1899 and 1907, the requirements being detailed in the Treaty of Versailles in the following terms:

ARTICLE 245
Within six months after the coming into force of the present Treaty the German Government must restore to the French Government the trophies, archives, historical souvenirs or works of art carried away from France by the German authorities in the course of the war of 1870–1871 and during this last war, in accordance with a list which will be communicated to it by the French Government; particularly the French flags taken in the course of the war of 1870–1871 and all the political papers taken by the

German authorities on October 10, 1870, at the chateau of Cercay, near Brunoy (Seine-et-Oise) belonging at the time to Mr Rouher, formerly Minister of State.

### ARTICLE 246

Within six months from the coming into force of the present Treaty, Germany will restore to His Majesty the King of the Hedjaz the original Koran of the Caliph Othman, which was removed from Medina by the Turkish authorities and is stated to have been presented to the ex-Emperor William II. Within the same period Germany will hand over to His Britannic Majesty's Government the skull of the Sultan Mkwawa which was removed from the Protectorate of German East Africa and taken to Germany. The delivery of the articles above referred to will be effected in such place and in such conditions as may be laid down by the Governments to which they are to be restored.

### ARTICLE 247

Germany undertakes to furnish to the University of Louvain, within three months after a request made by it and transmitted through the intervention of the Reparation Commission, manuscripts, incunabula, printed books, maps and objects of collection corresponding in number and value to those destroyed in the burning by Germany of the Library of Louvain. All details regarding such replacement will be determined by the Reparation Commission.

Germany undertakes to deliver to Belgium, through the Reparation Commission, within six months of the coming into force of the present Treaty, in order to enable Belgium to reconstitute two great artistic works:
(1) The leaves of the triptych of the Mystic Lamb painted by the Van Eyck brothers, formerly in the Church of St. Bavon at Ghent, now in the Berlin Museum;
(2) The leaves of the triptych of the Last Supper, painted by Dierick Bouts, formerly in the Church of St. Peter at Louvain, two of which are now in the Berlin Museum and two in the Old Pinakothek at Munich.

(Treaty of Versailles 1919)

The Louvain Library terms in Article 247 created a further interesting, and potentially valuable, precedent, as it provided for the return of comparable items in terms of type and value, not solely *in specie*, where the original object could not be traced and recovered. Under the terms of this, the Reparations Commission eventually ruled that substantial financial compensation should be paid to the university in respect of both items that could be neither recovered nor replaced by, for example, copies of the same works from German public collections, and for the serious damage to the library building itself.

Although the use of poison gas was prohibited by the 1925 Geneva Proto-col, proposals to develop rules to control aerial bombardment, which by then was beginning to emerge as a potential unprecedented danger to cultural property, failed. In 1923 a Draft Convention for Rules of Air Warfare was drawn up by a further Hague Conference of jurists representing a large number of countries. However, although the latter was closely modelled on the established rules relating to military and naval bombardment (and in partic-ular the Tenth Hague Convention of 1907 with its specific prohibition of the bombardment of religious and other cultural buildings), it was never adopted as an international instrument. The 1923 proposals included protec-tion for all non-military populations and areas, and specific provisions aimed at protecting cultural property in Articles 25 and 26:

> Art. 25. In bombardment by aircraft, all necessary steps must be taken by the commander to spare as far as possible buildings dedi-cated to public worship, art, science or charitable purposes, historic monuments, hospital ships, hospitals and other places where the sick and wounded are collected, provided such buildings, objects or places are not at the time used for military purposes. Such build-ings, objects and places must by day be indicated by marks visible to aircraft. The use of marks to indicate other buildings, objects, or places than those specified above is to be deemed an act of perfidy. The marks used as aforesaid shall be in the case of buildings pro-tected under the Geneva Convention the red cross on a white ground, and in the case of other protected buildings a large rect-angular panel divided diagonally into two pointed triangular por-tions, one black and the other white. A belligerent who desires to secure by night the protection for the hospitals and other privileged buildings above mentioned must take the necessary measures to ren-der the special signs referred to sufficiently visible.
>
> (International Committee of the Red Cross 1989: 127–39)

These principles were to have been amplified in considerable detail in the following Article, which provided for the establishment, international notifi-cation, and clear marking by both day and night of 'zones of protection' around important historic monuments, including a protective outer area up to 500 m in width beyond the actual boundaries of the historic site. Such designated and notified localities would thereby enjoy immunity from bom-bardment under all circumstances other than 'perfidy', (i.e. the misuse of either the location or the official identification marks or signs for military purposes – paralleling the perfidy provisions in the Hague and Geneva Con-ventions relating to the misuse for illegal military purposes of the Red Cross symbol or, for example, hospitals or prisoner of war camps). Had it been adopted, the protective regime established by the 1923 Instrument would have been backed up and enforced by an international inspection committee of persons from neutral states, including a representative of the neutral

Protecting Power representing the interests of the belligerent State (ibid.: 127–39).

The next major development grew out of what was initially the private initiative and campaign of a remarkable individual, Nicholas K. Roerich (Elbinger 1992; Brenner 1992). Born in St Petersburg in 1874, Roerich trained as an artist and worked across Europe as an artist and designer (the Paris première of the Diaghilev/Nijinsky ballet of Stravinsky's *Le Sacre du Printemps* was one of his theatre designs), before moving first to the US and then to India and the Himalayas. Becoming increasingly committed to mysticism and oriental religion, he used the Roerich Museum of his own paintings in New York as a base during his visits to the US.

As early as 1904 Roerich had developed proposals for an international pact for the protection of educational, scientific and artistic institutions and missions. In 1931 the first international conference was held in Bruges on the proposed 'Roerich Pact' and his proposal for a 'Banner of Peace' to be displayed to identify protected buildings and institutes of cultural importance. Soon afterwards the Montevideo conference of the Pan-American Union (the forerunner of the present-day Organization of American States) passed a unanimous resolution urging all American states to sign the Pact.

Roerich soon had the patronage and support of both Eleanor Roosevelt and US Secretary of Agriculture (and future presidential candidate) Henry Wallace. The result was the signing of the Roerich Pact as the Treaty of Washington on 15 April 1935 (Pan-American Day) by representatives of 21 American governments, and the adoption of Roerich's Banner of Peace as the official symbol of cultural protection. In presenting the Pact to the International Conference, President Roosevelt stated that 'This treaty possesses a spiritual significance far deeper than the text of the instrument itself' (Elbinger 1992).

When submitted to the US Congress, the Roerich Pact was accompanied by a detailed study by J.T. Schneider of issues relating to the protection of cultural property generally. In addition to a comprehensive review of the current US position and of the Roerich Pact itself, this study included a series of extremely valuable reviews of then current foreign legislations and structures – including, among others, detailed reviews of the situation in Belgium, France, Germany, Great Britain, Italy, Japan and Poland. Particularly interesting and important were the comments of Schneider on the purpose of the Washington Treaty itself:

> A forward step of Pan-American as well as of international importance was consummated with the signing on April 15, 1935, of a treaty, popularly known as the 'Roerich Pact', initiated by the Roerich Museum of New York in the United States, for the protection of artistic and scientific institutions and historic monuments. Its purpose is 'that the treasures of culture be respected and protected in times of war and peace.' The universal adopting of a flag is urged in order thereby to preserve in any time of danger

'all nationally and privately owned immovable monuments which form the cultural treasures of the peoples.' It is hoped that this treaty will be broadened so as to include all nations as signatory parties.

(Schneider 1935: 31)

Roerich's text was in fact very simple and direct, which may explain, at least in part, the remarkable speed with which it was processed and brought into force. (In the case of the US, all the Senate and presidential procedures that were needed for adoption of a new treaty, which can typically take several years, were completed in less than three months.) The full text of the Treaty (which is still in effect across all of North America and in most countries of Central and South America) sets out its essential elements in its opening Articles:

Article 1. The historic monuments, museums, scientific, artistic, educational and cultural institutions shall be considered as neutral and as such respected and protected by belligerents. The same respect and protection shall be due to the personnel of the institutions mentioned above. The same respect and protection shall be accorded to the historic monuments, museums, scientific, artistic, educational and cultural institutions in time of peace as well as in war.

Article 2. The neutrality of, and protection and respect due to, the monuments and institutions mentioned in the preceding Article, shall be recognized in the entire expanse of territories subject to the sovereignty of each of the Signatory and Acceding States, without any discrimination as to the State allegiance of said monuments and institutions. The respective Governments agree to adopt the measures of internal legislation necessary to insure said protection and respect.

Article 3. In order to identify the monuments and institutions mentioned in Article 1, use may be made of a distinctive flag (red circle – with a triple red sphere in the circle on a white background) in accordance with the model attached to this Treaty.

(International Committee of the Red Cross 1989: 31–2)

However, despite the high ideals and explicit commitments of the Pact, most States adopting the Washington Treaty did little or nothing to implement its provisions at the practical level. For example, only Mexico prepared and registered internationally a list of monuments and institutions for which they wished to seek protection in accordance with Article 4 of the Treaty. Also, this treaty was by definition only a Pan-American one, and not a global initiative (although some non-American countries, e.g. India shortly after it gained independence in 1947, made declarations supporting and adopting Roerich's text).

## WORLD WAR II

In Europe, the storm clouds of approaching war were gathering. In 1936 there were many reports of clear breaches of the principles of the 1907 Hague Convention in the widespread cultural destruction of the Spanish Civil War, including anticlerical acts such as attacks on church property by the Left, and extensive aerial bombing using new generations of German-designed heavy bombers and dive bombers by the forces of Franco, with direct intervention of the German air force itself at times (see, for example, Catalonia: Comissariat de Propaganda 1937; Thomas and Thomas 1971; Alvarez Lopes 1982).

As a consequence, the 6th Commission of the League of Nations, 'following many requests from members of the [League's] International Commission for Intellectual Co-operation' commissioned the International Museums Office to re-examine 'the problem of the protection of monuments and works of art in times of war or of civil disturbances'. [*the author's translations throughout*] (Office International des Musées 1939: 177). The ambition to add 'civil disturbances' to the categories of conflicts regulated was a most important change from the long-established principles of the laws and customs of war, and indeed on the absolute internal sovereignty of States. The Directory Board of the International Museums Office initiated work on the political, legal and technical issues involved, with the Professor of International Law at the University of Louvain, Professor Charles de Visscher, leading the legal study. Meeting in October 1936 under the presidency of Sir Eric Maclagan (Director of the Victoria and Albert Museum, London), the Board reviewed, adopted and remitted to the International Commission for Intellectual Co-operation a draft text intended to develop in far more detail the limited provisions of the 1907 Fourth and Ninth Hague Conventions and Regulations, and the more detailed proposals of the (unratified) 1923 Hague draft Rules of Air Warfare.

The title proposed was the International Convention for the Protection of Historic Building and Works of Art in Time of War, the full text of which was published by the International Museums Office in both French and English (ibid.: 180–201). Although never ratified, it is clear that many of the key provisions were eventually taken up in the post-war 1954 Hague Convention discussed later. The draft began by emphasizing the obligation on 'every Government' to prepare and arrange in peacetime for the protection of 'historic buildings and works of art' in wartime (Draft Convention Article 1), including both physical arrangements and military training. All High Contracting Parties would refrain from any act of hostility against designated pre-notified refuges, though these were to be limited in number, open to international inspection and:

> be situated at a distance of not less than 20 kilometres from the most likely theatres of military operations, from any military objective, from any main line of communication, and from any large

industrial centre (this distance may be reduced in certain cases in countries with a very dense population and small area).

(Article 4)

So far as monuments or groups of monuments were concerned, pre-notified monuments or groups of monuments not used directly or indirectly for purposes of national defence and at least 500 m from any military objective would be entitled to 'special protection' (Article 5), although, on a reciprocal basis, Contracting Parties could enter into special agreements to protect monuments 'of fundamental importance to the international community' which failed to meet the general criteria proposed (Article 6).

Other provisions included the use of a distinctive mark to identify cultural sites, the exemption of historic buildings and works of art from reprisals, and immunity during transport of works of art (including private collections) being transferred temporarily under international supervision to a third country for protection (Articles 7–10). Further proposed Articles provided for International Commissions of Inspection, for the High Contracting Parties to meet in general conference to decide on implementation measures and to appoint a Standing Committee and Secretariat, and for the 'Contracting States' together with the proposed Standing Committee having among its other functions the responsibility to work together with belligerents to resolve differences of interpretation and application.

The proposed Convention was to be supported by Regulations for Execution, covering issues such as the proposed International Verification Commission (Draft Regulations Articles 1–7), protection for national staff appointed to 'preserve and guard' refuges, museums and monuments (i.e. presumably including the curatorial and conservation staff) and practical aspects of the suggested temporary evacuation (Draft Regulations, Articles 8–10). There was a particularly detailed and comprehensive series of provisions for the proposed General Conference and Standing Committee including, for example, the possibility of removing the headquarters of the Secretariat to a neutral country in the event of the host country becoming a belligerent (Draft Regulations Article 12).

The Draft Convention was warmly received and endorsed by the League of Nations' International Commission for Intellectual Co-operation, and active efforts were made by the professional community to try to apply its principles in the rapidly escalating Spanish Civil War, while pressing at the same time for the convening of the Intergovernmental Conference needed to take the project forward.

The graphic demonstration of the implications of large-scale aerial bombardment using the new German warplanes of various types, including dive bombers and heavy bombers, together with other new types of heavy weapons, and the scale of the cultural (as well as human) atrocities in Spain, raised widespread alarm. In addition to protesting at the various Spanish attacks on historic cities and monuments, professionals and public authorities across much of Europe began to prepare air raid precautions for many museums and monuments, including plans for the physical evacuation to places of safety – along the lines proposed in the International Museums Office Draft Convention (see for example Museums Journal 1938a and b; British Museum 1939; Netherlands Government 1939).

As a second Europe-wide war appeared inevitable, on 1 September 1939 President Roosevelt of the US sent messages to the governments of Germany, France, Poland and the UK. Clearly referring to recent outrages such as those that had been happening in Spain, Roosevelt demanded explicit assurances from all potential combatants that in the event of armed hostilities breaking out, there should be no air attacks on civilian populations nor on unarmed towns, in effect adherence to the requirements of the (unratified) 1923 Hague Rules of Air Warfare:

> The cruel aerial bombardments of civilian populations in un-
> defended centres, in the hostilities that have raged in different
> parts of the world in the course of recent years and of which the
> consequence has been the mutilation and death of thousands of
> defenceless women and children, has wounded the hearts of all
> civilised men and women and has profoundly shocked the
> conscience of humanity . . . Consequently, I address this present
> appeal to the governments which could be engaged in the present
> hostilities that each one of them affirm publicly its determination
> not to proceed, in any case or circumstance, to an aerial bombing
> of civil populations or undefended towns, being understood that
> the same rules of war shall be scrupulously observed by all their
> adversaries. I ask you for an immediate response.
>
> (Office International des Musées 1939: 222)

The four potential belligerent states replied positively giving clear assurances on these and related points, and, in effect, guaranteeing protection of non-military targets by the (ancient and traditional) means of mutual exchanges and guarantees of the respective rules of engagement for the forthcoming hostilities. For example, on 1 September the German Chancellor, Adolf Hitler, insisted that:

> The views expressed in the message of President Roosevelt, namely
> to refrain in all circumstances from bombing non-military targets
> . . . is a humanitarian principle, corresponding exactly to my own
> views, as I have already declared . . . For my part, I presume that
> you have noted that, in my speech given today in the Reichstag,
> I announced that the German air force have received the order
> to limit their operations to military objectives. One obvious condi-
> tion for the continuation of these instructions is that the air forces
> opposing us observe the same rules.
>
> (Quoted in Office International des Musées 1939: 223)

The UK, French and Polish governments gave similar assurances on 1 September, with Lord Halifax, the British Foreign Secretary, stating that:

> His Majesty's Government welcomes the important and moving appeal of the President of the United States of America against the aerial bombing of civil populations or undefended towns. Profoundly impressed by the humanitarian considerations to which the proposals of the President refers, His Majesty's Government has, in advance, declared that its policy has will be, if it becomes involved in a conflict, to refrain from acts of this nature, and to strictly limit bombing to military targets, it being understood that the enemy scrupulously observes the same rules.
>
> (Office International des Musées 1939: 222)

With the start of the war on 3 September the British and French made public a Joint Declaration on aerial bombing which was much more detailed and explicit, including in addition to specific references to the avoidance of civilian populations, 'to preserve with all possible measures, monuments of human civilisation':

> The Governments of France and of the United Kingdom, solemnly and publicly affirm, their intention to conduct the hostilities which have been imposed upon them, with the firm desire to protect the civilian populations and to preserve, with every possible measure, the monuments of human civilisation. In this spirit they have welcomed with a profound satisfaction the appeal of President Roosevelt, on the subject of aerial bombing. Therefore, they have already sent express instructions to the commanders of their armed forces, under which they shall only bombard, by aerial or maritime means or by terrestrial artillery, strictly military targets, in the strictest meaning of the term.
>
> (Office International des Musées 1939: 225–6)

Likewise, the Declaration continued, in the case of bombardment by ground artillery:

> they will exclude objectives which do not present a clearly defined military objective, in particular, the large urban areas situated outside the battlefield and, similarly, will strive to avoid the destruction of areas and buildings of interest for civilisation . . . A demand will be addressed to the German Government to ascertain if they can give corresponding assurances. It goes without saying that if the enemy does not observe certain restrictions to which the governments of France and Great Britain have imposed on the operations of their armed forces, these governments reserve the right to have recourse to all the action they consider appropriate.
>
> (Office International des Musées 1939: 225–6)

The International Museums Office also moved quickly on the outbreak of
hostilities, and produced a very substantial (232-page) handbook on the protection of monuments and works of art in time of war (Office International des
Musées 1939). This detailed many practical examples of the recommended
measures for protecting museum collections and monuments, in part using
the Spanish Civil War experience. The book also included the texts (in both
French and English) of the Office's Draft Convention, and French translations of the exchanges between the US and the three principal belligerents
for reference and information.

The successes and failures at both the legal and practical levels to protect
cultural property in World War II have been extensively recorded and studied.[1]

However, it is important to record that, in marked contrast with the
German campaign on the Eastern Front which was fought throughout with
little or no regard to accepted standards of international conduct, in Western
Europe the exchanges of September 1939 of what amounted to the rules of
engagement between the belligerents were very largely respected for the first
two and a half years of the war. It is of course true that there were very
many civilian casualties during that period, but both sides seem to have
endeavoured to restrict their air attacks to legitimate military, communications and armaments-related industrial targets. The large number of human
and cultural casualties was largely if not wholly the result of collateral damage
to areas in close proximity to legitimate military or economic targets as a
result of the lack of accurate navigation and bomb-aiming aids, especially for
the increasingly prevalent night bombing. To take just one English example,
losses of civilian lives and of cultural property (especially historic churches
and other historic public buildings) were very severe in the 'Square Mile' of
the City of London. However, at a time when long-distance night bombing
on dark nights rarely achieved an accuracy of plus or minus 5 km, and bearing
in mind that no part of the 'Square Mile' was much more than 1 km from
the vitally important Pool of London between Tower and London Bridges
and contained three of the main railway terminals serving east coast ports, it
is difficult to argue that the severe cultural losses were the result of deliberate enemy action against the heritage.

A fundamental change of strategy came at the end of March 1942 with
the British firestorm test-bombing of the undefended historic city of Lübeck,
which immediately provoked a series of destructive German reprisal bombings (what were termed in England the 'Baedeker Raids') of April and May
1942 on the English cathedral cities of Exeter, Norwich, York and Canterbury.
Describing the Lübeck attack in his post-war memoirs, the creator of both
the UK's Bomber Command, and the 'strategic bombing' strategy, Sir Arthur
('Bomber') Harris was very open about his motives:

> On the night of March 28th–29th [1942] the first German city
> went up in flames. This was Lübeck, a rather distant target on
> the Baltic coast . . . from the nature of its buildings easier than

most cities to set on fire . . . It was not a vital target, but it seemed to me better to destroy an industrial town of moderate importance than to fail to destroy a large industrial city. However, the main object of the attack was to learn to what extent a first wave of aircraft could guide a second wave to the aiming point by starting a conflagration . . . In all, 234 aircraft were dispatched and dropped 144 tons of incendiaries and 160 tons of high explosives. At least half of the town was destroyed, mainly by fire. It was conclusively proved that even the small force I had then could destroy the greater part of a town of secondary importance.

(Harris 1947: 105)

In his post-war memoirs, Harris defended his actions (highly criticized at the time, not least by the US military, and more widely ever since) in switching the air attack to the German cities and hence the civilian population, making the astonishing claim that:

International law can always be argued pro and con, but in this matter of the use of aircraft in war there is, it so happens, no international law at all. There was never any agreement about it, with the single exception that about the time of the siege of Paris in the war of 1870 the French and Germans came to an agreement between themselves that neither side should drop explosives from free balloons.

(Harris 1947: 177)

In making this claim, Harris may have been right in relation to the stalled attempts to establish a specific international treaty concerning aerial bombing. However, his claim that 'there was never any agreement about it' totally ignores the mutual exchanges through the mediation of President Roosevelt in September 1939 agreeing severe restrictions on aerial bombing, and which clearly constituted a de facto exchange of the rules of engagement. Arguably the unilateral breach without prior notice of such agreed terms comes within the definition of 'perfidy' under customary law, allowing the other side to respond in kind without notice. This point was certainly not lost on the German military command, which immediately exercised its reserved right of retaliation and publicly presented its action in these terms.

The response was in the form of a deliberate attack on the Roman and medieval capital of the English West Country, the cathedral city of Exeter, followed over the next three weeks with heavy attacks on the historic hearts of the cathedral cities of Norwich, York and Canterbury (the latter two being the seats of the two Provinces of the Church of England), plus two more heavy raids on the centre of Exeter. (See also McDougal and Feliciano 1967: 686, for further discussion of the Lübeck bombing and Hitler's public response.)

This escalation of the war led to a revival of concern about the need to protect important monuments and collections, and these worries grew as the western allies began to prepare for the liberation of continental Europe. Also, by this time alarming information was beginning to emerge about the scale of German destruction and looting on the eastern front, especially in Poland and Russia, and later of state–organized looting in France and the other occupied territories.

In the 1943 campaign on the Italian mainland the Allied Supreme Commander in Europe, General Dwight D. Eisenhower, issued clear directions requiring his forces to respect and preserve cultural property. However, following widespread criticism of the destruction of the Monastery of Monte Cassino in February 1944, Eisenhower promulgated even more explicit rules of engagement on 26 May 1944 in advance of the Normandy landings:

> Shortly we will be fighting our way across the Continent of Europe in battles designed to preserve our civilization. Inevitably, in the path of our advance will be found historical monuments and cultural centers which symbolize to the world all that we are fighting to preserve. It is the responsibility of every commander to protect and respect these symbols whenever possible . . . [After referring to the enemy's use of Monte Cassino to 'shield his defense' he continues]: . . . where military necessity dictates, commanders may order the required action even though it involves destruction of some honored site. But there are many circumstances in which damage and destruction are not necessary and cannot be justified. In such cases, through the exercise of restraint and discipline, commanders will preserve cultural centers and objects of historical and cultural significance. Civil Affairs Staffs and higher echelons will advise commanders of locations of historical monuments of this type, both in advance of the front lines and in occupied areas. This information, together with the necessary instruction, will be passed down through command channels to all levels.
>
> (Quoted by Rorimer 1950: x)

The final years of World War II in Europe saw a further major development within the military command structure aimed at protecting cultural property, with the establishment of posts of Monuments, Fine Arts and Archives (MFAA) officers attached to the US, UK and Free French forces. Although very small in number these, usually academic experts or professionals in the field in civilian life, played a vitally important part in minimizing both direct war damage, through assisting in identifying areas to be protected (more than 400 were pre–listed in advance of the May 1944 invasion of Normandy, for example), and in supervising the protection of both buildings and collections during and after the battles. With the achievement of peace, the MFAA units switched their attention to the recovery and restitution of looted and otherwise illegally transferred cultural property. In support of this, one of the earliest pieces of martial law legislation adopted in occupied Germany was Military Government of Germany Law No. 52, which provided that:

no person shall import, acquire or receive, deal in, sell, lease, transfer, export, hypothecate or otherwise dispose of, destroy or surrender possession, custody or control of any property . . . which is a work of art or cultural material of value or importance, regardless of the ownership or control thereof.

(Rorimer 1950: 216)

First-hand accounts have been given by officers of all three nations, and detailed reports sector by sector on the war damages were published by all three allies: particularly valuable are those of the art historians Captain James Rorimer, the first American MFAA Officer (and later Director of the National Gallery, Washington) (Rorimer 1950), and of the distinguished archaeologist, Sir Leonard Woolley, who headed the UK's MFAA efforts (Woolley 1947). French legislation of 1949 'closed' most of the official records of Nazi art looting and the (partial) post-war recovery until the year 2000 (apparently on the grounds that the relevant files might contain personal information on the original owners or other private individuals). However, there is a (very much under-stated) published personal account called *Le Front d'Art* by Rose Valland. Valland was the Parisian curator who was officially attached to the German art looting centre in the Paris *Orangerie* throughout the Occupation, but who simultaneously carried out faithfully and at enormous personal risk the secret orders given to her by the Director of the Louvre to record in detail day by day the activities of the Rosenberg and other Nazi art appropriation and export operations (Valland 1961).

## FROM WORLD WAR II TO THE 1949 GENEVA CONVENTIONS

The five years between 1944 and 1949 saw a series of extremely important world developments and events which, though not specifically relating to the legal protection of cultural property at the international level, were to lay the foundations for the post-war world, for good or ill. On the negative side were the rapid escalation of the potential power and destructiveness of armaments. Most notable were the advances in aerial bombardment, first with the mass bombings using the new generation of heavy bombers creating unprecedented area devastation, culminating in the total destruction in February 1945 of the historic heart of Dresden, and then the first use of atomic weapons, first on Hiroshima and then on Nagasaki. On the positive side was the creation of new international organizations with supporting international law, and major new developments in international humanitarian law drawing on the negative experiences of World War II.

Moves to lay the foundations for the new post-war world order began with the Dumbarton Oaks international conference in 1944, and these aspirations were expressed in detailed form in the San Francisco Treaty of

26 June 1945 – the Charter of the United Nations. Although this introduced no new provisions specifically relating to culture, it had two major effects which were directly relevant. The first was the new structure for the making and maintenance of peace and of establishing pacific relations between States, and second were the provisions for the creation of additional intergovernmental organizations, which led directly to the establishment of the United Nations Educational, Scientific and Cultural Organization (UNESCO) less than five months later.

On 8 August 1945 the London Charter established the rules for the war crimes tribunals, particularly those held over the next three years in Nuremberg. This declared that the member states of the United Nations had the right to investigate, try and punish 'violations of the international law of war' as representatives of the world community, while in addition the occupying powers, as the victorious belligerents exercising supreme power in Germany, were entitled to exercise domestic jurisdiction over German nationals in place of the deposed German State. The London Treaty also established the rules for the investigation of war crimes – defined as (a) crimes against peace, (b) war crimes [contrary to both customary international humanitarian law and specific treaties, especially the Hague Conventions], and (c) 'crimes against humanity . . . whether or not in violation of domestic law' (O'Brien 1972: 195–6).

The subsequent Nuremberg war crimes trials clarified some issues relating to cultural property, particularly the cases brought against Goering and Rosenberg alleging both direct and indirect complicity in the direct looting and forced sales of tens of thousands of works of art and other items of movable cultural property. Of particular importance was the explicit statement of the Nuremberg Tribunal in the key general rulings concerning applicable law in the 'Nazi Conspiracy and Aggression' in 1947 and in relation to property in the 'I.G. Farben' case:

> The law of war is to be found not only in treaties, but in the customs and practices of states which gradually obtained universal recognition, and from the general principles of justice applied by jurists and practised by military courts. This law is not static but by continual adaptation follows the needs of a changing world.
>     . . . we are unable to find that there has been a change in the basic concept of respect for property rights during belligerent occupation of a character to give legal protection to the widespread acts of plunder and spoliation committed by Nazi Germany during the course of World War II. (Nazi Conspiracy and Aggression: Nuremberg Opinion and Judgement no. 51; *United States* v. *Krauch et al.* 1948).
>
> (Both quoted by Miller, 1975: 10)

In 1948, drawing on the revelations of the Holocaust that had emerged at the end of World War II, and particularly in the Nuremberg war crimes trials, the United Nations formally declared genocide to be a grave international crime. This was implemented in the Genocide Convention of 9 December 1948, which came into force in January 1951, and is equally applicable to situations of international armed conflict, civil wars, other internal armed conflicts and peacetime. This declared that 'the Contracting Parties confirm that genocide, whether committed in time of peace or time of war, is a crime under international law which they undertake to prevent and punish' (Convention on the Prevention and Punishment of the Crime of Genocide 1948) (United Nations).

Most regrettably, due to pressure from some major states such as France concerned about the potential implications for their current national language policies in relation to both their colonies and metropolitan minorities, the long-proposed fourth definition of genocide, that of 'cultural genocide' was removed from the final draft. The circumstances and pressures which led to the deletion of the explicit cultural genocide provision, and the serious consequences of this, have been examined in detail by Thornberry (1991: 70–5).

The following day, 10 December 1948, the General Assembly of the United Nations adopted the Universal Declaration of Human Rights, which included provisions in relation to cultural rights in Article 27: 'Everyone has the right freely to participate in the cultural life of the community, to enjoy the arts and to share in scientific advancement and its benefits' (United Nations 1988).

A year later, on the initiative of the International Committee of the Red Cross, the four 1949 Geneva Conventions were adopted. The First, Second and Third Geneva Conventions of 1949 were in many ways a continuation of the by then already long tradition of international law of war, especially the Hague Conventions of 1899 and 1907, and amplified the customary international law in relation to (among other things) the protection of non-combatants. Also, following the principles established in the 1945 Treaty of London and the Nuremberg War Crimes Tribunal proceedings, under the common provisions to all four Geneva Conventions (now accepted by virtually all independent States of the world, and in any case now regarded as binding customary law), all High Contracting Parties undertake to seek out and prosecute, regardless of their nationality, all persons alleged to have committed or to have ordered defined 'grave breaches' of the Geneva Conventions (Convention IV of 12 August 1949, International Committee of the Red Cross 1987).

However, this Fourth Geneva Convention broke new ground in that it covered specifically the international humanitarian law relating to the protection of civilians. Although there were no specific provisions relating to the protection of cultural property in Geneva IV, the Hague principles prohibiting the targeting of non-combatant populations and civilian property were reinforced particularly by Article 27 of the Fourth Geneva Convention of 1949. Also, one specific new provision which might be called in aid of the protection of cultural symbols, in so far as these are expressions of religious or cultural values, was adopted under the 'General Protection' provisions of the

Fourth Geneva Convention, 'Protected persons are entitled, in all circumstances, to respect for their persons, their honour, their family rights, their
religious convictions and practices, and their manners and customs . . .'.

The years following World War II have seen many reviews of the effectiveness or otherwise of both the practical and legal measures taken to protect
cultural property, including monuments, historic areas, museums, libraries,
archive repositories etc. Important original sources include the general reviews
of Woolley (1947) for a UK perspective, Rorimer (1950) for the experience
of US MFAA officers in Europe, and the French Government's (apparently
unpublished) sixty-six pages of evidence to the Nuremberg Tribunal on the
Nazi pillaging [Délégation française au Ministère Public – Section économique
Janvier 1946, *Expose du Ministère Publique: Le Pillage des Oeuvres d'Art dans
les Pays Occupés de l'Europe Occidentale*: Doc. ref. XIII, 51], and the shorter
published account apparently derived from this (Cassou 1947). For other
countries, key sources include the publication of the Hungarian Ministry of
Culture (Damna Scientiae Hungaricae 1947) for Hungary, the five volumes
of reports of the Polish Ministry of Culture (1945), Lorenz (1947, 1954 and
N.D.) and Polish Ministry of Culture (1949–53) for Poland. Later major
studies include Valland (1961) and Simon (1971) on France, Beseler and
Gottschow (1988) on West Germany and Berlin, and Varshavsky and Rest
(1985) on Leningrad, and the masterly overview of the Nazi programme of
art looting, confiscation and forced sales from 1933 to 1945: *The Rape of
Europa* by Lyn Nicholas (1995).

## THE 1954 HAGUE CONVENTION

In relation to international law, the pre-war work of the International
Museums Office for the League of Nations was taken up again by the Italian
government initially, but the lead responsibility was then passed to UNESCO.
Following a considerable period of preparatory work, including a detailed
development of the earlier proposals prepared by the Government of the
Netherlands, a Diplomatic Conference was formally convened at The Hague
in 1954. The verbatim record of the complex series of negotiations in both
plenary sessions and specialized commissions was eventually published as the
formal record of the Conference, and has recently been analysed in great
detail, and compared with the final text, by Dr Jiri Toman (1994).

The result was the adoption on 14 May 1954 of The Convention for the
Protection of Cultural Property in the Event of Armed Conflict, The Hague,
1954, which was amplified by detailed Regulations for the practical implementation of the Convention (which form an integral part of it), and a separate Protocol for the Protection of Cultural Property in the Event of Armed
Conflict. Despite much debate and many differences of opinion on the details,
particularly at the practical level, the 1954 Conference was clearly agreed on a
number of important principles, particularly the concept of a valid international

interest of the world community in cultural property as part of 'the cultural heritage of all mankind', requiring special legal measures at the international level for its safeguarding. Professor J.H. Merryman describes this innovation as 'a charter for cultural internationalism', and points out, with every justification, the profound significance of this new definition of the international interest for other areas of the law and policy concerning the international trade in and repatriation of cultural property (Merryman 1986: 837).

The Hague Conference adopted three formal Resolutions in addition to the Convention itself. The first of these:

> expresses the hope that the competent organs of the United Nations should decide, in the event of military action being taken in implementation of the Charter, to ensure application of the provisions of the Convention by the armed forces taking part in such action.
> (Hague Convention, 1954, Preamble, UNESCO 1985: 18)

The second Resolution recommended the establishment by each High Contracting Party of a National Advisory Committee for the application of the Convention, while the third Resolution asked the Director-General of UNESCO to convene a meeting of the High Contracting Parties (though this did not in fact take place until 1962).

The background and objectives to the Convention and Protocol are set out clearly at the beginning:

> The High Contracting Parties,
> Recognizing that cultural property has suffered grave damage during recent armed conflicts and that, by reason of the developments in the technique of warfare, it is in increasing danger of destruction;
> Being convinced that damage to cultural property belonging to any people whatsoever means damage to the cultural heritage of all mankind, since each people makes its contribution to the culture of the world;
> Considering that the preservation of the cultural heritage is of great importance for all peoples of the world and that it is important that this heritage should receive international protection;
> Guided by the principles concerning the protection of cultural property during armed conflict, as established in the Conventions of The Hague of 1899 and of 1907 and in the Washington Pact of 15 April, 1935;
> Being of the opinion that such protection cannot be effective unless both national and international measures have been taken to organize it in time of peace;
> Being determined to take all possible steps to protect cultural property;
> Have agreed upon the following provisions:
> (Hague Convention 1954: Preamble)

The Convention itself first defines within the single term 'cultural property' ('biens culturels' in the French version) three different conceptual categories: (1) both immovable and movable items which are themselves of intrinsic artistic, historic, scientific or other cultural value such as historic monuments, works of art or scientific collections, (2) premises used for the housing of movable cultural property, such as museums, libraries and archive premises, and (3) 'centres containing monuments' such as important historic cities or archaeological zones. Protection is also offered by the Convention (Article 2) to temporary wartime shelters, to authorized means of emergency transport in times of hostilities, and to authorized specialist personnel: concepts derived directly from the protection for civilian air-raid shelters, hospitals and ambulances in relation to humanitarian protection in the Geneva Conventions.

The language of the 1954 Convention is very uncomplicated in relation to the second of the two key concepts of its title and purpose: that of 'protection' of cultural property. This is simply defined as comprising 'the safeguarding and respect for such property'. However, the subsidiary definitions ('safeguarding' and 'respect') are rather odd. 'Safeguarding' is not used in the obvious sense of guarding and keeping safe that which is safeguarded (in this case cultural property) at all times, including the times of greatest danger (e.g. in this case during armed conflicts). Instead, in the Convention 'safeguarding' is explicitly defined as referring only to peacetime preparations for the possible effects of war or other armed conflicts:

> The High Contracting Parties undertake to prepare in time of peace for the safeguarding of cultural property situated within their own territory against the foreseeable effects of an armed conflict, by taking such measures as they consider appropriate.
>
> (Article 3)

Protection in times of war or internal armed conflict is instead merely termed 'respect'; a term that, at least in common English parlance, falls far short of the term 'protection' used in the overall definition. 'Respect' is defined in some detail, though with the main emphasis on 'refraining from' defined activities, rather than on the taking of active measures for 'safeguarding' during actual hostilities:

> The High Contracting Parties undertake to respect cultural property situated within their own territory as well as within the territory of other High Contracting Parties by refraining from any use of the property and its immediate surroundings or of the appliances in use for its protection for purposes which are likely to expose it to destruction or damage in the event of armed conflict, and by refraining from any act of hostility directed against such property.
>
> (Article 4(1))

Under customary international law the general staff and individual field commanders of invading and occupying forces have an established responsibility not merely to refrain from unlawful acts ('respect') but to ensure adequate military and/or civil police etc. control over not only their own forces, but also irregular forces and civilians within the occupied territory so as also to 'safeguard' (in the Hague Convention sense) both the lives and property of non-combatants. Indeed, in the current discussions about possible war crime cases in former Yugoslavia, the issue of field command and control over irregular forces and civilians in relation to the wilful destruction of property is seen as an important issue. It therefore seems reasonable to require attacking and occupying forces not merely to 'respect' but also to 'safeguard' positively cultural property in so far as this is practicable.

However, despite much discussion and counter-argument at the 1954 Hague Conference (see Nahlik 1967: especially 128 onwards; Toman 1994), all of these obligations were qualified by the retention of the long-established, but by then already controversial, doctrine of 'military necessity' for the benefit of both the attacking and defending powers:

> The obligations mentioned in paragraph 1 of the present Article may be waived only in cases where military necessity imperatively requires such a waiver.
>
> (Article 4 (2))

The 'military necessity' exception has, of course, a long history in international humanitarian law, being included in the 1907 Hague Conventions, following most if not all of the nineteenth-century texts, from the US' Lieber Code of 1863, where it is defined as 'those measures which are indispensable for securing the ends of war, and which are lawful according to the modern law and usages of war' (Article 14).

Few topics in relation to the humanitarian laws of war have attracted more comment and discussion than the exception for 'military necessity', and the limitations that international law places on this. It is generally accepted that the doctrine of 'military necessity' by no means gives unlimited and unrestrained power to either attacking or defending forces. For example, in his comprehensive review of the Nuremberg Principles, O'Brien (1972: 218) insists that 'the attitude that there are no legal restrictions on "military necessity" as defined by the responsible commander or government official is clearly rejected by the Hague Conventions of 1899 and 1907 and by the four Geneva Conventions of 1949', by 'numerous predecessors' of these and in the Nuremberg Principles. He draws particular attention to some explicit prohibitions and exceptions from the rights of 'military necessity' including the Hague prohibitions on attacks on 'non-military' targets, and the 1945 London [War Crimes] Charter and Nuremberg Judgements rulings that war crimes include 'wanton destruction of cities, towns or villages, not justified by military necessity'.[2]

There is a considerable danger of a circular argument here: prohibited acts cease to be prohibited simply because the military commander deems them necessary, so 'anything goes' if the commander claims that it is a question of 'military necessity'. This is an issue discussed at considerable length and in much detail by Adler in his study of the legal considerations of the choice of targets in war. In a key part of his analysis he argues:

> Although military necessity was a primary consideration in the Hague Conventions [i.e. those of 1899 and 1907, not the 1954 Convention, and with reference particularly to the Hague 1907 Annex], it was implicitly limited to the use of force which is required to attain a given objective. The rights of belligerents to adopt means of injuring the enemy is not unlimited.
>
> (Adler 1972: 295)

Discussing the 'military necessity' exception in the 1954 Hague Convention, Adler continues:

> Cultural Property is immune, except where military necessity prevents such immunity. The necessity relates to the actual use of the property, physical or tactical conditions of attack, and the capabilities and limitations of ordinance . . . an anomaly that would be removed by proper balancing of militarily necessary targeting with minimum incidental damage to nonmilitary targets. Such an approach would legitimize, for instance, the destruction of Monte Cassino and the Citadel at Hué in the Vietnam War unless alternative means were available to neutralise the military use of such institutions.
>
> (ibid.: 308)

In more direct language, General Eisenhower had set out his view of the limits of 'military necessity' in his Staff Orders of 29 December 1943 relating to the Italian mainland campaign:

> Today we are fighting in a country which has contributed a great deal to our cultural inheritance, a country rich in monuments which by their creation helped and now in their old age illustrate the growth of the civilization which is ours. If we have to choose between destroying a famous building and sacrificing our own men, then our men's lives count infinitely more and the buildings must go. But the choice is not always so clear-cut as that. In many cases the monuments can be spared without any detriment to operational needs. Nothing can stand against the argument of military necessity. That is an accepted principle. But the phrase 'military necessity' is sometimes used where it would be more truthful to speak of military convenience or even of personal convenience. I do not want it to cloak slackness or indifference.
>
> (Quoted in American Commission 1946: 48)

Referring to 'military necessity' in relation to non-combatants rather than cultural property (though the principles seem equally applicable), Adler concludes:

The question at all times is one of balancing military advantage with accidental damage. If a prosecution for the action is forth-coming it should be directed at he who placed the military target in a populated area.

(Adler: 309)

This last point is a most important one in relation to the 1954 Convention's concept of protection (and indeed has parallels under most codifications of international humanitarian law). The moment that the enemy uses an other-wise protected monument or other feature for a military purpose, or indeed places any form of the 'apparatus of war' (in the widest sense) in proximity to a protected place, that protection is temporarily lost. Consequently, the defending power has to remove or effectively neutralize and demilitarize everything that could be a legitimate military, political or economic target within the vicinity of the monument or other protected feature. If any monu-ment or other cultural feature is used for any kind of military purpose then the monument etc. immediately loses its protection under the 1954 Convention, and only regains protection when the military use ends. If this is not done, then no matter how important the feature, it becomes a legit-imate military target.

The (unadopted) 1923 *Rules of Air Warfare* and the International Museums Office draft of 1939 each recognized this, with their attempts to define minimum separation differences between protected areas and legitimate mili-tary targets. In the late 1950s and early 1960s, when the Holy See prepared proposals for the designation of the whole of the Vatican City as a 'centre containing monuments' with Special Protection under the 1954 Hague Convention, there had to be detailed negotiations with the government of Italy about the measures that it would be necessary for Italy to take in the event of threatened or actual hostilities. These necessary measures include diverting railway routes and neutralizing Italian military and political estab-lishments within a realistic zone of targeting error close to the boundaries of the Vatican City special protection zone.

More recently, in the Second Gulf War (the 'Desert Storm' campaign of 1991) the US claimed that the Iraqis had used cultural property within their control to shield military objects from attack:

A classic example is the positioning of two MiG-21 fighter aircraft at the entrance of the ancient city of Ur. Although the laws of war permitted their attack, and although each could have been destroyed utilizing precision-guided munitions, US commanders recognized that the aircraft for all intents and purposes were inca-pable of military operations from their position, and elected against their attack for fear of collateral damage to the monument.

(US Department of Defense statement to
Congress, 19 January 1993 – reproduced in
Boylan 1993: 201–6)

However, over the past half-century or more there has been a growing weight of opinion across the legal, political, humanitarian, and even military, spectrum that regardless of the conduct of the enemy, there have to be some absolutes in the conduct of war, which even the most pressing and urgent 'military necessity' cannot ever override. Following the atrocities of World War II, the 1949 Geneva Conventions placed absolute limits on the right of retaliation or counteraction against even the most heinous war crimes. A key Common Article in the various 1949 Geneva Conventions requires unconditional compliance with each Convention regardless of the perceived perfidy or alleged war crimes of the enemy, with States Parties undertaking 'to respect and ensure respect for the present Convention in all circumstances', while the First Additional Protocol to the Geneva Conventions of 1977 extends this absolute prohibition to reprisals against cultural property, with a specific cross-reference to the 1954 Hague Convention.

It is arguable that in comparison with the 1907 Hague Laws and Customs of War the abandonment of the universal 'military necessity' exception in the Geneva Conventions was the most important single advance in codified international humanitarian law for more than forty years. Consequently, and having seen the widespread acceptance of the Geneva Conventions four and a half years earlier, those preparing the working draft for the 1954 Hague Intergovernmental Conference followed the new principles established in Geneva, and therefore excluded the 'military necessity' exemption of the Fourth and Ninth Hague Conventions of 1907.

However, this issue became a major area of contention in the 1954 Hague Convention Diplomatic Conference. The military delegates of the US and the UK insisted on the addition of a 'military necessity' exception clause as a fundamental condition of their States' acceptance of the Convention. The position of the US at the Conference seems particularly illogical since it was (and remains) a Party to the 1935 Washington Pan-American Treaty ('Roerich Pact'), Article 1 of which requires unconditional 'respect and protection' with no hint of any 'military necessity' exemption.

The proposed inclusion of a 'military necessity' exception was opposed in a vote not just by the USSR and all other states of the 'socialist' block, but also by some Western European countries, including France, Greece and Spain. Other states, while opposing the principle of the proposed exemption, considered that the acceptance of the final treaty by both the US and UK was absolutely essential and, by a majority, the Conference agreed to add the 'military necessity' provisions, albeit with the qualification that this could in future only be invoked when 'the military necessity imperatively requires such a waiver' (See Government of the Netherlands 1961; Nahlik 1967 and 1988; Toman 1994).[3]

The general requirement of 'respect' (subject of course to imperative 'military necessity') was further clarified by two further clauses requiring effective measures against theft and pillage, and prohibiting reprisals against cultural property, respectively:

3. The High Contracting Parties further undertake to prohibit, prevent and, if necessary, put a stop to any form of theft, pillage or misappropriation of, and any acts of vandalism directed against, cultural property. They shall refrain from requisitioning movable cultural property situated in the territory of another High Contracting Party.

4. They shall refrain from any act directed by way of reprisals against cultural property.

(Article 4)

There is also an express prohibition of reprisals or otherwise prohibited acts whereby, even if another High Contracting Party fails to comply with the Convention, counteraction is still not allowed:

5. No High Contracting Party may evade the obligations incumbent upon it under the present Article, in respect of another High Contracting Party, by reason of the fact that the latter has not applied the measures of safeguard referred to in Article 3.

(Article 4)

Other important obligations accepted by the States Parties to the 1954 Convention are the provisions relating to Occupation. These require any Contracting State in occupation of all or part of the territory of another Party to support so far as possible the established structure of cultural property protection in the occupied lands. However, should the competent national authorities be unable to handle the tasks the occupying power itself must 'take the most necessary measures of preservation' (Article 5).

This is followed by a rather obscurely worded provision that:

Any High Contracting Party whose government is considered their legitimate government by members of a resistance movement, shall, if possible, draw their attention to the obligation to comply with those provisions of the Convention dealing with respect for cultural property.

(Article 5)

The intention appears to be to require the legitimate authority for an occupied territory, such as a government-in-exile, to draw the terms of the 1954 Convention to the attention of any internal resistance forces under its control or influence within the occupied territory. Ideally, all States Parties in a position to influence the conduct of irregular forces in an enemy (or indeed third) country should accept at least a moral obligation to try to apply this provision. However, the extent to which this obligation is binding on States Parties which may be in a position to influence, but claim not to have effective control – in the strict legal sense – of irregular forces would be a question of fact to be determined by appropriate legal process.

The other fundamental concept of the Convention is the obligation of States Parties in respect of peacetime preparation for the protection of cultural property, defined as 'safeguarding':

The High Contracting Parties undertake to prepare in time of peace for the safeguarding of cultural property situated within their own territory against the foreseeable effects of an armed conflict, by taking such measures as they consider appropriate.

(Article 3)

In 1954 and 1958 UNESCO published (French and English editions respectively) a very substantial practical handbook on recommended measures to be taken in relation to peacetime preparation, which was (and indeed still is) a valuable guide for action by both governments and individual cultural institutions and monuments (Lavachery and Noblecourt 1954; Noblecourt 1958). Also, the text of the Convention provides (in Article 26) for the High Contracting Parties to report to UNESCO on the action taken under the Convention, thus sharing information on the action each had taken in relation to, among other things, the peacetime preparation.

However, the wording of the undertaking in the 1954 Convention in respect of 'safeguarding' is so weak that a High Contracting Party could perfectly well decide that they need do virtually nothing, should they decide that this is what 'they consider appropriate', for any reason. For example, the government might believe (or may simply want its citizens and neighbouring states to believe) that there is no possibility of its involvement in any kind of armed conflict. This position, whether genuinely held or not, can of course be a serious barrier to the development of peacetime preparations for the possibility of war or other armed conflict in every area of national life, not solely in relation to the 1954 Convention.

Chapter I of the Convention concludes with important provisions requiring the peacetime training of the armed forces:

1. The High Contracting Parties undertake to introduce in time of peace into their military regulations or instructions such provisions as may ensure observance of the present Convention, and to foster in the members of their armed forces a spirit of respect for the culture and cultural property of all peoples.

2. The High Contracting Parties undertake to plan or establish in peace-time, within their armed forces, services or specialist personnel whose purpose will be to secure respect for cultural property and to co-operate with the civilian authorities responsible for safeguarding it.

(Article 7)

Chapter II (Articles 8–11) of the 1954 Hague Convention introduces and regulates the concept of 'Special Protection'. Under this, UNESCO, after consulting all High Contracting Parties, may place on a special list at the request of the state concerned, a limited number of temporary refuges or shelters for movable cultural property, and also 'centres containing monuments and other immovable property of very great importance', subject to the defending state being both able and willing to demilitarize the location and its surroundings.

Chapter III provides protection and immunity, modelled closely on that granted to ambulances under the Hague and Geneva Conventions, for official transport used in both internal and international transfers of cultural property, subject to prior authorization and international supervision of the movement (1954 Convention Articles 12–14; Regulations Articles 17–19).

Chapters IV-VII cover a wide range of provisions requiring belligerents to provide for the protection of authorized personnel engaged in the protection of cultural property (Article 16), details relating to the use of the official emblem of the Hague Convention (a blue and white shield), and issues relating to the interpretation and application of the Convention (Articles 15–18). Again, all of these are closely modelled on parallel provisions relating to humanitarian protection found in the 1949 Geneva Conventions.

Of particular, and growing, importance was the decision of the 1954 Inter-governmental Conference to follow Common Article 3 of the 1949 Geneva Conventions, and extend the protection of cultural property beyond the traditional definition of 'war' into the difficult area of internal armed conflicts, such as civil wars, 'liberation' wars and armed independence campaigns, and – probably – to major armed terrorist campaigns:

> 1. In the event of an armed conflict not of an international character occurring within the territory of one of the High Contracting Parties, each party to the conflict shall be bound to apply, as a minimum, the provisions of the present Convention which relate to respect for cultural property.
>
> 2. The parties to the conflict shall endeavour to bring into force, by means of special agreements, all or part of the other provisions of the present Convention.
>
> 3. The United Nations Educational, Scientific and Cultural Organization may offer its services to the parties to the conflict.
>
> 4. The application of the preceding provisions shall not affect the legal status of the parties to the conflict.
>
> (Article 19)

In the years since the adoption of the 1954 Convention, non-international armed conflicts, particularly those relating to internal strife along national, regional, ethnic, linguistic or religious lines, have become an increasingly common feature of the world order and in losses of monuments, museums, libraries and other cultural repositories. A cynic might argue that possibly the exploding 'heritage' movement that has developed in almost all parts of the world in the past half-century has done far too good a job in promoting the understanding of the cultural heritage, including museums, monuments, sites, archives and libraries, and in particular in presenting these as proud symbols of the cultural, religious or ethnic identity of nations, peoples and communities.

Whatever the reason, it is clear that the period since the end of World War II has seen deliberate iconoclastic attacks on, and destruction of, cultural heritage symbols unprecedented in modern times, more reminiscent of the religious conflicts of the Crusades, the Protestant revolution and religious wars of the sixteenth and seventeenth centuries. It can truly be said that while there have certainly been terrible losses of the cultural heritage and cultural identity in the two World Wars and many lesser conflicts of the nineteenth and first half of the twentieth centuries, the great majority of these losses have not been due to deliberate assaults on the cultures and identities of the territories fought over. However, what we have seen in successive Arab–Israeli conflicts from 1947 onwards, in partitioned Cyprus, in Afghanistan, and, above all, in former Yugoslavia (to give just four examples) shows that attacks on the cultural heritage have moved to a quite different plane: such destruction and mayhem are no longer unfortunate accidents of war due to ignorance or lack of care – instead, they have become primary war aims in their own right.

So far as dissemination of the 1954 Convention is concerned, the High Contracting Parties undertake to do so widely within their countries, certainly among the military, and if possible to the civilian population (Article 25), to communicate their national translations (beyond the French, English, Russian and Spanish texts of the 1954 Hague Conference) to other Parties (through UNESCO), and to submit periodic reports to UNESCO at least once every four years on the measures being taken to implement the Convention (Article 26). In fact it is evident that only a small minority of High Contracting Parties have made serious efforts to disseminate knowledge of the Convention more widely within their countries, and the same is true of the submission of the required periodic reports (Boylan 1993: 43, 89–90, 199–200).

Bearing in mind the importance of measures for enforcement, and indeed the Nuremberg War Crimes Tribunal rulings, the provisions for enforcement action and sanctions were remarkably weak and rather vague:

> The High Contracting Parties undertake to take, within the frame-
> work of their ordinary criminal jurisdiction, all necessary steps to
> prosecute and impose penal or disciplinary sanctions upon those
> persons, of whatever nationality, who commit or order to be
> committed a breach of the present Convention.
>
> (Article 28)

In fact, the Convention provides no explicit mechanism for resolving disputes about enforcement between States Parties to it nor for any form of specific international legal or extra-territorial action of the kind undertaken against, for example, Rosenberg in the Nuremberg war crimes trials. However, it must be stressed that the weakness of the Convention in this respect is the result of decisions of the Hague Conference to water down the original draft text, as is clear from both the procès-verbal of the Conference and the detailed analysis of the 1954 Conference and resulting text by Dr Jiri Toman (Government of the Netherlands 1961; Toman 1994).

The concluding Articles of the Convention dealt with a range of mainly legal issues, including a provision permitting the application of the Convention to colonies and other dependent territories, formalizing the relationship of the new Convention to the 1899 and 1907 Hague Conventions and the 1935 Washington ('Roerich') Pact, and including provisions relating to both individual denunciation by a High Contracting Party and for intergovernmental revision of the Convention and Regulations (Articles 28–40).

The 1954 Hague Regulations, which form an integral part of the Convention, set out first (Chapter I, Articles 1–10) the practical procedures to be followed in relation to the compiling by the Director-General of UNESCO of an international list of persons qualified to carry out the functions of Commissioners-General, and procedures to be followed in the event of armed conflict, including the arrangements for the appointment of cultural representatives, Commissioners-General and the responsibilities of the Protecting Powers (appointed in accordance with the Hague 1907 and Geneva 1949 principles).

The second part (Chapter II, Articles 11–16) of the Regulations deals with the practical arrangements and procedures for the granting and registration of 'Special Protection', including the notification of all proposals to every High Contracting Party and arrangements for the submitting of objections and for eventual arbitration on these if necessary, as well as provisions for the cancelling of 'Special Protection' where appropriate.

Chapter III of the Regulations (Articles 17–19) sets out in some detail the procedures for the transport of movable cultural property to a place of safety (possibly abroad) for protection, with the approval of the neutral Commissioner-General overseeing cultural heritage matters during the conflict.

The final part, Chapter IV, regulates the use of the Official Emblem and the identity cards and other identifying markers of persons duly authorized to undertake official duties in relation to the implementation of the Convention (Articles 20–21).

At a comparatively late stage in the 1954 Hague Conference proceedings it became clear that there was an irreconcilable split. The majority of Delegations wanted to include in the new Convention binding controls over transfers of movable cultural property within war zones and occupied territories. However, a number of countries argued strongly against this position, arguing variously that such measures would either damage the international art and antiquities trade, interfere with private property rights within their countries or, in most cases, both.

The final compromise over these objections was to separate out such measures into a separate legal instrument: the Protocol for the Protection of Cultural Property in the Event of Armed Conflict (now known as the First Protocol following the March 1999 Diplomatic Conference to update the Convention – see below). The 1954 Protocol has two unambiguous purposes. First, a State Party to the Protocol undertakes to take active measures to prevent all exports of movable cultural property as defined in the Hague

Convention from any territory which it may occupy during an armed conflict. Second, all High Contracting Parties undertake to seize and hold to the end of hostilities any cultural property from war zones which has been exported in contravention of the first principle of the Protocol. In marked contrast with the position taken by the US and Soviet Union at the Berlin (Potsdam) Conference of July–August 1945, less than a decade earlier, the Protocol also provides that such cultural property shall never be retained after the end of hostilities as war reparations.

## FROM THE 1954 HAGUE CONVENTION TO THE 1999 HAGUE DIPLOMATIC CONFERENCE

The 1954 Intergovernmental Conference was attended by official delegates of a majority of the Sovereign States in membership of the United Nations at that date, and most participating States signed the Final Act over the following months. However the number of States that formally ratified the Convention and Protocol was disappointing. Forty years on from the adoption of the 1954 Hague Convention, eighty-two countries (less than half of the United Nations member states) had become parties to the Convention itself, and of these fourteen had accepted only the main Convention, while rejecting the additional protection offered to movable cultural property by the Protocol. Thanks to a major effort by UNESCO, the situation has improved somewhat over recent years, although there are still substantial gaps. In particular, few African or Latin American countries have adopted the 1954 Convention, while the failure of three of the five permanent members of the UN Security Council – China, the UK and the US – to ratify the Convention undoubtedly greatly weakens its authority and effectiveness.

Those drafting the 1954 Convention probably envisaged war in terms of well-defined international conflicts between structured and well-disciplined military commands on the pattern of the two World Wars. However, looking back over history this was probably a mistake: more than half of all the armed conflicts resulting in fatalities that occurred between 1820 and 1945 were mainly internal rather than external conflicts, or mixed conflicts. Little (1975: 202), quoting L.F. Richardson's *The Statistics of Deadly Quarrels*, gives the figures for that 125-year period as 112 mainly internal, 33 mixed and 137 mainly external. According to these estimates, although the numbers of casualties were greatest in the two World Wars (between 3 million and 30 million fatalities – within a logarithmic scale), the next five in terms of the number of fatalities (between 300,000 and 3 million casualties each) were all internal or mixed, while within the 30,000 to 300,000 fatalities range the internal and mixed outnumbered international wars by fourteen conflicts to ten. Certainly, the great majority of the perhaps almost 200 armed conflicts that have occurred in the world since 1954 have been anything but traditional, well-organized and -commanded international wars. As long ago as 1972, O'Brien, a leading legal expert, commented '. . . sub-conventional and guerrilla warfare . . . has become the central form of contemporary armed conflict . . . there is a very real problem here that needs more clarification in positive international law on the one hand and more imagination and restraint on the part of belligerents on the other' (O'Brien 1972: 230).

Formal declarations of war are nowadays almost unheard of, as are formal exchanges of the respective rules of engagement (of the kind agreed between Britain, France, Germany and Poland in 3 September 1939). Protecting Powers in accordance with the Geneva Conventions etc. are rarely nominated and agreed, and only a very small proportion of the fighting in the many armed conflicts of the past 40 years have consisted of organized set-piece fighting, whether by land, sea or air, between two well-defined states.

In contrast with the clear assumptions of 1954, since the Hague Convention came into effect, perhaps only the 1956 Suez operation and the two subsequent Arab–Israeli Wars, and the two Gulf Wars of the past decade (Iran–Iraq, and the Iraq invasion of, and subsequent 'Desert Storm' expulsion from, Kuwait) were conducted along traditional lines (although even in these cases there were significant complications in the form of internal uprisings by racial, cultural or religious minorities, as with the Kurdish and Shiite uprisings in the north and south of Iraq respectively, for example). Most wars have had a major element of internal armed conflict even where there was a substantial international involvement as well, as with the Vietnam and Afghanistan conflicts.

One of the most marked features of the past quarter century has been the steady resurgence of internal conflicts of all kinds. At one extreme these include quasi-military operations by secret, irregular, terrorist campaigns by extremely small groups of political or religious extremists with little or no popular support from the population at large. They almost certainly do not meet the Red Cross definitions of armed conflicts and hence should probably be classed as simple criminal acts. For example, despite their self-declared title of the 'Irish Republican Army', the losses of, and damage to, important historic monuments in the 1992 and 1993 car-bombings of the City of London and the 1992 fire-bombing of the important regional military history museum in Shrewsbury Castle, also in England, could not be claimed as resulting from 'armed conflict', nor could the serious damage to Argentina's leading Hispano-American art museum (and national historic monument), the Fernando Blanco Museum in Buenos Aires, also in 1992, in the murderous car-bombing of the nearby Israeli Embassy by an unidentified terrorist group. The term 'armed conflict' is equally inapplicable to the cultural atrocity (accompanied by tragic loss of life) which occurred when religious fundamentalists tore down with their bare hands the historic Mogul period Great Mosque at Ayodhya, India, in December 1992.

However, from events such as these ranges a full spectrum of internal conflicts with a political, regional, cultural or religious basis, right through to full-scale civil wars, independence uprisings, and – increasingly frequently – mixed conflicts with either international intervention within a pre-existing internal conflict on the one hand, or a planned or opportunistic internal uprising by dissident groups or regions taking advantage of the country's involvement in an international conflict, on the other.

Even in the case of more organized and centrally directed military operations involving states or territory subject to the 1954 Hague Convention and Protocol, only rarely were its principles and detailed terms honoured by all parties during conflicts and subsequent occupations, including those affecting many regions of great cultural heritage. Well-known examples included the various conflicts in south-east Asia of the 1960s and 1970s, the Middle Eastern conflicts and occupations involving Israel, Egypt, Jordan, Lebanon and Syria from 1956 to the early 1990s, conflicts concerning Cyprus, and the bitter and destructive First Gulf (Iran–Iraq) War of the 1980s. Deliberate attacks on, and destruction of, cultural heritage sites and buildings frequently happened in such cases despite insistent promptings of actual and prospective belligerents of their obligations under the Hague Convention and the more general principles of customary international law by successive Directors-General of UNESCO, and often by neutral countries as well.

There were, however, some important advances in the protection of cultural property more generally during the 1970s and subsequently. For example, following long and difficult negotiations, the 1970 General Conference of UNESCO adopted the Convention on the Means of Prohibiting and Preventing the Illicit Import, Export and Transfer of Ownership of Cultural Property (UNESCO 1985), which aimed to outlaw the widespread trafficking in both smuggled and stolen works of art and other cultural property. Curiously, it includes no explicit reference to the 1954 Hague Convention and, especially, the Hague Protocol, even though it has been widely recognized for centuries that the risk of cultural losses through theft and smuggling are probably at their greatest during times of armed conflict and disorder, whether international or internal. In the 1970 Convention, UNESCO adopted a far more detailed definition of the term 'cultural property' than in the 1954 Hague Convention, and in the longer term it would be desirable for UNESCO to adopt common definitions for both wartime and peacetime protection of movable cultural property (Boylan 1993: 45, 49–51, 189–97).

Two years later UNESCO adopted the World Heritage Convention (1972), which provided for the designation of sites and zones of pre-eminent world importance as 'World Heritage Sites'. This Convention covers both cultural and, for the first time, natural sites. Once again the definitions adopted were quite different from those in the 1954 Convention, adding further to the difficulties and possibility of confusion. However, the World Heritage Convention included the important provision that States Parties to it must actively promote respect for the national and international patrimony throughout the population, and to establish and maintain adequate systems and organizational structures for the necessary practical measures.

Then, in 1977, some eighteen years after the adoption of the original 1949 Geneva Conventions, a Diplomatic Conference to review these was called by the International Committee of the Red Cross. It completed its work by consensus – that is, without a formal vote. The result was that the provisions of the Fourth Geneva Convention of 1949 were substantially widened by the First Additional Protocol relating to international armed conflicts and the Second Additional Protocol relating to non-international armed conflicts and serious civil disturbances (International Committee of the Red Cross 1989; Kalshoven 1987: 71–145).

In parallel provisions, each Protocol prohibits attacks on cultural or religious property 'which constitute the cultural and spiritual heritage of peoples' and the use of this for military purposes by either attacking or defending regular or irregular forces. However, the 1977 Additional Protocols have not yet gained the universal acceptance of the 1949 Conventions, and a number of major powers (including the US) still maintain objections to some aspects, particularly what is perceived to be an implied constraint in Protocol I on the use of nuclear weapons. More widely, the principles of Protocol II in relation to internal armed conflict are seen by some governments as limiting a state's powers in putting down internal revolutions and other attacks on the integrity and hence the very survival of the State itself.

More recently still, on the proposal again of the International Committee of the Red Cross, a further Geneva Convention on prohibitions or restrictions on the use of certain conventional weapons which may be deemed to be excessively injurious or to have indiscriminate effects was approved in October 1980. The Second Protocol to the 1980 Convention includes specific prohibitions on the use of booby-traps on cultural property, among other cases:

> Art. 6. Prohibition on the use of certain booby-traps
> 1. Without prejudice to the rules of international law applicable in armed conflict relating to treachery and perfidy, it is prohibited in all circumstances to use: . . .
> (b) booby-traps which are in any way attached to or associated with: . . .
>    (vii) objects clearly of a religious nature;
>    (ix) historic monuments, works of art or places of worship which constitute the cultural or spiritual heritage of peoples;
>                (International Committee of the Red Cross 1987)

A further development of considerable significance arose out of the international horror at, and protests about, the sheer savagery of the internal conflicts of the early 1990s, particularly in Yugoslavia (see, for example, Institute for the Protection of Cultural Monuments, 1992a and b; Maroevic 1995; Museum Documentation Centre 1991 and 1997). As a result, for the first time since the Nuremberg and Tokyo war crimes trials of 1945–48, allegations of

breaches of international law in relation to cultural property in the former
Yugoslavia are being actively investigated and prosecuted in specially established International Criminal Courts. By its Resolution 808 of 22 February
1993, the United Nations Security Council initiated formal procedures leading to the establishment of an international war crimes tribunal to investigate
and act on allegations of 'grave breaches and other violations of international
humanitarian law . . . including . . . destruction of cultural and religious property . . .'. It is difficult to over-emphasize the potential importance of any test
cases relating to 'cultural war crimes' under the planned United Nations proceedings, in order to demonstrate to the world the gravity of such allegations
(Boylan 1993: 47).

Public concern and horror mounted over the events in disintegrating
Yugoslavia from late 1990 onwards, particularly the extended sieges and bom-
bardments of Vukovar and the World Heritage city of Dubrovnik, both in
Croatia, and then of the historic centres of Sarajevo and Mostar (among many
other places) in Bosnia Herzegovina. By this time, UNESCO and a number
of key member governments had already turned their attention to the apparent ineffectiveness of the 1954 Hague Convention, and had decided to embark
upon a major review of the treaty. In 1992 the Executive Board of UNESCO
approved a report from the Director-General concerning the possible reinforcement of UNESCO's legal instruments for the protection of the cultural
heritage, prepared in response to a request from the last General Conference
of the organization. The Director-General's proposal was for a comprehensive
review of the 1954 Hague Convention and Protocol, particularly, though not
exclusively, in relation to its practical application (Prott 1994).

On the recommendation of the country's Ambassador to UNESCO, Dr
Johannes Sizoo, the government of the Netherlands offered UNESCO additional funds out of the Dutch budget for projects supporting the United
Nation's International Decade of International Law, 1990–99, to supplement
UNESCO's own budget for work on the Hague Convention. After discussions between Ambassador Sizoo and UNESCO, in September 1992 I was
approached by Dr Lyndel Prott, Head of International Standards in the
Cultural Heritage Division of UNESCO, and asked if I would carry out such
a review. The agreed basis of the research contract, which ran for approximately nine months from December 1992, was to review the 1954 Hague
Convention, Regulations and Protocol, not so much from the strictly legal
standpoint, but to try to identify the practical reasons for its apparent ineffectiveness in so many cases.

Through the period, in addition to much library and archive research, I
consulted as widely as possible, and at all levels, for example within the
United Nations and UNESCO, with a number of governments, with non-
governmental organizations such as the International Committee of the Red
Cross, the International Council of Museums (ICOM) and the International
Council on Monuments and Sites (ICOMOS) and with a wide range of
individual legal, cultural heritage and military experts. I drew on my personal

experience in managing museums, archives, monuments and sites, and of libraries, as well as my international experience in cultural heritage policy and operations through ICOM and UNESCO.

My report was considered first in draft form at a meeting of experts from nineteen countries held in the Ministry of Foreign Affairs, The Hague, in June 1993, where the total of more than forty recommendations addressed to governments, UNESCO, the United Nations and non-governmental organizations were reviewed. The finalized version of the Report in both English and French editions was presented to the autumn meeting of the UNESCO Executive Board, which agreed to its publication and widespread distribution free of charge (Boylan 1993). It was also agreed to invite all States Parties to the 1954 Convention to a formal meeting of States during the next UNESCO General Conference to discuss the issues raised. It was also agreed to redouble UNESCO's efforts to persuade more states to adopt the 1954 Convention and Protocol, and all countries that had not ratified or otherwise adopted them to do so without further delay – a move to which there was a moderately encouraging response.

In February 1994 a drafting group of experts met in Lauswolt, the Netherlands, to draw up specific proposals in the light of the Boylan Report and other recent consultations and considerations, and this meeting was followed by a further expert meeting in Stockholm at the invitation of ICOMOS Sweden, the Central Board of Antiquities and the Swedish National Commission of UNESCO, during which among other contributions Lyndel Prott outlined UNESCO's actions and current position on the updating of the 1954 Hague Convention, (Prott 1994), and I outlined the results of my UNESCO study and recommendations, emphasizing the need to develop new structures and adequate systems of information and communication as a prerequisite for the effective application of the Convention, and of any future development of it (Boylan 1994).

In the same year, discussions were initiated by Dr Leo Van Nispen on behalf of the International Council on Monuments and Sites (ICOMOS) on the establishment of a kind of 'Red Cross' for the Cultural Heritage, proposing the title 'International Committee of the Blue Shield' – the official symbol of cultural heritage protection under the 1954 Hague Convention being a blue and white shield. After initial meetings and seminars involving monuments and sites and museum and gallery specialists and organizations, particularly ICOMOS and the International Council of Museums (ICOM), Blue Shield (ICBS) was broadened to bring in the UNESCO-recognized bodies for the other two areas of cultural property protected by the Hague Convention; the International Council of Archives (ICA) and the International Federation of Library Associations and Institutions (IFLA). The ICBS was finally formally constituted as a standing emergency coordination and response committee of the four non-governmental organizations in 1996, with the two specially relevant intergovernmental organizations, UNESCO and the International Centre For Conservation, Rome, (ICCROM), as the closest possible partners and as permanent observers at all ICBS meetings. Following this there have been a growing number of moves to parallel the rapidly emerging cooperation and solidarity between the four ICBS professional bodies at the international level by the development of national Blue Shield organizations, beginning with Belgium and Canada.

During the 1995 biennial General Conference of UNESCO, a meeting of States Parties to the 1954 Hague Convention was convened, with all other member states of UNESCO and the UN (plus representatives of key non-governmental organizations) invited to attend as observers. This meeting supported the moves towards some kind of updating of the Convention, either by the revision of the Convention itself, or by the adoption of a new International Instrument linked to it, such as an Additional Protocol, under the international law of treaties; and the Lauswolt draft was referred to all interested parties for detailed analysis and comment. This in turn was followed by a further experts' drafting meeting hosted by the government of Austria and then a further meeting of States Parties and observers during the next UNESCO General Conference in 1997.

In the course of the latter meeting the government of the Netherlands formally announced that it intended to invite all UNESCO and UN member states to a formal Diplomatic Conference in The Hague to review and, if felt fit, revise or supplement the 1954 Hague Convention, as a further contribution to the World Decade of International Law. After some slippage in the Netherlands' provisional timetable due to delays in completing the negotiations for the establishment of a permanent International Criminal Court, finally agreed by a Diplomatic Conference in Rome in May–June 1998, invitations were issued in late 1998 by the Dutch Minister of Foreign Affairs calling a two-week Diplomatic Conference to revise or supplement the 1954 Hague Convention.

## 1999 SECOND PROTOCOL TO THE 1954 HAGUE CONVENTION

This Conference opened on 15 March 1999 in the Congress Centre, The Hague. This was a specially significant, even symbolic, location, being just a short distance from the Peace Palace where the original 1954 Convention had been drawn up, and on the same city block as the Courts of the International Criminal Tribunal for Yugoslavia, where criminal trials of men accused of both humanitarian and cultural war crimes were taking place. The 84 national delegations participating were made up of more than 300 diplomats and legal, military and cultural experts, and there were also representatives from both intergovernmental and non-governmental international organizations, including the International Committee of the Red Cross. The Conference Secretariat was provided by UNESCO's Division of Cultural Heritage, with much support from the Dutch Ministry of Foreign Affairs.

Also officially accredited to the Conference were the four leading UNESCO-linked international non-governmental organizations: the International Council on Archives (ICA); the International Federation of Library Associations and Institutions (IFLA); the International Council of Museums (ICOM); and the International Council on Monuments and Sites (ICOMOS), through a joint delegation under the auspices of the International Committee of the Blue Shield (ICBS). This delegation was led by myself, and supported from time to time by Manus Brinkman, Secretary-General of ICOM, and Mme Marie-Thérèse Varlamoff, the IFLA representative on the ICBS.

After two gruelling weeks, 15–26 March 1999, during which things often looked very bleak because of deep-seated differences between states, it was decided to adopt a new supplementary legal instrument to the 1954 Hague Convention on the Protection of Cultural Property in the Event of Armed Conflict, in the form of an Additional Protocol, named the Second Protocol (the original 1954 Protocol being renamed the First Protocol). The new measure was formally adopted by unanimous consensus of the Conference on the evening of Friday 26 March, with the heads of all national delegations taking part in the Diplomatic Conference signing the formal 'Final Act' (Boylan 1999). However, this does not automatically commit any State then to proceed to sign and ratify the new treaty itself. National legislative and other legal procedures vary considerably from country to country and usually require often prolonged consideration at the political level (and in this case consideration of the military aspects also) and, in most cases, major new primary legislation at the national level.

The new Protocol (Roberts and Guelff 1999; and reproduced as the appendix to this chapter) represents much the greatest advance in international cultural protection measures for decades – certainly since the 1972 World Heritage Convention and probably since the original 1954 Hague Convention. It is also the most substantial development in the general field of International Humanitarian Law since the drawing up of the Geneva Convention Additional Protocols of 1977. Both the World Heritage Convention and the 1977 Additional Protocols offered significant precedents (and in many places established forms of wording) for many of the innovations in the 1999 Second Protocol. The concepts behind the innovations and clarifications in turn reflected and attempted to respond to the long, and sad, experience of the failure of the world community to prevent great losses of important cultural property over the previous forty-five years, especially in the sort of 'dirty' armed conflicts such as civil wars that have been a constant feature of the post-war world, as identified in the 1993 Boylan Report for UNESCO and other critiques of the original 1954 Convention.

After the necessary preamble and definitions in Chapter 1, the new Chapter 2 greatly clarifies and amplifies the provisions of Hague 1954 in respect of 'protection' in general. There are now much clearer explanations of, for example, the very limited cases in which 'imperative military necessity' can be claimed in order to allow an attack on cultural property – in effect substantially reducing the possible use of this (a long-standing problem dating back to the original 1899 and 1907 Hague Laws of War). The obligations of States in relation to peacetime preparation and training have also been clarified and expanded, giving among many other things a major emphasis on the obligation to develop adequate inventories and catalogues of both monuments and sites and museum collections. The Chapter also clarifies (and limits very considerably) what an occupying power may do in relation to cultural property within occupied territories, placing very narrow limits on archaeological excavations and the alteration or change of use of cultural property, and requiring the occupying power to prohibit and prevent all illicit export, removal or change of ownership of cultural property.

Chapter 3 creates a new category of 'Exceptional Protection' for the most important sites, monuments and institutions. This will be an international des-ignation publicized in advance (rather along the lines of the World Heritage List under the 1972 World Heritage Convention). The detailed provisions restrict even further than the new Chapter 2 provisions the 1954 'Imperative Military Necessity' exemption: even in the case of gross misuse by the enemy, it will be lawful to attack or retaliate only if the cultural property is currently actually being used in direct support of the fighting etc., and even then there must be no reasonable alternative. Further, any military response must always be proportionate to the risk and strictly limited in both nature and time.

One of the two areas in which there is a very major advance in inter-national humanitarian law and international criminal law is the new Chapter 4. This establishes a range of five new explicit crimes in relation to breaches of cultural protection and respect contrary to either the original 1954 Convention, the First Protocol, or the cultural protection provisions of the 1977 Additional Geneva Protocols. States adopting the 1999 Protocol will have to legislate for these and in normal cases will be expected to prosecute such crimes in their normal civilian or military courts. However, there is also provision for universal international jurisdiction – giving the possibility of criminal prosecution anywhere else in the world, at least within a State Party to the Second Protocol, and the most serious new crimes will be extraditable. (These provisions, perhaps above all others, will require major new legisla-tion at the national level in the case of each country adopting it, and for this reason alone the process of ratification will inevitably be a relatively slow one.)

Chapter 5 deals with non-international conflicts, such as civil wars and internal 'liberation' conflicts, and aims to clarify and strengthen considerably the Hague 1954 provisions, which above all others have been consistently ignored by rebel and other irregular forces, as well as by the defending national forces at times. The 'cultural war crimes' provisions (including universal international jurisdiction) of Chapter 4 will apply unambiguously to such conflicts in future.

The other major advance and significant innovation is Chapter 6, which establishes for the first time permanent institutional arrangements in respect of the application of the 1954 Convention. There will be two-yearly meetings of the States Parties (compared with a 22-year gap between the 1973 and 1995 meetings!), and the States will elect a twelve member 'Committee for the protection of cultural property in the event of armed conflict', which will meet at least once a year and more frequently in cases of urgency. The Committee will have a duty to monitor and promote generally, and consider applications for both 'Exceptional Protection' and financial assistance from a (voluntary contributions) Fund to be established under the Protocol.

For the first time there will be a clear role for 'civil society' – represented by the non-governmental sector – within the Hague Convention system. The International Committee of the Blue Shield (by name) and its constituent 'eminent professional organizations' (i.e. the four UNESCO-recognized world NGOs for archives – ICA, libraries – IFLA, monuments and sites – ICOMOS and museums – ICOM), together with ICCROM and the International Committee of the Red Cross, will have important standing advisory roles in relation to the Committee and the regular meetings of States Parties. They will also be consulted on proposals such as the new 'Exceptional Protection' designation under Chapter 3, and an advisory role in the implementation of the new Second Protocol Committee and its work at all levels (directly paralleling the official role that ICOMOS and ICCROM have had under the World Heritage Convention since 1972).

Chapter 7 strengthens the 1954 provision in relation to information, training etc. about the Convention, Protocols and general principles of cultural protection. There is now a call for States to raise awareness among the general public and within the education system, not just among military personnel and cultural sector officials, as in the 1954 text. (This important development had to be non-binding in the final text because of the large number of federated states where the central government no longer controls or influences directly the school curriculum – although there remains a further important recognition of the importance and role attached to 'civil society' and public opinion nevertheless.)

As indicated above, with highly important constitutional issues to be addressed at the national level, such as the further extension of the principle of international jurisdiction for the most serious of the new, explicitly designated, war crimes, it will take a significant length of time for each country to go through the process of first gaining national government approval for the principles of the Second Protocol, and then legislating to bring it into effect. Further, the Protocol will only come into effect when at least twenty states have deposited formal instruments of ratification with the Director-General of UNESCO – a process that will clearly take several years. It was, however, encouraging to see that by Monday 17 May 1999, during the week of celebrations to mark the 100th anniversary of the 1899 Hague Peace Conference and Convention, and less than two months after the Diplomatic Conference, twenty-eight States were already able to pledge themselves to the eventual formal ratification and adoption of the Second Protocol, and hence sign it in a ceremony in the Peace Palace in the Hague. (There have been further signatures added subsequently.)[4] For a detailed legal commentary and analysis by a member of the International Committee of the Red Cross delegation to the Diplomatic Conference, see Henckaerts (1999).

## CONCLUSION

While the twentieth century certainly saw a most remarkable awakening of interest in the heritage of the world and its conservation, it equally saw the destruction of the physical evidence of that heritage on a scale certainly unparalleled since the European religious wars and iconoclasm of the sixteenth and seventeenth centuries, and probably the worst in history. This major uprating of the Hague Convention is an important step in seeking to ensure that history will not repeat itself in the twenty-first century. However, this will not be achieved unless we constantly keep at the forefront of our minds the opening words of the Constitution of UNESCO, adopted just months after the end of World War II: 'That since wars begin in the minds of men, it is in the minds of men that the defences of peace must be constructed'.

## ACKNOWLEDGEMENTS

The initial research which has led to this study was done for my 1993 UNESCO report (Boylan 1993) and the consent of UNESCO was given for me to rework, further develop and augment the relevant sections here. Well over 100 people have assisted me over the past years as consultees from 1992 onwards and as helpful critics of earlier versions of this and other written contributions and conference presentations, from the June 1993 expert meeting in The Hague through to the March 1999 Diplomatic Conference, at which the Second Protocol, based to a very considerable extent on my work, was finalised and adopted. However, I must acknowledge my special indebtedness for so much help, advice and personal encouragement, to a small number of colleagues and fellow travellers through all or most of that seven-year journey.

Dr Lyndel Prott, Head of International Standards in the Cultural Heritage Division of UNESCO, initiated and supervised the original research project, and the help and advice of both her and her colleagues, particularly Etienne Clément and Jan Hladik, have been absolutely invaluable in so many ways. From the Netherlands Government the key figures have been Adriaan Bos of the Ministry of Foreign Affairs (whose last major job before his retirement in June 1999 was to chair the Diplomatic Conference and then sign the Second Protocol in the name of his country) and Dr Sabine Gimbrère of the Ministry of Culture. Among the many military experts who have assisted, advised challenged and stimulated me, I am especially indebted to Colonel

W. Hays Parks of the US Department of Defense, Colonel Daniel Weisner of the Israel Defence Forces and Colonel Edmund Fokker of the Netherlands Army. Finally, but by no means least, I must thank the key figures within the four International Committee of the Blue Shield NGOs who have worked together to create and promote the ICBS, including in particular George Mackenzie of ICA, Marie-Thérèse Varlamoff of IFLA, Elisabeth Des Portes, Manus Brinkman, Christiane Logie, Ivo Maroevic and Branka Sulč of ICOM, and Leo Van Nispen, Dinu Bumbaru and Gaia Jungeblodt of ICOMOS.

## NOTES

1 See, for example, Beseler and Gottschow 1988; British Committee on the Preservation and Restitution of Works of Art 1946a, 1946b, 1946c, 1946d, 1946e; Cassou 1947; Commission de Récuperation Artistique 1946; Direction Générale de l'Economie 1947; Pape 1975; Polish Ministry of Culture and Art 1949–53; Rorimer 1950; Roxan 1964; Valland 1961; Woolley 1947.
2 Other relevant discussions include those of Kalshoven 1987: 64–7; while the permissible limits of international coercion, and specifically of the legitimacy of reprisals, are examined in detail by McDougal and Feliciano 1967; and Kalshoven 1971 and 1990.
3 The states who reluctantly voted for the 'military necessity' concession in order – as they thought – to secure the adherence of the US and the UK to the treaty were to be disappointed. Despite this major weakening of its provisions at their insistence, both signed the Convention in 1954 but then failed to present it for ratification under national law. However, in the case of the US, the President finally submitted the 1954 Convention to the Senate for ratification in January 1999, though ratification seems to be 'stalled' politically at the time of writing [2001].
4 As at 1 October 2000, the Second Protocol had been signed by 39 states and the necessary legislation for formal ratification was in active preparation in a number of these, though none has yet completed the process. The signatories (in alphabetical order) to date are: Albania, Armenia, Austria, Belarus, Belgium, Bulgaria, Cambodia, Colombia, Côte d'Ivoire, Croatia, Cyprus, Ecuador, Egypt, Estonia, Finland, Former Yugoslav Republic of Macedonia, Germany, Ghana, Greece, Holy See, Hungary, Indonesia, Italy, Luxembourg, Madagascar, Morocco, Netherlands, Nigeria, Oman, Pakistan, Peru, Qatar, Romania, Slovakia, Spain, Sweden, Switzerland, Syrian Arab Republic and Yemen.

## REFERENCES

Adler, G.J. 1972. Targets in War: Legal Considerations. Vol. 3, 281-326. In *The Vietnam War and International Law* (4 vols) 1968-1976. R.A. Falk (ed.). Princeton, N.J.: Princeton University Press.

Alvarez Lopes, A.J. 1982. *La politica de bienes culturales del gobierno republicano durante la guerra civil española*. Madrid: Ministerio de Cultura.

American Commission 1946. *Report of American Commission for the Protection and Salvage of Artistic and Historic Monuments in War Areas*. Washington DC: US Government Printing Office.

Bassiouni, M.C. 1983. Reflections on criminal jurisdiction in the international protection of cultural property. *Syracuse Journal of International Law and Commerce* 10 (2), 281–322.

Beseler, H. and N. Gottschow 1988. *Kriegsschicksale: Deutscher Architektur Ver luste – Schäden – Weideraufbau. Eine Dokumentation für das Gebeit der Bundesrepublik Deutschland* (2 vols). Neumünster: Karl Wachholtz Verlag.

Boylan, P.J. 1992. Revolutionary France and the foundation of modern museum management and curatorial practice. Part I. From Revolution to the First Republic, 1789–1792. *Museum Management and Curatorship* 11 (2): 141–52.

Boylan, P.J. 1993. *Review of the Convention on the Protection of Cultural Property in the Event of Armed Conflict (The Hague Convention of 1954).* Paris: UNESCO, Doc. Ref. CLT-93/WS/12. (Also French edition.)

Boylan, P.J. 1994. Information as complement to legal instruments. Report to UNESCO about the Hague Convention. *Svenska Unescoradets skriftserie* 4/1994, 35–53.

Boylan, P.J. 1999. New international treaty to strengthen protection of cultural property in the event of armed conflict. *International Preservation News (IFLA/PAC)* 19 (July), 6–7.

Brenner, L. 1992. Nicholas K. Roerich: Idealist and Visionary. *Foreign Service Journal* (USA) April 17, 1992, 20.

British Committee on the Preservation and Restitution of Works of Art 1946a. *Works of Art in Malta. Losses and Survivals in the War.* London: HMSO.

British Committee on the Preservation and Restitution of Works of Art 1946b. *Works of Art in Italy. Losses and Survivals in the War. Part II – North of Bologna.* London: HMSO.

British Committee on the Preservation and Restitution of Works of Art 1946c. *Works of Art in Greece: the Greek Islands and the Dodecanese. Losses and Survivals in the War.* London: HMSO.

British Committee on the Preservation and Restitution of Works of Art 1946d. *Works of Art in Germany (British Zone of Occupation). Losses and Survivals in the War.* London: HMSO.

British Committee on the Preservation and Restitution of Works of Art 1946e. *Works of Art in Austria (British Zone of Occupation). Losses and Survivals in the War.* London: HMSO.

British Museum 1939. *Air Raid Precautions in Museums, Picture Galleries and Libraries.* London: Trustees of the British Museum.

Burrows, G.S. 1984. *Montenegro Earthquake: the conservation of historic monuments and art treasures.* Paris: UNESCO.

Cassou, J. 1947. *Le Pillage par les Allemends des oeuvres d'art et des bibliothèques.* Paris: editions du Centre.

Catalonia: Comissariat de Propaganda 1937. *Le sauvetage du patrimoine historique et artistique de la Catalogne.* Barcelona: Generalita de Catalunya.

Chamberlin, R. 1983. *Loot! The Heritage of Plunder.* London: Thames and Hudson.

Commission de Récuperation Artistique 1946. *Les chefs-oeuvres des collections privées françaises retrouvés en Allemagne.* Paris: Musée de l'Orangerie.

Damna Scientiae Hungaricae 1947. *Devastationes in Bello Mundi Altero Ortae.* Budapest: Ministry of Culture and Public Education.

Direction Générale de l'Economie 1947. *Répertoire des biens spoliés en France durant la guerre, 1939–1945* (2 vols). Paris: Imprimerie Nationale.

Elbinger, L.K. 1992. The Neutrality of Art. The Roerich Pact's quest to protect art from the ignorance of man. *Foreign Service Journal* (USA) April, 1992, 16–20.

Government of the Netherlands 1961. *Intergovernmental Conference Convention on the Protection of Cultural Property in the Event of Armed Conflicts, The Hague, 1954: Records of the Conference.* The Hague: Staatsdruckkerij.

Government of the Netherlands 1991. *Cultuurbescherming in Buitengenwone Omstandigheden.* The Hague: Ministerie van VWC.

Hague Convention 1954. *Convention for the Protection of Cultural Property in the Event of Armed Conflict, The Hague, 1954.*

Hague Protocol 1954. *Protocol for the Protection of Cultural Property in the Event of Armed Conflict, The Hague, 1954.*

Hague Regulations 1954. *Regulations for the Execution of the Convention for the Protection of Cultural Property in the Event of Armed Conflict, The Hague, 1954.*

Harris, A.T. 1947. *Bomber Offensive.* London: Collins.

Henckaerts, J-M. 1999. New Rules for the Protection of Cultural Property in Armed Conflict. The Significance of the Second Protocol to the 1954 Hague Convention for the Protection of Cultural Property in the Event of Armed Conflict. *International Review of the Red Cross* 835 (Sept. 1999), 593–620.

Institute for Protection of Cultural Monuments 1992a. *War damages and destructions inflicted on the culture, monuments, sites and historical centers in Croatia (preliminary report – to April 02th [sic] 1992).* Zagreb: Ministry of Education, Culture and Sports.

Institute for Protection of Cultural Monuments 1992b. *War damage on cultural heritage in Croatia: damage and destruction in May and June 1992.* Zagreb: Ministry of Education, Culture and Sports.

International Committee of the Red Cross 1987. *Basic Rules of the Geneva Conventions and their Protocols.* Geneva: ICRC Publications.

International Committee of the Red Cross 1989. *International Law concerning the Conduct of Hostilities. Collection of Hague Conventions and some other Treaties.* Geneva: ICRC Publications.

Kalshoven, F. 1971. *Belligerent Reprisals.* Leiden: Sijthoff.

Kalshoven, F. 1987. *Constraints on the Waging of War.* Geneva: International Committee of the Red Cross.

Kalshoven, F. 1990. Belligerent reprisals revisited. *Netherlands Yearbook of International Law,* 43–80.

Lavachery, H.A. and A. Noblecourt 1954. *Les techniques de protection des biens culturels en cas de conflit armé* (Musées et Monuments, No. VIII). Paris: UNESCO. (For English edition, see Noblecourt, 1958.)

Little, R. 1975. *Intervention. External Involvement in Civil Wars.* London: Martin Robertson.

Lorenz, S. 1947. *Destruction of the Royal Castle in Warsaw.* Warsaw: Ministry of Culture and Art.

Lorenz, S. 1954. *Trésors Culturels de la Pologne.* Warsaw: Editions Sztuka.

Lorenz, S. (n.d.) *La Canada réfuse de rendre à la Pologne ses Richesses Culturelles* (2 vols). Warsaw: National Museum.

Maroevic, I. 1995. *Rat I Bastina u Prostoru Hvratske/Krieg und Kultur Erbe im Raum Kroatien* (Bilingual text, German and Croatian). Zagreb: Ogranak Petrinja.

McDougal, M.S. and F.P. Feliciano 1967. *Law and Minimum World Public Order: The Legal Regulation of International Coercion.* New Haven, Conn.: Yale University Press.

Merryman, J.H. 1986. Two ways of thinking about Cultural Property. *American Journal of International Law* 80 (4), 831–53.

Miller, R.I. 1975. *The Law of War.* Lexington, MA: Lexington Books.

Moynihan, D.P. 1993. *Pandaemonium: Ethnicity in International Politics.* Oxford: University Press.

Munro, D.C. 1912. *Translations and Reprints from the Original Sources of European History, Series 1, Vol 3:1 (rev. ed.).* Philadelphia: University of Pennsylvania Press (available online as Internet Medieval Source Book: http://www.fordham.edu/halsall/book. html).

Museum Documentation Centre 1991. *The destruction of museums and galleries in Croatia in the 1991 War.* Zagreb: Ministry of Education and Culture.

Museum Documentation Centre 1997. *War damage to Museums and Galleries in Croatia.* Zagreb: Muzejski documentacijski centar.

Museums Journal 1938a. Art Treasures of Spain. *Museums Journal* 37, 338–9.

Museums Journal 1938b. Air Raid Precautions and Museums. *Museums Journal* 38, 24.

Nahlik, S.E. 1967. Protection internationale des biens culturels en cas de conflit armé. *Recuil des Cours de l'Académie de Droit International de La Haye* 120, 61–163.

Nahlik, S.E. 1974. On some deficiencies of the Hague Convention on the Protection of Cultural Property in the Event of Armed Conflict. *Annuaire de l'Association des Anciens Auditeurs de l'Académie de La Haye* 1974, 100–8.

Nahlik, S.E. 1988. Protection of Cultural Property. In *International Dimensions of Humanitarian Law*, UNESCO, 203–15. Paris: UNESCO.

Nicholas, L.H. 1994. *The Rape of Europa: the fate of Europe's treasures in the Third Reich and the Second World War.* New York: Knopf.

Noblecourt, A. 1958. *Protection of Cultural Property in the event of armed conflict* (Museums and Monuments No. VIII). Paris: UNESCO.

O'Brien, W.V. 1972. The Nuremberg Principles. Vol. 3, 193-247. In *The Vietnam War and International Law* (4 vols) 1968-1976. R.A. Falk (ed.). Princeton, N.J.: Princeton University Press.

Office International des Musées 1939. *La Protection des Monuments et Oeuvres d'Art en Temps de Guerre.* Paris: Institut International de Coopération Intellectuelle.

Oxford Manual 1880. *The Laws of War on Land ('Oxford Manual').* New York and London: Institute of International Law.

Pape, M. 1975. Griechische Kunstwerke aus Kriegbeute und ihre oeffentliche Aufstellung in Rom. Unpublished Ph.D. thesis, University of Hamburg.

Polish Ministry of Culture and Art 1945. *Warsaw Accuses.* Warsaw: Ministry of Culture and Art.

Polish Ministry of Culture and Art 1949–1953. *Prace i MaterialyBiura Rewindykacji i Odszkodowan* vols. 9–13. [vol. 9: I. Malarstwo Obce (1949); vol. 10: Staty Wojenne Zbiorów Polskich w Dziedzinie Rekopisów Iluminowanych (1952); vol. 11: II Malarstwo Polskie (1951) – English translation as Polish Paintings (1953); vols 12 & 13: Staty Wojenne Zbiorów Polskich w Dziedzinie Rzemiosła Artystyczego – Praca Zbiorow I & II]. Warsaw: Ministry of Culture and Art.

Prott, L.V. 1994. Present work at UNESCO to reinforce the Convention for the Protection of Cultural Property in the Event of Armed Conflict (the Hague Convention 1954). *Svenska Unescoradets skriftserie* 4/1994, 55–63.

Roberts, A. and R. Guelff. 1999. *Documents on the Laws of War.* 3rd Revised Edition. Oxford: University Press.

Rorimer, J.J. 1950. *Survival. The Salvage and Protection of Art in War.* New York: Abelard Press.

Roxan, D. 1964. *The Jackdaw of Linz. The story of Hitler's art thefts.* London: Cassell.

Sandoz, Y. 1988. Implementing International Humanitarian Law. In *International Dimensions of Humanitarian Law*, UNESCO, 259–83. Paris: UNESCO.

Schneider, J.T. 1935. *Report to the Secretary of the Interior on the Preservation of Historic Sites and Buildings.* Washington, DC: US Dept of the Interior.

Simon, M. 1971. *The Battle of The Louvre. The Struggle to save French Art in World War II.* London: Cassell.

Thomas, A.V.W. and A.J. Thomas 1971. International aspects of the civil war in Spain 1936–39. Vol. 2, 111-78. In *The Vietnam War and International Law* (4 vols) 1968-1976. R.A. Falk (ed.). Princeton, N.J.: Princeton University Press.

Thornberry, P. 1991. *International Law and the Rights of Minorities.* Oxford: University Press.

Toman, J. 1994. *La protection des biens culturels en cas de conflit armé.* Commentaire de la Convention de La Haye du 14 mai 1954. Paris: Editions UNESCO. (English edition, 1996. *The Protection of Cultural Property in the Event of Armed Conflict.* Aldershot, Hants.: Dartmouth Publishing with UNESCO.)

Treaty of Versailles 1919. Online text of Treaty of Versailles, 28 June 1919. The Avalon Project at the Yale Law School. http://www.yale.edu/lawweb/avalon/int/menu.htm. (Reproduced from *The Treaties of Peace 1919–1923*. New York: Carnegie Endowment for International Peace, 1924.)

Treaty of Westphalia. Online text of Treaty of Westphalia, 24 October 1648. Tufts University Online Miscellaneous Historical Documents http://www.tufts.edu/fletcher/multi/texts/historical/westphalia.txt.

Treue, W. 1960. *Art Plunder: the fate of works of art in war, revolution and peace* (translation of *Kunsttraub* 1957). London: Methuen.

UNESCO 1985. *Conventions and Recommendations of UNESCO concerning the protection of the cultural heritage*. Revised edition. Paris: UNESCO.

UNESCO 1988. *International Dimensions of Humanitarian Law*. Geneva: Henry Dunant Institute; Paris: UNESCO.

United Nations 1951. Convention on the Prevention and Punishment of the Crime of Genocide, 9 December 1948. *United Nations Treaty Series No. 1021*. Vol. 78, 277. New York: United Nations.

United Nations 1988. *Universal Declaration of Human Rights*. New York: United Nations.

Valland, R. 1961. *Le Front de l'Art*. Paris: Librairie Plon. (New edition with brief biographical note, 1998, Paris: Réunion des Musées Nationaux.)

Varshavsky, S.P. and B. Rest 1985. *The Ordeal of The Hermitage. The Siege of Leningrad, 1941–1944*. Leningrad and New York: Aurora Art Publishers.

Villehardouin, G de. 1908. *Chronicles of the Crusades by Villehardouin and de Jointville.* Trans. F. Marzials. London. New Edition 1955 London: Dutton & Co.

Visscher, C. 1949. *International Protection of Works of Art and Monuments.* Washington DC: US Department of State.

Von Clausewitz, C. 1968. *On War* [Penguin Classics edition of 1908 J.J. Graham translation of extracts from original *Vom Kriege* of 1832]. London: Penguin Books.

Woolley, L. 1947. *A Record of the Work Done by the Military Authorities for the Protection of the Treasures of Art and History in War Areas*. London: HMSO.

Wright, Q. 1971. Francis Lieber's Code for Land Warfare. Vol. 2, 30-109. In *The Vietnam War and International Law* (4 vols) 1968-1976. R.A. Falk (ed.). Princeton, N.J.: Princeton University Press.

# APPENDIX

*Second Protocol to the Hague Convention of 1954 for the Protection of Cultural Property in the Event of Armed Conflict – The Hague, 26 March 1999*

The Parties,

Conscious of the need to improve the protection of cultural property in the event of armed conflict and to establish an enhanced system of protection for specifically designated cultural property;

Reaffirming the importance of the provisions of the Convention for the Protection of Cultural Property in the Event of Armed Conflict, done at The Hague on 14 May 1954, and emphasizing the necessity to supplement these provisions through measures to reinforce their implementation;

Desiring to provide the High Contracting Parties to the Convention with a means of being more closely involved in the protection of cultural property in the event of armed conflict by establishing appropriate procedures therefor;

Considering that the rules governing the protection of cultural property in the event of armed conflict should reflect developments in international law;

Affirming that the rules of customary international law will continue to govern questions not regulated by the provisions of this Protocol;

Have agreed as follows:

*Chapter 1 Introduction*

ARTICLE 1 – DEFINITIONS

For the purposes of this Protocol:

(a) 'Party' means a State Party to this Protocol;
(b) 'cultural property' means cultural property as defined in Article 1 of the Convention;
(c) 'Convention' means the Convention for the Protection of Cultural Property in the Event of Armed Conflict, done at The Hague on 14 May 1954;
(d) 'High Contracting Party' means a State Party to the Convention;
(e) 'enhanced protection' means the system of enhanced protection established by Articles 10 and 11;
(f) 'military objective' means an object which by its nature, location, purpose, or use makes an effective contribution to military action and whose total or partial destruction, capture or neutralisation, in the circumstances ruling at the time, offers a definite military advantage;
(g) 'illicit' means under compulsion or otherwise in violation of the applicable rules of the domestic law of the occupied territory or of international law.
(h) 'List' means the International List of Cultural Property under Enhanced Protection established in accordance with Article 27, sub-paragraph 1(b);
(i) 'Director-General' means the Director-General of UNESCO;
(j) 'UNESCO' means the United Nations Educational, Scientific and Cultural Organization;
(k) 'First Protocol' means the Protocol for the Protection of Cultural Property in the Event of Armed Conflict done at The Hague on 14 May 1954;

ARTICLE 2 – RELATION TO THE CONVENTION

This Protocol supplements the Convention in relations between the Parties.

ARTICLE 3 – SCOPE OF APPLICATION

1. In addition to the provisions which shall apply in time of peace, this Protocol shall apply in situations referred to in Article 18 paragraphs 1 and 2 of the Convention and in Article 22 paragraph 1.

2. When one of the parties to an armed conflict is not bound by this Protocol, the Parties to this Protocol shall remain bound by it in their mutual relations. They shall furthermore be bound by this Protocol in relation to a State party to the conflict which is not bound by it, if the latter accepts the provisions of this Protocol and so long as it applies them.

ARTICLE 4 – RELATIONSHIP BETWEEN CHAPTER 3 AND OTHER PROVISIONS OF THE CONVENTION AND THIS PROTOCOL

The application of the provisions of Chapter 3 of this Protocol is without prejudice to:

(a) the application of the provisions of Chapter I of the Convention and of Chapter 2 of this Protocol;

(b) the application of the provisions of Chapter II of the Convention save that, as between Parties to this Protocol or as between a Party and a State which accepts and applies this Protocol in accordance with Article 3 paragraph 2, where cultural property has been granted both special protection and enhanced protection, only the provisions of enhanced protection shall apply.

*Chapter 2  General provisions regarding protection*

ARTICLE 5 – SAFEGUARDING OF CULTURAL PROPERTY

Preparatory measures taken in time of peace for the safeguarding of cultural property against the foreseeable effects of an armed conflict pursuant to Article 3 of the Convention shall include, as appropriate, the preparation of inventories, the planning of emergency measures for protection against fire or structural collapse, the preparation for the removal of movable cultural property or the provision for adequate in situ protection of such property, and the designation of competent authorities responsible for the safeguarding of cultural property.

ARTICLE 6 – RESPECT FOR CULTURAL PROPERTY

With the goal of ensuring respect for cultural property in accordance with Article 4 of the Convention:

(a) a waiver on the basis of imperative military necessity pursuant to Article 4 paragraph 2 of the Convention may only be invoked to direct an act of hostility against cultural property when and for as long as:

(i) that cultural property has, by its function, been made into a military objective; and

(ii) there is no feasible alternative available to obtain a similar military advantage to that offered by directing an act of hostility against that objective;

(b) a waiver on the basis of imperative military necessity pursuant to Article 4 paragraph 2 of the Convention may only be invoked to use cultural property for purposes which are likely to expose it to destruction or damage when and for as long as no choice is possible between such use of the cultural property and another feasible method for obtaining a similar military advantage;

(c) the decision to invoke imperative military necessity shall only be taken by an officer commanding a force the equivalent of a battalion in size or larger, or a force smaller in size where circumstances do not permit otherwise;

(d) in case of an attack based on a decision taken in accordance with sub-paragraph (a), an effective advance warning shall be given whenever circumstances permit.

## ARTICLE 7 – PRECAUTIONS IN ATTACK

Without prejudice to other precautions required by international humanitarian law in the conduct of military operations, each Party to the conflict shall:

(a) do everything feasible to verify that the objectives to be attacked are not cultural property protected under Article 4 of the Convention;

(b) take all feasible precautions in the choice of means and methods of attack with a view to avoiding, and in any event to minimizing, incidental damage to cultural property protected under Article 4 of the Convention;

(c) refrain from deciding to launch any attack which may be expected to cause incidental damage to cultural property protected under Article 4 of the Convention which would be excessive in relation to the concrete and direct military advantage anticipated; and

(d) cancel or suspend an attack if it becomes apparent:

(i) that the objective is cultural property protected under Article 4 of the Convention;

(ii) that the attack may be expected to cause incidental damage to cultural property protected under Article 4 of the Convention which would be excessive in relation to the concrete and direct military advantage anticipated.

## ARTICLE 8 – PRECAUTIONS AGAINST THE EFFECTS OF HOSTILITIES

The Parties to the conflict shall, to the maximum extent feasible:

(a) remove movable cultural property from the vicinity of military objectives or provide for adequate in situ protection;

(b) avoid locating military objectives near cultural property.

ARTICLE 9 – PROTECTION OF CULTURAL PROPERTY IN OCCUPIED TERRITORY

1. Without prejudice to the provisions of Articles 4 and 5 of the Convention, a Party in occupation of the whole or part of the territory of another Party shall prohibit and prevent in relation to the occupied territory:

(a) any illicit export, other removal or transfer of ownership of cultural property;
(b) any archaeological excavation, save where this is strictly required to safeguard, record or preserve cultural property;
(c) any alteration to, or change of use of, cultural property which is intended to conceal or destroy cultural, historical or scientific evidence.

2. Any archaeological excavation of, alteration to, or change of use of, cultural property in occupied territory shall, unless circumstances do not permit, be carried out in close cooperation with the competent national authorities of the occupied territory.

*Chapter 3 Enhanced protection*

ARTICLE 10 – ENHANCED PROTECTION

Cultural property may be placed under enhanced protection provided that it meets the following three conditions:

(a) it is cultural heritage of the greatest importance for humanity;
(b) it is protected by adequate domestic legal and administrative measures recognizing its exceptional cultural and historic value and ensuring the highest level of protection;
(c) it is not used for military purposes or to shield military sites and a declaration has been made by the Party which has control over the cultural property, confirming that it will not be so used.

ARTICLE 11 – THE GRANTING OF ENHANCED PROTECTION

1. Each Party should submit to the Committee a list of cultural property for which it intends to request the granting of enhanced protection.

2. The Party which has jurisdiction or control over the cultural property may request that it be included in the List to be established in accordance with Article 27 sub-paragraph 1(b). This request shall include all necessary information related to the criteria mentioned in Article 10. The Committee may invite a Party to request that cultural property be included in the List.

3. Other Parties, the International Committee of the Blue Shield and other non-governmental organisations with relevant expertise may recommend specific cultural property to the Committee. In such cases, the Committee may decide to invite a Party to request inclusion of that cultural property in the List.

4. Neither the request for inclusion of cultural property situated in a territory, sovereignty or jurisdiction over which is claimed by more than one State, nor its inclusion, shall in any way prejudice the rights of the parties to the dispute.

5. Upon receipt of a request for inclusion in the List, the Committee shall inform all Parties of the request. Parties may submit representations regarding such a request to the Committee within sixty days. These representations shall be made only on the basis of the criteria mentioned in Article 10. They shall be specific and related to facts. The Committee shall consider the representations, providing the Party requesting inclusion with a reasonable opportunity to respond before taking the decision. When such representations are before the Committee, decisions for inclusion in the List shall be taken, notwithstanding Article 26, by a majority of four-fifths of its members present and voting.

6. In deciding upon a request, the Committee should ask the advice of governmental and non-governmental organisations, as well as of individual experts.

7. A decision to grant or deny enhanced protection may only be made on the basis of the criteria mentioned in Article 10.

8. In exceptional cases, when the Committee has concluded that the Party requesting inclusion of cultural property in the List cannot fulfil the criteria of Article 10 sub-paragraph (b), the Committee may decide to grant enhanced protection, provided that the requesting Party submits a request for international assistance under Article 32.

9. Upon the outbreak of hostilities, a Party to the conflict may request, on an emergency basis, enhanced protection of cultural property under its jurisdiction or control by communicating this request to the Committee. The Committee shall transmit this request immediately to all Parties to the conflict. In such cases the Committee will consider representations from the Parties concerned on an expedited basis. The decision to grant provisional enhanced protection shall be taken as soon as possible and, notwithstanding Article 26, by a majority of four-fifths of its members present and voting. Provisional enhanced protection may be granted by the Committee pending the outcome of the regular procedure for the granting of enhanced protection, provided that the provisions of Article 10 sub-paragraphs (a) and (c) are met.

10. Enhanced protection shall be granted to cultural property by the Committee from the moment of its entry in the List.

11. The Director-General shall, without delay, send to the Secretary-General of the United Nations and to all Parties notification of any decision of the Committee to include cultural property on the List.

ARTICLE 12 – IMMUNITY OF CULTURAL PROPERTY UNDER ENHANCED PROTECTION

The Parties to a conflict shall ensure the immunity of cultural property under enhanced protection by refraining from making such property the object of attack or from any use of the property or its immediate surroundings in support of military action.

ARTICLE 13 – LOSS OF ENHANCED PROTECTION

1. Cultural property under enhanced protection shall only lose such protection:
    (a) if such protection is suspended or cancelled in accordance with Article 14; or
    (b) if, and for as long as, the property has, by its use, become a military objective.
2. In the circumstances of sub-paragraph 1(b), such property may only be the object of attack if:
    (a) the attack is the only feasible means of terminating the use of the property referred to in sub-paragraph 1(b);
    (b) all feasible precautions are taken in the choice of means and methods of attack, with a view to terminating such use and avoiding, or in any event minimising, damage to the cultural property;
    (c) unless circumstances do not permit, due to requirements of immediate self-defence:
        (i) the attack is ordered at the highest operational level of command;
        (ii) effective advance warning is issued to the opposing forces requiring the termination of the use referred to in sub-paragraph 1(b); and
        (iii) reasonable time is given to the opposing forces to redress the situation.

ARTICLE 14 – SUSPENSION AND CANCELLATION OF ENHANCED PROTECTION

1. Where cultural property no longer meets any one of the criteria in Article 10 of this Protocol, the Committee may suspend its enhanced protection status or cancel that status by removing that cultural property from the List.

2. In the case of a serious violation of Article 12 in relation to cultural property under enhanced protection arising from its use in support of military action, the Committee may suspend its enhanced protection status. Where

such violations are continuous, the Committee may exceptionally cancel the enhanced protection status by removing the cultural property from the List.

3. The Director-General shall, without delay, send to the Secretary-General of the United Nations and to all Parties to this Protocol notification of any decision of the Committee to suspend or cancel the enhanced protection of cultural property.

4. Before taking such a decision, the Committee shall afford an opportunity to the Parties to make their views known.

*Chapter 4 Criminal responsibility and jurisdiction*

ARTICLE 15 – SERIOUS VIOLATIONS OF THIS PROTOCOL

1. Any person commits an offence within the meaning of this Protocol if that person intentionally and in violation of the Convention or this Protocol commits any of the following acts:

- (a) making cultural property under enhanced protection the object of attack;
- (b) using cultural property under enhanced protection or its immediate surroundings in support of military action;
- (c) extensive destruction or appropriation of cultural property protected under the Convention and this Protocol;
- (d) making cultural property protected under the Convention and this Protocol the object of attack;
- (e) theft, pillage or misappropriation of, or acts of vandalism directed against cultural property protected under the Convention.

2. Each Party shall adopt such measures as may be necessary to establish as criminal offences under its domestic law the offences set forth in this Article and to make such offences punishable by appropriate penalties. When doing so, Parties shall comply with general principles of law and international law, including the rules extending individual criminal responsibility to persons other than those who directly commit the act.

ARTICLE 16 – JURISDICTION

1. Without prejudice to paragraph 2, each Party shall take the necessary legislative measures to establish its jurisdiction over offences set forth in Article 15 in the following cases:

- (a) when such an offence is committed in the territory of that State;
- (b) when the alleged offender is a national of that State;
- (c) in the case of offences set forth in Article 15 sub-paragraphs (a) to (c), when the alleged offender is present in its territory.

2. With respect to the exercise of jurisdiction and without prejudice to Article 28 of the Convention:

(a) this Protocol does not preclude the incurring of individual criminal responsibility or the exercise of jurisdiction under national and international law that may be applicable, or affect the exercise of jurisdiction under customary international law;

(b) except in so far as a State which is not Party to this Protocol may accept and apply its provisions in accordance with Article 3 paragraph 2, members of the armed forces and nationals of a State which is not Party to this Protocol, except for those nationals serving in the armed forces of a State which is a Party to this Protocol, do not incur individual criminal responsibility by virtue of this Protocol, nor does this Protocol impose an obligation to establish jurisdiction over such persons or to extradite them.

## ARTICLE 17 – PROSECUTION

1. The Party in whose territory the alleged offender of an offence set forth in Article 15 sub-paragraphs 1 (a) to (c) is found to be present shall, if it does not extradite that person, submit, without exception whatsoever and without undue delay, the case to its competent authorities, for the purpose of prosecution, through proceedings in accordance with its domestic law or with, if applicable, the relevant rules of international law.

2. Without prejudice to, if applicable, the relevant rules of international law, any person regarding whom proceedings are being carried out in connection with the Convention or this Protocol shall be guaranteed fair treatment and a fair trial in accordance with domestic law and international law at all stages of the proceedings, and in no cases shall be provided guarantees less favorable to such person than those provided by international law.

## ARTICLE 18 – EXTRADITION

1. The offences set forth in Article 15 sub-paragraphs 1 (a) to (c) shall be deemed to be included as extraditable offences in any extradition treaty existing between any of the Parties before the entry into force of this Protocol. Parties undertake to include such offences in every extradition treaty to be subsequently concluded between them.

2. When a Party which makes extradition conditional on the existence of a treaty receives a request for extradition from another Party with which it has no extradition treaty, the requested Party may, at its option, consider the present Protocol as the legal basis for extradition in respect of offences as set forth in Article 15 sub-paragraphs 1 (a) to (c).

3. Parties which do not make extradition conditional on the existence of a treaty shall recognize the offences set forth in Article 15 sub-paragraphs 1 (a) to (c) as extraditable offences between them, subject to the conditions provided by the law of the requested Party.

4. If necessary, offences set forth in Article 15 sub-paragraphs 1 (a) to (c) shall be treated, for the purposes of extradition between Parties, as if they had been committed not only in the place in which they occurred but also in the territory of the Parties that have established jurisdiction in accordance with Article 16 paragraph 1.

## ARTICLE 19 – MUTUAL LEGAL ASSISTANCE

1. Parties shall afford one another the greatest measure of assistance in connection with investigations or criminal or extradition proceedings brought in respect of the offences set forth in Article 15, including assistance in obtaining evidence at their disposal necessary for the proceedings.

2. Parties shall carry out their obligations under paragraph 1 in conformity with any treaties or other arrangements on mutual legal assistance that may exist between them. In the absence of such treaties or arrangements, Parties shall afford one another assistance in accordance with their domestic law.

## ARTICLE 20 – GROUNDS FOR REFUSAL

1. For the purpose of extradition, offences set forth in Article 15 sub-paragraphs 1 (a) to (c), and for the purpose of mutual legal assistance, offences set forth in Article 15 shall not be regarded as political offences nor as offences connected with political offences nor as offences inspired by political motives. Accordingly, a request for extradition or for mutual legal assistance based on such offences may not be refused on the sole ground that it concerns a political offence or an offence connected with a political offence or an offence inspired by political motives.

2. Nothing in this Protocol shall be interpreted as imposing an obligation to extradite or to afford mutual legal assistance if the requested Party has substantial grounds for believing that the request for extradition for offences set forth in Article 15 sub-paragraphs 1 (a) to (c) or for mutual legal assistance with respect to offences set forth in Article 15 has been made for the purpose of prosecuting or punishing a person on account of that person's race, religion, nationality, ethnic origin or political opinion or that compliance with the request would cause prejudice to that person's position for any of these reasons.

## ARTICLE 21 – MEASURES REGARDING OTHER VIOLATIONS

Without prejudice to Article 28 of the Convention, each Party shall adopt such legislative, administrative or disciplinary measures as may be necessary to suppress the following acts when committed intentionally:

(a) any use of cultural property in violation of the Convention or this Protocol;

(b) any illicit export, other removal or transfer of ownership of cultural property from occupied territory in violation of the Convention or this Protocol.

*Chapter 5 The protection of cultural property in armed conflicts not of an international character*

ARTICLE 22 – ARMED CONFLICTS NOT OF AN INTERNATIONAL CHARACTER

1. This Protocol shall apply in the event of an armed conflict not of an international character, occurring within the territory of one of the Parties.

2. This Protocol shall not apply to situations of internal disturbances and tensions, such as riots, isolated and sporadic acts of violence and other acts of a similar nature.

3. Nothing in this Protocol shall be invoked for the purpose of affecting the sovereignty of a State or the responsibility of the government, by all legitimate means, to maintain or re-establish law and order in the State or to defend the national unity and territorial integrity of the State.

4. Nothing in this Protocol shall prejudice the primary jurisdiction of a Party in whose territory an armed conflict not of an international character occurs over the violations set forth in Article 15.

5. Nothing in this Protocol shall be invoked as a justification for intervening, directly or indirectly, for any reason whatever, in the armed conflict or in the internal or external affairs of the Party in the territory of which that conflict occurs.

6. The application of this Protocol to the situation referred to in paragraph 1 shall not affect the legal status of the parties to the conflict.

7. UNESCO may offer its services to the parties to the conflict.

*Chapter 6 Institutional issues*

ARTICLE 23 – MEETING OF THE PARTIES

1. The Meeting of the Parties shall be convened at the same time as the General Conference of UNESCO, and in coordination with the Meeting of the High Contracting Parties, if such a meeting has been called by the Director-General.

2. The Meeting of the Parties shall adopt its Rules of Procedure.

3. The Meeting of the Parties shall have the following functions:

(a) to elect the Members of the Committee, in accordance with Article 24 paragraph 1;

(b) to endorse the Guidelines developed by the Committee in accordance with Article 27 sub-paragraph 1(a);

(c) to provide guidelines for, and to supervise the use of the Fund by the Committee;

(d) to consider the report submitted by the Committee in accordance with Article 27 sub-paragraph 1(d);

(e) to discuss any problem related to the application of this Protocol, and to make recommendations, as appropriate.

4. At the request of at least one-fifth of the Parties, the Director-General shall convene an Extraordinary Meeting of the Parties.

### ARTICLE 24 – COMMITTEE FOR THE PROTECTION OF CULTURAL PROPERTY IN THE EVENT OF ARMED CONFLICT

1. The Committee for the Protection of Cultural Property in the Event of Armed Conflict is hereby established. It shall be composed of twelve Parties which shall be elected by the Meeting of the Parties.

2. The Committee shall meet once a year in ordinary session and in extraordinary sessions whenever it deems necessary.

3. In determining membership of the Committee, Parties shall seek to ensure an equitable representation of the different regions and cultures of the world.

4. Parties members of the Committee shall choose as their representatives persons qualified in the fields of cultural heritage, defence or international law, and they shall endeavour, in consultation with one another, to ensure that the Committee as a whole contains adequate expertise in all these fields.

### ARTICLE 25 – TERM OF OFFICE

1. A Party shall be elected to the Committee for four years and shall be eligible for immediate re-election only once.

2. Notwithstanding the provisions of paragraph 1, the term of office of half of the members chosen at the time of the first election shall cease at the end of the first ordinary session of the Meeting of the Parties following that at which they were elected. These members shall be chosen by lot by the President of this Meeting after the first election.

ARTICLE 26 – RULES OF PROCEDURE

1. The Committee shall adopt its Rules of Procedure.

2. A majority of the members shall constitute a quorum. Decisions of the Committee shall be taken by a majority of two-thirds of its members voting.

3. Members shall not participate in the voting on any decisions relating to cultural property affected by an armed conflict to which they are parties.

ARTICLE 27 – FUNCTIONS

1. The Committee shall have the following functions:

    (a) to develop Guidelines for the implementation of this Protocol;
    (b) to grant, suspend or cancel enhanced protection for cultural property and to establish, maintain and promote the List of Cultural Property under Enhanced Protection;
    (c) to monitor and supervise the implementation of this Protocol and promote the identification of cultural property under enhanced protection;
    (d) to consider and comment on reports of the Parties, to seek clarifications as required, and prepare its own report on the implementation of this Protocol for the Meeting of the Parties;
    (e) to receive and consider requests for international assistance under Article 32;
    (f) to determine the use of the Fund;
    (g) to perform any other function which may be assigned to it by the Meeting of the Parties.

2. The functions of the Committee shall be performed in cooperation with the Director-General.

3. The Committee shall cooperate with international and national governmental and non-governmental organizations having objectives similar to those of the Convention, its First Protocol and this Protocol. To assist in the implementation of its functions, the Committee may invite to its meetings, in an advisory capacity, eminent professional organizations such as those which have formal relations with UNESCO, including the International Committee of the Blue Shield (ICBS) and its constituent bodies. Representatives of the International Centre for the Study of the Preservation and Restoration of Cultural Property (Rome Centre) (ICCROM) and of the International Committee of the Red Cross (ICRC) may also be invited to attend in an advisory capacity.

ARTICLE 28 – SECRETARIAT

The Committee shall be assisted by the Secretariat of UNESCO which shall prepare the Committee's documentation and the agenda for its meetings and shall have the responsibility for the implementation of its decisions.

ARTICLE 29 – THE FUND FOR THE PROTECTION OF CULTURAL PROPERTY IN THE EVENT OF ARMED CONFLICT

1. A Fund is hereby established for the following purposes:

   (a) to provide financial or other assistance in support of preparatory or other measures to be taken in peacetime in accordance with, inter alia, Article 5, Article 10 sub-paragraph (b) and Article 30; and
   (b) to provide financial or other assistance in relation to emergency, provisional or other measures to be taken in order to protect cultural property during periods of armed conflict or of immediate recovery after the end of hostilities in accordance with, inter alia, Article 8 sub-paragraph (a).

2. The Fund shall constitute a trust fund, in conformity with the provisions of the financial regulations of UNESCO.

3. Disbursements from the Fund shall be used only for such purposes as the Committee shall decide in accordance with the guidelines as defined in Article 23 sub-paragraph 3(c). The Committee may accept contributions to be used only for a certain programme or project, provided that the Committee shall have decided on the implementation of such programme or project.

4. The resources of the Fund shall consist of:

   (a) voluntary contributions made by the Parties;
   (b) contributions, gifts or bequests made by:
       (i)    other States;
       (ii)   UNESCO or other organizations of the United Nations system;
       (iii)  other intergovernmental or non-governmental organizations; and
       (iv)   public or private bodies or individuals;
   (c) any interest accruing on the Fund;
   (d) funds raised by collections and receipts from events organized for the benefit of the Fund; and
   (e) all other resources authorized by the guidelines applicable to the Fund.

*Chapter 7 Dissemination of information and international assistance*

ARTICLE 30 – DISSEMINATION

1. The Parties shall endeavour by appropriate means, and in particular by educational and information programmes, to strengthen appreciation and respect for cultural property by their entire population.

2. The Parties shall disseminate this Protocol as widely as possible, both in time of peace and in time of armed conflict.

3. Any military or civilian authorities who, in time of armed conflict, assume responsibilities with respect to the application of this Protocol, shall be fully acquainted with the text thereof. To this end the Parties shall, as appropriate:

(a) incorporate guidelines and instructions on the protection of cultural property in their military regulations;
(b) develop and implement, in cooperation with UNESCO and relevant governmental and non-governmental organizations, peacetime training and educational programmes;
(c) communicate to one another, through the Director-General, information on the laws, administrative provisions and measures taken under sub-paragraphs (a) and (b);
(d) communicate to one another, as soon as possible, through the Director-General, the laws and administrative provisions which they may adopt to ensure the application of this Protocol.

## ARTICLE 31 – INTERNATIONAL COOPERATION

In situations of serious violations of this Protocol, the Parties undertake to act, jointly through the Committee, or individually, in cooperation with UNESCO and the United Nations and in conformity with the Charter of the United Nations.

## ARTICLE 32 – INTERNATIONAL ASSISTANCE

1. A Party may request from the Committee international assistance for cultural property under enhanced protection as well as assistance with respect to the preparation, development or implementation of the laws, administrative provisions and measures referred to in Article 10.

2. A party to the conflict, which is not a Party to this Protocol but which accepts and applies provisions in accordance with Article 3, paragraph 2, may request appropriate international assistance from the Committee.

3. The Committee shall adopt rules for the submission of requests for international assistance and shall define the forms the international assistance may take.

4. Parties are encouraged to give technical assistance of all kinds, through the Committee, to those Parties or parties to the conflict who request it.

## ARTICLE 33 – ASSISTANCE OF UNESCO

1. A Party may call upon UNESCO for technical assistance in organizing the protection of its cultural property, such as preparatory action to safeguard

cultural property, preventive and organizational measures for emergency situations and compilation of national inventories of cultural property, or in connection with any other problem arising out of the application of this Protocol. UNESCO shall accord such assistance within the limits fixed by its programme and by its resources.

2. Parties are encouraged to provide technical assistance at bilateral or multilateral level.

3. UNESCO is authorized to make, on its own initiative, proposals on these matters to the Parties.

*Chapter 8 Execution of this protocol*

ARTICLE 34 – PROTECTING POWERS
This Protocol shall be applied with the cooperation of the Protecting Powers responsible for safeguarding the interests of the Parties to the conflict.

ARTICLE 35 – CONCILIATION PROCEDURE
1. The Protecting Powers shall lend their good offices in all cases where they may deem it useful in the interests of cultural property, particularly if there is disagreement between the Parties to the conflict as to the application or interpretation of the provisions of this Protocol.

2. For this purpose, each of the Protecting Powers may, either at the invitation of one Party, of the Director-General, or on its own initiative, propose to the Parties to the conflict a meeting of their representatives, and in particular of the authorities responsible for the protection of cultural property, if considered appropriate, on the territory of a State not party to the conflict. The Parties to the conflict shall be bound to give effect to the proposals for meeting made to them. The Protecting Powers shall propose for approval by the Parties to the conflict a person belonging to a State not party to the conflict or a person presented by the Director-General, which person shall be invited to take part in such a meeting in the capacity of Chairman.

ARTICLE 36 – CONCILIATION IN ABSENCE OF PROTECTING POWERS
1. In a conflict where no Protecting Powers are appointed the Director-General may lend good offices or act by any other form of conciliation or mediation, with a view to settling the disagreement.

2. At the invitation of one Party or of the Director-General, the Chairman of the Committee may propose to the Parties to the conflict a meeting of their representatives, and in particular of the authorities responsible for the protection of cultural property, if considered appropriate, on the territory of a State not party to the conflict.

ARTICLE 37 – TRANSLATIONS AND REPORTS

1. The Parties shall translate this Protocol into their official languages and shall communicate these official translations to the Director-General.

2. The Parties shall submit to the Committee, every four years, a report on the implementation of this Protocol.

ARTICLE 38 – STATE RESPONSIBILITY

No provision in this Protocol relating to individual criminal responsibility shall affect the responsibility of States under international law, including the duty to provide reparation.

*Chapter 9 Final clauses*

ARTICLE 39 – LANGUAGES

This Protocol is drawn up in Arabic, Chinese, English, French, Russian and Spanish, the six texts being equally authentic.

ARTICLE 40 – SIGNATURE

This Protocol shall bear the date of 26 March 1999. It shall be opened for signature by all High Contracting Parties at The Hague from 17 May 1999 until 31 December 1999.

ARTICLE 41 – RATIFICATION, ACCEPTANCE OR APPROVAL

1. This Protocol shall be subject to ratification, acceptance or approval by High Contracting Parties which have signed this Protocol, in accordance with their respective constitutional procedures.

2. The instruments of ratification, acceptance or approval shall be deposited with the Director-General.

ARTICLE 42 – ACCESSION

1. This Protocol shall be open for accession by other High Contracting Parties from 1 January 2000.

2. Accession shall be effected by the deposit of an instrument of accession with the Director-General.

ARTICLE 43 – ENTRY INTO FORCE

1. This Protocol shall enter into force three months after twenty instruments of ratification, acceptance, approval or accession have been deposited.

2. Thereafter, it shall enter into force, for each Party, three months after the deposit of its instrument of ratification, acceptance, approval or accession.

ARTICLE 44 – ENTRY INTO FORCE IN SITUATIONS OF ARMED CONFLICT

The situations referred to in Articles 18 and 19 of the Convention shall give immediate effect to ratifications, acceptances or approvals of or accessions to this Protocol deposited by the parties to the conflict either before or after the beginning of hostilities or occupation. In such cases the Director-General shall transmit the communications referred to in Article 46 by the speediest method.

ARTICLE 45 – DENUNCIATION

1. Each Party may denounce this Protocol.

2. The denunciation shall be notified by an instrument in writing, deposited with the Director-General.

3. The denunciation shall take effect one year after the receipt of the instrument of denunciation. However, if, on the expiry of this period, the denouncing Party is involved in an armed conflict, the denunciation shall not take effect until the end of hostilities, or until the operations of repatriating cultural property are completed, whichever is the later.

ARTICLE 46 – NOTIFICATIONS

The Director-General shall inform all High Contracting Parties as well as the United Nations, of the deposit of all the instruments of ratification, acceptance, approval or accession provided for in Articles 41 and 42 and of denunciations provided for Article 45.

ARTICLE 47 – REGISTRATION WITH THE UNITED NATIONS

In conformity with Article 102 of the Charter of the United Nations, this Protocol shall be registered with the Secretariat of the United Nations at the request of the Director-General.

IN FAITH WHEREOF the undersigned, duly authorized, have signed the present Protocol.

DONE at The Hague, this twenty-sixth day of March 1999, in a single copy which shall be deposited in the archives of the UNESCO, and certified true copies of which shall be delivered to all the High Contracting Parties.

# 4 Law and the underwater cultural heritage: a question of balancing interests

SARAH DROMGOOLE

## INTRODUCTION

Shipwrecks, the main constituents of the underwater cultural heritage, have the potential to give rise to significant conflicts of interest. The most obvious tension is between the interests of archaeologists on the one hand and those of salvors on the other, which arises from the juxtaposition of archaeological and commercial value that may be found in wrecks. One of the fundamental tenets of archaeology – that remains should be preserved *in situ* wherever possible – clearly conflicts with the purpose of salvage work, which is to recover property of value and return it to commercial use. There are other groups too who have interests in the underwater cultural heritage which may not be compatible.[1] The general public as a whole has an interest in access to its heritage; sport divers will be interested in access to sites for purposes of recreation and possibly to collect souvenirs; insurers and other parties may claim ownership rights to a valuable cargo or other artefacts; and States may well assert some form of interest, which may not necessarily be motivated by a desire to protect the cultural value of the remains.

The possibility that conflicting interests might arise in shipwrecks began to be recognized in the 1960s, when wrecks in shallow coastal waters first became accessible to sport divers. It became clear that there was a need for legal mechanisms to prevent the plunder and destruction of historic wreck sites. Since then, many States have legislated to protect such sites within their territorial remit. In framing their legislation, States have been influenced by their own particular legal traditions and, as a result, treatment of the different interest groups varies considerably. At one extreme, some domestic laws favour the archaeological interest to the extent that access to underwater sites and recovery of material is all but prohibited; at the other end of the spectrum, there are laws which favour commercial interests to such an extent that they positively encourage the recovery and sale of historic material. However, neither of these two extremes facilitates the preservation of the underwater cultural heritage. A largely unregulated system is obviously likely to lead to the exploitation and destruction of important archaeological sites and dispersal of material at auction, but experience also suggests that draconian restrictions are unlikely to be respected and may end up being flagrantly abused. Fortunately, it is being increasingly recognized that the key to successful legislation in this field is to take into account the various interests concerned and to try to achieve an appropriate balance between them. Apart from creating a legal regime which is effective and enforceable, this approach can also afford other benefits from a cultural point of view. The encouragement of responsible sport diver involvement, for example, may greatly assist in monitoring sites and in archaeological fieldwork, and the encouragement of the public's interest can create a useful income stream for cash-starved museums and other institutions.

In recent years technologies have become available which have enabled the location and recovery of wrecks in the deepest of waters. For the first time deep water wrecks are vulnerable to human interference and are now the subject of considerable attention and speculation. At present there is little legal protection available for wrecks located beyond traditional territorial jurisdiction. However, the need for a mechanism to control activities in respect of such wrecks has been recognized by UNESCO, the cultural wing of the UN, and this organization is currently in the process of finalizing an international treaty for this purpose.

This essay examines the interests of those directly involved in the underwater cultural heritage and considers how far they are likely to be, and should be, taken into account in any new international legal regime in this field. The body of the work is divided into three sections: the first outlines the nature of each of the interests involved, the second considers how domestic laws treat these interests, and the third examines the international law position to date. A suggestion as to how the most difficult issue of all – the conflict between archaeological and commercial salvage interests – may be resolved, is examined in the conclusions.


## INTEREST GROUPS

### Private owners

Ownership of property is not lost simply because it sinks to the bottom of the sea. Unless the property has been abandoned by its owner or is subject to some form of lawful expropriation, the ownership rights will continue to exist. This is the case even for long-lost wrecks. In many cases, the owner will be a private individual or body which has acquired ownership by succeeding to the rights of the original owner or insurer of the property. The motivation for such owners asserting their rights over a wreck or its contents is likely to be financial. In particular, a successor in title to the original owner or insurer may assert title to a valuable cargo. Exceptionally the motivation may be personal – for example, where a descendant of a passenger or member of the crew on board a vessel claims an ancestor's personal possessions. Even in the case of quite elderly wrecks, it is not unheard of for private owner-ship claims of these kinds to be made. Indeed, the Salvage Association, which represents the interests of wreck owners, maintains records dating back as far as 1860 regarding sunken vessels and their cargoes and will assert claims to such property if it believes that it is in the interests of the owners to do so.

The interest of insurers in wrecks is often referred to. What exactly is the nature of their interest? Under marine insurance law, where insurers pay out on an actual total loss they are subrogated to all the rights and remedies of the assured in the vessel or other insured property. This means that they become entitled to take over the owner's interest in the property, for example by claiming the benefit of any salvage. Where the vessel is a constructive total loss, the owner may abandon the vessel to the insurers, treat the loss as if it were an actual total loss and be indemnified in full. Again the insurer will become entitled to take over the interest of the owner in whatever may remain of the property insured. Insurers may therefore become the property owners.[2]

Considerable difficulties may arise in attempting to assert an ownership claim to long-lost property. The claimant will need to prove its line of succession from the original owner and, in the case of an insurer, will need to prove that the original insurer exercised its right to take over the benefit of the property insured. The claimant will also need to show that its interest has not been abandoned. Physical abandonment of a vessel by itself is not enough for the owner to lose its property rights. Instead, the owner must show an *intention* to relinquish ownership rights. Such an intention may be expressed, or it may be implied through lapse of time and absence of action to recover the property. For example, if a wreck has been lying easily accessible on a foreshore for many years with no attempt being made at recovery, this may well lead to the im-plication of abandonment. If, on the other hand, a ship sank in deep water and its precise location is unknown, the fact that there has been no attempt at recovery will not necessarily lead to such implication.

The difficulty of proving an ownership claim was illustrated in recent litigation in the US courts concerning the SS *Central America*.[3] The vessel sank in 1857 carrying gold valued at the time at $1,219,189 (O'Keefe 1994: 7). A claim by salvors to ownership of the gold was challenged by a number of US and UK insurance companies. However, these companies had diffi-culty proving their ownership claims because they were unable to produce any official records showing that they had insured the cargo or paid out on the loss. Instead, they relied merely on contemporary newspaper reports that they had done so. The absence of documentation was a significant factor leading the District Court judge to conclude that the insurers had abandoned any claim they might have had.[4] The difficulties faced by these insurers in proving claims to property lost as recently as 1857 suggest that private claims to property lost *before* the nineteenth century will generally be impossible to prove.

Claims by commercial parties such as insurers, if upheld, will usually result in the property being sold at auction to obtain the best commercial price possible. Where a private individual claims personal effects, the claimant may well wish to keep the item in his or her personal and private possession. A conflict is therefore likely to arise between the interests of the claimant, and the interests of archaeologists who will wish that recovered artefacts are made available for research purposes and public display. The adoption of a cut-off date or age for ownership rights is sometimes advocated as a mechanism for resolving this conflict. In cultural heritage legislation, 100 years is often used as the age that defines the scope of any special protective regime and it is sometimes argued that ownership rights should not be recognized in material over this age. However, those representing the interests of owners and insurers argue that many wrecks over 100 years of age are of legitimate commercial interest and that using a cut-off date or age is an arbitrary method of confiscating private property rights. In any event, it may not be necessary to remove these rights in order to protect cultural interests. Instead, it may be as effective to continue to recognize the rights but to impose restrictions upon them in relation to methods of recovery and disposal.

*States*

Most claims to ownership of wrecks will in fact be made by States. States are more likely to be able to prove their line of succession in respect of long-lost wrecks than private bodies or individuals and will also have less difficulty in showing that their rights have not been abandoned. While State rights will undoubtedly be asserted in respect of warships and other government vessels which have been lost in relatively recent years, many States will also claim rights in respect of State vessels lost in earlier centuries. In support of their claims they will assert that their ownership rights in respect of warships, and possibly other State vessels, may be lost only by a formal statement of abandonment, rather than by implication. States may also assert ownership rights in certain commercial vessels where the State has succeeded to the rights of the original owners. The Dutch government claims ownership of the wrecks of Dutch East Indiamen owing to the fact that it took over the assets and liabilities of the Dutch East India Company (VOC) when it was liquidated in 1798. It also appears that the British government may have some interest in the vessels of the East India Company as a consequence of provisions of the Government of India Act 1958 (now repealed) (Dromgoole and Gaskell 1998: 155–6).

Succession is not the only mechanism by which States acquire ownership rights in historic wrecks. Some States have historical prerogative rights to wreck material that has been recovered and brought ashore, in cases where no private owner establishes a claim. Such rights, which were intended to create an extra source of revenue for the Crown, date back to feudal times and may later have become enshrined in statute law. Domestic legislation may also enable a State to claim ownership of wrecks located in its territorial waters, most commonly where the owner has, or is deemed to have, abandoned its ownership rights. Under the US Abandoned Shipwreck Act of 1987, the individual states claim ownership of certain abandoned wrecks lying on or in state submerged lands, although the Act makes no attempt to define abandonment. Under other legislation, abandonment may be deemed to have occurred if the owner does not exercise its rights within a certain period from a vessel's sinking. The time limit may be short. Spain, for example, claims ownership of any wreck whose owner does not exercise its rights within three years of the vessel sinking (O'Keefe and Nafziger 1994: 395).

There are a variety of reasons why States will assert ownership rights in wrecks. Maintaining the sanctity of any human remains on board a vessel may be the primary concern, particularly where the vessel was lost during a military campaign or where close relatives may still be alive. In some cases States may assert their rights as a means of preserving those rights. For example, in 1989 the US government asserted title to the Confederate raider, *Alabama*, which is located in French territorial waters, apparently in order to reinforce its official position that abandonment of its warships could not be implied merely by the passage of time. In 1989 the British government asserted its interest in the wreck of HMS *Birkenhead*, which sank in 1852 off the South African coast, by negotiating a formal agreement with the South African government in respect of the wreck. The terms of the agreement indicate that in this case the British government had a variety of motives for asserting its interest. For example, the agreement included provision for the respectful treatment of the wreck as a war grave, for the return of artefacts to the various British Army regiments with whom they could be identified, and for the sharing of gold salvaged from the wreck. Indeed, in many cases a State's motivation for its assertion of rights will be financial. In South America, the Caribbean and the Far East, governments have contracted deals with salvors whereby they award salvage contracts in return for a share of the proceeds of sale from the auction of cultural artefacts. The adoption of such a practice will clearly bring governments into conflict with cultural interests.

A State may, of course, assert its ownership interests as a means of protecting part of its cultural heritage. This appears to be the motivation of the Netherlands for regularly claiming its rights in respect of wrecked VOC vessels. Indeed, the historical and cultural interest of the Netherlands was formally recognized in the agreement made in 1972 between the Netherlands and Australia in respect of several Dutch East Indiamen located off the coast of Western Australia. By contrast, Spain has been reluctant to claim any interest in its historical vessels and from a cultural point of view this has led to some unfortunate consequences. In particular, in the absence of any claims from Spain the US federal and state governments have fought, and frequently lost, legal battles with salvors over rights to Spanish galleons wrecked off Florida. However, the recent claim by Spain to the Spanish frigates *La Galga* and the *Juno* (lost in 1750 and 1802 respectively) (for details see O'Keefe, Chapter 5) may signify a welcome change in policy. It certainly means that the ultimate fate of artefacts recovered from the two wrecks will be under the control, not of the salvors, but of the Spanish government.[5]

Rather than claiming ownership of a wreck, a State may claim the right to exercise jurisdiction over the wreck. There are several bases for such claims. States have a right to exercise jurisdictional control over activities affecting wrecks in their territorial waters[6] and a number also claim the right to exercise control over such activities further afield.[7] The domestic legislation under which such control is exercised often applies even to wrecks which have no direct historical connection with the coastal State. For example, under the UK Protection of Wrecks Act 1973 the criterion for protection is that a wreck must be of 'historical, archaeological or artistic importance': no national interest or connection needs to be shown. Clearly there is potential for a dispute to arise between the coastal State in whose territorial waters a wreck lies and a State which has a close national interest, as to which has the right to control activities affecting the wreck. Although flag States have some jurisdictional rights over vessels which are afloat, whether or not such rights continue once a vessel has sunk is a difficult and controversial question. Some States certainly claim that flag State jurisdiction continues in respect of sunken *warships*, even if they lie in the territorial waters of another State. Consequently they are entitled to sovereign immunity and therefore cannot be interfered with except with the express consent of the flag State. In view of the legal uncertainty and political sensitivity surrounding such claims, some coastal States have entered into bilateral agreements with flag States in respect of wrecks located in their territorial waters. Such agreements include those regarding the *Birkenhead* and the *Alabama*, and the US is currently in negotiations with France in respect of *La Belle*.[8] States have also started to negotiate regional agreements regarding wrecks located in *international* waters in an attempt to control interference.[9] Such agreements are based on the exercise of accepted principles of international jurisdiction allowing a State to control the activities of its nationals and flag vessels, and to control the use of its port facilities, etc.

The assertion of State interests, appropriately motivated, may be an extremely valuable method of protecting historic shipwrecks. The negotiation of inter-State agreements can resolve potential disputes between States and provides a useful device to afford some means of protection to wrecks in international waters.

*General public*

The term 'cultural heritage' embodies the notion of a vested public interest in historical and archaeological remains. The nature of this interest is poorly defined but it includes some sense of both proprietorship and custodianship. In general terms, the cultural heritage is the inheritance of us all and we are all entitled to share in its benefits. Equally, we have a duty to look after the heritage in order that it can be handed on to our descendants. As far as the underwater cultural heritage is concerned, the general public is apt to associate historic shipwrecks with treasure. This association is encouraged by the media, which tends to emphasize and glamorize the treasure aspects of any new discovery, rather than focusing on its archaeological and cultural significance. Nonetheless public interest extends beyond the concept of treasure. The immense popularity of the *Mary Rose* and the *Vasa* museums illustrates that even vessels which do not contain enormous treasures in a monetary sense are capable of exciting public interest. The motivation behind the public interest will usually be to learn something about the past, to be excited and entertained. It may also extend to acquiring some form of souvenir, such as a book about the wreck, or a small duplicate or replica artefact. Furthermore, the huge public interest in the auctioning of porcelain from the *Geldermalsen* demonstrates that it is not just serious collectors who may have an interest in acquiring more culturally significant artefacts.

To benefit fully from its heritage, the public needs to be educated to appreciate the historical and archaeological significance of the remains. Research findings need to be interpreted and presented in a publicly accessible and lively format. This task is made easier by modern technologies, especially the Internet which is accessible from homes, schools and museums, and can be updated regularly. Catering for the public's interests by providing sources of education and entertainment, while a valuable end in itself, can also provide direct benefits to the heritage. Greater knowledge of the harm that treasure-hunting can cause may shift public attitudes towards treasure-hunters, and this would undoubtedly assist in the fight against the plundering and destruction of sites. Harnessing the public's natural enthusiasm for, and interest in, shipwrecks can also give rise to significant income-generating possibilities for museums and archaeologists, as well as States. Entrance fees to exhibitions, sale of books, videos and film rights, and the sale of replicas and other souvenirs have considerable revenue-raising potential. The creation of popular tourist attractions can also have a significant impact on local and even national economies, especially in poorer parts of the world (Throckmorton [1990] 1999: 179–83).

*Archaeologists*

Shipwrecks are particularly valuable archaeological remains. Unlike many archaeological sites on land, they are 'closed deposits' – in other words, all the remains in the deposit will be associated in time. Furthermore, natural decay processes may be considerably slowed down by the marine environment. As with all archaeological deposits, archaeologists are concerned with extracting as much information about the past as possible from the remains, often by the use of painstaking and time-consuming methods. Their interest is in the information that can be gleaned from the remains, rather than in the remains per se. The following quotation gives some indication of the archaeological viewpoint:

> The totality of the information is crucial and that is why archaeologists take pains to record the relationships and associations of

structure and contents and take samples of substances which are
of no interest to treasure hunters at all. The most mundane items
and fragile organic traces can provide just as much information as
commodities such as gold and porcelain.

(Hutchinson 1996: 288)[10]

Archaeologists will therefore have an interest in aspects of the wreck which
are of little or no commercial value. A cargo of gold bullion may well be
of less archaeological interest than the remains of the vessel on which it was
carried, or the personal possessions of the passengers and crew. Contextual
information, including the location of objects and their proximity to one
another, will be of importance to archaeologists, but of little commercial
significance.

While archaeologists are concerned with the gathering and analysis of information, it would not be true to say that they have no long-term interest in
the material remains themselves. The following quotation makes clear that
archaeologists are concerned that remains continue to be accessible for research
purposes:

Archaeologists . . . try to keep assemblages together in case future
research questions are posed which can only be answered by a re-
examination of the original material.

(ibid.: 289)

The need to retain access to artefacts is justified further by the fact that:

Regardless of the quality of the original fieldwork and how well
the artefact is recorded, unless the artefacts are available for restudy
and reinterpretation the original archaeological work can only be
considered unscientific because no future independent verification
can take place.

(Murphy 1997: 33)[11]

Preservation *in situ* is now the prime archaeological mantra and is advocated
in all cases except where recovery is considered necessary for research purposes
or a site faces some physical threat. Excavation is destructive: it 'changes a
site forever and destroys the potential for future data collection' (Abbass 1999:
262). It should therefore be undertaken only where the highest archaeological
standards can be maintained and suitable conservation and storage facilities
provided. Excavation in the marine environment is an extremely costly
business. The need to hire vessels, crew and special equipment and the requirements for specialized conservation and curation of artefacts mean that the
budget for underwater excavation could be 20–50 times that of a land
excavation (Strati 1999a: 63). There are other factors too which are used to
justify the principle of protection *in situ*. Current generations are merely custod-
ians of the heritage on behalf of future generations. Furthermore, it is undoubtedly the case that in the future more sophisticated archaeological techniques
will be available, enabling the extraction of greater information.

Just how much of the evidence of human history that exists underwater should be preserved is a difficult question, which in turn gives rise to more questions. How old does a wreck or artefact need to be to be of archaeological interest? The layperson might imagine that archaeological interest would not extend to remains which are less than 100 years old and certainly not to remains that are only a few decades old. However, in the maritime context, vessels lost during both World Wars are undoubtedly of historical interest, as are the remains of great passenger liners such as the *Titanic* and the *Lusitania*. Does the fact that they are of historical *interest* of itself mean that they should be legally protected and preserved, or should the degree of interest be taken into account? Legal protection inevitably interferes with the rights and interests of owners, divers and other users of the sea. The importance, or significance, of the remains may therefore need to be weighed in the balance to determine whether their preservation justifies restrictions on other interests.

In respect of material that has been recovered from a site and brought ashore, similar questions arise in determining how much of the material should remain available for future study. Again, the archaeological importance of a particular site, and consequently of any material raised from it, is a significant factor:

> Commercial operators make money from historic shipwrecks by selling the finds from the sites. For many sites of archaeological value that is unacceptable but for less significant sites there may be little justification for insisting that the assemblage must remain intact.

> (Hutchinson 1996: 289)

In some cases the preservation of a representative sample of artefacts as part of the project archive may be sufficient, especially in view of the difficulties museums face in providing storage facilities.

In 1996 the International Council for Monuments and Sites (ICOMOS) produced a Charter on the Protection and Management of Underwater Cultural Heritage, which is intended to supplement the ICOMOS Charter for the Protection and Management of the Archaeological Heritage 1990.[12] The 1996 Charter sets out a number of fundamental principles to be applied in the protection and management of the underwater cultural heritage, including that preservation *in situ* should be considered as a first option and non-intrusive techniques should be encouraged in preference to excavation. The Charter also recognizes that the underwater cultural heritage is a finite and non-renewable resource, that it requires sensitive management, and that it can play a positive role in the promotion of recreation and tourism. It provides that '[a]rchaeology is a public activity; everybody is entitled to draw upon the past in informing their own lives, and every effort to curtail knowledge of the past is an infringement of personal autonomy.' It also states that public access should be encouraged. These provisions in the Charter constitute significant formal recognition by archaeologists of the legitimacy of the public's interest. Nonetheless, there is potential for conflict between the interests of the public and those of archaeologists. For example, access by the public to underwater sites for purposes of recreation and cultural tourism may be seen as a threat to the archaeological integrity of a site, and public access to material recovered from a site may be excluded, restricted or delayed on the ground that the collection must be readily available for scientific study. The potential for conflict between the interests of the public and those of archaeologists is evident not just in relation to access but also in respect of publications. Archaeologists can provide a valuable public service by publishing interpretative literature, but there is a risk that they may become so absorbed in esoteric research output that they neglect to produce non-technical reports.

*Sport divers*

Over the last 35 to 40 years, sport diving has become an immensely popular pastime and wrecks are inevitably a focus of attention for divers. In terms of categorization, sport divers may be viewed as a sub-set of the 'general public' category. They are members of the public who are able to dive and can therefore gain direct physical access to the underwater cultural heritage.

The interests of sport divers in wrecks are various. Many divers are motivated by the desire for recreation, exploration and excitement. Some are motivated by the desire to recover and collect souvenirs. Others may be in more serious pursuit of 'treasure', motivated by the excitement that the concept of treasure engenders and also no doubt by the desire to profit financially. A growing number of sport divers are interested in history and archaeology, and some will have had basic archaeological training.

The fundamental requirement of sport divers is *access*. Access for the purpose of exploration only is unlikely to cause damage unless a site is particularly sensitive. Indeed, the legitimacy of access by sport divers to the majority of underwater sites on a 'look but don't touch' basis is widely recognized by marine archaeologists. In some cases access may need to be monitored. The creation of underwater parks and trails can play a public role by promoting recreation and tourism, as well as acting as a 'honeypot' to attract divers away from archaeologically sensitive sites. Experience in various parts of the world (Jeffery 1999: 11; Le Gurun 1999: 61; Strati 1999b: 80; O'Connor 1999: 98; Kowalski 1999: 123–4; Dromgoole 1999: 193; Blake 1999: 178–9) has shown that the education of sport divers to understand the archaeological significance and value of wreck sites may well prove more effective in deterring damage to sites than the enactment of severe restrictions on diving. Furthermore, it has been found that 'educated' sport divers can play a valuable role in reporting discoveries and monitoring sites. Where sport divers wish to participate actively in archaeological fieldwork, again experience has shown that they can form an enthusiastic and valuable workforce to supplement the limited number of professional marine archaeologists.

*Commercial salvors*

The concept of salvage and the principles on which it is based have ancient origins. A highly reputable professional salvage industry has developed over the years to provide a salvage service to seafarers whose property is in danger at sea. The service may be rendered with or without the prior agreement of the owner of the property, but its purpose is to return the property to its rightful owner, who is required to pay a reward – 'salvage' – for the service rendered. Salvage rewards are calculated by the courts taking into account a number of factors, including the risks faced by the salvors, the degree of skill and labour involved, the length of time taken, etc. The reward is traditionally available on a 'no cure no pay' basis, never exceeding the value of the property saved. The underlying public policy factor which has influenced the development of salvage law has been the desire to encourage salvors to assist others in recovering maritime property in danger and returning it to the 'stream of commerce'. This is seen to be an extremely valuable service and for this reason salvors have been granted extensive legal rights and are amply rewarded for their efforts.

The traditional salvage industry has an interest in property which is still afloat but in immediate peril, and also in property which has sunk. In the latter case, salvage will usually be undertaken on the instructions of the owner. However, there has long been discussion in legal circles about whether property which has been lying on the seabed for a period of years can be the subject of salvage: after all, is it really in any 'danger'? Where the original owner still exists, or where there is a clear and direct line of succession between the claimant and the original owner, it can be argued that the sunken property is at risk in the sense that the owner may be permanently deprived of its use. In the case of long-lost wrecks where there are no immediate commercial interests, it may still be argued that the property is in danger in the sense that it is lost to the stream of commerce. However, in counter-argument it can be said that a wreck which has been lying on the seabed for a number of years is likely to be well preserved by its marine environment and salvage operations may in fact destabilize the site and put it in peril.

The traditional salvage industry needs to be distinguished from another group of salvors who also have a commercial motive: the treasure salvage industry. The latter is engaged in the location and recovery of valuable cargoes of porcelain, gold and silver coins, jewellery and other artefacts, and bullion. Until recently treasure-salvage operations were largely confined to the southeast coast of the US, but they are now increasingly taking place on a global scale. Such activities have been fuelled by the technological developments which have made accessible wrecks located on the deep seabed. Magnetometers, side-scan sonars and remote-controlled submersibles are used to search for potentially lucrative wreck sites. Once a site is found, explosives and propeller-wash deflectors capable of creating large holes in the seabed are used to gain access to valuables. Some 'hauls' are worth vast sums on the open market. For example, gold and silver coins, jewellery and other artefacts from the Spanish galleons *Atocha* and *Santa Margarita* fetched $3 million at auction, while porcelain from the Dutch East Indiaman *Geldermalsen* and the Asian trading ship *Vung Tau* fetched $16 million and $7.2 million respectively (Kaoru and Hoagland 1994).

In the US a significant amount of litigation has come before the courts in which salvors have sought to obtain legal rights to their finds. The salvors' claims have been challenged by both the federal government and the states in attempts to protect historic shipwrecks. The salvors have adopted two lines of argument. First, they have argued that, under the law of finds, they are entitled to be awarded title to their finds on the basis that there is either no known owner of the wreck, or the wreck has been abandoned. Second, the salvors have argued that salvage law applies and that they are entitled to a generous reward for returning the property to its owner. The federal and state governments have tried to counter these claims by arguing either that they own the wreck, or that heritage protection laws displace the application of the laws of salvage and finds.[13] In general, the federal admiralty courts have found for the salvors, in many cases adopting the traditional commercial argument that:

> The law acts to afford protection to persons who actually endeavour
> to return lost or abandoned goods as an incentive to undertake
> such expensive and risky ventures.[14]

Archaeological and cultural considerations have been largely ignored, although good archaeological practice has been recognized as an element to be taken into account in the assessment of a salvage reward.[15]

To launch an expedition to undertake deep water search and recovery operations is an immensely expensive business. Many treasure salvors have managed to raise financial backing for their activities by launching themselves on the stock market, attracting investors motivated by the possibility of huge monetary reward. While the auctioning of valuable finds is the most obvious source of revenue for such groups, treasure salvors have not been slow in realizing that financial exploitation of a wreck site can take a variety of forms: the exhibition of artefacts; the sale to the public of books, videos of work on the site, replicas of artefacts or small items of material; the commercial sale of photographs and film rights; and the operation of tours to the site. The public's interest in wrecks will ensure a good return from such activities and members of the public may potentially gain educational and recreational benefits.

Treasure-salvors often employ marine archaeologists to give them archaeological advice. In some cases their motivation for doing this may be simply to add a veneer of respectability to their operations; in others it may be a genuine attempt to adopt archaeological recovery methods. Some treasure salvors advocate the possibility of more formal collaboration with archaeologists on certain projects. In attempting a reconciliation of interests, they are developing 'ethical' codes of practice and 'fair share' agreements. They have also identified a category of 'trade goods', which they believe can be distinguished from material of cultural significance (for further details see O'Keefe, Chapter 5). From the viewpoint of archaeologists, there may be some advantages to collaboration, especially on deep-water wrecks. In particular, it provides the opportunity to participate in well-funded and exciting projects which would otherwise be beyond their reach. Furthermore, while salvage activity in international waters remains unregulated, there is a danger that unless archaeologists collaborate they will be excluded altogether from access to deep-sea wrecks, which will be exploited and destroyed without any archaeological record being made. Despite the potential benefits, however, archaeology and treasure hunting appear to be fundamentally antithetical activities. Is it really possible to reconcile the interest of treasure salvors merely in items of value and the interest of archaeologists in the whole deposit, in associations and context? Will fair share agreements or similar proposals provide a satisfactory solution to the conflicting views regarding disposal? How can one reconcile the commercial need to operate as speedily as possible so as to minimize the costs of recovery with the archaeological need to adopt time-consuming techniques to extract information? Can the salvor's primary aim of recovery and the archaeological principle of *in situ* protection ever be practically reconciled? While efforts are being made to overcome these differences, it seems inevitable that significant tensions will remain.

## DOMESTIC LAW BACKGROUND

In the process of developing an international legal regime on any subject, regard will be paid to domestic laws in the field. There is much to learn from the experiences that States have had in implementing national legislation and equally the domestic law background of the States involved in negotiating an agreement will have an impact on the positions they adopt and the eventual shape of the agreement. Not least among their considerations, negotiating States will be keen to ensure that the implementation of any new treaty would not necessitate a large number of changes to their domestic law.

In many fields of law, there is a clear distinction in the approach adopted by common law States and civil law States. This arises from their very different legal backgrounds and traditions. For example, the treatment of property, including cultural property, differs markedly between the two systems. The common law pays considerable regard to private rights and interests, and endeavours to restrict the impact of regulation on those interests. By contrast, the civil law tends to favour public interests over private interests, and will restrict private interests to a considerable extent in the interests of, for example, heritage protection. This fundamental difference of approach to property is reflected in attitudes to the protection of underwater cultural property and has an impact on many issues, including the extent to which private ownership rights are respected, application of salvage law, extent of restrictions imposed upon divers and salvors, severity of penalties, and the bringing of prosecutions.

States with a civil law tradition regard their duty to protect the public's interest in the cultural heritage as of such importance that it justifies the restriction of private property interests. Cultural property is generally considered to be part of the public domain and is usually subject to the principle of inalienability. Should an antiquity be discovered, it becomes the property of the State. In respect of finds of more recent origin, where private ownership rights may be recognized, provision is made for expropriation where this is considered to be in the public interest. Some States have introduced laws establishing a statutory presumption of abandonment of ownership rights after the lapse of a fairly short period of time. Special legal regimes in respect of cultural property displace the application of maritime laws, including salvage law, and in most cases finds must be left *in situ*. Many civil law States have adopted a blanket form of protection of the cultural heritage, including the underwater cultural heritage, which permits interference only by qualified archaeologists and imposes severe penalties for infringement of the regulations. The underwater cultural heritage is widely defined and sport diving and recovery are strictly limited. Despite the severity of the restrictions and penalties, however, many civil law States find it difficult to control illegal excavation of underwater archaeological sites and the flow of material to the black market. For example, in relation to Greece, Strati has stated that:

> many sites in shallow water have been plundered. This is primarily due to the inability of Greece to monitor its 15,000 km coastline, as well as to the reluctance of private individuals to comply with the strict rules which offer no real incentive for co-operation.
>
> (Strati 1999b: 80)

It appears that the position may be even worse in other countries bordering the Mediterranean Sea, including France and Italy, where – according to Strati – 'the vast majority of sites in shallow water have been plundered' (ibid.: 84).

States with a common law tradition have generally adopted a very different approach. Historically, the private interests of owners and salvors may have been preserved through the operation of a receiver of wreck service, regulated by statutory provisions deriving from UK Merchant Shipping legislation. Under this system, all wreck material recovered and brought ashore was required to be reported to the receiver in order that entitlement to it could be determined. Ownership rights were upheld, subject to the payment of a salvage reward to the finder. Where no ownership claim was made, or a claim was unproven, the wreck would be awarded to the Crown, again subject to the payment of salvage. In such cases, the wreck would usually be sold and the proceeds (less salvage) paid into the Exchequer. In more recent times, heritage protection laws have been grafted on top of this system and attempts have been made to distinguish between the treatment of modern wreck and 'historic' wreck. In some States, historic wreck has been removed altogether from the wreck and salvage law system; in others the law has simply been adapted to take account of the special nature of historic material. Generally speaking, the heritage protection laws provide some level of protection for sites judged as being of *special* historical significance, but operate a permit system which may allow excavations to be undertaken by sport divers and commercial salvors subject to varying conditions.

The archetypal common law system is of course that found in the UK. Here, the receiver service now operates under the *Merchant Shipping Act* 1995. All wreck brought ashore in the UK, including historic wreck, has to be reported to the receiver, who will determine entitlement to it. Nearly 50 wreck sites are deemed to be of sufficient historical importance as to warrant protection under the *Protection of Wrecks Act* 1973. This statute prohibits unauthorized interference with the site. Licences may be granted to 'competent, and properly equipped' persons to carry out salvage operations in a manner 'appropriate to the historical, archaeological or artistic importance' of the wreck. In practice, the licence provisions have been interpreted quite liberally. Licences have been granted at one time or another for the majority of designated sites and have been issued to amateur divers and commercial salvage operators. The reasoning behind this practice is that it is considered preferable for such persons to work within the legal framework so that their activities can be monitored and archaeological guidance provided, rather than that they work surreptitiously and without supervision. The Merchant Shipping provisions apply even to wreck brought ashore from designated sites, but in relation to any 'historic' wreck, i.e. wreck over 100 years of age, the provisions are now administered with some sensitivity. However, the purpose of the provisions continues to be to protect the private interests of the finder and owner. Where these interests conflict with the public – cultural – interest, the private interests take precedence. For example, while finders are encouraged to waive their salvage rights in order that finds can be donated to a museum, where a finder is unwilling to do so the material may have to be sold, at a price based on its current commercial valuation (Dromgoole 1999). Furthermore, there is no statutory presumption of abandonment and therefore it is at least theoretically possible for ownership rights to be upheld even in the most ancient of wrecks. There have been few prosecutions under either the Merchant Shipping provisions or the Protection of Wrecks Act. Instead, the policy has been to try gradually to change attitudes among the sport diving community through a process of education.

The fact that very different approaches have been adopted by civil law and common law States in respect of the various interests involved in the underwater cultural heritage makes the task of concluding a successful international agreement in the field a difficult one. While the development of an international regime that bridges the divide would be logical and desirable, experience in the negotiation of other conventions suggests that the proponents of one approach tend to sway the outcome and in consequence those

States with opposing views will simply refrain from signing the convention. However, undoubtedly the greater the understanding that each negotiator has of the law and practice of others, the more likely it is that an acceptable compromise position can be achieved.

## DEVELOPMENTS IN INTERNATIONAL LAW

It has long been recognized that there is a need for some form of international legal regime for the protection of the underwater cultural heritage. Of particular concern has been the absence of an effective legal framework to control interference with historic wrecks situated in international waters. The traditional principle of freedom of the high seas has meant that anyone is free to recover sunken property on the high seas, subject to the application of the ordinary rules of salvage (O'Keefe and Nafziger 1994: 397, 399; Strati 1995: 215–17).[16] The UN Convention on the Law of the Sea 1982 makes some general provision for the protection of historically significant remains, but provides few practical devices to achieve this. However, a process of negotiating a specific international convention for this purpose is now under way.

### UN Convention on the Law of the Sea 1982

The only provisions of international law to make specific reference to the underwater cultural heritage are contained in the UN Convention on the Law of the Sea 1982 (hereafter the LOS Convention),[17] which came into force in November 1994. This Convention has two provisions on the underwater cultural heritage, Articles 149 and 303. These articles are of such a general nature that, by themselves, they have little practical impact on salvage activities in international waters. However, they provide the parameters within which any new convention on the underwater cultural heritage will have to operate. They therefore need to be examined to see how far they recognize, and provide for, the various interests in the underwater cultural heritage.

Article 149 states:

> All objects of an archaeological and historical nature found in the Area shall be preserved or disposed of for the benefit of mankind as a whole, particular regard being paid to the preferential rights of the State or country of origin, or the State of cultural origin, or the State of historical and archaeological origin.

The LOS Convention created the 'Area' – that is, that part of the seabed under the high seas but outside other maritime zones. Article 149 applies only to this area. In relation to objects of an archaeological and historical nature found in the Area, it recognizes the interests of mankind as a whole, and also the 'preferential' rights of certain States from which the objects originated. Many questions arise as to the meaning and effect of this article. What exactly does '. . . preserved or disposed of for the benefit of mankind as a whole . . .' mean? How should mankind benefit? What does 'disposal' mean? In particular, does it include sale? Certainly the article does not expressly exclude sale, but it might be argued that certain forms of sale, e.g. sale by auction, would be prohibited since it can hardly be said to be in the interests of mankind to disperse collections of archaeological material. Other forms of sale, e.g. the sale of duplicates, might be acceptable. Just how far sale is permitted will clearly have an impact on whether or not commercial salvors will be able to continue participating in activities affecting the underwater cultural heritage.

Article 149 refers to the preferential rights of States. An earlier draft of this article expressly recognized ownership rights, as well as preferential rights of States. The fact that the reference to ownership rights was excluded in the final text suggests that ownership rights to objects of an archaeological and historical nature found in the Area would not be recognized and therefore the preferential rights of States would be rights less than ownership and would be something nearer to cultural rights. The fact that such rights appear to be accorded to several different types of State of origin may potentially lead to claims being made by more than one State to the same material. Also, the interrelationship between the rights accorded to mankind by the article and to the State(s) of origin is far from clear. At its simplest, it may mean that mankind in a preferential State should receive the benefit, perhaps through the objects being deposited in that State.

The second article on the underwater cultural heritage, Article 303, states:

1 States have the duty to protect objects of an archaeological and historical nature found at sea and shall cooperate for this purpose.

2 In order to control traffic in such objects, the coastal State may, in applying article 33,[18] presume that their removal from the seabed in the zone referred to in that article without its approval would result in an infringement within its territory or territorial sea of the laws and regulations referred to in that article.

3 Nothing in this article affects the rights of identifiable owners, the law of salvage or other rules of admiralty, or laws and practices with respect to cultural exchanges.

4 This article is without prejudice to other international agreements and rules of international law regarding the protection of objects of an archaeological and historical nature.

The location of Article 303 in the 'General Provisions' section of the Convention means that, other than paragraph 2 which specifically refers to the contiguous zone,[19] the article applies to *any* area of the sea, including the 'Area'. The primary value of the article in so far as it applies to any area of the sea is that it makes it clear that States have a duty to protect underwater cultural heritage. The provision that States shall cooperate for this purpose is also valuable since it should encourage the negotiation of inter-State agreements in respect of wreck sites. A difficult question is how does

Article 303 square with Article 149 in relation to the Area? For example, Article 303(3) upholds the law of salvage and other rules of admiralty. Surely there is potential for conflict between the application of salvage law, which encourages the recovery and sale of material, and the principle laid down in Article 149 that objects found in the Area shall be preserved or disposed of for the benefit of mankind as a whole? Further potential difficulty arises from the fact that Article 303(3) specifically reserves ownership rights, yet the historical development of Article 149 suggests that it does not recognize such rights. Which article takes precedence in this respect? There may be no satis-factory answers to these questions.

While it is often said that Articles 149 and 303 of the LOS Convention are disappointingly weak in terms of the protection they afford to the under-water cultural heritage (see O'Keefe in this volume, p. 137), these provisions are nonetheless of value. They make it clear that States have a duty to protect the underwater cultural heritage in whatever area of the sea it is located. They establish a principle of cooperation between States and provide some basis for controlling activities in the contiguous zone. They also provide a basis for States to assert a cultural interest in particular wrecks. Furthermore, in the view of the author these articles provide a flexible and unrestrictive framework for the development of a specific international agreement on the underwater cultural heritage.[20] Indeed, Article 303(4) appears to invite the creation of such a convention.

## UNESCO Draft Convention on the Protection of the Underwater Cultural Heritage

The UNESCO Draft Convention on the Protection of the Underwater Cultural Heritage is discussed in some detail by O'Keefe in Chapter 5. Two drafts have been produced to date.[21] The first, referred to here as 'the 1998 draft', was produced by the UNESCO Secretariat for discussion at a meeting of government experts in June/July 1998.[22] The second, referred to here as 'the 1999 draft', resulted from a second meeting of government experts, in April 1999. Although this second draft was considered at a third meeting of experts, which took place in July 2000, no formal changes were made at that meeting.[23] It is still very much open to discussion and includes some wording in square brackets which merely represents suggestions which are not yet the subject of agreement. Nonetheless, it provides a useful indication of how the various interests in the underwater cultural heritage may be treated by any new international regime which emerges from the negotiations.

The primary purpose of the Draft Convention is to introduce mechanisms to regulate and control activities affecting the underwater cultural heritage in international waters. A particular intention behind the Convention is to curtail the freedom of salvors to operate on the high seas in the interests of preserving the cultural heritage. The aim of the Convention is to ensure that as far as possible intrusive activity is conducted only if in conformity with archaeo-logically acceptable standards. Rules incorporating such standards will be

annexed to the Convention. These are based on the ICOMOS International
Charter on the Protection and Management of Underwater Cultural Heritage.[24] The Rules make it clear that preservation *in situ* should be considered
as a first option and that excavation should be authorized only when it would
make 'a significant contribution to knowledge, protection and [/or] enhance-
ment of underwater cultural heritage'. Where an excavation is authorized,
the Rules emphasize the need for any artefacts raised to be kept together
and made available for scientific study. Conformance with archaeological standards and principles is therefore at the core of the Convention.

The Draft Convention lays down as a general principle that the underwater cultural heritage shall be preserved 'for the benefit of humankind'.[25]
This echoes the principle set out in Article 149 of the LOS Convention,
although the Draft Convention refers only to preservation and not to disposal.
Non-intrusive public access, 'where practicable', is encouraged.[26] The Preamble refers to the 'conviction' of States Parties that information and education
'will enable the public to appreciate the importance of underwater cultural
heritage to humanity and the need to preserve it'. Article 15 of the 1999
text states that:

> Each State Party shall endeavour by educational means to create
> and develop in the public mind a realization of the value of the
> underwater cultural heritage as well as the threat to this heritage
> posed by violations of this Convention and non-compliance with
> the Rules of the Annex.

The Annex itself requires that archaeological projects provide for 'popular'
presentation of their results[27] and is also likely to require that project archives
be made publicly accessible within a certain period of the completion of
fieldwork.[28] The general public's interest in the underwater cultural heritage
will therefore be accorded priority by the new Convention.

The text of the Draft Convention makes no specific reference to sport
divers. However, the Preamble refers to the necessity for cooperation of
divers and the need for responsible diving in order that the underwater cultural
heritage can be protected and preserved. The interests of sport divers are also
taken into account in the provisions for public access,[29] and the benefits that
the sport diving community can bestow from a heritage point of view are
recognized by the provision made for education[30] and training.[31] The absence
of direct reference to sport divers in the text may be due to the fact that
the Convention is primarily concerned with controlling activities in international waters. In the past, the nature of the equipment available to sport
divers has meant that their activities have been restricted to fairly shallow
coastal waters. However, the development of mixed gas and rebreather equipment means that sport divers are operating in ever deeper waters. Furthermore,
the Convention makes provision not just for international waters but for
territorial waters too. Therefore, some specific acknowledgement in the text
of the role that sport divers can play in safeguarding the underwater cultural

heritage would not be inappropriate and would undoubtedly provide reas-
surance to divers that their interests are being taken into full account.

Under the 1998 draft, the Convention would have been applicable only
to underwater cultural heritage which had been abandoned[32] and provision
was made for abandonment to be deemed in certain circumstances.[33] This
was felt to be a mechanism which would preserve reasonable ownership rights
while at the same time precisely defining the concept of abandonment
(O'Keefe and Nafziger 1994: 406; Strati 1999a: 17). However, the provisions for deemed abandonment proved to be among the most controversial
of the 1998 draft owing at least partly to the different national approaches
to this particular issue. In the 1999 draft all references to abandonment have
been excluded and therefore, under its terms, the Convention would apply
to underwater cultural property whether abandoned or not, and the extent
of property rights is left to be determined by national laws. If the Convention
is to be acceptable to common law, as well as civil law, States, this is probably the best approach.

As far as the interests of States are concerned, one of the most contentious
issues in the negotiations has been whether or not warships and other State-
owned or -operated vessels should be included within the scope of the
Convention. A provision in the 1998 draft excluding such vessels is the subject
of ongoing discussion. Such an exclusion would undermine the whole purpose
of the Convention since it would result in a considerable proportion of the
underwater cultural heritage falling outside the Convention's remit. The
greatest concern of States is the possibility that the Convention could bestow
rights on other States in respect of their warships and other vessels. However,
it should not be beyond the capability and resourcefulness of the negotiators
to find a means of overcoming this concern. For example, the Convention
could set a time limit for sovereign immunity of, say, 150–200 years and
could require that the coastal State consult with the flag State in relation to
any activities on older wrecks. States are also concerned about the need to
protect the sanctity of war graves. However, there is no reason why provisions designed to control interference with wrecks should compromise the
sanctity of human remains. Indeed, under the Convention, wrecks will be
preserved *in situ* wherever possible. Where intervention is permitted, the sanctity of human remains can be ensured by appropriate provision being made
in the rules of the Annex.[34]

The Draft Convention makes various references to the interests that States
may have in particular underwater cultural remains. For example, provision
is made for States to enter into regional or bilateral agreements for the preservation of 'common underwater cultural heritage'.[35] Use of the word 'common'
suggests that the provision would apply to States which shared a special
interest in the underwater cultural heritage, perhaps through some historical
or cultural connection. However, it appears that the provision is intended to
allow agreements to be concluded between States bordering the same sea for
the preservation of heritage located there.[36] These States may therefore have

no special connection with the wreck beyond the fact that it is located within their vicinity. These regional and bilateral agreements may also be open to 'States of cultural origin and States of historical and archaeological origin',[37] and clearly these would have a special connection with the wreck. The Draft Convention also makes provision for the seizure of underwater cultural heritage which has been excavated in a manner not in conformity with the Rules in the Annex,[38] and provides that States known to have a 'cultural heritage interest' in such material shall be notified of its seizure.[39] Furthermore, provision is made for the interests of States with a 'national heritage interest' to be taken into account when the ultimate disposition of seized material is decided,[40] and States are exhorted to consider collaborating with States who have expressed such an interest in particular underwater cultural heritage.[41] The recognition of State interests going beyond the traditional ownership and jurisdictional interests is useful, as is the provision for cooperation through the negotiation of bilateral and regional agreements. However, the use of a variety of phrases to refer to these interests is bound to lead to confusion.

How far the activities of commercial salvors should be allowed to continue, if at all, is one of the most thorny questions faced by the drafters of the Convention. Neither the 1998 nor the 1999 drafts include an express exclusion of salvage law,[42] but instead they include a provision which states that:

> States Parties shall provide for the non-application of any internal law or regulation having the effect of providing commercial incentives or any other reward for the excavation and removal of underwater cultural heritage.[43]

The insertion of a provision in this form, rather than an express exclusion of salvage law, was no doubt intended to appear as a compromise. However, it could well have much the same effect in practice. There is also provision in the general principles set out in the Annex to the 1999 draft that:

> The commercial exploitation of underwater cultural heritage for trade or speculation . . . or its irretrievable dispersal is fundamentally incompatible with the protection and proper management of the underwater cultural heritage. Underwater cultural heritage shall . . . not be traded, sold, bought and bartered as items of commercial value.[44]

The precise scope of these two provisions is far from clear. Exactly what would count as a 'commercial incentive' or as 'commercial exploitation . . . for trade'? A commercial incentive would clearly include payment of a salvage reward, but would it include the award of title under the law of finding? Arguably, application of the law of finding may lead to even worse consequences from the point of view of the cultural heritage than the application of salvage law. 'Commercial exploitation . . . for trade or speculation' would clearly include the sale of artefacts, but would it also include the sale of videos of an underwater site, or artefact replicas?

These provisions represent something of a fudge. Arguably, in their place it would be preferable for a provision to be included expressly excluding from the application of salvage law, and the law of finds, underwater cultural heritage to which the Convention applies.[45] Neither is appropriate for dealing with the underwater cultural heritage and the exclusion of salvage law has been widely called for. Such a provision would not, of itself, exclude the involvement of commercial salvors in recovery activities. Consideration would need to be given as to whether any commercial involvement should be permitted. The draft as it presently stands appears virtually to prohibit commercial activities on all underwater sites over 100 years old.[46] Arguably, this sways the balance too far in the direction of archaeological interests and may well lead to clandestine excavations and the development of a larger black market in artefacts from marine sites. Presumably, not all underwater sites over 100 years of age are worthy of preservation. Rather than having this blanket-cover approach, it might be preferable for the Convention to adopt a significance criterion, for example so that it applies to underwater cultural heritage which is of archaeological 'importance', 'value' or 'significance'. Admittedly, there are difficulties in this approach as the significance of particular remains is likely to be variously interpreted and in some cases would undoubtedly give rise to disputes. However, even if it is concluded that a significance criterion is unworkable, surely it would be reasonable to allow some level of participation by commercial salvors? Properly structured and regulated, such participation could be of benefit to archaeologists and the general public as a whole. Certainly it would not compromise the general principle of protection *in situ* to allow cooperation between archaeologists and salvors on sites which are under threat, or where excavation is necessary for research purposes. Any cooperative ventures would naturally be required to conform with the archaeological standards laid down in the Annex. However, if commercial salvors were involved, they would obviously require to be recompensed for their endeavours. While in certain cases funding may be found to do this without requiring the sale of artefacts, this may not always be the case. Is a total ban on all trading in underwater cultural heritage, as currently provided for in the Annex, actually the best approach? Or is it possible to identify certain categories of artefacts which, after appropriate study, would not need to be kept in the project archive but which could be returned to the stream of commerce? There appeared to be some agreement at the first meeting of government experts held in June/July 1998 that commercial interests in archaeology might in some circumstances be legitimate and that the concept of partnerships might be useful.[47] However, the matter was not considered in any detail at the second meeting of government experts in 1999 and, although discussed at the third meeting in 2000, no consensus was reached.[48]

## CONCLUSIONS

In the Preamble to the UNESCO Draft Convention reference is made to the belief that:

> cooperation among States, marine archaeologists, museums and other scientific institutions, salvors, divers and their organizations is essential for the protection of the underwater cultural heritage.

The Draft Convention therefore explicitly recognizes the need to take into account non-archaeological interests in the underwater cultural heritage and the advantages that may arise from so doing. In the case of most such interests, it should be possible to achieve a workable compromise which does not prejudice the primary aim of the Convention which is to protect the underwater cultural heritage. However, the question remains of how far, if at all, any form of concession should be made to commercial salvors?

On this point, it may be helpful to draw on the experience of US statute law and practice. The US *Abandoned Shipwreck Act* of 1987 was designed to resolve the long-running conflict between state governments and federal admiralty courts as to who should control salvage activities on state land (Giesecke 1988: 379–89). The primary purpose of the Act is to recognize the authority of the states to control recovery of historic shipwrecks (Giesecke 1988: 387). While the preferred policy under the Act is for *in situ* preservation (Varmer 1999a: 283), it has as its basis the recognition of multiple uses of the underwater cultural heritage, including commercial recovery operations. Interestingly, however, the law of salvage and finds is expressly excluded from applying to shipwrecks to which the Act applies. These are abandoned shipwrecks embedded in state submerged lands, and those located on state submerged lands and determined to be historic. Under the Act, the US asserted title to these wrecks, and then transferred that title to the underlying states. The states are placed under a duty to protect the shipwrecks and to develop policies to:

(A) protect natural resources and habitat areas;

(B) guarantee recreational exploration of shipwreck sites; and

(C) allow for appropriate public and private sector recovery of shipwrecks consistent with the protection of historical values and environmental integrity of the shipwrecks and the sites.

The Act requires that the National Park Service develop guidelines, in consultation with appropriate public and private sector interests, for assisting states in undertaking their responsibilities under the Act. The Act requires that the guidelines seek to, *inter alia*:

• foster a partnership among sport divers, fishermen, archeologists, salvors, and other interests to manage shipwreck resources . . .;

• facilitate access and utilization by recreational interests;

- recognize the interests of individuals and groups engaged in shipwreck discovery and salvage.

The Act therefore recognizes multiple interests in the underwater cultural heritage and seeks to foster a 'partnership' with these interests to manage shipwreck resources.[49]

The Act was the result of a compromise: salvage law would be excluded in return for the recognition of multiple users, including professional salvors and sport divers (Varmer 1999a: 283–4). The inclusion of professional salvors among the interests recognized by the Act was a radical decision. The Act makes it clear that any recovery must be 'consistent with the protection of historical values and environmental integrity of the shipwrecks and the sites'. Presumably with this requirement in mind, the Guidelines make provision for the recovery of shipwrecks by the private sector on behalf of the public sector subject to appropriate control and advises that the unscientific use of treasure hunter technology should be prohibited.[50] Despite these safeguards, inevitably there is a significant degree of tension in the legislation between the need to protect cultural and natural resources and to facilitate recreational access, and the possibility of wreck recovery. No doubt such tension is also reflected in the practical application of the Act.

Nonetheless, the drafters of the UNESCO Convention might consider whether the compromise that forms the basis of the *Abandoned Shipwreck Act* could form an effective basis for a consensus between civil and common law States, and between archaeologists and salvors.[51] After all, the principle of multiple use management is widely employed to regulate the use of other finite resources. However, if it was adopted, it would be vital that the interests of commercial salvors should not be given such weight that they threaten the fundamental purpose of the legislation to protect the underwater cultural heritage. Whether the *Abandoned Shipwreck Act* provides the right balance between the interests involved can be determined only by a close examination of how the Act operates in practice.[52]

Action to provide protection for underwater cultural heritage in international waters is urgently required. New wreck sites are being discovered all the time. If the current unregulated regime continues, many sites which are of great archaeological interest will be 'excavated' without the participation of archaeologists. However, to be effective in ensuring that any recovery activities in international waters are undertaken in accordance with agreed archaeological standards, a new convention must achieve *widespread* support. The possibility of achieving such support is made particularly difficult by the divergence in national approaches to the topic. If a successful agreement is to be achieved, there must be significant concessions on both sides. The exclusion of salvage law in return for the recognition of multiple uses might provide the basis for compromise. The danger is that civil law States may view the adoption of a principle taken from US legislation as meaning that the balance has been swayed too far in the direction of the common law approach. However, the reality is that, in many fields including this one, US law has adopted a novel and practical approach which deserves serious consideration.

## ACKNOWLEDGEMENT

The author would like to acknowledge the support of the University of Leicester in awarding her study leave enabling her to write this essay.

## NOTES

1 This article focuses on groups which have direct interests in the underwater cultural heritage. However, there are others who have indirect interests – for example, fishermen and those involved in dredging, pipeline and cable-laying, oil and gas exploration, etc. These groups may well be affected by any legal regime protecting the underwater cultural heritage and their interests must be taken into account. Unfortunately, space constraints mean that they are not considered here.

2 For a detailed examination of insurers' interests, and of ownership issues generally, see Dromgoole and Gaskell 1998: 152–78.

3 *Columbus-America v The Unidentified Wrecked and Abandoned Sailing Vessel* [1992] *American Maritime Cases* 2705, [1995] *American Maritime Cases* 1985 (4 Cir.).

4 On appeal the decision on abandonment was reversed, primarily it seems because the insurers had come before the court to assert their interests (O'Keefe 1994: 7–12).

5 *Sea Hunt Inc. and the Commonwealth of Virginia v. Unidentified Shipwrecked Vessel or Vessels* 221 F.3d 634 (4th cir., 2000), petition for writ of certiorari to the US Court of Appeals for the Fourth Circuit denied, 121 S. Ct. 1079 (2001).

6 The majority of States claim a territorial limit of 12 nautical miles, in line with the UN Convention on the Law of the Sea 1982, Art. 3, which refers to the right of States to establish a territorial limit up to 12 nautical miles from baselines. A number of States claim a wider limit (see Shaw 1997: 402 f.n. 64).

7 For example, France has extended its jurisdiction so as to exercise control over the 24 mile contiguous zone, in line with Art. 303(2) of the Law of the Sea Convention (see further below, p. 125). Italy appears to be in the process of doing the same. While Australia, Ireland and Spain exercise control over their continental shelves, the legal basis for their claims is contentious.

8 This vessel was being used by the French explorer La Salle to transport French colonists, when she sank in Matagorda Bay, Texas, in 1686. The wreck was discovered in 1995. For further details, see http://www.thc.state.tx.us/belle/index.html

9 In 1995 an agreement was signed by the governments of Estonia, Finland and Sweden to protect the wreck of the ferry *Estonia*, which sank in 1994 while travelling from Tallinn to Stockholm with the loss of almost 900 lives. A draft agreement has also been prepared by the US State Department regarding the wreck of the *Titanic* and it is envisaged that the US, UK, France and Canada will be signatories.

10 At the time of writing, Hutchinson was Curator of Archaeology at the National Maritime Museum, London.

11 At the time of writing, Murphy worked for the Submerged Cultural Resources Unit of the National Park Service, Santa Fe, New Mexico.

12 The 1996 Charter was ratified by the 11th ICOMOS General Assembly, held in Sofia, Bulgaria, in October 1996. Its text can be found at http://www.international.icomos.org/icomos/under_e.htm

13 In the US there are both federal and state preservation statutes. The foremost federal statute is the *Abandoned Shipwreck Act* of 1987, which delegates responsibility for many coastal wrecks to individual states. For further details, see Conclusions.

14 *Treasure Salvors Inc v The Unidentified, Wrecked And Abandoned Sailing Vessel* (Salvors III) [1981] *American Maritime Cases* 1857, 1874.

15 See, for example, *Columbus-America Discovery Group v Atlantic Mutual Insurance Co. (The Central America)* (1992) 974 F. 2d 450, 468; *Chance v Certain Artifacts Found and Salvaged* (1984) 606 F. Supp. 801, 808–9; *Klein v Unidentified, Wrecked and Abandoned Sailing Vessel* (1985) 758 F. 2d 1511, 1515. Fairly flimsy evidence of 'good archaeological practice' has, however, been accepted. See O'Keefe in this volume, Chapter 5.

16 While there is some academic debate on the point, the weight of opinion seems to be that this is the position even in the case of sunken warships (Dromgoole and Gaskell 1999: 184).

17 [1982] 21 *International Legal Materials* 1261.

18 Article 33 established a contiguous zone extending from the outer boundary of the territorial sea to 24 nautical miles from the coast and provided that a coastal State may exercise control over this area to prevent and punish infringement of its customs, fiscal, immigration or sanitary regulations occurring within its territory.

19 Article 303(2) aims to provide coastal States with an international legal basis for action to control traffic in material found in the contiguous zone. See note 18 above.

20 However, the extent to which these provisions, and in particular Art. 303, restrict a later agreement is contentious. While Art. 303(4) states that Art. 303 is without prejudice to other international agreements, there is considerable debate about whether this refers only to antecedent agreements, or whether it also covers subsequent agreements. If the former, it could be argued that Art. 303(3) precludes a future agreement that does not recognize ownership rights or that excludes the application of salvage law.

21 This essay was written prior to July 2001 when a further draft was produced. See further note 23.

22 The 1998 draft was based on an earlier text drafted by the International Law Association, which was submitted to UNESCO for consideration in 1994. See further O'Keefe in this volume, Chapter 5.

23 At the fourth and final meeting of experts, which took place in two sessions from 26 March to 6 April 2001 and from 2 to 7 July 2001, a final text was agreed. This text will be put before the 31st session of the UNESCO General Conference, which takes place in October/November 2001 for final debate and possible adoption.

24 See note 12 above. Exactly how the provisions of the Charter should be made applicable has been the subject of some debate. In the draft produced in 1998 the Charter itself was annexed to the Convention. In the meeting of government experts held in 1999 it was decided that it would be more appropriate to use the general standards set out in the Charter to formulate a set of rules for annexation to the Convention.

25 1999 draft, Art. 3. This point is reiterated in the Preamble to the Draft Convention.

26 Annex, para. 7.

27 Annex, para. 34.

28 Annex, para. 31 suggests that this will be a period of five years.

29 Annex, paras. 7 and 31.

30 1999 draft, Art. 15.

31 1999 draft, Art. 16.

32 1998 draft, Art. 2(1).

33 1998 draft, Art. 1(2).

34 At the April 1999 meeting of experts it was agreed that the Draft Convention would deal with the war grave issue 'in one way or another': UNESCO, *Final Report of the Second Meeting of Government Experts*, 19–24 April 1999 (CLT.99/CONF.204) para. 24. Any provision that is made should ensure that *all* human remains receive appropriate treatment. There is little justification for distinguishing between those whose lives were lost in battle and others whose lives were lost at sea.

35 1999 draft, Option 1 Art. 5(4), Option 2 Art. 2 ter, Option 3 Art. 2 ter.

36 UNESCO, *Final Report of the Second Meeting of Government Experts*, para. 35, op. cit. note 34.

37 Provision is made to this effect in square brackets in the 1999 draft after a request was made that the agreements be open to such States at the meeting of experts held in 1999: UNESCO, *Final Report of the Second Meeting of Government Experts*, para. 35, op. cit. note 34.

38 1999 draft, Art. 9.

39 1999 draft, Art. 11.

40 1999 draft, Art. 12(1).

41 1999 draft, Art. 13(1).

42 Unlike the earlier draft text produced by the International Law Association: see note 22 above.

43 Article 12(2). The words 'or any other reward' were not included in the version of Art. 12(2) in the 1998 draft.

44 Annex, para. 2. Furthermore, the Annex provides that '[p]roject funding shall [should] not require the sale ... of underwater cultural heritage': para. 19.

45 As has already been noted (see note 20 above), there is some question about whether Art. 303(3) of the LOS Convention precludes the exclusion of salvage law in a new convention on the underwater cultural heritage. There may also be potential difficulties in relation to the Salvage Convention 1989 (see Dromgoole and Gaskell 1999: 189–90).

46 It should be noted that States Parties would also be able to designate material within their jurisdiction which had been underwater for less than 100 years.

47 UNESCO, *Report of the Meeting of Government Experts on the Draft Convention for the Protection of the Underwater Cultural Heritage*, 29 June–2 July 1998 (Doc. CLT-98/CONF.202/7), para. 33.

48 See now Article 4 of final draft text agreed at the fourth meeting of experts (see note 23 above) and Rule 2 of the Annex. Both the final text and the Annex are contained in UNESCO Doc. 31 C/24, 3 August 2001.

49 Since the Act applies only to abandoned shipwrecks, the interests of private owners do not need to be taken into account.

50 55 Fed. Reg. 50132 (1990).

51 The suggestion that this compromise could be adopted by any new international treaty was first proposed by Varmer (1999a).

52 It would also be useful to look at the US national marine sanctuary underwater cultural heritage programme, which operates under the *National Marine Sanctuaries Act* of 1972, and is based on similar principles. See further Varmer 1999b.

# REFERENCES

Abbass, D. 1999. A marine archaeologist looks at treasure salvage. *Journal of Maritime Law and Commerce* 30, 261–8.

Blake, J. 1999. Turkey. In *Legal Protection of the Underwater Cultural Heritage: National* and *International Perspectives*, S. Dromgoole (ed.), 169–80. London: Kluwer Law International.

Dromgoole, S. 1999. United Kingdom. In *Legal Protection of the Underwater Cultural Heritage: National and International Perspectives*, S. Dromgoole (ed.), 181–203. London: Kluwer Law International.

Dromgoole, S. and N. Gaskell 1998. Interests in Wreck. In *Interests in Goods*, N. Palmer and E. McKendrick (eds), 141–204. London: Lloyd's of London Press.

Dromgoole, S. and N. Gaskell 1999. Draft UNESCO Convention on the Protection of the Underwater Cultural Heritage 1998, *International Journal of Marine and Coastal Law* 14, 171–206.

Giesecke, A. 1988. The Abandoned Shipwreck Act: Affirming the Role of the States in Historic Preservation. *Columbia-VLA Journal of Law and the Arts* 12, 379–89.

Hutchinson, G. 1996. Threats to underwater cultural heritage. The problems of unprotected archaeological and historic sites, wrecks and objects found at sea. *Marine Policy* 20, 287–90.

Jeffery, B. 1999. Australia. In *Legal Protection of the Underwater Cultural Heritage: National and International Perspectives*, S. Dromgoole (ed.), 1–17. London: Kluwer Law International.

Kaoru, Y. and P. Hoagland. 1994. 'The value of historic shipwrecks: conflicts and management'. *Coastal Management* 22, 195–213.

Kowalski, W. 1999. Poland. In *Legal Protection of the Underwater Cultural Heritage: National and International Perspectives*, S. Dromgoole (ed.), 119–32. London: Kluwer Law International.

Le Gurun, G. 1999. France. In *Legal Protection of the Underwater Cultural Heritage: National and International Perspectives*, S. Dromgoole (ed.), 43–63. London: Kluwer Law International.

Murphy, L. 1997. Archaeological record. In *British Museum Encyclopaedia of Underwater and Maritime Archaeology*, J. Delgado (ed.), 33. London: British Museum Press.

O'Connor, N. 1999. Ireland. In *Legal Protection of the Underwater Cultural Heritage: National and International Perspectives*, S. Dromgoole (ed.), 87–99. London: Kluwer Law International.

O'Keefe, P. 1994. Gold, Abandonment and Salvage: *The Central America*. *Lloyd's Maritime and Commercial Law Quarterly*, 7–12.

O'Keefe, P. and J. Nafziger. 1994. The Draft Convention on the Protection of the Underwater Cultural Heritage. *Ocean Development and International Law* 25, 391–404.

Shaw, M.N. 1997. *International Law*. Cambridge: Grotius.

Strati, A. 1995. *The Protection of the Underwater Cultural Heritage: An Emerging Objective of the Contemporary Law of the Sea*. The Hague: Martinus Nijhoff.

Strati, A. 1999a. *Draft Convention on the Protection of Underwater Cultural Heritage: A Commentary prepared for UNESCO*. (UNESCO Doc. CLT-99/WS/8, April 1999). Paris: UNESCO.

Strati, A. 1999b. Greece. In *Legal Protection of the Underwater Cultural Heritage: National and International Perspectives*, S. Dromgoole (ed.), 65–85. London: Kluwer Law International.

Throckmorton, P. 1990. The world's worst investment: the economics of treasure hunting with real life comparisons. *Underwater Archaeology Proceedings from the Society for Historical Archaeology Conference 1990* 6–10; reprinted in L.V. Prott and I. Srong (eds) 1999, *Background Materials on the Protection of the Underwater Cultural Heritage*, 179–83, Paris and Portsmouth: UNESCO/Nautical Archaeology Society.

Varmer, O. 1999a. The case against the 'salvage' of the cultural heritage. *Journal of Maritime Law and Commerce* 30, 279–302.

Varmer, O. 1999b. United States of America. In *Legal Protection of the Underwater Cultural Heritage: National and International Perspectives*, S. Dromgoole (ed.), 205–221. London: Kluwer Law International.

# 5 Negotiating the future of the underwater cultural heritage

Patrick J. O'Keefe

Some 200 governmental experts met in Paris, 19–24 April 1999, to discuss and negotiate a Draft Convention on the Protection of the Underwater Cultural Heritage. This was the second such meeting. It represented a further step in a process designed to establish a legal and administrative regime whereby underwater cultural heritage beyond the territorial sea of States would be treated in accordance with agreed international standards.

## THE PROBLEM

Recent years have seen numerous examples of objects being raised from great depths beyond the territorial sea of any State. For example, numerous articles have been raised from RMS *Titanic*, found in 1985 at a depth of approximately 2.5 miles and some 300 miles from Newfoundland. A large quantity of gold and certain artefacts have been taken from the SS *Central America*, found in 1987 lying 160 miles off the South Carolina coast at a depth of about 1.5 miles. The American explorer Robert Ballard removed artefacts for dating purposes from Roman wrecks he had found in deep water north-west of Sicily during an expedition in 1977. In February 1999, newspapers carried a report that the wreck of the Japanese submarine *I-52*, sunk during World War II, had been found in the mid-Atlantic about 1,200 miles west of Cape Verde and 3.2 miles down. Shoes found near the wreck were raised for presentation to an association of the families of sailors who perished in the sinking. The technology now in use is capable of reaching 98 per cent of all ocean floors.

However, law has not kept pace with these technological developments. Beyond the territorial sea, it is rudimentary and incapable of ensuring that remains constituting underwater cultural heritage are treated so as to extract the greatest possible amount of knowledge. There is general agreement that the United Nations Convention on the Law of the Sea 1982 (hereafter the LOS Convention) is inadequate in this regard. It has a provision (Article

303(2)) which allows States to take some action regarding 'archaeological and historical objects' between 12 and 24 miles from the baselines from which they measure their territorial seas (i.e. the contiguous zone), but very few have implemented the provision. In the area between the 24-mile line and the deep seabed, Article 303(1) may apply. For example, Migliorino considers that Article 303 only applies to the contiguous zone (1995: 485). But all it says is that States 'have the duty to protect objects of an archaeological and historical nature found at sea and shall cooperate for this purpose'. There is no indication of what this duty is or how it applies. For the deep seabed, Article 149 is relevant:

> All objects of an archaeological and historical nature found in the Area shall be preserved or disposed of for the benefit of mankind as a whole, particular regard being paid to the preferential rights of the State or country of origin, or the State of cultural origin, or the State of historical and archaeological origin.

The defects with this provision will be obvious: the limited nature of the material covered; the juxtaposition of 'preserved or disposed' and the difficulty of assessing the interests of States.

In the vacuum left by the LOS Convention, national courts have attempted to provide some rules. For example, courts in the US have purported to take jurisdiction over, and issue orders concerning, the *Central America* and the *Titanic*, even though both of these lie outside the territory of that country. However, there is no way to enforce those orders against persons who have no contact with the US other than by those in whose favour the orders have been given going to a foreign court and asking that court to enforce them. The problem has been vividly illustrated recently in relation to the *Titanic*. Exclusive salvage rights had been granted to an American company, RMS Titanic Inc., by the district court in the Eastern District of Virginia. In 1998, Deep Ocean Expeditions (DOE), a British Virgin Islands company with headquarters on the Isle of Man, began marketing a programme of public visits to the *Titanic* using a Russian research vessel and her submersibles. RMS Titanic Inc. sought an injunction preventing DOE, among others, from visiting and photographing the wreck site. This was granted by the District Court.[1] However, DOE simply ignored the injunction and conducted its planned expedition. It is unlikely that a court on the Isle of Man would have enforced the American injunction under the doctrine of comity.

In order to make salvage a more acceptable method for dealing with underwater cultural heritage, some courts in the US have included among criteria used in assessing a salvage award that of whether the work was done according to archaeological standards. In *Columbus-America Discovery Group v. Atlantic Mutual Insurance Company*,[2] the Court of Appeals for the Fourth Circuit says of the six criteria that the US Supreme Court has listed for fixing a salvage award: 'We thoroughly agree with all six and, in cases such as this, would add another: the degree to which the salvors have worked to protect the

historical and archaeological value of the wreck and items salved'. Unfortunately, the emphasis in judgments leaves much to be desired from the viewpoint
of professional archaeology.

The District Court noted further that Columbus-America had published a
book and promoted a television account of its endeavours, and had provided
educational materials to schools interested in teaching their students about
the *Central America* and its history. The court found that 'the efforts to preserve
the site and its artefacts have not been equaled in any other case. . . .'[3]

But the unreported judgment of the District Court shows that the experts
were only aboard the search vessel 'from time to time' rather than contin-
uously supervising operations. One commentator has stated:

> No overall site photographs, a site map, or any other archaeo-
> logical information has been released. . . . Archaeological study and
> documentation of *Central America* would be particularly significant
> because no detailed record of a Panama Route steamship of the
> period exists. More importantly, the apparent high degree of preser-
> vation of passenger baggage, which is very similar to that observed
> at the *Titanic* wreck site, would offer a detailed opportunity to
> assess the material culture of the period, and its use and trans-
> portation on a vessel travelling from the 'frontier' of Gold Rush
> California, and could be compared with collections of the same
> period from the wrecks of *Bertrand* and *Arabia*.
>
> (Delgado 1997: 93–4)

The courts have also emphasized archaeological aspects in the salvage work
on the *Titanic*: 'the archaeological preservation of the wreck itself as well as
the recovered artefacts is of extreme importance to this Court'.[4] But, once
again, the court exhibits only a partial understanding of what constitutes
archaeology; emphasizing conservation of artefacts, exhibitions and maintenance of the collection. It ignores the absence of any professional archaeologist
on site, the failure to assemble an archive of dive data and the failure to
prepare an archaeological report (Fewster and Valliant 1997: 29). Emphasis
appears to be on entertainment, not information.

## THE BUENOS AIRES DRAFT CONVENTION

It was against this developing background that the Cultural Heritage Law
Committee of the International Law Association (ILA) decided, in 1988, to
prepare a draft international convention dealing with the issues. In doing this,
it could draw on the work done by the Council of Europe in the period
1978–85 when it tried to prepare a European Convention on Protection of
the Underwater Cultural Heritage. That effort failed when Turkey objected to
the territorial scope of application of the draft (Strati 1995: 87). However, the
ILA Committee and the Council of Europe were dealing with fundamentally

different areas of the sea. The latter was concerned with protection of the underwater cultural heritage within State jurisdiction; the former was primarily interested in protection of that outside the territorial seas of States.

Bederman has stated that the ILA is 'an international organization of academic international law specialists' and that during the work of the Committee 'no input was invited from any person or entity other than those concerned with historic preservation values' (1999: 331). This appears to be an attempt to denigrate the work of the Committee and is inaccurate. Half of the members of the Committee were practising lawyers or government officials. During the six years that the Committee worked on the topic, various organizations were consulted including the International Maritime Organization, the United Nations, the Comité Maritime International and other Committees of the ILA concerning sovereign immunity and the law of the sea.

The Committee completed its work in 1994 when the Sixty-sixth Conference of the ILA held at Buenos Aires adopted the draft it had prepared. At the same time, the International Committee on Underwater Cultural Heritage Inc. of the International Council on Monuments and Sites (ICO-MOS) had prepared a Charter for the Protection and Management of the Underwater Cultural Heritage,[5] which was attached to the ILA Draft. The Secretary-General of the ILA forwarded the Draft with the attached Charter and the Committee's three Reports to UNESCO for consideration.

## ACTION IN UNESCO

In 1993, the UNESCO Executive Board invited the Director-General to make a study of the legal instruments protecting the cultural heritage. One conclusion of this survey was the need for a legal instrument to protect the underwater cultural heritage. The Executive Board endorsed that view and the UNESCO Secretariat prepared a feasibility study using the ILA Draft as a basis. This was considered by the Executive Board of UNESCO at its meeting in May 1995. The Board decided that States needed to examine further the jurisdictional aspects. The views of States were sought and later that year were put before the General Conference of UNESCO, which reacted favourably but decided further discussion was needed. In accordance with its wishes, a meeting of experts representing expertise in archaeology, salvage and jurisdictional regimes was held in Paris, 22–24 May 1996. The views of this meeting were sent to all Member States of UNESCO and to those with observer status – then the UK and the US. On 12 November 1997, the UNESCO General Conference adopted Resolution 29C/6.3 to the effect that 'the protection of the underwater cultural heritage should be regulated at the international level and that the method adopted should be an international convention'. The Director-General was invited to prepare a draft convention, circulate this to States for comment and observations and then convene a group of governmental experts 'representing all regions together with representatives of the competent international organizations in order to consider this draft convention for submission to the General Conference at its thirtieth session' in 1999. A document[6] containing the Draft Convention on the Protection of the Underwater Cultural Heritage was circulated to Member States of UNESCO and others in April 1998. The first meeting of governmental experts to consider the Draft was held 29 June–2 July 1998 (hereafter 1998 meeting) and the second, as already noted, 19–24 April 1999 (hereafter 1999 meeting). The latter resolved to ask the Director-General of UNESCO to convene a further meeting 'as soon as possible'.[7]

## ROLE OF UNESCO

> The preservation of the world's cultural heritage is one of the essential functions laid on the Organization by its Constitution. It calls for the adoption of appropriate legislation defining the nature and scope of the protection to be provided, specifying the property involved and setting out the measures which will afford such protection. Of comparatively recent date, this legislation is being built up gradually.[8]

The Draft Convention on the Protection of the Underwater Cultural Heritage is the latest attempt to add to this body of international law. However, during the second meeting of governmental experts, Norway expressed the view that the matter should be dealt with in the context of law of the sea negotiations in New York. There was no support for this position and the Resolution adopted by the meeting specified that the next meeting should be held at UNESCO headquarters in Paris. It seems likely that the Norwegian view was motivated by political considerations – seeing the New York venue as more congenial to their position on jurisdiction. It should also be noted that the text of the Draft Convention presented at the 1998 meeting was 'proposed by UNESCO and the United Nations Division of Ocean Affairs and Law of the Sea (DOALOS) with the advice of the International Maritime Organization (IMO)'. There was no such description in the Draft presented to the 1999 meeting. As the previous meeting had adopted that draft as the basis of future work towards a Convention, it was now the draft of the experts. However, at the 1999 meeting the US indicated that DOALOS had withdrawn its support for the Draft. In reply, the DOALOS representative stated that, in accordance with a General Assembly Resolution that office had given its assistance to another Agency of the United Nations system to ensure coherence in the law of the sea and that it was at the meeting to continue to give that assistance. DOALOS stated that it was not its function to interpret the LOS Convention. In light of the different interpretations given to that Convention by the Parties to it, DOALOS could hardly say otherwise.

## RELATIONS WITH THE LAW OF THE SEA CONVENTION

As explained above, the LOS Convention has two Articles dealing with 'archaeological and historical objects' and these are generally considered to be inadequate. However, in debate and commentary a number of States have said that the Draft Convention must not disturb the 'delicate balance' achieved in the LOS Convention. Indeed, in November 1998, the General Assembly of the United Nations stressed the 'importance of ensuring that the instrument to be elaborated is in full conformity with the relevant provisions of the Convention'.[9]

The LOS Convention is indeed one of the great achievements of international law making. Nevertheless, it has already been altered twice – once in respect of the deep seabed mining regime and also as regards fish that move backwards and forwards over the relevant zones. Moreover, what little attention was paid to underwater cultural heritage during the drafting of the LOS Convention was concentrated on wrecks near the coastline. The technology allowing access to wrecks virtually anywhere has changed the picture dramatically. Is preservation of the heritage to be held back by the dead hand of the past?

One of the problems in drafting the Convention on the Protection of the Underwater Cultural Heritage while insisting on compatibility with the LOS Convention is that there is no universally agreed interpretation of what the latter requires. States who argue that the current Draft Convention, particularly those provisions dealing with jurisdiction over the continental shelf and in the exclusive economic zone (commonly known as the EEZ), is incompatible with the LOS Convention, have yet to point out precisely where this occurs. One line of argument appears to be that, since during negotiations for the LOS Convention there were proposals entailing coastal State control over archaeological material on the continental shelf which were not adopted, any proposal applying to the continental shelf cannot now be accepted. This reads into the Convention something that is not there and exists only in the view of the States concerned. The fact is that the LOS Convention does not deal with underwater cultural heritage on the continental shelf in any meaningful way. Italy expressed this succinctly at the 1999 meeting when it said:

> The coastal State should be entitled to be informed of, to regulate and to authorize all activities relating to underwater cultural heritage found on its continental shelf (or in its exclusive economic zone). This is the best way to promote the preservation of the heritage and to ensure the disposal of it for the public benefit. Rights of this kind are neither specifically allowed, nor prohibited by UNCLOS. It is the filling of an UNCLOS gap, as permitted by UNCLOS itself.

## MAJOR POINTS OF DISCUSSION

Debate during the production of the ILA Draft and the meetings of experts, both UNESCO and governmental, has shown some matters to be of primary significance in the preparation of the Draft Convention: jurisdiction; treatment of warships and other vessels entitled to sovereign immunity; scope of the Convention; the role to be given commercial interests; contents of the Charter/Annex.

### Jurisdiction

The Draft Convention contains several provisions dealing with different aspects of jurisdiction. One of these – Article 4 – concerns underwater cultural heritage in internal waters, archipelagic waters and the territorial sea. However, an imperative formulation was adopted, requiring that all activities in these areas comply with the operative provisions of the Charter. At the 1999 meeting, there was unresolved debate on whether the provision should be made more flexible using such words as 'should take all necessary measures to ensure' the rules in the Annex be applied. Some States also wanted an additional provision on underwater cultural heritage in the contiguous zone – the area between 12 and 24 nautical miles from the low water mark. This already appears in Article 303(2) of the LOS Convention, although what that provision means is unclear. Ignoring the precise wording, most States appear to regard it as simply giving the right to take control of underwater cultural heritage up to 24 miles. The ambiguity is reflected in the current text of the Draft Article as is once again whether States 'shall' or 'should' require compliance with the rules in the Annex. However, the most controversial issue is in Article 5 which gives a coastal State some jurisdiction over underwater cultural heritage on the adjoining continental shelf and in its EEZ. There are also Articles dealing with jurisdiction over nationals and ships flying the flag of the State concerned and port State jurisdiction – in other words, the ability of a coastal State to control who uses its ports.

At the conclusion of the 1999 meeting, three options dealing with jurisdiction were on the table but the position of all States was reserved. Option 1, supported by the majority of States present, allows States to regulate underwater cultural heritage in their EEZ or on their continental shelf. In other words, States are permitted, but not required, to do this. A proposal made by Canada would sharpen the application of the provision by restricting it to 'activities directed at' the underwater cultural heritage. This is a welcome innovation which overcomes problems associated with activities such as cable laying which are permitted by the LOS Convention. In addition, States may forbid activities directed at underwater cultural heritage where these have the effect of interfering with the exploration or exploitation of their natural resources or any other rights or jurisdiction that they might have under the LOS Convention. Finally, States shall require that any discovery relating to underwater cultural heritage occurring in their EEZ or on their continental shelf be reported to their competent authorities.

Option 2, proposed originally by the UK and supported by, among others, Norway, the US and Germany, would require States, in exercising their sovereign rights in the EEZ and on the continental shelf, 'as provided for in the UN Convention on the Law of the Sea', to 'take account of the need to protect underwater cultural heritage in accordance with this Convention'.

Option 3 was originally proposed by the Chairman of the Working Group set up to discuss issues of jurisdiction. This starts by requiring any activity or discovery relating to underwater cultural heritage in a State's EEZ or on its continental shelf to be notified to that State. Then follow provisions setting out what the State is to do with this information. A State may authorize 'protective intervention and scientific research of the discovered underwater cultural heritage'. There must be consultation with the competent authorities of the State of the nationals or the flag State of the vessel concerned. The authorization must ensure compliance with the rules of the Annex and involve participation by experts of the coastal State.

Option 1 is a significantly modified version of the original ILA Draft. Gone is any reference to a 'cultural heritage zone'. The provision is now tied closely to the LOS Convention and its natural resources regime. It is further refined by restricting its operations to activities directed at underwater cultural heritage. Option 2 would place a duty on States to consider the underwater cultural heritage in whatever they do or authorize in their EEZs or on their continental shelves. However, it does not indicate any specific actions a State should take and appears to go little further, if at all, than Article 303(1) of the LOS Convention. States and individuals would thus be free to continue current practices.

At the 1999 meeting, Italy stated that it 'would be meaningless to simply repeat the provisions of the UNCLOS, including their shortcomings, without bringing any improvements'. Would giving the coastal State jurisdiction over activities directed at underwater cultural heritage on its continental shelf or in its EEZ be an improvement? It is true that some coastal States will not have the ability to police activities in these areas adequately. They will lack the personnel, equipment and funds to exert control. But this did not stop States gaining control of fisheries in similar circumstances in the LOS Convention. Moreover, what are the alternatives? The commonly suggested alternatives – port state, nationality and flag state jurisdiction – also suffer from major defects.

> It is often assumed that this [the law of the flag of the ship] is a
> straightforward question of discovering the place of registry of a
> vessel and that this is practically the same as referring to its nation-
> ality. It may not always be so clear if registration is optional, where
> the vessel has dual registration under one of the new bareboat
> registries, or (perhaps) where the vessel is registered in a flag of

convenience State with which its beneficial owners have no real connection.

(Dromgoole and Gaskell 1997: 106)

In spite of these defects, there appears to be a broad agreement that, for activities directed at underwater cultural heritage in areas beyond continental shelves and EEZs, the only methods of control are through the forms of jurisdiction mentioned. They are indirect. Even if a Convention is agreed at the UNESCO General Conference in 2001, it will be some years before the network of States Party develops to such an extent that it is capable of effectively limiting the activities of those who do not choose to abide by the rules in the Annex when dealing with underwater cultural heritage. At the 1999 meeting, some States indicated that they had problems with nationality jurisdiction. For example, Canada has concerns about the practical implications for enforcing the prohibition of the activities of nationals in the Area (i.e. the deep seabed, that part outside continental shelves and EEZs) and would prefer that there be an obligation to make it an offence for nationals to carry on such activities. Others appear to be motivated more by a basic philosophical notion against taking jurisdiction over nationals in these circumstances. France seems to be in this category. As France also opposes coastal State jurisdiction over activities directed at underwater cultural heritage on the continental shelf or in the EEZ, it is difficult to see how that country sees the Convention as operating.

All three Options provide for the making of regional agreements with more stringent rules and regulations than those adopted at global level. This may be seen as an excess of caution. On the other hand, it could provide support for those States that are already thinking of regional arrangements e.g. those bordering the Mediterranean and the Baltic are possibilities. There is a proposal that such agreements should also be open to States of cultural origin and States of historical and archaeological origin. This would be regrettable. Identifying such States is extremely difficult and their inclusion would dilute the regional solidarity underlying such agreements. It would be preferable to require such agreements to contain a provision obligating notification of such a State, if identifiable, when a find is made. Another proposal would require regional agreements to be consistent with international law. Presumably this means consistent with the proposer States' interpretation of the LOS Convention, which, as we have seen, is controversial.

*Sovereign immunity*

This phrase encapsulates the notion that government-owned property cannot be interfered with by the government of another State. Applying this doctrine, in Article 2(2) the Draft Convention stated it did not apply 'to the remains and contents of any warship, naval auxiliary, other vessel or aircraft owned or operated by a State and used, at the time of its sinking, only for non-commercial purposes'. Current practice 'suggests that public vessels used for non-commercial purposes and warships retain their status as State property so that their recovery may require the consent of the flag State' (Strati 1999: 22). Consequently, the relationship of the Convention to such vessels must be spelt out in the Convention itself. This will require a decision on several difficult points.

One is the precise meaning of the term 'warship'. For example, in past centuries there was the privateer – 'a privately owned and armed ship commissioned by a government to make reprisals, to gain reparation for specified offences in time of peace, or to prey upon the enemy in time of war' (Encyclopaedia Britannica 1986: 464). Is this a warship or not? The definition of warship in the LOS Convention[10] would exclude it but that definition is framed for modern conditions. Some of the problems would be solved if there were a cut-off date, but what would that be? Some years ago, the US indicated that in 'the absence of an express transfer or abandonment of a US warship sunk in the near past (e.g. in the World War II era), it should be presumed that title to such vessels remains in the US. Title to vessels sunk in the more distant past (such as during the seventeenth and eighteenth centuries) would, of course, still be determined by the more conventional interpretation of abandonment of that period'.[11]

Another significant problem concerns vessels engaged by governments during the colonial period to communicate between the home government and the colonies. For example, it is alleged that a number of wrecks in South American waters were engaged in non-commercial operations for the Spanish Government during the period of colonial rule and should be protected by sovereign immunity. The debate on this provision at the 1999 meeting was inconclusive. Spain, not surprisingly, made a proposal that the Convention should only apply to the remains of vessels 'owned or operated by or on behalf of a State' with the express consent of that State. This was opposed by numerous South American States. In the Declaration of Santo Domingo,[12] these States had declared that underwater cultural heritage 'is the property of the State in which it is found'. In their view, if the wrecks concerned were excluded from the Convention, 'the nations of the Americas would have virtually no right to salvage any shipwrecks dating from the above stated time period'. Spain does not appear to have made any claim to the numerous wrecks found in Caribbean waters over the past 40 or so years or to those of the Armada found off the UK and Ireland.[13] However, it did lay claim to two wrecks of 1750 and 1802 off Virginia. The District Court in the Eastern District of Virginia ruled in April 1999[14] that the later wreck is indeed Spanish property, never having been abandoned. However, the earlier wreck, the *La Galga*, was abandoned under a treaty of 1763 whereby Spain transferred all its North American territories and property to Britain at the conclusion of the French and Indian war. This assertive action by Spain and its stance in the 1999 meeting probably signals a change in Spanish attitude to all these early wrecks.

At the 1999 meeting, the US submitted a proposal whereby title to warships and vessels used for government non-commercial purposes could only be lost if there was express abandonment and not through mere passage of time. It is interesting to note that in *Treasure Salvors Inc. v. Unidentified, Wrecked and Abandoned Sailing Vessel* the US Court of Appeals for the Fifth Circuit said that '[d]isposition of a wrecked vessel whose very location has been lost for centuries as though its owner were still in existence stretches a fiction to absurd lengths'.[15] There the Court was referring to the *Nuestra Señora de Atocha*, a Spanish vessel which sank off the Marquesas Keys in 1622 en route from the Havana to Cadiz with a cargo containing bullion and precious stones for the Spanish Crown.

*Scope of the Convention*

A number of States consider that the scope of the Convention is too broad. This is in spite of the fact that its origins are impeccable. The main provision in the Draft Convention reads:

> 'Underwater cultural heritage' means all traces of human existence underwater for at least 100 years, including:
> (i) sites, structures, buildings, artefacts and human remains, together with their archaeological and natural contexts; and
> (ii) wreck such as a vessel, aircraft, other vehicle or any part thereof, its cargo or other contents, together with its archaeological and natural context.

A State Party may also decide that certain traces of human existence which have been underwater for less than 100 years constitute underwater cultural heritage.

The inspiration for this definition came from the Draft European Convention on the Protection of the Underwater Cultural Heritage 1985,[16] the European Convention on the Protection of the Archaeological Heritage 1969[17] and the European Convention on the Protection of the Archaeological Heritage (Revised) 1992.[18] Elements from each of these instruments were melded to make the definition for the Draft Convention. For example, 'traces of human existence' comes from the 1969 Convention and was adopted in the 1985 Draft Convention. References to 'context' appear in the Revised Convention. The many States party to these Conventions would not appear to have had problems in dealing with the concepts and their experience should be examined by those who argue for other wording. The US suggests that 'all traces of human existence' be replaced by 'objects of prehistoric, archaeological, historical or cultural significance found underwater on or under the seabed'. This also suffers from a number of defects. For example, the emphasis should be on sites, not objects if protection is to be efficient. Second, significance often cannot be established until a site underwater has been excavated. If it has not been correctly excavated but the object is found to be significant then the information that could have been obtained is lost. There is also the archaeological principle that sites should only be excavated for scientific purposes, they should otherwise be left alone. How is significance to be established if the site is not to be touched?

The 100 years underwater criterion has also been questioned. Some find this an arbitrary figure which would exclude underwater cultural heritage of more recent date, particularly, at this point of time, that from the two world wars. Nevertheless, the criterion is found in much national legislation relating to sites on land and provides an effective basis for administrative procedures. For problem cases, there is the alternative procedure permitted by the definition.

The Greek delegation wanted the Draft Convention to cover an ancient object lost at sea in modern times e.g. supposing a 3,000 year old statue being sent from Athens to an exhibition in New York was lost when the aircraft carrying it crashed and sank on the continental shelf of France. But the Greek concern here is misplaced. This is not a situation requiring an archaeological investigation – at least not for 100 years! Normally a salvage company would be engaged to undertake recovery operations in accordance with standard rules and specifications ensuring safety of the cargo.

Other delegations wanted the definition amended to cover traces of human existence 'which have been partially, totally or periodically' underwater for at least 100 years. Once again, this concern does not really seem to be relevant. The basic purpose of the Draft Convention is to protect underwater cultural heritage beyond the territorial sea of States. As such, there are likely to be few situations where the heritage is not completely submerged.

The Draft Convention contained a definition of 'abandonment' and stated that it applied only to underwater cultural heritage that had been abandoned. It is now clear that there is an almost universal wish among States to delete this definition and the restriction. There was criticism of its content. Some States seemed to think that it took away their rights because they did not have access to the relevant technology; whereas it would only do this if, in fact, they were the owner of the underwater cultural heritage. Others considered that the concept of abandonment of wrecks was not part of their legal system. Yet others were of the view that this definition led the Draft Convention into questions of ownership and raised issues that were beyond its scope. It is therefore almost certain that the Convention which eventually emerges from the negotiations will not have a definition of 'abandonment'.

Some States have questioned the necessity for specifically including cargo in the definition. The reason is that an important aspect of dealing with shipwrecks is to make sure that the appurtenances of the ship, its cargo and personal articles on board are covered. For example, this problem arose in Norway following the discovery of the wreck of the *Akerendam* – a Dutch East Indiaman – in 1972. In the wreck were large quantities of gold and silver coins from chests aboard the vessel at the time it was wrecked. The Norwegian *Protection of Antiquities Act* 1951 at that time provided rules relating to 'vessels, ships' hulls, and objects pertaining thereto or parts of such objects . . .'. It was argued that:

the coins were part of the *Akerendam's* cargo and thus did not fall within the scope of the rules of the Antiquities Act . . . The only debatable point was whether the *Akerendam's* treasure chests were cargo or whether they were to be classed as ship's appurtenances, because, for example, they constituted the master's funds for the voyage.

(Braekhus 1976: 63)

In 1974 the Norwegian Act was amended to include among the objects covered 'cargo and other material that has been carried on board'.

*Commercial interests*

The ILA Draft Convention stated simply that: 'Underwater cultural heritage to which this Convention applies shall not be subject to the law of salvage'. The commentary accompanying the Draft saw the major problem with salvage to be its economic motivation: 'the salvor is often seeking items of value as fast as possible rather than undertaking the painstaking excavation and treatment of all aspects of the site that is necessary to preserve its historic value'.[19] This brought a severe reaction from apologists for salvors although no attempt was made to explain the numerous examples of destruction on record. Some pointed to the requirement by certain courts in the US that 'archaeological standards' be taken into account in assessing the salvage reward. As has already been indicated, those courts have an idiosyncratic view of what constitutes such standards. Perhaps Bederman lets the cat out of the bag when he explains:

> Indeed, United States courts have made express that the potential salvor's fidelity to archaeological values is among the elements to be considered in granting a salvage award. This is not to say, of course, that commercial salvors have been held to exactly the same technical standards as adopted by nautical archaeologists.

(Bederman 1999: 345)

Organizations other than the ILA have misgivings with salvage law in the context of heritage preservation. For example, English Heritage has recently commented: 'it is widely agreed that current salvage law in the UK and in international waters is not wholly consistent with best management of the marine cultural heritage'.[20]

At the Paris Meeting of Experts in 1996 it became clear that the exclusion of salvage law was a topic needing further negotiation. In response to views expressed at this meeting and by States, the Draft Convention did not adopt the ILA formulation but introduced a new provision in Article 12(2):

> States Parties shall provide for the non-application of any internal law or regulation having the effect of providing commercial incentives or any other reward for the excavation and removal of underwater cultural heritage.

At the 1998 meeting, there was some discussion of this provision with the majority seeming to favour a return to a provision along the lines of the ILA Draft. As Strati notes: 'There are many aspects of salvage law, quite apart from the application of commercial incentives, which are inconsistent with the regime established by the Charter' (1999: 56). At the 1999 meeting, this issue was raised but not considered in any detail. The US introduced an interesting proposal that the Draft Convention should exclude application of the laws of salvage and finds to underwater cultural heritage but that this could be subject to a reservation by a State at the time of becoming party. States entering such a reservation would have the opprobrium of having done so and they would still be bound to apply the rules in the Annex. Due to time constraints, this proposal unfortunately received little attention. It may, of course, be raised again at the next meeting.

For some States, salvage law is not a problem since after a short period of time a wreck is no longer regarded as capable of salvage in the legal sense. States in this position must realize, however, that effective world-wide protection of the underwater cultural heritage has to take into account the impact of salvage and finders law. When used by a court exercising extraterritorial jurisdiction, these can influence what happens to the heritage thousands of miles from the seat of the court.

Much work remains to be done in establishing a relationship between commercial interests and archaeology. The former cannot be dismissed. They have the equipment and often the funding to reach the ocean depths. In their normal work, sites of importance to the history of humanity may be found. More specifically, there is a small group of organizations formed with the primary purpose of searching for and excavating historic shipwrecks. This activity is not in itself reprehensible. The problem is what is done when the wreck is found.

It must be remembered that the ICOMOS Charter contains two provisions with a direct commercial connotation and others that cut across the activities of commercial operators. The latter are the so-called 'fundamental principles' that, first, the 'preservation of underwater cultural heritage *in situ* should be considered as a first option' and, second, that 'non-destructive techniques, non-intrusive survey and sampling should be encouraged in preference to excavation'. These would appear to require any excavation to be justified in terms of adding to the corpus of knowledge about a particular era, shipbuilding technique, person etc. The other two provisions of the Charter mentioned above are found in Article 3:

> Project funding must not require the sale of underwater cultural heritage or the use of any strategy that will cause underwater cultural heritage and supporting documentation to be irretrievably dispersed.

and Article 13:

Underwater cultural heritage is not to be traded as items of commercial value.

This assumes that all underwater cultural heritage, once excavated, must be kept as a unit for the preservation of knowledge. But such may not necessarily be the case. ProSEA[21] distinguishes a category of what it calls 'trade goods', comprising those goods which can be identified as cargo and which can be distinguished by any one of three criteria:

1  Number of duplicates on site.
2  Ease of recording or replicating artefacts.
3  Archaeological value versus value of return to the stream of commerce.

What is meant by these categories is described by Stemm, President of ProSEA, in these words:

1. Number of duplicates on site
This is simply an evaluation of the number of artefacts of that particular type available from the site. We recommend maintaining a minimum 10% to 20% sample of the multiple artefacts in the permanent cultural collection. This will depend on the analysis of the project archaeologist.

2. Ease of recording or replicating artefacts
In the ProSEA Code of Ethics, it states that those artefacts that cannot be 'documented, photographed, moulded or replicated in a manner that allows reasonable future study and analysis' must be kept together. An obvious example is a coin, which can be easily photographed in high resolution, weighed and the dimensions given, which will provide virtually all the data necessary for further study of the coin. The one exception would be an analysis of the metal in the coin, but that can be accomplished for the most part from the sample collection of similar coins in the permanent collection.

3. Archaeological value versus value of return to stream of commerce.This is a subjective judgement, but can be illustrated by example:
In the case of 10,000 similar gold coins from the late 18th Century, the market value of those coins could easily reach $10,000,000 US. In terms of the archaeological value, there are many of the same coins already widely circulated throughout the coin collectors marketplace, so there is very little that can be learned incrementally about 18th Century culture that can't be learned from records and data which are already in existence. This is especially true when coupled with a representative sample plus photos and documentation of the coins that are dispersed.
    In this case, a reasonable conclusion could be drawn that the tiny incremental value of the archaeological knowledge that could

be gained from keeping the collection together does not warrant preventing a return of $10,000,000 to the stream of commerce.

On the other hand, a large collection of pithoids from a Mediterranean bronze-age site would probably not have a very large intrinsic value. However, so little is known of trade from this era, that minor variations in markings on the pithoids, as well as data that can be gleaned from the remains of their contents, may provide data that can be gathered in no other way.

In this case, a reasonable conclusion could be drawn that the low commercial value would not warrant breaking up this collection.[22]

These ideas need further elaboration, and the way the underlying philosophy is presented may be questioned, but the concept is worthy of further investigation and study. This is particularly the case at a time when government funding for storage of collections is contracting in many countries. The problem of adequate care for collections has been addressed elsewhere and the recommendation made that the Director-General of UNESCO be asked to set in motion the machinery for establishing guidelines for disposal from collections (O'Keefe 1997: 74).

Other matters affecting commercial interests also need to be considered. One of these is photography of a wreck. Another is the right to take members of the public to view the site. These are potentially valuable interests which could fund a substantial part of the work on certain sites if marketed professionally. In *RMS Titanic Inc. v. Wrecked Vessel*,[23] the US District Court for the Eastern District of Virginia held that a salvor in possession – such as RMS Titanic Inc. – was entitled to an injunction prohibiting others from visiting the site and photographing it. Commentators were critical of the decision, some calling the ruling 'an extraordinary leap in the application of intellectual property principles – probably quite unintended' (Bederman and Prowda 1998). The decision was subsequently reversed on appeal.

## The Charter/Annex

The ILA Draft envisaged a document attached to the Convention setting out archaeological principles for the management of underwater cultural heritage. States would use this as a standard to measure activities affecting the heritage. In order to take account of changing technology and developing professional practices, it was thought desirable to allow ICOMOS to revise the Charter when the organization felt this was necessary. Any change would be subject to notice of non-acceptance by States that did not agree. States have accepted the rationale for such a document but not the role of ICOMOS as many felt this would compromise their sovereignty. At the 1998 and 1999 meetings it became clear that States wanted the document to be an Annex to the Convention. Although the content of the Annex was discussed at length and largely agreed during the 1999 meeting, there was little debate on the substantive provision in the Convention itself referring to the Annex.

Canada presented the 1999 meeting with a document containing the substance of the Charter adjusted to fit the context of the Convention. This was used as the basis for discussion in a working group. Following further discussion in plenary session, the Annex now consists of thirty-six paragraphs divided into fourteen sections with the headings: general principles; project design; preliminary work; project objective, methodology and techniques; funding; project duration – timetable; competence and qualifications; conservation and site management; documentation; safety; reporting; curation of project archive; dissemination; international cooperation. In summary, the Annex seeks to ensure that activities directed at underwater cultural heritage are planned and performed by competent persons with the results recorded and disseminated.

As already indicated, the Charter had various provisions dealing with commercial trade in underwater cultural heritage. The current provision in the redrafted Annex reads:

> The commercial exploitation of underwater cultural heritage for trade or speculation [leading to its irretrievable disposal] is fundamentally incompatible with the protection and management of the underwater cultural heritage. Underwater cultural heritage shall [should] not be traded, sold, bought and bartered as items of commercial value.

There is some argument that this is too important a provision to appear in the Annex and should be transferred to the Convention. As noted, there was little substantive discussion of the salvage/commercial exploitation provisions in the Convention at the 1999 meeting. Much more analysis of this issue is needed.

The provision on curation should be read in the same context. It requires that the project archive, 'including any underwater cultural heritage removed', 'should as much as possible be kept together and intact as a collection in a manner that it can be available for scientific and public access as well as the curation of the archive'. Does this require that the archive be kept physically intact or does it mean that the collection should, or must be, capable of reassembly if need be?

## OTHER PROVISIONS

There was brief comment on these by delegates in the first plenary session at the 1999 meeting. The Chairman presented a set of revised Articles based on his assessment of views expressed by delegates. However, there was no substantive discussion of these or the original formulation in the Draft Convention.

It is worthwhile here to set out the plan of the ILA Draft which was in many respects closely followed by the Draft Convention. States would be

able to issue permits in advance of excavation allowing entry into their territory of underwater cultural heritage provided there was compliance with the
Charter. This meant that a person wishing to excavate a site could have clearance in advance for entry of what was recovered. Complying with the Charter
would require, in most cases, the presence of archaeological expertise, conservators etc. However, there was also provision for a person who excavated
without a permit. A State could provide a permit allowing entry of the
material if that person could persuade the authorities that the excavation and
retrieval activities had been conducted in accordance with the Charter. It is
essential to note that the permit is not a permit to excavate; it is a permit
allowing entry of recovered material into the territory of a State.

The Draft Convention would require States Parties to seize underwater
cultural heritage brought within their territory, either directly or indirectly,
where its excavation or retrieval has not been in conformity with the Charter.
The reference to indirect entry was intended to catch situations where material
was brought ashore in a State not party to the Convention and then transferred to a State Party.

States would also be required to impose sanctions on persons responsible
for importing underwater cultural heritage subject to seizure and would cooperate with each other in the enforcement of those sanctions.

There are other provisions in the Draft Convention – dealing, for example,
with collaboration, notification, training, education, technical services, dispute
settlement – but they will not be dealt with here in light of the little attention they received at the 1999 meeting.


## CONCLUSION

Negotiations for the future of the underwater cultural heritage stand at a
crossroads. The major issues should now be clear to all States. However,
negotiation will have to be done and compromises made. Some States seem
to be taking the view that they are so important that the Convention will
fail if their views are not adopted. This may well lead to failure to achieve
a multilateral agreement and proliferation of regional instruments.


## POSTSCRIPT

The Third Meeting of Governmental Experts was held in Paris, 3–7 July 2000.
The same major points – extent of coastal State control, warships and the
role of commercial treasure seekers – were still in contention. The Chairman
of the Working Group on coastal State control put forward a proposal
which, while it gained some acceptance, would seem to be impractical. There
appeared to be a consensus that warships would be under the control of the
coastal State but that any activity in relation to the wreck would be subject to

authorization by the flag State. No agreed formula was reached on the role of treasure seekers. It was unfortunate that one delegation was basically responsible for delay on procedural grounds that lost more than a day from the substantive discussion. However, a resolution was adopted that a fourth and final meeting of experts should be held in the first six months of 2001. (See Dromgoole, Chapter 4, note 21.)

## NOTES

1 Reversed on appeal – see later discussion.
2 (1992) 974 F.2d 450, 468.
3 (1995) *American Maritime Cases* 1985, 2008.
4 *RMS Titanic v. Wreck* 1996 *American Maritime Cases* 2481, 2493.
5 A modified version of this, entitled the *International Charter on the Protection and Management of Underwater Cultural Heritage*, was ratified by the ICOMOS General Assembly at its meeting in Sofia, 9 October 1996. Copies are available from ICOMOS Headquarters in Paris.
6 UNESCO Doc. CLT-96/CONF.202/5.
7 This will probably take place early in 2000. See Postscript.
8 UNESCO *Conventions and Recommendations of Unesco Concerning the Protection of the Cultural Heritage* (UNESCO, Paris, 1985) 7.
9 Para. 20, Resolution of 3 November 1998 on Oceans and the Law of the Sea.
10 Article 10: 'a ship belonging to the armed forces of a State bearing the external marks distinguishing such ships of its nationality, under the command of an officer duly commissioned by the government of the State and whose name appears in the appropriate service list or its equivalent, and manned by a crew which is under regular armed forces discipline.'
11 Letter from Department of State to Maritime Administration, December 30, 1980, reprinted in US Department of State, 8 *Digest of United States Practice in International Law* 999, 1004 (1980).
12 Endorsed by the Forum of Ministers of Culture and officials responsible for Cultural Policies of Latin America and the Caribbean, Barbados, 4–5 December, 1998.
13 Some of these were commandeered vessels and not under Spanish ownership (see further Dromgoole and Gaskell 1997: 117).
14 *International Herald Tribune*, 7 May 1999, p.6 – official report not yet available.
15 (1978) 569 F.2d 330, 337.
16 The Draft European Convention was never adopted but sections of it are reproduced in Strati (1995: 87).
17 European Treaty Series No. 66.
18 European Treaty Series No. 143.
19 International Law Association *Report of the Sixty-Sixth Conference, Buenos Aires, Argentina* (ILA, London, 1994) 438.
20 English Heritage *Towards a Policy for Marine Archaeology: An English Heritage and RCHME Discussion Paper*, Consultation Draft March 1999, 10.
21 Professional Shipwreck Explorers Association Inc. ProSEA is described as a non-profit organization which represents members throughout the world active in legitimate and ethical shipwreck exploration. It was formed to provide self-regulation to those companies and individuals who seek to preserve and protect the world's shipwreck resources. Among its members are some of the largest deep ocean exploration companies, including Oceaneering, Comex, Odyssey Marine Exploration and Nauticus.

22  Personal communication, 26 April 1999.
23  1998 *American Maritime Cases* 2421.

## REFERENCES

Bederman, D.J. 1999. The UNESCO Draft Convention on Underwater Cultural
Heritage: a critique and counter-proposal. *Journal of Maritime Law and Commerce*
30: 331.
Bederman, D.J. and J.B. Prowda 1998. In 'Titanic' Case, IP and Admiralty Laws
collide. *The National Law Journal*, 19 October.
Braekhus, S. 1976. Salvage of wrecks and wreckage: legal issues arising from the
Runde find. *Scandinavian Studies in Law* 20: 39, 63.
Delgado, J.P. (ed) 1997. *Encyclopaedia of Underwater and Maritime Archaeology* 93–4.
London: British Museum.
Dromgoole, S. and N. Gaskell 1997. Interests in wreck. *Art Antiquity and Law* 2:
103–36.
*Encyclopaedia Britannica* 1986. (15th edn) Vol. 9: 464. Chicago, Encyclopaedia Britannica.
Fewster, K.J. and J.R. Valliant 1997. Titanic: delving beneath the surface. *Museum
News* 29 (May/June).
Migliorino, L. 1995. *In Situ* Protection of the Underwater Cultural Heritage Under
International Treaties and National Legislation. *International Journal of Marine and
Coastal Law* 10: 483.
O'Keefe, P.J. 1997. *Trade in Antiquities – Reducing Destruction and Theft*. Paris and
London: UNESCO and Archetype Publications.
Strati, A. 1995. *The Protection of the Underwater Cultural Heritage: An Emerging Objective
of the Contemporary Law of the Sea*. The Hague: Martinus Nijhoff.
Strati, A. 1999. *Draft Convention on the Protection of Underwater Cultural Heritage: A
Commentary Prepared for UNESCO*. UNESCO Doc. CLT-99/WS/8, April 1999.
Paris: UNESCO.

## APPENDIX

*Charter on the Protection and Management of Underwater Cultural Heritage
(1996)*
(ratified by the 11th ICOMOS General Assembly, held in Sofia, Bulgaria,
from 5–9 October 1996)

INTRODUCTION

This Charter is intended to encourage the protection and management of
underwater cultural heritage in inland and inshore waters, in shallow seas and
in the deep oceans. It focuses on the specific attributes and circumstances of
cultural heritage under water and should be understood as a supplement to the
ICOMOS Charter for the Protection and Management of Archaeological
Heritage, 1990. The 1990 Charter defines the 'archaeological heritage' as that
part of the material heritage in respect of which archaeological methods provide
primary information, comprising all vestiges of human existence and consisting
of places relating to all manifestations of human activity, abandoned structures,

and remains of all kinds, together with all the portable cultural material associated with them. For the purposes of this Charter underwater cultural heritage is understood to mean the archaeological heritage which is in, or has been removed from, an underwater environment. It includes submerged sites and structures, wreck-sites and wreckage and their archaeological and natural context.

By its very character the underwater cultural heritage is an international resource. A large part of the underwater cultural heritage is located in an international setting and derives from international trade and communication in which ships and their contents are lost at a distance from their origin or destination.

Archaeology is concerned with environmental conservation; in the language of resource management, underwater cultural heritage is both finite and non-renewable. If underwater cultural heritage is to contribute to our appreciation of the environment in the future, then we have to take individual and collective responsibility in the present for ensuring its continued survival.

Archaeology is a public activity; everybody is entitled to draw upon the past in informing their own lives, and every effort to curtail knowledge of the past is an infringement of personal autonomy. Underwater cultural heritage contributes to the formation of identity and can be important to people's sense of community. If managed sensitively, underwater cultural heritage can play a positive role in the promotion of recreation and tourism.

Archaeology is driven by research, it adds to knowledge of the diversity of human culture through the ages and it provides new and challenging ideas about life in the past. Such knowledge and ideas contribute to understanding life today and, thereby, to anticipating future challenges.

Many marine activities, which are themselves beneficial and desirable, can have unfortunate consequences for underwater cultural heritage if their effects are not foreseen. Underwater cultural heritage may be threatened by construction work that alters the shore and seabed or alters the flow of current, sediment and pollutants. Underwater cultural heritage may also be threatened by insensitive exploitation of living and non-living resources. Furthermore, inappropriate forms of access and the incremental impact of removing 'souvenirs' can have a deleterious effect.

Many of these threats can be removed or substantially reduced by early consultation with archaeologists and by implementing mitigatory projects.

This Charter is intended to assist in bringing a high standard of archaeological expertise to bear on such threats to underwater cultural heritage in a prompt and efficient manner.

Underwater cultural heritage is also threatened by activities that are wholly undesirable because they are intended to profit few at the expense of many. Commercial exploitation of underwater cultural heritage for trade or speculation is fundamentally incompatible with the protection and management of the heritage. This Charter is intended to ensure that all investigations are explicit in their aims, methodology and anticipated results so that the intention of each project is transparent to all.

### ARTICLE 1 – FUNDAMENTAL PRINCIPLES

The preservation of underwater cultural heritage *in situ* should be considered as a first option.

Public access should be encouraged.

Non-destructive techniques, non-intrusive survey and sampling should be encouraged in preference to excavation.

Investigation must not adversely impact the underwater cultural heritage more than is necessary for the mitigatory or research objectives of the project.

Investigation must avoid unnecessary disturbance of human remains or venerated sites.

Investigation must be accompanied by adequate documentation.

### ARTICLE 2 – PROJECT DESIGN

Prior to investigation a project must be prepared, taking into account:

the mitigatory or research objectives of the project;

the methodology to be used and the techniques to be employed;

anticipated funding;

the time-table for completing the project;

the composition, qualifications, responsibility and experience of the investigating team;

material conservation;

site management and maintenance;

arrangements for collaboration with museums and other institutions;

documentation;

health and safety;

report preparation;

deposition of archives, including underwater cultural heritage removed during investigation;

dissemination, including public participation.

The project design should be revised and amended as necessary.

Investigation must be carried out in accordance with the project design. The project design should be made available to the archaeological community.

### ARTICLE 3 – FUNDING

Adequate funds must be assured in advance of investigation to complete all stages of the project design including conservation, report preparation and dissemination. The project design should include contingency plans that will ensure conservation of underwater cultural heritage and supporting documentation in the event of any interruption in anticipated funding.

Project funding must not require the sale of underwater cultural heritage or the use of any strategy that will cause underwater cultural heritage and supporting documentation to be irretrievably dispersed.

## ARTICLE 4 – TIME-TABLE

Adequate time must be assured in advance of investigation to complete all stages of the project design including conservation, report preparation and dissemination. The project design should include contingency plans that will ensure conservation of underwater cultural heritage and supporting documentation in the event of any interruption in anticipated timings.

## ARTICLE 5 – RESEARCH OBJECTIVES, METHODOLOGY AND TECHNIQUES

Research objectives and the details of the methodology and techniques to be employed must be set down in the project design. The methodology should accord with the research objectives of the investigation and the techniques employed must be as unintrusive as possible.

Post-fieldwork analysis of artefacts and documentation is integral to all investigation; adequate provision for this analysis must be made in the project design.

## ARTICLE 6 – QUALIFICATIONS, RESPONSIBILITY AND EXPERIENCE

All persons on the investigating team must be suitably qualified and experienced for their project roles. They must be fully briefed and understand the work required.

All intrusive investigations of underwater cultural heritage will only be undertaken under the direction and control of a named underwater archaeologist with recognized qualifications and experience appropriate to the investigation.

## ARTICLE 7 – PRELIMINARY INVESTIGATION

All intrusive investigations of underwater cultural heritage must be preceded and informed by a site assessment that evaluates the vulnerability, significance and potential of the site.

The site assessment must encompass background studies of available historical and archaeological evidence, the archaeological and environmental characteristics of the site and the consequences of the intrusion for the long term stability of the area affected by investigations.

## ARTICLE 8 – DOCUMENTATION

All investigation must be thoroughly documented in accordance with current professional standards of archaeological documentation.

Documentation must provide a comprehensive record of the site, which includes the provenance of underwater cultural heritage moved or removed in the course of investigation, field notes, plans and drawings, photographs and records in other media.

## ARTICLE 9 – MATERIAL CONSERVATION

The material conservation programme must provide for treatment of archaeological remains during investigation, in transit and in the long term.

Material conservation must be carried out in accordance with current professional standards.

## ARTICLE 10 – SITE MANAGEMENT AND MAINTENANCE

A programme of site management must be prepared, detailing measures for
protecting and managing in situ underwater cultural heritage in the course
of and upon termination of fieldwork. The programme should include public
information, reasonable provision for site stabilisation, monitoring and protection against interference. Public access to in situ underwater cultural heritage
should be promoted, except where access is incompatible with protection
and management.

## ARTICLE 11 – HEALTH AND SAFETY

The health and safety of the investigating team and third parties is paramount.
All persons on the investigating team must work according to a safety policy
that satisfies relevant statutory and professional requirements and is set out in
the project design.

## ARTICLE 12 – REPORTING

Interim reports should be made available according to a timetable set out in
the project design, and deposited in relevant public records.

Reports should include:

an account of the objectives;

an account of the methodology and techniques employed;

an account of the results achieved;

recommendations concerning future research, site management and curation of underwater cultural heritage removed during the investigation.

## ARTICLE 13 – CURATION

The project archive, which includes underwater cultural heritage removed
during investigation and a copy of all supporting documentation, must be
deposited in an institution that can provide for public access and permanent
curation of the archive. Arrangements for deposition of the archive should
be agreed before investigation commences, and should be set out in the
project design. The archive should be prepared in accordance with current
professional standards.

The scientific integrity of the project archive must be assured; deposition
in a number of institutions must not preclude reassembly to allow further
research. Underwater cultural heritage is not to be traded as items of commercial value.

## ARTICLE 14 – DISSEMINATION

Public awareness of the results of investigations and the significance of underwater cultural heritage should be promoted through popular presentation in a range of media. Access to such presentations by a wide audience should not be prejudiced by high charges.

Cooperation with local communities and groups is to be encouraged, as is cooperation with communities and groups that are particularly associated with the underwater cultural heritage concerned. It is desirable that investigations proceed with the consent and endorsement of such communities and groups.

The investigation team will seek to involve communities and interest groups in investigations to the extent that such involvement is compatible with protection and management. Where practical, the investigation team should provide opportunities for the public to develop archaeological skills through training and education.

Collaboration with museums and other institutions is to be encouraged. Provision for visits, research and reports by collaborating institutions should be made in advance of investigation.

A final synthesis of the investigation must be made available as soon as possible, having regard to the complexity of the research, and deposited in relevant public records.

## ARTICLE 15 – INTERNATIONAL COOPERATION

International cooperation is essential for protection and management of underwater cultural heritage and should be promoted in the interests of high standards of investigation and research. International cooperation should be encouraged in order to make effective use of archaeologists and other professionals who are specialised in investigations of underwater cultural heritage. Programmes for exchange of professionals should be considered as a means of disseminating best practice.

# 6     Perceptions of marine artefact conservation and their relationship to destruction and theft

## Amanda Sutherland

## INTRODUCTION

The potential for access to wrecks has expanded greatly in the past decade, not only with the advent of technology for mixed-gas diving but, more importantly, the development of deep-sea submersibles or remotely operated vehicles (Fenwick 1998: 1–2) and 'grabs' (Harrison 1997: 65). Salvage companies employ increasingly sophisticated methods backed heavily by financial sponsors. Commercial companies have been involved for some time now, in developing conservation treatments and disseminating them to others. Developed outside professional conservation, these treatments lack the underpinning of a professional approach or regulation and consequently do not ensure the responsible and safe handling of archaeological material. Many simply 'reinvent the wheel' in that they indisputably cause damage and have long since been discarded by professional archaeological conservators for just this reason. Additionally, since these treatments are frequently based on methodology devised by those with no formal conservation training, the ethics concomitant with responsible conservation are not being incorporated and this raises serious issues.

Arguably, maritime archaeology is a younger discipline than archaeology carried out on the land and this is clearly reflected in conservation practice (Sutherland 1998: 30). Historically the fields have developed separately and are distinct from the practice of professional salvage, as the latter is characterized by the dispersal of artefact assemblages through sale (*Express* 1997). Wrecks have a propensity for preservation which is rarely surpassed by any of the material found on land. However, material recovered from the marine environment has proved in the past to be highly unstable. This has been regarded as an inherent characteristic rather than the more likely derivative of poor handling immediately post-excavation. As a result, undue emphasis has been placed on the need for chemical stability at all costs. Such costs have included the historical integrity of an artefact, with the potential complete destruction of any associated archaeological evidence, conservation being seen as a simple one-step process comprising both cleaning and stablization (Cussler 1993: 174; Carlin and Keith 1996: 38). The consequent loss of information, as for example, archaeometallurgical evidence, which can never be retrieved, ultimately affects the value, both financial and historical of any artefact or assemblage. Indeed, there is little awareness of even the most fundamental of professional ethics; minimal intervention and reversibility (Horie 1987) of treatment. As recently as 1997, the definition of marine artefact conservation was still shown to be skewed (Delgado 1997: 106). This is possibly because, on a global scale, the emphasis in marine archaeology has been in ship construction and technology, whereas the principal interest in salvage has resided in cargo. To some extent therefore, finds assemblages from wrecks have been largely incidental to the aims of professional archaeological excavation. On a larger scale, the potential for destruction and looting of sites is linked to the issue of the perceived cost of conservation since the latter affects attitudes towards archaeological planning and the management of underwater cultural heritage. Sites which could be contributing to current knowledge and the public enjoyment of history are not being excavated. In the ensuing hiatus such sites are left vulnerable to looting or damage. Additionally, conservation precepts are being used in arguments both in support of and against the salvage of wrecks in deep-water environments. Seabed technology is developing fast (Pleydell-Bouverie 1997) and, coupled with today's passion for 'art', this renders shipwrecks in international waters or beyond the territorial seas a unique target for the avid collector (Meyer 1974; *International Herald Tribune* 1998).

As long as wrecks continue to be discovered, monitored or salvaged (Johnston 1993: 53–60) artefacts continue to be raised. Thus remains the need for conservation and there are a clearly a number of perceptions about how this can be achieved. Although the issues presented here relate principally to wooden wrecks rather than 'modern' ones, the principles expounded apply loosely to all marine artefacts.


## FINANCE

The financing of marine artefact conservation is complex, both in terms of sourcing and attitude. This has ramifications for the way in which material is treated, by whom and where. Salvage is heavily backed by financial sponsors enabling project-related 'conservation' to be carried out. Conversely, in the world of archaeology underwater, the associated costs of preservation have risen within the archaeological mind. The associated perceived costs have also ostensibly been exemplified by well-known wreck projects such as the *Mary Rose* (Mouzouras *et al.* 1990: 173–88) and *Wasa*. However, there is little evidence that the differences between the costs of the preservation of hull structures and the preservation of their associated artefact assemblages have been recognized. The attitude that conservation is highly expensive now prevails, so that any proposition of undertaking such work may automatically price professional excavation out of the market. Consideration of how this attitude has arisen throws some light on the current precarious position of wrecks with regard to destruction and theft.

Archaeology underwater has developed largely from the study of the construction of ships and the history of shipbuilding. Given such emphasis it is not surprising that the perception regarding the cost of conservation is associated principally with vessel hulls. Costs for the preservation of either ships' timbers or artillery are certainly relatively expensive, running into the tens if not hundreds of thousands of pounds sterling. This, however, has created a financial back-drop with regards to the perceived potential costs of conservation, which appears to have held sway ever since the early days of archaeological investigation. Within this scenario archaeological activities have become increasingly limited to monitoring.

In the UK, many of the 48 sites designated as Historic Wreck sites (Fenwick and Gale 1998) are currently monitored by local dive groups (Oldham et al. 1993: 323–30) and already have a small associated extant assemblage, recovered whilst the site was originally the subject of curiosity and efforts to identify it. Funding is required for the conservation treatment of these small assemblages even if they are never enlarged. Funding provision is also necessary for the treatment of any finds recovered in the future (DCMS 1998a). One of the consequences of the emphasis on hulls and the implicit cost of raising them is that cost-effective methods of information retrieval and suitable archiving methods for artefact assemblages have not been pursued. A further hindrance is the idea that conservation is a single-stage process with one visible and chemical outcome. At present the perception prevails that all finds are automatically to be conserved to display standard because there is widespread ignorance that any other approach exists, despite several recognized levels of conservation (Watkinson and Neal 1998: 3) to which objects can be conserved, depending on their ultimate use, which is not necessarily display.

From the literature dating back 30 years it is clear that the situation has not advanced. As early as 1981, Robinson was lamenting 'the lack of financial support available' for conservation of marine finds (1981: 27–30). Item 4 of 'Heritage at Sea' a consultation paper produced by the Joint Nautical Archaeology Policy Committee (JNAPC) in 1989 states: 'Conservation of underwater material is expensive, sometimes demanding a higher proportion of excavation and post-excavation funds than land sites.' In project planning for proposed excavations using public funding and grants, professional practising conservators have rarely been consulted and since few sites have actually been fully excavated to date (English Heritage 1999: 4) with the full involvement of an archaeological conservator, there is little data to substantiate these claims. Additionally, most costings have also included the supposition that an entirely new laboratory be built, naturally increasing the assumed overheads by hundreds of per cent. In fact, conservation laboratory facilities in which archaeological conservators work, both in the private and public sector, have existed up and down the country for many years and it is not clear why this resource has not been used. Also, experience has shown that potential conservation costs are increased if conservation is only factored in at the end of a project rather than at the beginning. As Green has pointed out: 'It is unacceptable to conduct an excavation and then allow archaeological material to be destroyed simply because it is impossible to conserve' (1990: 162). What Green is implying here is that archaeological conservation is often forgotten until material has been physically raised, rendering the situation far more complex and potentially more expensive, than if storage, record systems and conservation facilities had been established at an early stage with cross-referencing.

Archaeological conservators who have worked extensively in the field on land sites will verify that high-standard work is possible on a 'shoe-string' budget – in other words, hundreds rather than thousands of pounds sterling. Ironically, the costs of resourcing an outfit for the investigation of a wreck, including provision for dive equipment, dive boat, fuel and ongoing maintenance, may far exceed this. Admittedly, the costs for the conservation of marine artefacts (as opposed to ships' timbers) may be higher than for terrestrial small finds, but poor planning has contributed greatly to the perceived high costs of conservation, since conservation expenditure then becomes reactionary and haphazard. The ramifications of this perception are enormous. There is now little ambition to excavate since the costs of conservation are simply seen as too prohibitively high. This leaves marine sites or even those which lie in the tidal zone vulnerable to damage from a variety of sources including erosion, fishing nets, seabed development and looting. Indeed an extreme has been reached recently, wherein it is deemed preferable to allow objects to be lost for ever, due to erosion from the seabed, rather than to raise them without funds for their conservation.

Marine sites are more difficult to safeguard than scheduled monuments on land because of the physical environment in which they are located. There is the additional dilemma of 'going public' with the location and significance of a site in order to raise funds for its complete conservation and, just as in museums, attempted theft to order is not unknown. Within the past few years divers in the Channel Islands have been offered sums in the region of £50,000 per gun for theft to order from a known site (personal communication).

Further work on suitable procedures for the conservation of small assemblages of marine artefacts would ultimately reduce costs and encourage the investigation of certain categories of site. Coupled with work in recent years on the efficacy of reburial of wooden timbers *in situ*, for example, this would not only enable extensive recording of a site without the associated requirement to lift the hull, but would also allow retrieval of the portable antiquities vulnerable to loss or theft, even if a site is protected by law or monitored regularly.

## ARCHAEOLOGICAL PLANNING

Lack of funding has led to a restriction in virtually all aspects of archeological investigation. This could in some respects be responsible for the current trend in policy towards preservation *in situ* (Corfield *et al.* 1996; English Heritage 1999: 6). However, the latter avenue should not be seen as the only alternative to complete excavation and lifting. There has been extensive work on the efficacy of reburial of ship timbers for long-term preservation and these areas should be considered in conjunction with improved measures for the handling and conservation of small finds recovered during excavation. Item 5 of 'Heritage at Sea' (JNAPC 1989) states: 'Controlled sampling and survey may provide a cost-effective alternative to complete excavation of a site, possibly followed, where practicable, by re-burial of the remains.' Green advocates uncovering and recording of timbers without dismantling, at the end of which he suggests they are either fully recovered and dismantled, as in the approach which is often taken, or that they are re-buried in specially-built underwater storage pits (1990: 162). This latter approach would allow for 'modest' investigation and intervention, whilst recovering the portable heritage, but without the overwhelming cost of preservation of large-scale waterlogged structures. Indeed, not all large-scale structures survive and the only indication of many sites may be the remaining scatter field of artefacts. Marine finds then, once secured and treated, would also enhance the understanding of the relationship of a wreck site to the local landscape by engaging the public interest in a rewarding and educational way (English Heritage 1999: 6). This approach would at least make the conservation of an assemblage a real possibility and would reap great benefits in terms of site interpretation and public display (Throckmorton 1990: 6–10). Abroad, this approach would help greatly by supporting the use of marine assemblages for long-term sustainability within the tourist industry. At present, the quick-fix solution is defined in the terms of concession to salvage because governments are given the impression they are 'getting a good deal' in that an assemblage is usually split 50:50 between government and treasure hunters (*Express* 1997; McKay 1998). In some cases as much as 75 per cent is afforded to the salvor (*Chicago Tribune* 1997). This leaves irreplaceable cultural material in the waters of Third World countries particularly vulnerable to dispersal through sale. Most recently, Article 3 of the draft UNESCO Convention (UNESCO 1998) states: 'State parties shall preserve underwater cultural heritage for the benefit of humankind'. The draft is based on the precepts of the ICOMOS Charter (ICOMOS 1996), which maintains that 'conservation shall be undertaken to accepted professional standards'. Where deeds of concession have been granted, even in accordance with Article 21 of the UNESCO 'Recommendation on International Principles Applicable to Archaeological excavations, adopted by the General Conference at its Ninth Session' (New Delhi, 5 December 1956), the statutes of the deeds have not been monitored. Experience has shown that in Third World countries, artefacts recovered from salvage concessions and belonging to *both salvor and government*, have been left rotting in buckets, no longer with labels and therefore no longer with context.

Other more detailed aspects of archaeological planning for maritime sites also deserve to be reviewed. For instance, the efficacy of conservation is far more dependent on the finds records system than for terrestrial sites: labelling and packing tend to be far more complicated (that divers are rarely able to evaluate finds underwater has an impact); difficulties can then arise with phys-ical storage on account of inappropriate or poorly planned registration systems. Additionally, if a site has a high public profile which, given experience seems likely, then artefacts will be required to be viewed by the public while in 'holding' or during conservation. This can place both objects and the public at risk if not properly planned: a professional conservator is in the best possi-ble position to advise. Finally, a further key element is the increased need for appropriate X-radiographic facilities. In larger, pre-planned projects it is essential that an industrial X-ray unit is acquired for the work or that, at least, unlimited access to a suitable unit is established. In the UK, all iron from terres-trial sites is routinely X-radiographed immediately post-excavation in compli-ance with widely-accepted standards (Walker 1990; English Heritage 1991; IFA 1991). Many iron corrosion products migrate in solution and it is therefore the nature of coastal and marine sites that small finds are impregnated with iron corrosion products (Argo 1981; MacCleod 1991: 222–34). This is exacerbated by the presence of iron as artillery, fittings, ballast, or vessel hulls (Morris 1984b: 71–6), so that the need for routine X-radiography of marine assemblages is all the greater. There has been a tendency in recent years for field projects to rely on X-radiographic facilities in local hospitals. These are usually inadequate for a number of reasons, the principal one being that the voltage setting required for marine artefacts is far higher than that for human bone. Other difficulties may also be encountered: the shelf-life of developing chemicals and film may be unreliable, water purity and temperature for film processing and power sup-plies may vary and the equipment may be so poorly maintained as to make the readings on the dials completely inaccurate (as advised by hospital staff on one occasion). Finally, since the examination of human casualties clearly takes precedence, quite rightly, over the use of such facilities for marine material, access within specific time-limits can be limited.

Although comparatively expensive to begin with, X-radiographic equip-ment designed to the right specification and secured as a basic prerequisite to archaeological excavation would go far in offsetting the current perceived costs of conservation by negating the need for much of the ensuing inter-ventive work currently pursued.

## ETHICS

Archaeological conservation, as practised today, has been associated with the development of archaeology carried out on the land and as a profession has been established for at least 40 years. The training to qualify as a conservator is extensive and is usually undertaken at university degree level. Dissemination of information is undertaken through professional conservation literature and ethics are the mainstay of sound professional practice, since interference of any kind with archaeological artefacts changes their nature, history and value. Similarly, any artefact with a history of burial can be defined as being archaeological. At this level then there is no difference between artefacts from a terrestrial context and those from the sea. There should therefore be no difference in the approach to their conservation.

The potential of marine artefact assemblages to reveal information (Cronyn *et al.* 1985) may be damaged or destroyed beyond the point of recovery, either by ill-devised treatments or by those based on skewed or outmoded objectives. These factors become more crucial in the light of the variety of some of the chemical reagents and methods currently used. Not only are the effects of the reagents on the substrates poorly understood (Rodgers 1992), but there is also little comprehension of the residual effects that the introduced chemicals may have. The epithet of 'a little knowledge is a dangerous thing' holds true here, since well-meaning but poor intervention is often far more damaging than doing nothing at all. Whilst in recent years there has been much emphasis and research (Muncher 1991: 335–49) on the chemistry and stabilization of sites (Babits and Van Tilburg 1998) there has been little on either the potential for information retrieval from finds (Morris 1984a), or cost-effective archiving methods. It is not really clear why this should be so, since it is without question that wreck sites may surrender huge quantities of material in almost unbelievably good condition (Bass 1998).With regard to the latter, both chemically and physically this should theoretically reduce the amount of treatment necessary, rather than increase it, when compared with other archaeological material.

There is still much confusion between archaeological conservation and other types of conservation such as gilding, textiles or paintings conservation. Ethical concerns form an important backdrop to the field, as do the applied practical skills necessary for carrying out the work. Based on materials science, conservation aims to *preserve* and retrieve information rather than to *restore*. Professional conservation involves a diagnosis of the condition of an object prepared as a report, much like a doctor would assess an individual patient. Once the condition has been assessed then an appropriate treatment can be devised or tailored to suit the needs of the object. No one artefact will behave exactly like another, since the definition of the burial environment at any point is uniquely dependent on the juxtaposition of every item in the vicinity. This has ramifications for the way in which treatments are devised and the decision-making process at the start of and throughout interventive conservation treatment. A practitioner is also expected to have sound knowledge of the advantages and disadvantages of all the treatments at his or her disposal in order to make an informed decision (Jaeschke 1996). Ideally, only treatments which can be reversed (Horie 1987) are carried out. It is also expected that only the 'minimum interference' necessary will be undertaken to effect the desired result. This requires consideration of the possibilities for long-term interference: a proposed treatment may destroy the potential for future chemical or physical analysis.

Many practitioners have come into 'marine conservation' from a variety of backgrounds and consequently do not operate to any known professional standards; it is probably fair to say that membership of professional conservation bodies is also rare. The knowledge on which marine artefact conservation decisions is based is therefore disparate. Further, incomplete conservation knowledge is now being disseminated by those who have carried out or developed conservation treatments without recognizing the limits of their skills (Tubb 1997: 41–50). Testing seems rarely to be undertaken and the approach of many to marine artefacts, even in the literature, seems to be limited to the recommendation of standardized procedures for basic types of material – for example, copper, iron or ceramics – rather than being based on the composition of the whole, the condition of which varies from object to object as a result of burial and manufacturing technology, even throughout cargo of the same type. As an example, an interesting case involved a group of archaeologists who had had conservation training for only 2–3 months, yet who persisted in carrying out severe chemical and electrical treatments on marine metal artefacts without the slightest idea of the definition of a metal alloy. They therefore could not have possibly understood the consequences of the treatment.

Such lack of awareness of conservation ethics means that the standard professional approach, which demands that any evidence of manufacture, burial or context (English Heritage 1991) be retained on or within the object, is usually overlooked. This is alarming since an extensive array of information can survive in, or attached to, an archaeological artefact, and this needs to be recorded before it is disturbed, damaged or destroyed (Janaway and Scott 1989; la Neice and Craddock 1993).

## CURRENT CONSERVATION METHODOLOGIES

It is well recognized that marine artefacts can be prone to swift, highly visible deterioration. This, more often than not, is the result of poor post-excavation maintenance, but has unfortunately led to an overemphasis on chemical stabilization and cleaning, at the expense of historical integrity. Article 9 of the ICOMOS Charter (1996) states that 'Material conservation must be carried out in accordance with current professional standards', but this is patently not done. Treatment tends to be regarded as a process intent on stabilization, rather than a treatment tailored to suit an object. There is also much emphasis on restoring the 'original' appearance of an artefact. Severe and highly interventive treatments are now regarded as the norm, although a professional archaeological conservator would not contemplate using them, and the side-effects of which seem rarely to be considered. An example is the employment of high concentrations of chemicals for *days* such as in a treatment used in the US for the removal of iron corrosion staining from porcelain (personal communication). The necessity for the removal of such staining is, in any case, debatable, but the time period involved implies that the treatment selected is not working fast enough to offset the chance of any secondary reactions occurring, and would indicate that an improved treatment needs to be found. Neither does it take into account the residues of any such chemicals which, by the time of completion of treatment, would have penetrated deeply into the artefact.

Electrical and high-temperature treatments are another favourite. In some firms these treatments are regarded as so 'successful' that they are being extended for use on terrestrial artefacts, somewhat ironically, since they were discontinued several decades ago due to the damage they caused. In one case the attempt to record a collection of rare early sixteenth-century wrought iron swivel guns was doomed by the treatment they had been afforded by the owner after acquisition through sale. High-temperature hydrogen reduction had been undertaken by an industrial firm and the barrels, although ostensibly chemically stable, had melted, buckled and warped. Bore and length measurements, indicative of the size and type of vessel at the wreck site, could no longer be taken, neither was archaeometallurgical analysis possible, needed to discover more about the early technology used in producing such guns (Scott 1991). In another instance, a beautifully conserved wooden artefact was presented for comment some years ago. It had been freeze-dried to a high standard but then coated with raw linseed oil to make it look more 'original'. A professional conservator would have known that the oil film cross-links with time, becoming sticky, brittle and unsightly, eventually discolouring and, more importantly, becoming well-nigh impossible to remove without causing damage to the underlying surface.

## CONSERVATION IN THE FIELD AND FIRST-AID

At present there are two recognized stages of handling for both terrestrial and marine finds within conservation: first-aid, followed by full treatment. However, one of the difficulties concomitant with the treatment of marine finds is the way in which these two stages are frequently confused. A first-aid field facility, whether for terrestrial archaeological sites or marine sites in no way encompasses all the facilities necessary for full conservation treatment (Stanley-Price 1995). Interestingly enough, in US projects, the 'first-aid' facility in the field is usually referred to as the 'laboratory' or 'lab', probably adding to the confusion, which does not lend itself well to the consistent development of conservation practice.

Seawater can be thought of as one vast pool of electrolyte because it is so concentrated in potential chemical reactants, chloride ions in particular. It is because of this that marine finds are probably more susceptible to extensive changes immediately post-excavation than are finds from terrestrial sites, but the causes of these changes are not well-enough appreciated. Most marine artefacts are frequently allowed to undergo some level of drying immediately upon retrieval. Lamentably, it is often the rarest finds which are the most vulnerable to damage since these are the ones which generate the most excitement. Even the imperceptible drying caused by the handling and passing around of an exciting find for only seconds or minutes prior to re-immersion, can result in immense damage and immediate decay. Subsequent to this, finds will either be allowed to dry out completely on the decks of research vessels, or, in better circumstances, they will be transferred to storage in a purer form of water such as tap water. Here though they will often continue to suffer quite extensive post-excavation changes which can only apparently be slowed by the addition of an inhibitor or by changing the pH. Since most finds are made of composite material this can threaten the survival of associated evidence within an artefact. However, a principal component of this supposed post-excavation instability must be the failure to remove all residual seawater upon retrieval. Lack of appropriate rinsing, as differentiated from 'desalination' where the aim is to remove soluble salts from within the fabric of an artefact, will mean that finds remain immersed in a potentially highly reactive solution which creates an ideal environment for rapid change. Further, the problems which often ensue have been exacerbated by commonly storing mixed materials together. Finds from terrestrial sites are usually stored in separate boxes to avoid contamination and potential chemical interference. With finds stored in solution the need is all the greater since the solution has the capacity to act as an electrolyte. However, when visiting facilities in tropical countries, the author has found it to be common practice for the finds from a single marine site to be stored together in one or two large concrete tanks. Artefacts may therefore cause contamination of others, interfering with the potential for future analysis. Further, galvanic cells may be established between different metals or metal alloys, setting up rapid preferential dissolution of those areas of metal objects with a lower electro-potential within the storage environment. This again may be a principal cause of continuing corrosion immediately post-excavation and is a factor probably not sufficiently well recognized in the development of counter-measures.

Current standards for the first-aid of marine finds have largely developed through extrapolation of the methodology used for terrestrial finds (UKIC Archaeology Section 1983) and in many ways do not take the issues described above into account. They may therefore frequently prove to be inadequate, which, at face value is somewhat surprising, given that marine finds, particularly some metals, are frequently found in a more physically sound and less porous state than their terrestrial cousins.

It therefore appears that, for these reasons, marine finds have earned a perceived reputation for extensive chemical instability which is regarded as inherent rather than circumstantial and which must be addressed at all costs.

This perception has largely governed the development of conservation methodology within this area since the severe treatments described above appear to have been developed to counteract this. However, many facilities do not have the resources and funding necessary to carry out immediate full conservation treatment and where project funding is acquired it may not be available consistently throughout the course of post-excavation work. Additionally it must be recognized that it may take a number of years to conserve fully a large assemblage in its entirety and so it is likely that there will always be projects in which finds will be put 'on hold' for a number of years prior to being afforded treatment. First-aid methodology at present seems inadequate in enabling a large assemblage to be easily stored, accessed, handled, maintained and most importantly, prioritized during the period of years over which most projects take place. Finds therefore continue to be stored in solution for this duration but are then, by definition, no longer in the realms of 'first-aid'.

It would appear then, that a new and third stage of conservation handling must be introduced. This would be interposed between that of first-aid as currently carried out immediately post-excavation and full treatment. Such a concept, referred to here for ease of reference as 'holding', would go far in offsetting the ramifications of the highly invasive treatments discussed above. For example, sound non-ferrous metal finds could be washed thoroughly to remove residual seawater and then stored desiccated to minimize the risk of further change. Robust ceramics could be routinely desalinated and subsequently stored dry. This would help to avoid, for example, the risks of biological attack or dissolution of glazes whilst in solution. Storing some classes of material in a dry state rather than a wet state, until such time as full treatment could be undertaken and provided that appropriate steps had been taken in drying, would greatly facilitate, for instance, not only storage maintenance and access, but also the X-radiography necessary for prioritizing an assemblage. Such an approach would, of course, need to be properly researched. However, in the event that such a stage of treatment were to be recognized as crucial and in some ways unique to marine finds, it is likely that the current perceived costs of conservation would be mitigated. The proper maintenance of a wet-storage facility is highly time-, space- and labour-consuming and the quantities of water and chemicals involved can be expensive.

Such recognition would also enable archaeological conservation within site projects of any size to be properly planned, managed, prioritized and carried through to completion. This would not only allow the full investigation of a site, in order to contribute to current archaeological and historical knowledge, but would also help to ensure the recovery of the portable finds vulnerable to loss. This is particularly critical since the assessment of many sites in recent years has been reduced simply to surveying and recording.

Other areas of current methodology also need attention, such as records. Often, no conservation records are created because the treatment afforded during excavation is not seen as part of the conservation process: conservation being interpreted only as that which is carried out in full treatment. Thus even the concentrations and changes of frequently used storage solutions are not recorded. This is critical since the lack of proper records creates serious difficulties both in terms of the interpretation of the future behaviour of unstable artefacts and in terms of health and safety. Where conservation records do exist they are frequently inadequate because phrasing and terminology are ambiguous. This constitutes poor practice professionally. Conservation records should comprise an unambiguous written account of the history of artefacts from the point of excavation, reinforced with black and white photographic records, as a minimum standard.

One other area which requires serious attention is that of lifting. In 1992, techniques were published which demonstrated methods by which marine artefacts could be lifted more safely (Daley and Murdock 1992: 133–45). There still is considerable evidence that such literature is being overlooked (Empereur 1996).

## CONCLUSION

The situation on a global scale with regard to the archaeological conservation of marine artefacts appears to be one of 'all or nothing'. The 'all' frequently comprises the selection and undertaking of extensive, expensive and severe treatments on a vast scale and at vast cost, with little monitoring. The 'or nothing' derives from a perceived cost of conservation beyond the realistically obtainable, consequently stifling any archaeologically invasive action on a site.

The situation gives further cause for concern in the area of training. As courses develop in marine artefact conservation, the attitude that the conservation of marine material is a discipline separate from that of archaeological conservation is promulgated. If appropriate ethics are not soon introduced then the already existing gap can only widen. It is therefore now the responsibility of those involved as practitioners to research the literature properly and draw on the experience of professional conservation. Likewise, proper examination by trained professional conservators of the issues involved may provide an opportunity to change the perception as regards the cost of conservation and thus the cost of carrying out archaeology. This would also help to prevent the ubiquitous 'reinvention of the wheel'. The latter is sadly apparent in the treatments already developed and the costs, in terms of destruction of evidence within artefacts, must be enormous. Many of the areas discussed within the literature for marine artefact conservation have already been extensively researched within archaeological conservation for terrestrial finds. The premise of 'developing new frontiers' in the preservation of cultural objects, as so often quoted by commercial companies, is therefore simply not true.

Additionally, issues of provenance must not go unregarded (Throckmorton 1996: 103); the law both nationally and internationally is complex (Tubb

1995) and many conservation practitioners might argue that their first priority should simply be to an 'artefact' in order to effect its survival (Tubb and Sease 1996: 193–8). However, given the potential increase in financial value imbued by conservation, the responsibilities of conservation practitioners cannot be divorced from provenance and the associated destruction of irreplaceable underwater cultural heritage.

There is still clearly a need to address the wrongs accorded to marine cultural heritage. However, with current gaps in the perceptions of marine artefact conservation, training and experience, it remains to be seen how this can be achieved. Current conservation practice for marine archaeological artefacts must be brought in line with standard archaeological practice and at the earliest opportunity if an important and crucial part of the world's cultural heritage is to be preserved.

## BIBLIOGRAPHY

Argo, J. 1981. On the nature of 'ferrous' corrosion products on marine iron. *Studies in Conservation* 26: 42–4.

Ashley-Smith, J. 1999. *Risk Assessment for Object Conservation*. Oxford: Butterworth-Heinemann.

Babits, L.E. and H. Van Tilburg 1998. *Maritime Archaeology: a Reader of Substantive and Theoretical Contributions*. (The Plenum series in underwater archaeology). New York: Plenum Press.

Ballard, R.D. 1989. *The Discovery of the Titanic*. Toronto: Madison Press Books.

Bass, G. (ed.) 1998. *Ships and Shipwrecks of the Americas*. London: Thames and Hudson.

Blot, J-Y. 1995. *Underwater Archaeology – exploring the world beneath the sea – new horizons*. London: Thames and Hudson.

Buglass, J. 1994. *Museums and Maritime Archaeology – dealing with maritime finds*. Newcastle upon Tyne: North of England Museums Service.

Cameron, E., S. Watkins and D. Watkinson 1988. *Provision for Archaeological Conservation in England and Wales: a review*. London: United Kingdom Institute for Conservation Archaeology Section.

Carlin, W. and D. Keith 1996. Technical communication. An improved tannin-based corrosion inhibitor-coating system for ferrous artefacts. *International Journal of Nautical Archaeology* 25(1): 38–45.

Carpenter, J. and I. D. MacLeod 1993. Conservation of corroded iron cannon and the influence of degradation on treatment times. In *ICOM 10th Triennial Meeting, Washington DC, USA, 22–27 Aug*. 759–67. Paris: ICOM Committee for Conservation.

Cheek, P. 1986. Conservation of cannon at Chatham Historic Dockyard – Notes and News. *International Journal of Nautical Archaeology*. 15(3): 253–4.

*Chicago Tribune* 1997. Scientists show relics from ship fit for pirate, possibly Blackbeard. Knight-Ridder. 30 October.

Corfield, M., P. Hinton, T. Nixon and M. Pollard (eds) 1996. *Preserving Archaeological Remains In Situ*. Proceedings of the conference of 1–3 April 1996. London: Museum of London Archaeology Service.

Cronyn, J., E. Pye and J. Watson 1985. The recognition and identification of traces of organic materials in association with metal artefacts In *The Archaeologist and the Laboratory*, P. Phillips (ed.), 24–7. CBA Research Report No 58.

Croome, A. 1992. The United States' Abandoned Shipwreck Act goes into action – a report. *International Journal of Nautical Archaeology* 21(1): 39–53.

Cussler, C. 1993. *Treasure*. London: Harper Collins Publishers.

Daley, T.W. and L.D. Murdock 1992. Excavating and raising artifacts from a marine environment. In *Retrieval of Objects from Archaeological Sites*, R. Payton (ed.), 133–45. Wales: Archetype Publications.

Dean, M. 1988. *Guidelines on Acceptable Standards in Underwater Archaeology*. The Scottish Maritime Studies Development Association [no publisher location given] 18–19.

Dean, M., B. Ferrari, I. Oxley, M. Redknap and K. Watson 1992. *Archaeology Underwater: the NAS guide to principles and practice*. London: NAS and Archetype Publications.

Delgado, J.P. 1997. Conservation. In *British Museum Encyclopedia of Underwater and Maritime Archaeology*, 106–8. London: British Museum Press.

DCMS (Department of Culture, Media and Sport) 1998a. *Advisory Committee on Historic Wreck Sites 1998 Annual Report*. London: DCMS.

DCMS (Department of Culture, Media and Sport) 1998b. *Portable Antiquities Annual Report 1997–98*. London: DCMS.

Department of the Environment (DoE) 1990. *Policy and Planning Guideline: Archaeology and Planning 16*. London: DoE.

Department of the Environment (DoE) 1999. Protection of Wrecks Act. In *Background Materials on the Protection of the Underwater Cultural Heritage*. L.V. Prott and I. Srong (eds), 63–7. Paris and Portsmouth: UNESCO and Nautical Archaeology Society.

Empereur, J-Y. 1996. Raising statues and blocks from the sea at Alexandria. *Egyptian Archaeology* 9: 19–22.

English Heritage 1991. *Management of Archaeological Projects*. London: English Heritage.

English Heritage 1996. M. Fulford, T. Champion and A. Long, (eds), *England's Coastal Heritage: a survey for English Heritage and the RCHME*. London: English Heritage.

English Heritage 1999. *Towards a Policy for Marine Archaeology: an English Heritage and Royal Commission on the Historic Monuments of England discussion paper, March 1999*. London: English Heritage.

*Express* 1997. Is this the start of £4bn gold rush? (Foreign Service). 22 March.

Fenwick, V. 1998. Editorial. *International Journal of Nautical Archaeology* 27(1): 1–2.

Fenwick, V. and A. Gale 1998. *Historic Shipwrecks: Discovered, Protected and Investigated*. Stroud, Gloucestershire: Tempus Publishing.

Gilberg, M.R. and N.J. Seeley 1981. The identity of compounds containing chloride ions in marine iron corrosion products: a critical review. *Studies in Conservation* 26: 50–6.

Gillard, R.D., S.M. Hardman, R.G. Thomas and D.E. Watkinson 1994. The mineralization of fibres in burial environments. *Studies in Conservation* 39: 132–40.

Green, J. 1990. *Maritime Archaeology – A Technical Handbook*. London: Academic Press.

*Guardian* 1999. Ship find swells mania for Charles I (Gerard Seenan, Martin Wainwright, Maev Kennedy). 29 January.

Hamilton, D.L. 1976. *Conservation of Metal Objects from Underwater Sites: a Study in Methods*. Texas Memorial Museum Miscellaneous Papers 4. Austin, Texas: Texas Memorial Museum.

Harrison, S. 1997. Treasures of the SS John Barry – an American liberty ship lying at a depth of 2600 meters in the Arabian Gulf – the deepest ever bulk recovery from the sea bed. *Museums in Britain* 1: 65.

Heritage Office, New South Wales, Australia 1994. *Underwater Heritage: principles and guidelines*. Sydney: Heritage Office.

Horie, C.V. 1987. *Materials for Conservation: organic consolidants, adhesives and coatings*. Oxford: Butterworth-Heinemann.

ICOMOS 1996. Charter on the Management of Underwater Cultural Heritage.

Institute of Field Archaeologists (IFA) 1991. *Guidelines for Finds Work*. IFA.

*International Herald Tribune* 1998. An old salt [Mel Fisher] outlives his era (Jim Carrier, New York Times Service). 11 May.

Jaeschke, H.F. 1996. The conservation of looted antiquities and the responsibilities of conservators. In *Archaeological Conservation and Its Consequences: preprints of the contributions to the Copenhagen Congress, 26–30 August 1996*, A. Roy and P. Smith (eds), 82–6. London: IIC.

Janaway, R. and B. Scott (eds) 1989. *Evidence Preserved in Corrosion Products: New Fields in Artifact Studies*. UK Institute for Conservation Occasional Paper No. 8. London: UKIC.

Johnston, P.F. 1993. Treasure salvage, archaeological ethics and maritime museums. *International Journal of Nautical Archaeology* 22(1): 53–60.

Joint Nautical Archaeology Policy Committee (JNAPC) 1989. *Heritage at Sea: Proposals for the Better Protection of Archaeological Sites Underwater*. London: JNAPC.

Joint Nautical Archaeology Policy Committee (JNAPC) 1993. *Still at Sea*. London: JNAPC.

Joint Nautical Archaeology Policy Committee (JNAPC) 1995. *Code of Practice for Seabed Developers*. Swindon: Royal Commission on the Historical Monuments of England.

Joint Nautical Archaeology Policy Committee (JNAPC) 2000. *Underwater Finds – Guidance for Divers*. London: JNAPC.

Lang, J. and A. Middleton 1997. *Radiography of Cultural Material*. Oxford: Butterworth-Heinemann.

La Niece, S. and P. Craddock (eds) 1993. *Metal Plating and Patinations, Cultural, Technical and Historical Developments*. Oxford: Butterworth-Heinemann.

Laures, F.F. 1986. More details about rapid drying of wood by 'frying' it in poly-ethylene glycol. *International Journal of Nautical Archaeology* 15(1): 68.

Li, G. 1998. Ancient Chinese anchors: their rigging and conservation. *International Journal of Nautical Archaeology* 27(4): 307–12.

McKay, R. 1998. Pirate's treasure exhibition sinks leaving £250,000 debt. *Scotland on Sunday,* 15 November.

MacLeod, I.D. 1987. Conservation of corroded iron artifacts – new methods for on-site preservation and cryogenic deconcreting. *International Journal for Nautical Archaeology and Underwater Exploration* 16(1): 49–56.

MacLeod, I.D. 1991. Identification of corrosion products on non-ferrous metal arti-facts recovered from shipwrecks. *Studies in Conservation* 36(4): 222–34.

Meyer, K. 1974. *The Plundered Past – Traffic in Art Treasures*. London: Hamish Hamilton.

Morris, R. 1984a. News and notes – ferrous clib concretion on small guns. *International Journal of Nautical Archaeology* 13(1): 65–70.

Morris, R. 1984b. News and notes – finds in clib at Colossus wreck. *International Journal of Nautical Archaeology* 13(1): 71–6.

Mouzouras, R., A.M. Jones, E.B.G. Jones and M.H. Rule 1990. Non-destructive evaluation of hull and stored timbers from the Tudor ship *Mary Rose*. *Studies in Conservation* 35(4): 173–88.

Muncher, D.A. 1991. Technical communication: the conservation of WLF-HA-1: the WHYDAH shipwreck site. *International Journal of Nautical Archaeology* 20: 335–49.

Museum and Galleries Commission 1992. *Standards in the Care of Archaeological Collections*. London: MGC Publications.

Museums and Galleries Commission & English Heritage 1998. Hedley Swain (ed.), *A Survey of Archaeological Archives in England*. London: MGC Publications.

North, N.A. 1982. Corrosion products on marine iron. *Studies in Conservation* 27: 75–83.

O'Keefe, P.J. 1996. Protection of the underwater cultural heritage: developments at UNESCO. *International Journal of Nautical Archaeology* 25: 169–76.

O'Keefe, P.J. 1997. *Trade in Antiquities: Reducing Destruction and Theft*. London and Paris: Archetype Publications and UNESCO.

Oldham, N., M. Palmer and J. Tyson 1993. The Erme Estuary, Devon, historic wreck site, 1991–93. *International Journal of Nautical Archaeology* 22(4): 323–30.

Payton, R. 1987. Conservation of objects from one of the world's oldest shipwrecks: the Uluburun, Kas Shipwreck, Turkey. In *Recent Advances in the Conservation and Analysis of Artifacts*, J.Black (ed.), 41–9. London: Summer Schools Press, University of London.

Pearson, C. (ed.) 1987. *Conservation of Marine Archaeological Objects*. London: Butterworth.

Pitman, A.J., A.M. Jones and E.B.G. Jones 1993. The wharf-borer *Nacerdes melanura* L., a threat to stored archaeological timbers. *Studies in Conservation* 38(4): 274–84.

Pleydell-Bouverie, J. 1997. Curlywurly cable plumbs the depths: a marine salvage team can now recover cargoes from wrecks in deeper waters than ever before. *New Scientist* 10 May: 29.

Prott, L.V. 1997. Safeguarding the underwater cultural heritage: UNESCO moves ahead. *Museum International* 49(1). Paris: UNESCO.

Robinson, W. 1981. *First Aid for Marine Finds*. London: National Maritime Museum.

Robinson, W. 1998. *First Aid for Underwater Finds*. London & Portsmouth: Nautical Archaeology Society and Archetype Publications.

Rodgers, B.A. 1992. *The ECU Conservator's Cookbook*. Greenville, North Carolina: East Carolina University.

Royal Commission on the Historical Monuments of England (RCHME) 1996. *The National Inventory of Maritime Archaeology for England*. Swindon: Royal Commission on the Historical Monuments of England.

Scott, D.A. 1991. *Metallography and Microstructure of Ancient and Historic Metals*. California: John Paul Getty Trust.

Scott, D.A. and N.J. Seeley 1987. The washing of fragile iron artifacts. *Studies in Conservation* 32: 73–6.

Stambolov, T. 1985. *The Corrosion and Conservation of Metallic Antiquities and Works of Art*. Amsterdam: Central Research Laboratory for Objects of Art and Science.

Stanley-Price, N. (ed.) 1995. *Conservation on Archaeological Excavations*. Rome: ICCROM.

Sutherland, A.J. 1998. Maritime and coastal archaeology and conservation. *Conservation News* 66: 29–31.

Throckmorton, P. (ed.) 1996. *The Sea Remembers*. London: Chancellor Press.

Throckmorton, P. [1990] 1999. The world's worst investment: the economics of treasure hunting with real life comparisons. In *Background Materials on the Protection of the Underwater Cultural Heritage*, L.V. Prott and I. Srong (eds), 179–83. Paris and Portsmouth: UNESCO and Nautical Archaeology Society.

Tubb, K.W. (ed.) 1995. *Antiquities Trade or Betrayed: Legal Ethical and Conservation Issues*. London: Archetype/UKIC.

Tubb, K.W. 1997. Focusing beyond the microscope: ethical considerations in conservation. *Art, Antiquity and Law* 2(1): 41–50.

Tubb, K.W. and C. Sease 1996. Sacrificing the wood for the trees – should conservation have a role in the antiquities trade? In *Archaeological Conservation and Its Consequences: preprints of the contributions to the Copenhagen Congress, 26–30th August 1996*, A. Roy and P. Smith (eds), 193–8. London: IIC.

Tylecote, R.F. 1988. *A History of Metallurgy*. London: The Metals Society.

Tylecote, R.F. 1977. Durable materials for sea water: the archaeological evidence. *International Journal for Nautical Archaeology and Underwater Exploration* 6(4): 269–83.

UNESCO 1998. Draft Convention on the Protection of Underwater Cultural Heritage. Paris: UNESCO.

United Kingdom Institute for Conservation (UKIC) Archaeology Section 1984. *Environmental Standards for the Permanent Storage of Excavated Material from Archaeological Sites*. Archaeology Section Guidelines 3. London: UKIC.

United Kingdom Institute for Conservation (UKIC) Archaeology Section 1983. *Packing and Storage of Freshly Excavated Artefacts from Archaeological Sites*. Archaeology Section Guidelines No. 2. London: UKIC.

Walker, K. 1990. *Guidelines for the preparation of excavation archives for long-term storage*. London: UKIC Archaeology Section.

Watkinson, D. and V. Neal 1998. *First Aid for Finds*. London: Rescue and UKIC Archaeology Section.

Wingood, A.J. 1986. Sea Ventura: Second interim report – part 2: the artefacts. *International Journal of Nautical Archaeology* 15(2): 149–59.

# 7 Metal detecting in Britain: catastrophe or compromise?

## PETER V. ADDYMAN AND NEIL BRODIE

The advent of cheap and effective metal detectors in the 1970s was initially regarded by archaeologists in Britain as an unmitigated and potentially over-whelming disaster. Britain is a country where archaeological sites may average as many as ten per square kilometre, and are so frequent in places that the concept of archaeological landscapes had to be invented to comprehend them (Stoertz 1997). The prospect of large bands of archaeologically untrained metal-detecting hobbyists systematically hoovering up artefacts from them promised loss of archaeological information on an unprecedented scale. It seemed likely to lead to increased uncontrolled intervention in archaeological sites, removal of artefacts from stratified archaeological contexts, disassociation of objects from their find spots (Addyman 1995: 167) and the disappearance of the artefacts themselves into unnamed private collections, the antiquities trade and abroad.

Metal detecting proved to be one of the growth hobbies of the 1980s, particularly after the development of high-resolution instruments which were able to eliminate background 'noise' caused by finely dispersed iron minerals in the soil. Sales of detectors suggested that hundreds of thousands of Britons had at some time used one. Statistics provided by the national metal-detecting magazines *Treasure Hunting* and *The Searcher* seemed to imply that as many as one million and possibly two million objects were being recovered annually. Under Britain's permissive antiquities laws only objects of gold and silver ('treasure trove') – and since the *Treasure Act 1996*, coins and objects found with gold, silver and coins – were subject to state control, while metal detecting was prohibited only on the 13,000 or so Scheduled Ancient Monuments and Areas of Archaeological Importance (*Ancient Monuments and Archaeological Areas Act 1979*), a tiny part of the known archaeo-logical landscape.

An initial knee-jerk reaction – a STOP! Campaign to try to persuade the nation against metal detecting – probably did more harm than good. It fomented wordy battles between archaeologists and detectorists, vilification in both the archaeological and treasure-hunting press, lack of comprehension, loss of sympathy and the polarization of attitudes. Meanwhile, metal detecting became ever more popular. Detecting rallies on selected sites could attract over 1,000 detectorists. Internationally marketed treasure tours to Britain promised richly rewarding detecting holidays.

Also during this period some detectorists began digging illegally on private land or scheduled sites to recover saleable artefacts and hoards ('treasure'). Early in the 1980s fifteen or more Roman bronze masks, beasts and figures were taken from a farmer's field at Icklingham in Suffolk, and are now in a private collection in the US (Browning 1998). In 1985 treasure hunters descended upon the Romano-British site of Wanborough in Surrey and are thought to have removed 5,000 or more coins which were dispersed abroad on the international market (CBA 1985). Also in 1985 the Salisbury Hoard was illegally excavated by two detectorists in Wiltshire. It was a unique find of some 500 bronze objects of various ages, some dating back to the beginning of the Bronze Age, which had been buried together sometime around 200 BC. Again, it was broken up on the market although a subsequent collaboration between the police and staff of the British Museum led to the recovery of about two-thirds, with the remainder having disappeared abroad (Stead 1998). The British Museum purchased a similarly mixed assemblage of bronze age material in 1989 (the 'Batheaston Hoard') and learned in 1992 that it had probably also been first obtained illegally in south Wiltshire (ibid.: 120).

More hopefully, however, some detectorists began to heed the need to record context, and the best of them turned themselves into skilled, perceptive and responsible avocational archaeologists. Significantly, too, the national metal-detecting associations began to argue that there might be positive archaeological value in much that the detectorists were doing. First, it was pointed out that most detecting was carried out on arable land where objects had been moved out of context by ploughing and were open to attack by chemical fertilizers (Dobinson and Denison 1995: 51). Second, it was demonstrated that large numbers of artefacts were lost through the surface stripping that preceded excavation, and that a competent detector survey could eliminate this loss almost completely (Gregory and Rogerson 1984).

In light of all this, the Council for British Archaeology was commissioned by English Heritage to carry out a systematic survey which was published as *Metal Detecting and Archaeology in England* (Dobinson and Denison 1995). This confirmed that the number of finds made by hobby detectorists annually was colossal, possibly, the report thought, amounting to 400,000 pre-1600 finds each year, but that only a tiny proportion were ever seen by archaeologists or museums (ibid.: 8, 11). Most of these finds were made by detectorists working with full permissions, but detecting also proved to be rife on scheduled ancient monuments which are protected by law and archaeological excavations where no permission to detect had been given (Denison 1995: 8).

Very few scheduled sites receive more than a monthly or even yearly inspection so that evidence of illicit digging is hard to identify, small holes rapidly fill in or are overgrown, or are ploughed out; furthermore, much illicit detecting takes place at night and the so-called nighthawks are rarely caught red-handed (Dobinson and Denison 1995: 54). The position with unscheduled or previously unknown sites is even worse. Nevertheless, it was reported that during the period 1988–94, 188 scheduled monuments had suffered from illicit detecting, although the true number, for reasons outlined above, was in all probability much larger (ibid.). A survey of professional archaeological units showed that 37 out of the 50 surveyed had suffered raids during the course of their excavations (ibid.). Units based in the south suffered more than those in the north, while those in the south-west were largely unaffected (ibid.: 56), a pattern which corresponds largely to the distribution of arable land in England. Some sites, such as the Roman period Caistor-by-Norwich, suffered from what the authors termed 'quasi-industrial' looting (ibid.: 55), with Roman sites generally being most vulnerable. Entries from the daybook of Corbridge Roman fort and town in north England revealed 24 incidents between April 1989 and September 1993, when it was necessary to hire a private security firm to protect the site (ibid.: 56).

More positively, however, the report suggested that for some categories of objects, such as iron age coins and Roman brooches, the huge spate of new finds being brought to museums for identification was resulting in large gains in archaeological knowledge, even though evidently these reported finds were only a tiny proportion of the total. It seemed likely that even of potential 'treasure trove' finds, only 5 per cent were being reported.

A national Standing Conference on Portable Antiquities (SCOPA) representing all Britain's main archaeological bodies reviewed the report and gave its support to the tightening of the Treasure Trove law in the new Treasure Act 1996, which came into operation in 1997. SCOPA also adopted a statement of principles for the protection of portable antiquities which emphasized the non-renewable nature of the archaeological resource and the valid public interest in having the discovery of archaeological finds reported and recorded. From this lead the government, after consultation, promoted a voluntary scheme for the recording of portable antiquities. The pilot scheme *Recording Our Past* commenced operation in 1997 in six trial areas, and was extended early in 1999 to eleven, covering about half of England and Wales. The hope is ultimately to extend it to cover both countries completely with a complement of thirty-two finds liaison officers and a central support staff of six (Bland 1999: 203).

The aims of this pilot scheme are:

1 To advance our knowledge of the history and archaeology of England and Wales.
2 To initiate a system for recording of archaeological finds and to encourage and promote better recording practice by finders.
3 To strengthen links between the detector users and archaeologists.
4 To estimate how many objects are being found across England and Wales and what resources would be needed to record them.

Two years' experience shows the scheme to be at least partially effective. All finds are inspected by a finds liaison officer and details are entered on to a database and awarded a unique identification number. Important finds are drawn and photographed, but objects made later than 1800 are not recorded unless deemed to be of special interest. The scheme is designed to record all archaeological finds made by members of the public, but the overwhelming majority to date have been metal detector finds (87 per cent in 1999; DCMS 1999: 46). Findspot information varies from an eight-figure grid reference to parish, but by 1999 58.6 per cent of objects were recorded with at least a six-figure grid reference – an accuracy of 100 square metres or better (ibid.: 42). Ninety-one per cent of objects were recovered from cultivated land (ibid.: 44). There is evidence that the 1995 estimate of 400,000 metal-detecting finds annually may have to be revised upwards; in 1998 it was estimated that 100,000 finds might be made each year in Kent alone (DCMS 1998: 27) and the national figure may be closer to one million. No data recording scheme is likely to be able to cope with this, but information recovered through voluntary recording is already beginning to inform major academic studies of artefacts, artefact types, distributions and especially numismatics, confirming the worth of the initiative. Efforts now are being concentrated on making the resultant information widely available and easily accessible, and to encourage its use, so as to justify the considerable expenditure in terms of benefit to the public. The database is freely accessible on a website at *www.finds.org.uk* and it is envisaged that it will allow the data to be used by schools or any interested member of the public (Bland 1999: 194).

It is probably too soon for this new scheme to have made a serious impact on illegal detecting, and reports of this continue to filter through. In February 2000 the British Numismatic Trade Association reported the existence of an undeclared hoard of third-century AD Roman coins, perhaps more than 10,000, which had been offered for sale in London and New York, apparently with a newly invented 'European' provenance. Two months later on the internet auction site E-Bay, 500 (probably unrelated) uncleaned Roman coins were advertised for sale in New York as '. . . found with metal detectors in England and they still have the British dirt on them . . .'. The large number of Roman coins offered for sale on E-Bay with a 'Bulgarian' or 'Black Sea' provenance has also aroused suspicion (Lufkin 2000). Wanborough in Surrey continues to be attacked, most recently in March 2000. One night in 1997 local residents reported seeing a lorry with no lights driving past loaded with soil, apparently to be more thoroughly searched elsewhere. In September 1999 the *First Annual English Style Metal Detecting Rally* was held in Colorado and offered 25 acres seeded with genuine British coins for treasure hunters to search. A second was announced for September 2000 with the promise of 10,000 British coins, from ancient to modern (pre-1942). It is difficult to say how many of these coins are archaeological and might have been recently removed from the UK.

The Janus-like nature of metal detecting in England today, with, on the one hand, responsible detectorists working with archaeologists but, on the other, nighthawks looking towards the market, is best illustrated by the experience of the British Museum at Snettisham. Here in 1990 a detectorist discovered a hoard of iron age gold objects, which he reported to the Norfolk Archaeology Unit. The British Museum was called in to investigate the site further, with the help of the detectorist who renounced any further financial interest, and in the course of a five-week project five more hoards were discovered. It seems that one was missed, however, as in 1991 nighthawks visited the site and removed a hoard of about 6,000 iron age coins – mainly silver but some gold – which were subsequently dispersed unseen on the market (Stead 1998: 145–7).

In 1995 the authors of *Metal Detecting and Archaeology in England* made seven recommendations for future action:

1 Improve liaison between archaeologists and the detecting community.
2 Improve communications among archaeologists themselves.
3 Investigate ways of managing a large increase in finds-reporting.
4 Investigate new methods of protecting scheduled sites from illicit metal detecting.
5 Investigate the relationship between illicit detector finds and the antiquities market.
6 Educate archaeologists about the metal detector.
7 Investigate finds erosion in ploughsoil.

The voluntary scheme *Recording our Past* has successfully addressed recommendations 1, 3 and perhaps 6, but the others remain to be met. The need to investigate movement of illicit finds through the antiquities market is particularly urgent as the market ultimately provides the incentive for nighthawks to continue their depredations. But the way ahead is seen as education and persuasion rather than coercion. There could be initiatives to encourage the responsible use of metal detectors, to encourage the reporting and to encourage the depositing of important artefacts in public collections, rather than their sale on the open market. A climate of opinion in which people generally want to do the right thing would leave the law to deal solely with the least tractable situations. A similar approach to the problem of export of small antiquities of British origin is probably advisable, with the emphasis on the recording of objects rather than the prohibition of export. An export reviewing committee might then advise on objects which should be retained in Britain in the national interest, using criteria of archaeological significance rather than financial value. Here, as in so many aspects of the catastrophe engulfing Britain's portable antiquities, compromise is likely to bring the best rewards.

# REFERENCES

Addyman, P.V. 1995. Treasure trove, treasure hunting and the quest for a portable antiquities act. In *Antiquities Trade or Betrayed: Legal, Ethical and Conservation Issues*, K.W. Tubb (ed.), 163–72. London: Archetype/UKIC.

Bland, R. 1999. The Treasure Act and Portable Antiquities Scheme: a progress report. *Art, Antiquity and Law* 4, 191–203.

Browning, J. 1998. An individual's struggle to reclaim stolen property. In *Recovery of Stolen and Looted Works of Art*. Leicester: Institute of Art and Law.

CBA 1985. Detector looting results in rescue excavation. *CBA Newsletter* 9(7), 55–6.

DCMS 1998. *Portable Antiquities 1997–8*. London: Department of Culture, Media and Sport.

DCMS 1999. *Portable Antiquities 1998–9*. London: Department of Culture, Media and Sport.

Denison, S. 1995. Finders, keepers and losers. *British Archaeology* 1, 8–9.

Dobinson, C. and S. Denison 1995. *Metal Detecting and Archaeology in England*. London: Council for British Archaeology and English Heritage.

Gregory, T. and A.J.G. Rogerson 1984. Metal-detecting in archaeological excavation. *Antiquity* LVIII, 179–84.

Lufkin, M. 2000. Web sales of ancient coins raise legal questions. *Art Newspaper* no. 100, 62.

Stead, I. 1998. *The Salisbury Hoard*. Stroud: Tempus.

Stoertz, C. 1997. *Ancient Landscapes of the Yorkshire Wolds*. Swindon.

## 8    *Britannia waives the rules? The licensing of archaeological material for export from the UK*

Neil Brodie

## INTRODUCTION

In the UK the trade in archaeological and other cultural material is clandestine and not readily amenable to public exposure. Provenances (find spots) or ownership histories of objects are not routinely provided and so cover is provided for the entry on to the market of material which was obtained originally by illicit means. Many reasons are offered for this reluctance to reveal the pedigree of an object offered up for sale, from the wish of a collector to remain anonymous to that of a dealer not to reveal a source. But, nonetheless, for whatever reason, licit and illicit material become hopelessly mixed and, in consequence, it is not possible to identify which unprovenanced objects on offer in the salerooms of London might originally have been obtained illicitly.

This suppression or erasure of provenance-related information makes it difficult to mobilize public opinion against the marketing of illicit cultural material. Although it is clear that all around the world archaeological sites and cultural institutions are being looted to supply the market, it is hard to demonstrate with any degree of accuracy the magnitude of the trade in looted material or the scale of the material damage caused. Without such indicators it is difficult to convey to the general public the gravity of the situation, or to gain their sympathy. Furthermore, while details of provenance are withheld, a well-meaning collector cannot choose only to buy licit material, but must instead take pot luck.

The 1970 UNESCO Convention on the Means of Prohibiting and Preventing the Illicit Import, Export and Transfer of Ownership of Cultural Property and 1995 UNIDROIT Convention on Stolen and Illegally Exported Cultural Objects have been drafted specifically to combat the illicit trade in cultural material but, until December 2000, the UK Government had consistently refused to ratify either one. Again, it is difficult for those concerned about the effects of the trade in illicit cultural material to bring quantifiable arguments to bear when relevant information about ownership histories and find spots is deliberately withheld or obscured by members of the trade who argue, without revealing their sources, that the volume of the trade in illicit material is in fact small and does not justify the cost to the taxpayer of ratification. Thus, those who stand to lose from ratification are in the happy position of being able to withhold information which has a direct bearing on Government policy, and are able to stifle any properly informed discussion of the issues involved. The UK Government is then reluctant to take action to curtail what it sees to be a profitable and legitimate – and largely harmless – trade.

However, the ramifications of suppressed provenances go far beyond politics. There is increasing evidence that drug barons and other criminals are able to take advantage of the secrecy in which the international trade carries on for laundering the proceeds of their crimes. In recent years there have been several seizures in Miami of stolen or smuggled antiquities, most recently of material from Corinth museum, and Miami seems to have become a centre of the illicit trade on account of the large quantities of 'dirty money' in circulation there (Tasker 1999). The withholding of provenance for purposes of client confidentiality cannot be justified in such an environment.

London and, by extension the UK, is a major transit point for the trade. The export of cultural material from the UK is controlled and subject to licensing by the Department of Culture, Media and Sport (DCMS). In theory, this is one area where the hidden flows of the trade must come out into the light, to be recorded, described and quantified. However, the DCMS does not allow public access to its records, nor can it provide detailed information upon request. This study, compiled largely from secondary sources, suggests that, in addition, the operation of the licensing system is far from perfect and that there is evidence of widespread misunderstanding or evasion of its requirements.

In what follows an account is provided of the export licensing system of the UK insofar as it applies to archaeological material. It has two objectives. First, to obtain data which might be used to assess the scale and reveal the organization of the trade. Second, to argue that the licensing system does nothing to hinder the trade of illicit material.

## HISTORY

Tombs have been robbed of their precious contents for millennia, but it has been suggested that it was the appearance of individual production in Classical Greece that first created the necessary conditions for an art market, and that the plunder of archaeological sites for their 'art' soon followed (Schnapp 1996: 58). It then fell to the Italian heirs of the classical tradition to pass the first law protecting archaeological remains when, in 1162, Trajan's Column in Rome was declared a protected monument. By the fifteenth century Pope Pius II had extended protection to all monuments or their remains, and in 1462 he passed what is perhaps the earliest portable antiquities law when he prohibited the export of works of art from the Papal States (Bator 1983: 37; Schnapp 1996: 94). Today, control of archaeological material by regulation of its export is practised in most countries of the world, except those such as the US which are wealthy enough to buy back material on the open market.

In his discussion of the international trade in art, Bator distinguished between two different types of export regulation, which he termed total embargo and screening (ibid.: 38). He argued that any system of total embargo, by which he meant the complete prohibition of export, was bound to fail. The cost and intrusion of its administration would render it unenforceable while, by failing to satisfy international demand, a black market would emerge to be fed by a profitable illicit trade (ibid.: 42). In contrast, he felt that screening, which usually operates by means of a licensing system and acts to retain important objects, would allow the majority of intended exports to leave and thus was likely to be more successful. International demand would be satisfied without the creation of a black market and the amount of material retained so small that enforcement would be possible (ibid.: 39, 45).

Bator considered the British system of screening to be effective, in that it is generally complied with, and thus discourages an illicit trade, and he went on to examine the reasons for its apparently successful operation. He observed that the British system operates in a generally law-abiding and – crucially – affluent society. This latter factor allows the domestic market to mount effective opposition to international competition so that a significant quantity of material is retained. But Bator's study is focused upon art, not archaeology, and he also pointed out that in the UK the large part of material is owned (art and antiques), not found (antiquities), and that archaeological looting is not – or, at least, was not at the time of his study – a problem (ibid.: 46, 48). Export regulation by screening would be irrelevant in a country suffering from the indiscriminate looting of its archaeological sites (ibid.: 49).

Nevertheless, despite Bator's reservations, the British system is often held up as a paradigm for other countries to emulate, offering as it does minimum bureaucracy, protection of the more significant pieces, and the benefit derived by the nation's economy from a thriving art trade (Morrison 1995: 206). Commentators on both sides of the 'antiquities trade fence' stress that it is pragmatic, or fair (Anderson 1996: 123; Weihe 1996: 65; Ede 1998: 129), so much so that in 1994 the curator-in-chief of the Louvre appealed for France to adopt the British system (Merryman 1996: 14). However, a study directed specifically towards the protection of portable antiquities concluded that the British system was '. . . lamentably inadequate to prevent loss of antiquities . . .' (Bennett and Brand 1983: 162) and its effectiveness in obstructing the illicit trade has never been seriously examined, a woeful omission given London's status as a major centre of the antiquities trade.

## THE WAVERLEY REPORT

During the eighteenth and nineteenth centuries of its economic predominance, the UK amassed large quantities of cultural material of all kinds and from all quarters of the globe. By the beginning of the twentieth century, however, its fortunes were on the slide and what had by then come to be seen as the nation's heritage was beginning to be bought up by wealthy collectors and institutions abroad. In 1913 the Curzon Committee reported that over 500 important paintings had been lost to the nation, although it recommended that no system of export control be instituted (Maurice and Turnor 1992: 274). Subsequent calls for control in 1921 and 1922 were rejected by the Chancellor of the Exchequer and no action was taken (ibid.: 274).

The present system of export control dates back to the 1939–45 war when the Import, Export and Customs Powers (Defence) Act 1939 was enacted to prevent any flow of capital out of the country, thereby protecting the foreign exchange reserves of the UK. In 1940, antiques and works of art became subject to this control and at the end of the war it was realized that the Act could be used to stop the export of cultural material (ibid.: 274). The operation of this export control was not well established, however, so in 1949 a committee under the chairmanship of Viscount Waverley was appointed by the Chancellor of the Exchequer to investigate means of controlling the export of works of art. Its report, known now as the 'Waverley Report', was published in 1952 (Committee on the Export of Works of Art etc. 1952).

The primary objective of the Waverley Committee was to design a system of export control which would prevent the loss from the UK of what were termed 'national treasures', without at the same time placing undue hindrance upon the free trade of other cultural material. 'National treasures' is a term used frequently in the Waverley Report, which is focused largely on paintings and antique furniture; there is little specific mention of archaeological material. Indeed, with regard to antiquities and ethnographic material, the Report recommended that:

> Export control is an unsuitable means of safeguarding objects of this type . . . and that, if experience shows that any categories can be freed from control altogether, that step should be taken as soon as it is possible to do so.
>
> (ibid.: 42)

During its deliberations the Waverley Committee consulted widely and invited comment from a range of interested parties and expert witnesses. Only four paragraphs of the Report (which extends to over 400) were devoted exclusively to the particular problems of archaeological material. Although various points were made by witnesses called upon to advise the Committee only two are listed (ibid.: 42):

- The undesirability of returning type specimens to places where there are no facilities for looking after them, or where the climatic environment is unfavourable.
- Antiquities are always being dug up and that archaeologists are usually prepared to come to terms about the distribution of types.

The identities or interests of these witnesses were not revealed, and whatever archaeological opinion would have made of these statements in 1952 it is certain that today there is little to recommend them. There is no mention of assemblage, context or provenance – all now key concepts in archaeological practice.

A further eleven paragraphs of the Waverley Report were devoted to the problem of re-exports. It noted cases where export licences had been refused for objects which had only recently been imported and recognized the deleterious effect of such decisions on the trade and the confidence of buyers in the British market. The Committee emphasized that it was concerned with export control from the point of view of safeguarding national treasures and recommended the establishment of a fifty-year time limit so that export of objects imported within that period could be claimed as of right and a licence automatically granted (ibid.: 42). The volume of the antiquities trade at the time seems to have been small. The British Museum for instance advised that the majority of Greek and Roman antiquities exported were from long-established British collections (ibid.: 12).

Since the Waverley Report there has been increasing concern over the fate of archaeological, and indeed of other types of collections, but until the Palmer enquiry (Palmer 2000), there had been no positive initiative from the UK Government. The licensing system today is still focused on the concept of the individual object as a treasure or work of art and there is no regard to the cultural meaning or historical significance of its original context.

In general, the Waverley Committee felt that export control should be confined to limited categories of objects of high importance and recommended two mechanisms by means of which importance could be assessed. One was, quite simply, the monetary value of an object. A series of monetary thresholds were proposed for different categories of material and only objects of a price exceeding the relevant threshold would require a licence. If this criterion of monetary value was met, then the licence application would be referred to an expert adviser, who might assess the cultural or historical importance of an object by reference to the Waverley criteria (ibid.: 36). The criteria are:

I.   Is the object so closely connected with our history and national life that its departure would be a misfortune?
II.  Is it of outstanding aesthetic importance?
III. Is it of outstanding significance for the study of some particular branch of art, learning or history?

The judgement of the expert adviser would then be subject to the further arbitration of an appointed Reviewing Committee, which would also be responsible for overseeing the operation of the control. In practice, only a few licence applications for archaeological objects are referred to the Reviewing Committee, and deferrals are usually granted after satisfaction of the third criterion. Interestingly, though, in the Waverley Report, archaeological material was only mentioned in connection with the first criterion which, it was thought, might apply to '. . . such archaeological discoveries as the Battersea Shield and the Sutton Hoo Ship Burial in the British Museum, which are not protected by the law of Treasure Trove' (ibid.: 37).

Mention of the Sutton Hoo burial carries an implicit understanding of the importance of assemblage and context, which is not otherwise mentioned, as it is the context, and not the individual items, which provides the connection with British history and which imbues the objects with a historical rather than aesthetic importance. If Sutton Hoo had been excavated illegally, without record, most if not all of the objects individually might be licensed for export, although, as an assemblage, they would not.

As a result of the Waverley Report, two separate categories of foreign material are now recognized by the licensing system: material which has been in the UK for over 50 years and material imported within that time. Thus a distinction is drawn between what is considered to be part of the national heritage – material in the UK for more than fifty years – and what is considered to be traded material – in the UK for less than fifty years. The operation of the licensing system pays great attention to the first category – indeed, the system is designed specifically to protect the national heritage so that many objects will be reviewed individually. For the second category, however, the traded material, the requirements are less stringent and licences are granted more or less automatically. A cynical commentator might be forgiven for observing that the system functions to protect the heritage of the UK while at the same time allowing the British economy to benefit from marketing the heritage of others.

## EC REGULATION NO. 3911/92

The system of export control changed in 1993 with the implementation into British law of EC Regulation No. 3911/92 on the export of cultural goods. This Regulation was drafted in response to the emergence of the European single market with few internal border controls (Goyder 1996).

Although Article 34 of the Treaty of Rome – which established the European Union – prohibits any restriction or control of trade between member states, it is qualified by Article 36, which allows for the control of 'national treasures possessing artistic, historic or archaeological value'. Thus it is left for each member state to control the export of cultural material from its own territory, and all member states have legislation which places some degree of control (ibid.: 2). Nonetheless, with the gradual disappearance of internal border controls, these laws have become increasingly difficult to police, and the spectre is raised of archaeological material flowing from states (such as Italy) with a prohibitive regime into those more liberal countries (such as the UK) and from there out of the European Union. Thus the Regulation was intended to establish a uniform system of control for all cultural material exported outside the European Union, no matter what its EU state of origin.

The EC Regulation imposes a zero monetary threshold on all archaeological material and so requires that all antiquities exported to destinations outside the European Union, whatever their value, and whatever their origin, should be subject to licence. However, while it was being drafted, in the UK this aspect of the Regulation attracted opposition from commercial interests for what Brian Cook has called two reasons and an excuse (1995: 189). The reasons were first, that it would be bad for the London art market and, second, that the massive increase in licence applications would place an insupportable burden upon the government department called upon to administer the system; the excuse was that it would commit the UK to enforcing the export laws of other countries. Under pressure from the trade, the UK Government negotiated an exclusion clause.

The Government had been prepared to block negotiations in Brussels over this issue of licensing archaeological exports and as a result it was successful in obtaining an amendment to the Regulation so that objects of limited archaeological or scientific importance are now excluded from licensing requirements (Morrison 1995: 208–9). In response to concerns over illicit exports expressed by various Mediterranean countries the Reviewing Committee (1991: 6) responded that '. . . the trade in cultural goods is an important area of trade and . . . the UK art trade operates a voluntary code of practice, agreeing not to handle objects which it has reasonable cause to believe are of dubious provenance'. Some later Reports have taken a less sanguine view (1994: 9, 11) and in 1992 the Committee felt that 'It may be . . . preferable to handle only objects of clearly identified provenance even if that would mean restricting the business to the contents of the sculpture gallery of Charles Towneley and the Duke of Marlborough's gem cabinet' (1992: 4). Needless to say, this happy circumstance has not materialized.

At present the licensing system is administered by the Export Licensing Unit of the DCMS and the Reviewing Committee reports to the Secretary of State for Culture, Media and Sport. Guidelines to the operation of the system are set out in the 1997 booklet *Export Licensing for Cultural Goods*. In general, exports to destinations outside the European Union require an EC licence while exports to destinations within the European Union require a UK licence. The EC licence was introduced in 1993 with the implementation into British Law of EC Regulation 3911/92.

**Table 8.1**  Total value in thousands of pounds of exports of cultural material (Reviewing Committee 1995: 61; 1996: 57; 1997: 55; 1998: 51)

|         | Total exports | Exports outside the EU | Percentage |
|---------|---------------|------------------------|------------|
| 1994–95 | 1,269,057     | 1,171,490              | 92.3       |
| 1995–96 | 1,298,144     | 1,189,532              | 91.6       |
| 1996–97 | 1,312,281     | 1,261,421              | 96.1       |

DCMS figures show that the large majority of exports (of all classes of cultural material, and so presumably also antiquities) are directed outside the European Union (Table 8.1).

## EXPORT LICENSING REQUIREMENTS FOR ARCHAEOLOGICAL MATERIAL FOUND IN UK SOIL OR ITS TERRITORIAL WATERS

### Requirements

At the present time all archaeological material more than 50 years old found in UK soil or its territorial waters, whatever its value, requires a licence for export and is subject to expert review.

### Procedure

Licence application forms are obtained from the Export Licensing Unit, and completed forms are returned to the Unit. A description of the object to be exported must be provided but there is no requirement for an accurate statement of provenance. Applications are then forwarded to an expert adviser, who will decide whether a licence should be granted or the application deferred. The adviser will judge the application by reference to the Waverley criteria, and if the object fails to satisfy any of the criteria then the licence is granted. If, however, the object is of Waverley standard (i.e. satisfies one or more of the Waverley criteria), the licence application is referred to the Reviewing Committee on the Export of Works of Art. If the Reviewing Committee agrees that the object is of Waverley standard, it recommends to the Secretary of State that a decision on the licence application should be deferred for a specified period so that a British institution might come forward to purchase the item at a fair price, thereby guaranteeing its retention within the UK. If, on the other hand, the Reviewing Committee decides that the object in question is not of Waverley standard, it recommends that an export licence be granted.

Staff at the British Museum's Departments of Prehistoric and Roman Antiquities and Medieval and Later Antiquities act as expert advisers. They regularly review the catalogues of the major auction houses (Sotheby's, Christie's, Bonhams and Phillips), but not of smaller dealers. They occasionally see licence applications from smaller dealers but not routinely.

### Discussion

It is of interest to know what quantity of material might be moving out of the country without licence. Table 8.2 shows the number of export licences issued per year for archaeological material of UK origin over a nine-year interval. It is clear that the numbers are not high, and the conclusion must follow that many objects are exported without a licence. Some cases of this sort are quite well known. The Icklingham Bronzes for instance, bought by

**Table 8.2**  Licences granted for archaeological material of UK origin

| Year | Prehistoric and Romano-British | Medieval and Later |
|------|------|------|
| 1989–90 | 1 | 81 |
| 1990–91 | 21 | 4008 |
| 1991–92 | 12 | 9 |
| 1992–93 | 3 | 14 |
| 1993–94 | 54 | 18 |
| 1994–95 | 369 | 5 |
| 1995–96 | 88 | 28 |
| 1996–97 | 117 | 201 |
| 1997–98 | 175 | 63 |

*Note*: The bar indicates the introduction of the EC licence in 1993. (The reason for the inflated figure noted under Medieval and Later for the year 1990–91 is not clear, but it might have been caused by the temporary export of material for exhibition)

the Ariadne Galleries of New York, were shipped to the US without any licence being issued (Stead 1998: 151). Many objects from the Salisbury Hoard were also exported but not a single licence application was made (ibid.: 151).

Sometimes, at least, the failure to obtain a licence might owe more to uncertainty over licensing requirements than to deliberate evasion. One US company, for instance, organizes treasure hunting tours to the UK and is careful to meet all legal requirements and works in collaboration with British museums. In the past, however, it has only applied for export licences for objects which would be designated under English law as 'treasure', and was unaware of the need to license all objects. It estimates that for one of its tour groups, comprising about 40 metal detectorists, it would require many thousands of licences, which gives some idea of the amount of unlicensed material which has left the country. In 1999, however, after consultation with the Export Licensing Unit, a system was established whereby everything discovered during this particular company's tours will be listed and passed by the British Museum and a licence will be issued. Nonetheless, other tours continue to operate unlicensed. If, in any one year, only a couple of hundred licence applications are reviewed while at the same time thousands of objects are exported by a single tour group, the true scale of unlicensed export is a matter only for speculation.

There is no necessary relationship between the monetary value of an antiquity and its archaeological significance – low-value objects might come from important sites – but it is clear from the recently established DCMS reporting scheme that huge numbers of low-value antiquities, which have often been found out of context, and which in consequence might be of little significance, are now being found in the UK (DCMS 1999). Unknown quantities of these finds are exported and, in theory, due to the zero monetary threshold, they all should require a licence. In practice, however, this is not happening.

It has been suggested in consequence that the Government might look again at the zero threshold, but to date it has not been revised (Morrison 1995: 208).

## EXPORT LICENSING REQUIREMENTS FOR ARCHAEOLOGICAL MATERIAL FOUND IN SOIL OR WATERS OUTSIDE THE UK AND ITS TERRITORIAL WATERS

*Requirements*

If an antiquity to be exported to a destination outside the European Union is more than 100 years old, and from any country in the world outside the UK, then a licence is required. However, objects considered to be in one of the following categories of limited archaeological or scientific interest do not require a licence:

- numismatic items of a standard type which are published in a reference work on numismatics;
- objects, other than numismatic items, which possess no special or rare features of form, size, material, decoration, inscription or iconography, and which are not in an especially fine condition for the type of object.

Objects falling within these categories do not require a licence provided that:

- they do not form part of a recognized archaeological collection of special historical significance;
- they are not the direct product of excavations, finds and archaeological sites within a member state [of the European Union], i.e. they have not come straight onto the market after being recently discovered;
- they are lawfully on the market. Objects which are stolen would not qualify;
- they do not fall within any other category of the Annex [of EC Regulation 3911/92]. Category A2 in particular may be relevant. That category covers elements forming an integral part of a dismembered monument more than 100 years old.

It is worth emphasizing this last point, made in the DCMS leaflet *Guidance to Exporters of Antiquities*, that elements forming an integral part of artistic, historical or religious monuments of an age exceeding 100 years which have been dismembered are subject to a zero monetary threshold and *cannot* be excluded from licensing requirements on the grounds of limited interest. Thus, the large number of architectural fragments from Gandharan, Tibetan, Cambodian etc. temples, palaces and monasteries which are presently flowing through the UK should all be licensed – but whether they are or not is not known.

Objects which have been imported from any country within 50 years of the date of export from the UK and which require a licence, are automat-

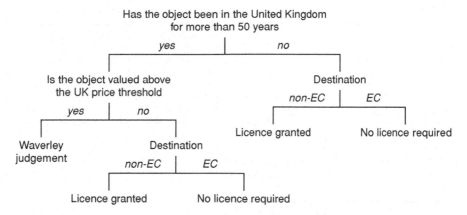

**Figure 8.1** Export licensing requirements for archaeological material not of UK origin and not of limited interest

ically granted one. For an object which has been exported from another EU country after 1 January 1993, an application for a licence has to be accompanied by documentary proof of legal despatch from the EU country of origin. If the requirement for a licence is waived then no check is made on the legality of its previous export.

If an object to be exported has been in the UK for more than 50 years, is more than 50 years old, and is valued at over £39,600, an expert adviser will judge the application by reference to the Waverley Criteria, and a licence is required.

The system is summarized in Figure 8.1.

*Procedure*

In practice, auction (and some dealers') catalogues are circulated to expert advisers in relevant museums who decide in advance of a sale which lots would require a licence for export, or might satisfy one or more of the Waverley criteria and be referred to the Reviewing Committee. Lists of lots requiring licences can be obtained at pre-sale viewings. For dealers who do not produce a catalogue, licence applications are left to their own discretion and they provide the Export Licensing Unit with quarterly returns.

*Discussion*

In theory, the only antiquities not of UK origin which are judged by the Waverley criteria are those which have been in the UK for more than 50 years and which are valued over the relevant monetary threshold (which in 2000 was £39,600). In practice, this seems usually to be the case.

The DCMS cannot reveal how many, or what percentage of, antiquities of non-UK origin are licensed for export. However, at the public viewings which precede auctions printed lists are available to indicate which lots will

**Table 8.3** Number of lots for sale by auction requiring a licence for export

|  | No. of lots | No. requiring licence | Percentage |
|---|---|---|---|
| Bonhams 25.11.1999 | 310 | 13 | 4.2 |
| Bonhams 22.4.1999 | 741 | 68 | 9.2 |
| Bonhams 13.4.2000 | 458 | 57 | 11.7 |
| Christie's 12.4.2000 | 385 | 71 | 18.4 |

**Table 8.4** Total number of cultural objects (in the UK for less than 50 years) licensed for export

|  | No. of objects licensed |
|---|---|
| 1995–96 | 6,869 |
| 1996–97 | 7,728 |
| 1997–98 | 8,151 |

need a licence for export. The figures for some recent auctions (for antiquities not of UK origin) are noted in Table 8.3.

A preliminary conclusion to be drawn from these figures is that something in the region of 11 per cent of all antiquities not of UK origin exported should require a licence.

It is not possible to estimate how many antiquities which arrived in the past 50 years (i.e. traded) are exported in any one year, although in 1993 the dealers themselves suggested that upwards of half a million objects a year were leaving the country (Morrison 1995: 208). Assuming that half a million objects a year are indeed exported, and from the previous paragraph it is assumed that perhaps 11 per cent require a licence, then something in the order of 55,000 licences a year should be issued. This is not the case. The total number of licences issued per year by the Export Licensing Unit are shown in Table 8.4, and these figures are for all classes of cultural material, including fine art and antique furniture, not just antiquities.

Clearly, the number of licences issued for antiquities must be lower, and considerably lower than the expected 55,000. There are three possible explanations:

- There is widespread evasion of the licensing system.
- The figure of half a million objects suggested by the trade in 1993 was grossly inflated, perhaps to over-emphasize the economic importance of the trade so as to discourage the government from implementing fully the EC Regulation.
- The major part of antiquities sold are not exported, in which case it is difficult to see how their sale can benefit the UK economy as the trade continues to maintain.

It is not certain to what degree dealers comply with, or even understand, the present system of export control. In 1999 one dealer stated that a licence is only applied for when an object is sold for more than £39,600, which is clearly in contravention of present rules and harks back to the pre-1993 system. Another dealer, when approached, merely stated that the UK only operates the system out of selfish interest – it wants to keep the best pieces for itself!

Any cultural object which has come into the UK from another EU member state since 1993 must have valid export documentation from its country of origin before the DCMS will issue a licence for its export. This is to stop material from parts of Europe with a stringent export regime being exported from those (particularly the UK) with a more liberal regime. In practice, however, there seem to be few checks on original documentation because, as pointed out above, most non-UK material is excluded from EC licensing requirements, presumably on the grounds of limited importance. If an auction lot does not require a licence, it can be exported without any check being made on its original documentation.

A study of classical Greek and Italian pottery offered for sale at the four recent auctions referred to above showed that, out of a total of 151 lots, only 24 had any kind of a provenance and of the remaining 127 only 9 required a licence for export. Thus, 118 lots (183 pots) could have been exported without being passed through the licensing procedure, and with no check being made on their recent history. Included in this number were at least nine Apulian vases. These vases, made during classical times in the area of what is now Puglia, Italy, have been exhaustively studied and catalogued by Australian scholars. This means that any Apulian vase appearing on the market today without a provenance has almost certainly been looted. Official Italian statistics of illegal excavation show that between 1993 and 1997, of all Italian regions, Puglia was probably the hardest hit. Twenty-one per cent of all looted antiquities recovered nationwide by the Carabinieri were from this area (Elia 2001).

The failure in the UK of expert advisers to ask that such material be licensed means that the original documentation of antiquities such as the Apulian vases is not checked – there is no check made on the legality of their original export from Italy. This seems to undermine the purpose of the EC Regulation which is to prevent the illegal export of cultural material from one member state to another, and it can only facilitate the movement of illicit material through the market. In the case of Italy, its archaeological heritage is ultimately protected, if that is the right word, by the weak British control rather than the stronger Italian, and it is incorrect to argue that the large illicit trade in Italian material is the direct result of Italy's draconian export regime.

It was suggested above that the licensing system was failing for archaeological material of UK origin because, at zero, the monetary threshold is too low, and the huge number of licences which in theory are needed would make the system difficult to administer, although in practice the requirements seem often to be evaded, deliberately or not. For material not of UK origin, however, the reverse seems to be case. The exclusions negotiated at the time of drafting the EC Regulation allow the major part of exported antiquities to leave the country unlicensed. Presumably many of these antiquities are from looted sites. There seems to be a good case for withdrawing the exclusions and replacing them with a fixed monetary threshold, above which all antiquities exported should be licensed.

## DEPARTMENT OF TRADE AND INDUSTRY STATISTICS

The annual reports of the Reviewing Committee also provide export statistics derived from HM Customs and Excise trade data, although there is little correspondence between these statistics (compiled by the Department of Trade and Industry (DTI)) and those which record the value of export licences issued by the DCMS. As shown in Table 8.5 the DTI figures are consistently lower, and by significant amounts.

The DTI figures are taken from the Standard International Trade Classification (SITC) Category 896 (Works of Art, Collectors Pieces and Antiques), which encompasses most cultural material licensed for export (including paintings etc.), so there should be a broad measure of agreement between the two sets of statistics. If anything, the value of material licensed should be lower than the value of material exported, as not all material exported is licensed. It should not be almost three times as high, as it is in the figures for 1995–97.

When approached, the DCMS suggests that objects between 50 and 100 years of age are excluded from the DTI figures, and perhaps aeroplanes and motor cars too. Other classes of material recorded by DCMS but not listed in SITC Category 896 might also be suggested: books; scientific drawings, manuscripts; photographs; scientific material. But still, over the years in question here (1994–97), these classes together only accounted for about five to eight per cent of the total value of material of British origin licensed for export, which is not enough to explain the discrepancy. The DCMS statistics also include material from National Museums and Galleries leaving the country temporarily for exhibition, but it is not clear what proportion of the total can be accounted for by loans. Again, however, it is not likely to account for the large size of the discrepancy.

**Table 8.5** Value in thousands of pounds of cultural material licensed (DCMS) and exported (DTI) (Reviewing Committee 1995: 12; 1996: 14; 1997: 55)

|         | DTI       | DCMS      |
|---------|-----------|-----------|
| 1994–95 | 1,269,057 | 3,133,835 |
| 1995–96 | 1,298,144 | 3,371,449 |
| 1996–97 | 1,312,281 | 2,976,291 |

**Table 8.6** Annual value of exports from the UK to the US of SITC category 896.50. Official US trade statistics for imports and UK statistics for exports

|  | 1996 | 1997 | 1998 |
| --- | --- | --- | --- |
| Total value of exports to US in thousands of pounds | 22,320 | 18,214 | 33,172 |
| Total value of imports from UK in thousands of dollars | 9,100 | 13,700 | 13,700 |

However, the DTI statistics themselves are far from convincing. The DTI allows public access to trade statistics, although for cultural material the SITC classification is far from ideal as the recording categories are too broad and imprecise. Nevertheless, figures for exports to the US of category 896.50 (collections and collectors pieces of zoological, botanical, mineralogical, anatomical, historical, archaeological, palaeontological, ethnographic or numismatic interest) are shown in Table 8.6. Unfortunately, however, the official US trade statistics which record the value of imports from the UK for the same category (896.50), also shown in Table 8.6, do not agree with the equivalent figures provided by the DTI for UK exports.

Clearly, there is a huge discrepancy between the figures provided for US imports from the UK, and those for UK exports to the US. UK exports are valued at something like two to three times more than US imports. The DTI can list thirteen reasons for discrepancies such as these, which include reporting timelags, differences in SITC categorization and fraudulent declarations. The cause of the discrepancy in this particular case is not immediately clear.

## DISCUSSION

In his study of the art trade, Bator argued that a strong export control would be likely to encourage the development of an illicit trade, and his argument has been taken up since by those who favour unregulated trade of cultural material (e.g. Merryman 1996: 36). However, in answer to this argument, it has been pointed out that although an illegal trade, almost by definition, is caused by an export embargo, the total amount of material lost to a country might still be much lower than to those with a more liberal export regime (Prott and O'Keefe 1989: 482; Coggins 1998: 55). The issue is looting, not the legality or otherwise of the ensuing trade, and the cultural heritage of nations with liberal or no export laws is still looted, notably the US (Vitelli 1996: 111).

There seem to be two reasons for this. First, collectors are interested in the unique, not the mundane, and would not want to buy the large quantities of what, from the art trade's point of view, are low-quality objects (Coggins 1996: 51). Thus, the looting would continue in pursuit of the unique. Certainly, the high quality of much of the material known to have left Turkey illegally in recent years has been remarked upon (Blake 1997: 250).

On the other hand, and in seeming contradiction, one feature of the growth of the trade has in recent years been the move 'downmarket' (Tubb and Brodie 2001). Large quantities of low-value objects are sold at regional fairs, by mail order or on the Internet. The April 2000 sale of antiquities and fossils at London's exclusive emporium Fortnum and Mason's is another sign of this. Deliberate attempts are being made to create a sales environment which is less forbidding to the new customer, and objects are being marketed as items of decoration rather than works of art, albeit decorations with an intellectual or cultural edge. This is, in essence, the second reason why export deregulation will not work. Proponents of export deregulation assume a finite or inelastic demand, which might be met by a moderate increase in supply. Experience has shown, however, that demand is highly elastic, and that the market in cultural material is supply led. Marketing strategies aimed at increasing the customer base for lower value objects are but one sign of this. Another is the massive and recent growth in the Asian and Tribal 'art' markets, which are composed largely of archaeological or ethnographic material. Thus, relaxation of export controls might increase the supply of licit material, but this would be used to create a larger demand, so that the looting would continue, and – in all probability – increase.

But this still leaves the problem of Italy. How is it that a relatively wealthy country with a strict export regime suffers badly from the ongoing looting of its archaeological and cultural heritage? The answer is now clear: in an integrated Europe, Italy's export control is only as strong as that of its most liberal EU partner, in this case the UK. Yet the UK routinely allows the export of Italian archaeological material with no check whatsoever on its origin. Unprovenanced and unlicensed Italian vases have been noted in this study, and although it cannot (and in all likelihood never will) be known for certain what proportion were originally looted, it is hardly credible that none were. Certainly it is known that in the past vases of the kind shown here not to require a licence (nor a check on origin) have been excavated illegally, smuggled and sold openly in London (Watson 1997: 183). Thus Italy, not out of choice, actually has quite a liberal export control, and so the plunder goes on.

However, Italy's heritage isn't the only one to suffer from the UK's lax export control. There is increasing evidence to suggest that pre-Hispanic material from Central and South America is being routed through the UK, presumably because US customs officers will not subject shipments from British ports to the same degree of scrutiny. In 1997 the London market was reported to be glutted with smuggled pre-Hispanic antiquities with 60 per cent of sales revenue coming from the US (Windsor 1997). After the rich Moche tomb at Sipán, in Peru, was sacked in the 1980s large quantities of material were first moved to the UK, before being passed on to the US (Kirkpatrick 1992: 100).

In May 2000 the DCMS appointed a panel of enquiry to advise the UK Government upon the trade in illicit cultural material. Among other things, it observed that the export licensing system offers a '. . . currently under-used means of imposing constraints on the movement of those cultural objects which have recently entered the UK after their illegal exportation from an overseas country.' (Palmer 2000: 27). It went on to recommend the formation of a sub-committee of the Reviewing Committee which would oversee the function of the export licensing system as regards the trade in illicit cultural material. It is proposed (ibid.: 28) that this sub-committee could usefully:

(a) advise from time to time on types of cultural property currently subject to looting and therefore needing extra checks on provenance before export licences are granted;

(b) monitor the illegal unlicensed outflow of archaeological material from the UK, including material offered for sale on the Internet;

(c) advise on the information on provenance that should be requested from applicants for export licences;

(d) advise on the due diligence that should be required from applicants;

(e) advise on declarations about provenance and due diligence that should be made by applicants, particularly whether it should continue to be voluntary whether to declare recent exports and imports;

(f) press the European Commission to redesign the export licence form so as to make the requirements for statements about provenance clearer;

(g) press the European Commission to enable export licence applications to be made electronically;

(h) advise on the extent to which expert advisers should investigate or comment on matters of provenance for different categories of material;

(i) monitor the impact, problems and benefits of the 'limited importance' exemption and to advise on the criteria that should be applied to judge whether items of 'limited importance' are legally on the market;

(j) advise what action should be taken if the staff of the Export Licensing Unit or expert advisers have any suspicions about the provenance of an object;

(k) consider whether some of the information collected during the export licensing process could be made available for the benefit of scholarship and particularly for the recording of portable antiquities found in England and Wales, without compromising legitimate considerations of confidentiality;

(l) advise on the most useful ways of presenting an annual statistical report on the export of cultural property from the UK and the volume and detailed categories of items licensed for export.

The panel further proposed that in the case of objects imported into the UK within the last 50 years for which an export licence is sought, the same checks should be carried out as are currently made for objects that have been imported from another EU state (ibid.: 28). It also noted 'that individual owners may have legitimate reasons for not wishing their names to be published in [auction] catalogues, we feel that it is desirable to publish provenance histories even without naming individual owners'.

These proposals, if implemented, will institute a comprehensive system of export record and control, which will also make information available for public and political debate. The EC Licence application form requires a description of the object to be exported, which for objects originating outside the UK goes some way towards providing a provenance. Thus, the information collected would allow material flows to be identified and quantified. Clearly, however, the large volume of material exported every year precludes total coverage; the resources are not available to allow a check to be made on every object passing out of the country. Rather than be guided by monetary thresholds, with the distortion they entail, favouring object value over context, the panel has wisely suggested that the system could be administered by a programme of spot checks, so that, in effect, a random sample of material will be passed through the licensing system. Thus, a deterrent will be maintained at limited cost to the taxpayer.

It is also interesting to note that the Financial Action Task Force (an intergovernmental body established by the 1989 G-7 summit in Paris to combat money laundering) noted in 1998 that an effective regime of export control deters the use of cultural objects for money laundering.

In closing, the Waverley Report called for general cooperation between museums, collectors and dealers, and recommended in particular that dealers provide information and guidance regarding sales (Committee on the Export of Works of Art etc. 1952: 64). It was intended that such cooperation would reduce the burden on the Reviewing Committee, but the policy of nondisclosure promoted by the trade as a professional principle would seem to fly in the face of this recommendation.

## ACKNOWLEDGEMENTS

Thanks are due to Roger Bland, John Cherry, David Gurney, Lynn Gates, Stuart Needham, James Normandi and Graham Suggett for information supplied. The opinions expressed, however, remain my own.

## REFERENCES

Anderson, M.L. 1996. Art market challenges for American museums. In *Legal Aspects of the International Trade in Art,* M. Briat and J.A. Freedberg (eds), 121–4. The Hague: Kluwer Law International.
Bator, P.M. 1983. *The International Trade in Art.* Chicago: University of Chicago Press.
Bennett, G.J. and C.M. Brand 1983. Conservation, control and heritage – public law and portable antiquities. *Anglo-American Law Review* 12, 141–73.

Blake, J. 1997. Export embargoes and the international antiquities market – the Turkish experience. *Art, Antiquity and Law* 2, 233–50.

Coggins, C. 1996. A licit international traffic in ancient art? In *Legal Aspects of the International Trade in Art*, M. Briat and J.A. Freedberg (eds), 47–56. The Hague: Kluwer Law International.

Coggins, C. 1998. United States and cultural property legislation: observations of a combatant. *International Journal of Cultural Property* 7, 52–68.

Committee on the Export of Works of Art etc. (1952). *The Export of Works of Art, etc. Report of a committee appointed by the Chancellor of the Exchequer.* London: HMSO.

Cook, B. 1995. The antiquities trade: a curator's view. In *Antiquities Trade or Betrayed: Legal, Ethical and Conservation Issues*, K.W. Tubb (ed.), 181–92. London: Archetype/UKIC.

DCMS 1999. *Portable Antiquities. Annual Report 1997–98.* London: DCMS.

Elia, R.J. 2001. Analysis of the looting, selling, and collecting of Apulian Red-Figure vases: a quantitative approach. In *Trade in Illicit Antiquities: the Destruction of the World's Archaeological Heritage*, N.J. Brodie, J. Doole and C. Renfrew (eds), 145–53. Cambridge: McDonald Institute for Archaeological Research.

Goyder, J. 1996. The E.C. Regulation and directive and their effect on continental export control regimes. In *Art Export Licensing and the International Market.* Leicester: Institute of Art and Law.

Kirkpatrick, S.D. 1992. *The Lords of Sipán: a True Story of Pre-Inca Tombs, Archaeology and Crime.* New York: Henry Holt.

Maurice, C. and R. Turnor 1992. The export licensing rules in the United Kingdom and the Waverley Criteria. *International Journal of Cultural Property* 1: 273–95.

Merryman, J.H. 1996. A licit international trade in cultural objects. In *Legal Aspects of the International Trade in Art*, M. Briat and J.A. Freedberg (eds), 3–46. The Hague: Kluwer Law International.

Morrison, C.R. 1995. United Kingdom Export Policies in relation to antiquities. In *Antiquities Trade or Betrayed: Legal, Ethical and Conservation Issues*, K.W. Tubb (ed.), 205–10. London: Archetype/UKIC.

Palmer, N. 2000. *Ministerial Advisory Panel on Illicit Trade.* London: Department for Culture, Media and Sport.

Prott, L.V. and P.J. O'Keefe 1989. *Law and the Cultural Heritage. Volume 3, Movement.* London: Butterworths.

Reviewing Committee 1991. *Export of Works of Art 1990–91. Thirty-seventh Report of the Reviewing Committee.* London: HMSO.

Reviewing Committee 1992. *Export of Works of Art 1991–92. Thirty-eighth Report of the Reviewing Committee.* London: HMSO.

Reviewing Committee 1993. *Export of Works of Art 1992–93. Thirty-ninth Report of the Reviewing Committee.* London: HMSO.

Reviewing Committee 1994. *Export of Works of Art 1993–94. Fortieth Report of the Reviewing Committee.* London: HMSO.

Reviewing Committee 1995. *Export of Works of Art 1994–95. Forty-first Report of the Reviewing Committee.* London: HMSO.

Reviewing Committee 1996. *Export of Works of Art 1995–96. Forty-second Report of the Reviewing Committee.* London: HMSO.

Reviewing Committee 1997. *Export of Works of Art 1996–97. Forty-third Report of the Reviewing Committee.* London: HMSO.

Reviewing Committee 1998. *Export of Works of Art 1997–98. Forty-fourth Report of the Reviewing Committee.* London: HMSO.

Schnapp, A. 1996. *The Discovery of the Past.* London: British Museum Press.

Stead, I. 1998. *The Salisbury Hoard.* Stroud: Tempus Publishing.

Tasker, F. 1999. Lowbrow art smugglers target a 'hot' South Florida market. *Miami Herald*, 19 September.

Tubb, K.W. and N.J. Brodie 2001. The Antiquities Trade in the United Kingdom. In *Destruction and Conservation of Cultural Property*, R.L. Layton, P.G. Stone and J. Thomas (eds), 102–16. London: Routledge.

Vitelli, K.D. 1996. An archaeologist's response to the draft principles to govern a licit international traffic in cultural property. In *Legal Aspects of the International Trade in Art*, M. Briat and J.A. Freedberg (eds), 109–12. The Hague: Kluwer Law International.

Watson, P. 1997. *Sotheby's: Inside Story*. London: Bloomsbury.

Weihe, H.K. 1996. Licit international trade in cultural objects for art's sake. In *Legal Aspects of the International Trade in Art*, M. Briat and J.A. Freedberg (eds), 57–66. The Hague: Kluwer Law International.

Windsor, J. 1997. Potted history up for sale. *The Independent*, 31 May, Long Weekend.

## 9 Mexico's archaeological heritage: a convergence and confrontation of interests

ENRIQUE NALDA

### INTRODUCTION

In Mexico, the debate over the significance, protection and management of the archaeological heritage is plagued by clichés. This would not be worthy of attention except for the fact that some of these clichés seem to have inspired fundamental aspects of the Mexican legislation that protects this heritage.

Mexican law today considers that everything generated by pre-Hispanic cultures found within the country's borders is archaeological heritage. This includes 'human remains, and those of flora and fauna, that are related to such cultures'. Underpinning this definition is the idea that everything that can contribute to an understanding of Mexican history is of national and social interest; the archaeological heritage is seen to be an object of study rather than one of protection. This is borne out by the word order of the preamble to the law: 'Research, protection, conservation, restoration and recuperation of archaeological monuments are of public interest . . .' (*Ley Federal de Monumentos y Zonas Arqueológicos, Artísticos e Históricos*, Chapter 1, Article 2).

The present legal framework was promoted by Mexican archaeologists who were inspired by the belief that there was a Mexican history to be written, one that could configure and reinforce national identity, one that would allow a better understanding of the present and provide the basis for more informed proposals for future self-achievement. Today, as in the 1970s when the law was passed, few archaeologists have any doubts about the reality of these objectives, the possibility of achieving them, or their apparent benefits.

Yet there are inconsistencies and obstacles in these positions, and they contradict other principles which are equally adhered to by the same archaeological community.

## ARCHAEOLOGICAL HERITAGE AND ACADEMIA

In defence of the idea that research should be privileged, Mexican archaeologists scorn other activities that, in the broader perspective of social interest,
can be considered as priorities. In reality, it is an extreme position from which
attempts to defend, protect and present the archaeological heritage and to
recover looted goods are seen as less important objectives, and it reflects
nothing but a concern with the professional character of the archaeological
community.

Many archaeologists seem to believe that excavation-based research comes
before everything else. The tasks of cataloguing and processing, even of
mapping archaeological sites, are perceived as indulgent concessions granted
to the institution with which they are affiliated. Archaeologists seem to be
unaware of the impossibility of doing research on something that does not
exist, unaware that the study of the past is only as important as the preservation of its remains. They neglect this obvious fact by repeating that, before
anything else, they are researchers.

This apparent dichotomy between research and 'everything else' is perhaps
best exemplified by the issue of reconstruction, or restoration, of archaeological monuments. Save for a few exceptions, archaeologists generally regard
this work as one step removed from archaeology's *raison d'être*, a position
clearly reflected by the distinction, very prevalent in the archaeological
community, between those 'who stick together stones' and those who are
'scientific'. This idea is also shared by almost every foreign researcher working
in Mesoamerica, who believe that it is up to local authorities to enhance the
social value of archaeological monuments – it is an 'archaeology for tourism',
a lesser activity. It enables them to survey large structures without having to
restore them, let alone present them to visitors. The advantages are obvious:
significantly lower costs of archaeological research and less complex work
teams. Archaeological excavations can end simply by backfilling pits and
trenches although, in the case of larger interventions, like Nohmul in northern
Belize, excavations are simply left open. There, a few years after the conclusion of work, it is now impossible to distinguish between the excavations of
'scientific archaeologists' and the products of massive looting.

A second aspect of this supposed division between 'tourist archaeology'
and 'scientific archaeology' is the dissemination of research. The publication
of research has always been of crucial concern to archaeologists yet, however
legitimately, they seem to be more concerned with achieving recognition
among peers than with attempting to repay the people who, ultimately, make
possible their excavations. Archaeologists are hardly encouraged to pursue
their stated objective, and justification, of making modern society easier to
understand by examination of its origins.

It is not surprising, in this context, that archaeologists regard the *mise en
valeur* of monuments and sites as a marginal activity. For them, prestige among

peers is what matters and this is gained through publication in scientific journals and debate over issues such as excavation accounts, presentation of findings and analysis of recovered materials; such recognition is not conferred to the presentation of conservation and restoration reports. The monuments and the archaeological zones are the domain of the non-specialist and – despite manifestos – seemingly do not deserve the immediate and concentrated attention of archaeologists. Thus, possibly the most effective means of promoting the history of Mexico is shunned. This, of course, is essential to those involved with issues of education and national identity; for obvious reasons, it cannot be the main concern of foreigners undertaking research in Mexico. This adds to their traditional lack of interest for conservation and restoration operations. There are, of course, a few exceptions and it should be remembered that the only case of research headed by a foreign institution that concluded with the restoration of an important number of monuments was financed by the Mexican government: Carnegie's work at Chichén Itzá.

What is curious is that the issues of restoration of a site for presentation to future visitors are clearly, on the one hand, compatible with an archaeology that is highly technical, theoretical and well developed in the field, while, on the other, not adding any major effort or workload on to archaeologists apart from the increased expense.

The scorn that many Mexican archaeologists have for anything that does not belong to the realm of research can only be compared to the energy of their drive to find data. It seems that the underlying thesis here is that a true history will emerge unaided at the end of an inductive process – a hope that quantity will turn into quality through the accumulation of data. The undesirable consequence is that all archaeological projects become automatically justified: data on a given region or period will never be sufficient and, unless objectives are defined a priori, all data are equally important. Thus, it is not surprising that archaeologists at the end of a field season frequently conclude, or pretend to conclude, that they have 'found very interesting data'.

This reflects the fact that archaeologists see themselves as producers of histories: before them there was nothing; after, some past aspect of a region or locality has been revealed. Yet few of them realize that before they arrived on the scene a history already existed, and that their own version has done little to change it. Few understand that their so-called 'scientific' history is simply a particular, transitory and detached interpretation of the social reality of a region or locality – a reality that they do not even attempt to understand.

The defence of excavation-based research as the central focus – and, in practice, the only focus – of archaeological practice not only leads to the isolation of academia, but also produces a distancing from the community. For Mexican archaeologists, who have been trained in a tradition where archaeology is seen as an anthropological discipline and formed in a school of anthropology whose practitioners are both members of academia and activists of social transformation, such isolation is paradoxical.

## ARCHAEOLOGICAL HERITAGE AND IDENTITY

This zeal to produce a pre-Hispanic history of a locality or, by the same token, of ancient Mexico, poses the question of 'which history is this?'. In other words, if history can define and reinforce an identity which induces social cohesion around a specific project, which project can this be? One should never forget that the project and its supporting discourse change through time, through specific junctures, by the confrontation of interests of the main social groups. Although a permanent and unchanging factual core does exist, the variants and reinterpretations of some facts can diverge by degrees that make an official history unrecognizable, either through the trans-formation of contents or simply by the marginalization of certain aspects.

For many years, the dominant political discourse in Mexico focused on the need to build a country with no underdevelopment, one firmly rooted in an indigenous past and a *mestizo* (mixed-race) future, constructed around a single language, a single shared history – the national history – and a single model of social well-being and growth. In this discourse, uniformity was a necessary condition of progress – indigenous communities could retain only those traits of their own culture compatible with this new model of growth. Otherwise, it was argued, the backwardness in which they found themselves could not be beaten.

This national project had its heyday during the period that followed the end of the Mexican Revolution. Not only did it stand against *caudillismo* (the rule of political bosses) and the ensuing political and territorial fragmenta-tion, but it also created a barrier to anything non-Mexican, strengthening the defence of the country's resources and reinforcing the decision to combat all forms of foreign intervention. The image that best reflects this era and spirit is the massive and unconditional support that the Cárdenas administration received from all Mexicans, regardless of social position or ethnic origin, when in 1938 it decided to expropriate the oil industry from the foreign companies that then operated in Mexico.

This discourse also provided an effective defence for the interests of the national bourgeoisie and the mid-twentieth century economic project, in which development was based on a relatively autonomous technology – a protected national industry and state-led development of infrastructure.

This drive to promote solidarity only gave way in the 1970s, when it was felt necessary to reduce excessive centralization and break away from the subsequent inequality of regional development, fundamentally for reasons of political control. Official history and the discourse of resistance and confronta-tion with foreign powers – once again curiously predicated on the defence of the national oil industry – remained topical. But, in parallel, the recogni-tion of the importance and particularities of each region led towards a celebration of their virtues. This was the era when regional museums prolif-erated. Between 1982 and 1985 Mexico built, restored or modernized at least one museum in each capital city of all but four states. A total of thirty-one museums were built, some of them represented large-scale investments with new buildings that were later endowed with exceptional collections. The Federal District – where the capital of the Republic is located – received a similar treatment with the erection of the Museo del Templo Mayor.

It was an era which celebrated local heroes, one that reconsidered and even rehabilitated villains in light of the circumstances of history. Previously unknown events suddenly became foci of attention and their importance magnified. It was a time when everybody seemed to have participated equally in the development of a national history – even those regions physically and politically distant from central Mexico. This experience had a positive effect on the democratic development of the country but it did not last long as the country's political continuity relied upon the existence of a monolith whose cement was the concentration of power at the centre. Once unleashed, decentralization efforts proceeded timidly at first, but ultimately centralized power became threatened by the same forces it had set free. The 1985 earthquake in Mexico City ended all dreams of democracy without any loss of political control: in response to the demands imposed by the catastrophe, the population became organized and expressed a solidarity that contrasted with the inefficiency of the state and the insensitivity of the government. Questioned by the political opposition and abandoned by politicians disillusioned by the loss of constituencies they regarded as their own, the Government and the State fell into a discredit from which they would not rise. Decentralization, the rehearsal of democracy, and the monolithic state disappeared all in one blow.

The most recent elaboration of official discourse was the so-called 'universalization of our achievements.' In this context the history of Mexico was, before anything else, the sum of all its contributions to human development. Nahoa 'philosophy', Maya legends, knowledge of mathematics and astronomy, and skills in certain artistic techniques now replaced heroes and battles. All features which were compatible with globalization were underscored, while the profile of everything that reaffirmed national sovereignty was softened. This new variant of the official discourse, nonetheless, did not reach the point of introducing coherent representations in museums or school textbooks since, during the Mexican government's attempt to integrate the country into a new economic order based on free trade, 'neozapatism' emerged, demanding – among other things – the recognition of indigenous rights.

Neozapatism called for equality and support of a diversity that dissolved the old definition of Mexican – namely, *mestizo*, Spanish speaking and progressive. It opposed the view of a cultural universality to which Mexico was but one contributor. Or, at least, it marginalized that view by placing the histories of individual communities, with their own traditions and values, at the core. This stance was rapidly integrated into the new museums, especially those located in areas with a strong indigenous presence. Indigenous communities were no longer represented as the roots and backward reality of modern Mexico – instead, they were depicted as peoples struggling for unsatisfied demands and as a dignified vanguard for the entire country.

Of course, this shift towards the region and the locality, towards particular communities, not only implies a recovery of things forgotten, but it also
masks other differences and relegates the defence of national sovereignty to
a secondary status. By highlighting indigeneity it rejects other shared experiences that override difference: in this discourse indigenous Mexicans seem
to share little with the *mestizos* that live in urban centres and who have been
equally exploited and marginalized. At the same time, the image of a single
country, diverse but cohesive, one that responds monolithically to any threat
to its resources and lifestyle, becomes blurred. Finally, essentially, it faces
problems and opportunities squarely. The tendency is for indigenous communities to be considered as equals and potential allies, a status denied to
other communities which share the same past of oppression and underdevelopment in the eyes of those outside Mexico.

## ARCHAEOLOGICAL HERITAGE AND THE COMMUNITY

As part of their programme of demands, indigenous communities have played
out old arguments about the relationship between the archaeological heritage
and local communities. According to present laws, archaeological sites are
federal property.[1] The reason is obvious: it is a heritage that 'gives meaning'
to the nation, one that belongs equally to all Mexicans; a heritage that
everyone has the responsibility of defending and the right to enjoy, in all
possible senses; one that should not be hostage to any one social sector.
Naturally, lawsuits filed by the states against the Federation in order to obtain
the custody of archaeological heritage have been rejected.

In the past, this controversy turned about the issue of the sovereignty of
the states in relation to the Federation. However, today there are two arguments. First, there is the demand that archaeological remains located in *ejido*[2]
or communal lands should be seen as yet another resource to be tapped for
the benefit of the corresponding community. In a situation where a broader
social interest, that of the nation, confronts an important, but smaller, social
sector, one would expect the former to be favoured – the reaffirmation of
federal control of archaeological heritage. Yet, the *ejido* – like archaeological
heritage – is owned by the nation.[3] It has a special legal status, was one of
the most important products of the 1910 Mexican Revolution and is also
one of the most significant spheres of political control. The confrontation,
therefore, is not one between two unequal forces. To understand what this
implies, it should be noted that the government has for many years bought[4]
*ejido* land containing archaeological remains – the irony being that in order
to prevent the destruction of archaeological remains by agricultural or urban
expansion, it now needs to repurchase land that it first came to own through
the revolution, and that it subsequently redistributed by creating the very
*ejido* system. It is bought despite existing use restrictions for land with archaeological remains because, following the logic of private ownership, it is

impossible to place restrictions *on the right to* possession or ownership of land, an inalienable right enshrined by the very Constitution. (In the case of private lands the procedure is the same, with the advantage that the legal arrangements needed for the transfer of rights are much less complicated and involve a lower political risk.)

Second, it is argued that because the inhabitants of a region are the direct descendants of the people who produced the heritage in dispute, it is only fair compensation that the Federation give the administration of archaeological sites to the communities living in close proximity to them. This line of argument leads, in turn, to the idea that artefacts taken from such sites should remain in the custody of the same communities. The San Andrés Larrainzar agreements between the federal authorities and representatives of the EZLN (Ejército Zapatista de Liberación Nacional, a guerilla group in Chiapas) are very explicit in this respect. They stipulate a federal obligation to train the indigenous people in the management of archaeological sites; in this way, local communities are endowed with the right to benefit from any tourism associated with their land's archaeological sites. This implies, in particular, the right to collect fees for visits to the sites, although at no point does this challenge federal control of archaeological heritage.

The question of the relationship between archaeological sites and the communities in their vicinity is one that can be analysed from a variety of angles. One is the authenticity of the claim, and here there is enormous variability. It ranges from a community that demands respect for its sacred sites to the demands of merchants who have no connection to the history of the sites. The latter attempt to demonstrate a relationship that will justify their claims by organizing ceremonies that have more to do with bodily energy than with indigenous cosmovisions and origins myths. For example, at one extreme, there are the legitimate demands of the Pápagos (O'odham) to Quitovac, the place in which, according to their beliefs, the ethnic group was created, or that of the Huichols to the road used to procure peyote. At the other extreme is the claim of the merchants established near the Teotihuacán ruins to be the descendants of the people who built the large pre-Hispanic urban centre 1,500 years earlier, even though at present it is not known which ethnic groups integrated the Teotihuacán population during the so-called 'Classic' period. In any case, the merchants have nothing in common with the few inhabitants of modern towns near the site that could securely claim an indigenous link, such as the Nahoas. Despite the invalidity of their claim, however, the arguments have served to unite the merchants in their struggle to preserve their sales pitches, to the detriment of the archaeological heritage.

Another angle to consider is the long history of 'despoiled' heritage suffered by communities to the benefit of the Museo Nacional de Antropología (MNA), located in the capital city. Because it was the first museum to be established and has since been the most important one, the MNA was until recently the repository of all artefacts produced by archaeological investigations, as well as by donation and confiscation. After more than a century of accumulation, the MNA had acquired large collections that could not be found elsewhere in the country, not even in the place of origin of the pieces. This situation became patent during the 1980s when the programme of regional museums discussed above was launched. The collections for the new museums were obtained from the MNA, in the face of reluctant curators who argued that the museum was being dismantled, but approved by the people from provinces that witnessed the return of some of the most important regional pieces. Today, because it is common practice for pieces to reside in the region or locality of their discovery, it has become difficult for the federal government to control material without the knowledge and consent of provincial authorities. A recent case illustrates this well. The Instituto Nacional de Antropología e Historia (INAH) tried to support *The Mayas* exhibition that opened at the Palazzo Grassi, Venice, by providing artefacts from the Palenque site museum. When the proposed loan to Venice became known, a large crowd assembled outside the museum to stop a possible case of theft, convinced that the pieces would never return to Palenque. This type of collective response, one that previously occurred only occasionally, and in very specific regions such as Oaxaca, is now relatively common in Mexico.

Of course there are other extremes at play also. The Palenque case has much to do with collective identity. Perhaps a few years ago this kind of reaction would not have occurred, at least not in the decisive and tumultuous way in which it did, but, with the resurgence of neozapatism in the region a change in the self-esteem of the indigenous populations and further opposition to central power has occurred. Both these factors have transformed the defence of the ancient Mayan archaeological heritage into a vital issue for the indigenous groups in the region. There is, however, another aspect to be considered. The Palenque Museum, with its excellent collections and first-class facilities, is one of the most important Mexican museums, a special stop in the tour of the archaeological zone and, as such, a stimulus to the economy of the modern town of Palenque. Degradation of the collection through partial loss is intolerable to those who inhabit the town and the region, thus the defence of the collection has an important economic motive.

A similar case recently occurred at Frontera, this time involving a predominantly Chol population that lives on the Usumacinta river, downstream from the archaeological site of Yaxchilán, which can only be reached by river on boats controlled by the Frontera Chol, or by air. A group of Chol requested federal authorization to take into their town a stela located in a forest area which was threatened by looting. At first sight, this concern with the protection and conservation of an undoubtedly important archaeological monument would seem to have been genuine, and it is clear that it inspired the petition; however, there was another equally justifiable reason – a desire to place a piece in the future Frontera museum that would entice more tourists to make the river trip to Yaxchilán, rather than travel by air. In a similar vein, the Chols are now building a hotel at Frontera.

The attitude of the Frontera Chols contrasts with that of the indigenous people from the region of Usumacinta where an unusually well-preserved altar was found six years ago – the famous Altar No. 4 of El Cayo, Chiapas, which has been studied by Peter Mathews. They stopped it from being moved to the regional museum in the state capital, thought necessary in order to prevent its deterioration through exposure. The archaeologists in charge of the move had informed and obtained the authorization of the communities around Yaxchilán necessary to carry out the operation. However, while attempting to move it, they were confronted by a large and menacing group of indigenes. Fortunately, they managed to escape a lynching but the altar has since disappeared and there is a suspicion that it has now entered an illegal network dedicated to the smuggling of archaeological pieces.

Abundant examples from the Maya area bear out the connection between claims to the ancestors' goods and an expectation of improved living conditions, whether by negotiating with the federal authorities for a 'road, hospital or school in exchange for an archaeological piece', or by hoping to develop a future tourist attraction – which in many cases is the only way of achieving regional development. Of these two possibilities, the latter offers the opportunity of a more permanent development of the community, as well as true decentralization and a more effective defence of the archaeological heritage, as will be discussed below. In northern Mexico, where the potential for tourism based on archaeological resources is significantly lower, it is no surprise that there are fewer disputes over the control of sites and artefacts.

Only a handful of indigenous groups in Mexico can claim a direct relationship to the archaeological remains found in their locality; even fewer can argue for a long occupation in the region where they live; modern Mayas, for instance, can prove that Late Classic Palenque was the work of their ancestors because Maya (Chol or Yucatec variants) is the language used in the inscriptions found in stone monuments at the site. Yet, some of the strongest and best-argued and more convincing demands for the ruling of 'sacred sites' do not come from any of these culture areas, but from northern Mexico, from groups that entered the pre-Hispanic scene in relatively recent times and are making no claim on anything that may be considered a tourist attraction. This state of affairs suggests that, in general, claims over sacred places constitute part of a broader resistance and have more to do with responses to specific situations and less to do with respecting ancestors or ways of life. It is a latent issue that appears when needed as a useful political instrument to confront interests that challenge the persistence and well-being of the community. The Lacandón claim to sites like Yaxchilán, a place they often visit to place copal offerings on wooden palettes, illustrates the point well. They cannot claim a direct relationship to Yaxchilán because they arrived in the area only recently. Their argument, however, has successfully empowered them making them beneficiaries of one of the most important territorial allotments recorded during the distribution of agricultural lands in Mexico.

## ARCHAEOLOGICAL HERITAGE AND LOOTING

In the eyes of Mexican archaeologists, the communities living in the vicinity of sites not only ignore their own history, but are also agents of heritage degradation who are frequently responsible for looting. This latter claim needs to be qualified. Although it is true that the people living at or near an archaeological site facilitate looting – they know where artefacts can be found and when and how one can search for them – it is also the case that these same people are in the best and most effective position to prevent looting. They may be enemies but are potentially also the most important allies in the defence of the archaeological heritage. The question is, how can the latter be achieved while avoiding the former?

The answer is not straightforward. The type and intensity of looting is different in every country, it changes with time, and depends on specific regional and local conditions. In the case of central Mexico, even if the frequent plundering practices of prehistoric times are set aside, looting has been going on for a long time and, until recently, was notoriously intense. Little can be said about the archaeological remains under Mexico City because the most important remains of Tenochtitlan-Tlatelolco were rapidly destroyed with no intention of preserving any evidence for posterity. The task then at hand was to hide, to bury what was being fought over. Later, many of the remains that survived the material and spiritual conquest were looted as part of treasure hunting that started in the mid-nineteenth century and continued until the 1930s. Although gold was never found, artefacts did end up in the hands of collectors. It is still possible to find old timers from the villages of central Mexico who tell how landowners or rich people would hire them to excavate the largest mounds for a few cents a day. Large shafts penetrated the centres of mounds. By the 1960s, the intensity of looting was such that in Morelos and Querétaro, for example, not a single mound was left without a hole.

Less naïve looters dug tombs for saleable artefacts, and behind these efforts there was always someone who had promised to buy what was found. Much of this contraband ended up in the hands of collectors and dealers abroad. In the poorest localities, looting reached truly alarming levels. In others, the demand for antiquities led to counterfeiting. Many pieces today both inside Mexico and abroad are the product of a lack of equilibrium between supply and a demand which fluctuates cyclically with the rhythms of inflation and the corresponding search for secure investments capable of resisting devaluation.

In addition to profit-oriented or organized looting 'to order', non-profit destruction of heritage also took place. Reutilization of pre-Hispanic materials for the construction of houses or fences, the extraction of stones from ancient structures to produce lime, adobe and bricks, the lining of roads with debris, the levelling of land for the introduction of irrigation and mechanized agriculture, and digging to set the foundations of buildings were among the most common activities of this type. They were, and continue to be, a systematic and relatively uncontrolled form of destruction that today is possibly of greater magnitude than genuine looting, and cannot easily be dismissed. Only in the case of major construction projects such as dams, roads, large buildings in urban centres, and developments near declared zones does the Mexican government intervene directly, using its own archaeologists to conduct rescue operations.

In central Mexico, looting continued throughout the twentieth century. It is enough to record that large portions of the Teotihuacán fresco are presently abroad, the result of illegal excavations that took place in the 1960s and possibly the 1970s. However, in comparative terms, in this region the phenomenon seems now to be in decline. Looting has diminished as there is not much left to plunder. The large centres of pre-Hispanic populations have been engulfed by urban and agricultural territorial processes that are part of an unprecedented demographic expansion in the region.

The case of the Maya area is different. Non-profit looting and destruction have increased during recent years, reaching worrying proportions, especially in the centre and south of the Yucatán peninsula. Until 30 years ago, when settlement intensified, there were large areas of the rainforest in which archaeological remains had remained hidden in very dense vegetation, untouched for millennia and subject only to the vandalizing action of dealers in search of precious pieces. Population density was minimal and there were vast and completely uninhabited areas. During the 1960s, however, a large number of new *ejidos* were created to attract settlers from remote regions, most of them with no connection whatsoever to Maya culture, and who required land for cropping and cattle raising, which led to a massive stripping of vegetation and reduction of the rainforest. Archaeological remains that for many years had resisted looting were exposed, and the same long processes undergone by central Mexico many years previously began: the archaeological heritage was destroyed as materials were reutilized, obstacles to agricultural production were eliminated, and a modern infrastructure was constructed.

Up to now, however, the settlement of the rainforest has not lived up to initial expectations. In terms of social well-being, the inhabitants of the new population centres are in the same situation of poverty and insecurity that they had known before their move to the Yucatán peninsula. They are victims of sharp fluctuations in prices that, year after year, affect their agricultural products, which are often monocultures; they suffer from a lack of adequate commercialization channels, from poorly organized production, and insufficient credit. The colonizers rely on governmental assistance programmes that are by all accounts insufficient. It should surprise no one that the proportion of people from these new population centres that seek better job opportunities in the US is higher than that of their own communities of origin, which were formerly among the most important providers of manual workers in the country.

Perhaps, then, the worst frustration – if not tragedy – has been the destruction of archaeological heritage caused by the settlement of the rainforest.

With some few very important exceptions, the new model of agricultural exploitation is based on the premise that the rainforest is an enemy to be subdued. Consequently, everything that exists, including precious timber, is slashed and burned, and with the destruction of plant cover there is a consequent disappearance of fauna. In the pursuit of this model, the sign of victory is the establishment of grasslands, a guarantee that the rainforest will not recover for many years. It seems impossible for the majority of peasants and regional governments to envisage sustainable harvesting of rainforest resources or to adopt strategies that ensure its recovery.

Hand in hand with environmental damage, human repopulation of the rainforest has caused a destruction of the archaeological heritage which finds its only parallel in central Mexico during the first century of the Colonial period. With land clearance, intact remains of pre-Hispanic Maya buildings appeared – ruins that had survived the passing of years, the climate and the action of plants rooted into them. Extraction of material to build the new settlements nearby also unearthed artefacts of all types. These finds started the looting, that ranged from the recovery of chance finds to a professional search for antiquities (Figure 9.1). In defiance of market laws, a growing supply of antiquities effectively expanded demand; the inefficacy of the restrictions imposed by the Mexican legislation and the favourable conditions for sale abroad resulted in a majority of artefacts leaving the country, a process that continues today.

**Figure 9.1**  Looters' trench in one of the buildings of Plaza Yaxná in Kohunlich. The building was trenched on all four sides; the looters were not successful but damaged the building to a point where its restoration became practically impossible

One part of the recent looting in the Maya area that cannot be dismissed can be blamed on the newly arrived inhabitants. Landless peasants, beguiled by the offer of participation in the newly formed *ejidos*, arrived with the idea of earning sufficient capital to allow them to return to their communities of origin and buy land that formerly they could not afford. For them, the migration was seen as temporary and the place of arrival as totally foreign. The landscape and the remains of a regional history seemed strange and difficult to understand. Worse still, the peasants would become interested in this new environment only if they could obtain better returns from their allotted lands.

After a few years, however, the immigrants did become settled. Looting stopped being a profitable activity for the new settlers, possibly because the artefacts were no longer found so often and so easily, or because the international market contracted or became more demanding, perhaps because they were never able to accumulate sufficient money to purchase land in their places of origin, feasibly because the cemeteries of the new population centres began to receive their own dead, possibly because little by little the place began to seem familiar and part of their own history. In any event, today most looting is conducted by outsiders who only rarely are supported by locals.

However, in the most remote parts of the region, known to only a handful of people, the looting is on another scale and occurs under very different conditions. In the south of Quintana Roo, for example, sites have been plundered by work teams that camp for extended periods in their vicinity (Figure 9.2). Their excavations seem to be directed by people who have worked with professional archaeologists. They have communication equipment and they are surely armed – despite the fact that this does not seem strictly necessary because the proximity of international borders allows them to cross over, thereby avoiding any police or military raids. The remains left behind by these looters (broken but complete monochrome ceramic pots; Figure 9.3) suggests that the market they are working to supply is composed of foreign collectors with sufficient resources to acquire sophisticated artefacts, artefacts normally found in 'royal' tombs: jade and shell objects, polychrome ceramics, decorative elements of civic-religious buildings, stelae and altars. The proximity of clandestine landing strips suggests that part of this booty at least leaves the country through drugs trafficking networks. This suspicion is supported by the fact that objects stolen from museums – for example those taken from the Museo de Antropología of Mexico City in 1985 – have later passed through such networks.

Faced with these economic and social realities, what can be done? In the case of intermittent and unselective small-scale plundering by locals, the simple answer is nothing: it seems best to accept it as a palliative in times of duress, undesirable but unavoidable. It is almost impossible to contain such looting, especially given the hundreds of thousands of sites in Mexico with visible structures (i.e. excluding hunter-gatherer sites) and the fact that communal solidarity precludes collecting information that would lead to the punishment of these looters. Rather, the best and fairest course of action would seem to

**Figure 9.2** Looters' trench in one of the buildings of a site in the south of Quintana Roo, Mexico. The trench went all the way to the centre of the building; its position suggests that the looters had previous experience and success in the discovery of 'royal' Maya tombs

be to focus efforts on combating the organized and systematic looting that takes place in remote areas, away from population centres. The difficulty, however, is that it is impossible to distinguish between the two types of looting except in the most extreme cases.

There is another problem with this proposal, however, which cannot be avoided, in that the acceptance or rejection of one particular type of looting, whatever its nature, undermines the principle of defending the country's archaeological heritage and the interests of the communities that participate in looting activities. Heritage is both a non-renewable resource that disappears from the public domain once it reaches the hands of private collectors, and a set of symbolically charged objects that should be respected as such, especially when communities can claim legitimately to have a relationship with the people who produced the objects. While we are still able to distin-

**Figure 9.3** Monochrome ceramic left by looters next to a Maya tomb in a site in the south of Quintana Roo. The looters no doubt removed the more precious and easier to sell jade artefacts and polychrome ceramics

guish between originals and replicas, the original objects have a special interest that can be realized in projects of economic development, fundamentally through tourism, for both the locality and the region.

Justice, then, should be tempered with common sense. This is perhaps the most frustrating aspect of this subject: the impossibility of setting up a legal framework that punishes not so much those who loot to survive, but rather the professional looters and unscrupulous merchants who cause the plundering.

## ARCHAEOLOGICAL HERITAGE AND TOURISM

The prevailing view among the majority of Mexican archaeologists is that the fewer the people that visit an archaeological site, the better. From the limited perspective of site conservation they are clearly right: the effects of tourism on an archaeological site can be devastating. The very history of so-called cultural tourism in Mexico clearly demonstrates that the arrival of visitors at archaeological zones brings with it speculation in land prices, an invasion of hotels and businesses, the destruction of cultural and natural resources, visual pollution, the development of new social inequalities and the intensification of inter-community conflicts.

Faced with the prospect of a promissory future for the regional economy, those who own land in and around a site capitalize on expectations, relinquishing their rights over land on advantageous terms, or becoming part of the business of selling services and crafts themselves, all of which – for good or bad – slowly detach them from their condition as peasants. In the case of souvenirs, non-local merchants often arrive on the scene quickly. These merchants manage their commodities on a national scale and have their own ideas about what tourists will want to buy. Given their larger resources and better organization, they impose their own products (usually of deplorable quality and taste) and inhibit local craftsmanship, leading to the extinction of local craft traditions.

When new sites are opened, tourist services arrive, new roads are built, power and telephone lines are put in place, 'undesirable' vegetation is eliminated, hotels that seek to command the best views are erected, and shops are placed both between the tourist and the site and inside the site itself (Figure

**Figure 9.4** Teotihuacán. Entrance leading to the Pyramid of the Sun, lined up with stores selling souvenirs to the tourists. An example of visual aggression to the site, in this case to its main structure

9.4). The most noticeable consequence of this is the destruction of heritage, especially at the larger sites (Figure 9.5). If tourist services were to respect the totality of the archaeological remains, they would have to place themselves at a great distance from the site, a situation they will not accept. In the case of Teotihuacán, for example, the closest land outside that totality is almost three kilometres away.

Increased tourism leads to the expansion and encroachment of hotels upon monumental architecture, to an increase in the number of shops, and to the emergence and subsequent multiplication of street vendors, who eventually become fixed by moving into an extension of established shops (shop owners have argued that this is the only way of countering the unfair competition attendant on mobility). The vicious circle seems endless: at Teotihuacán, there are close to a few hundred street vendors on any single weekend; at Chichén Itzá, there is an equivalent and constantly growing number of small shops which have even been erected only a few metres away from the site's structures; at Tulum, merchants have seized the prehistoric wall surrounding the site as if it belonged to them (Figures 9.6 and 9.7). Given enough time all these groups become political forces that either align themselves with or confront local governments, depending on whether their demands are accepted or rejected. In time, there is frequent complicity between parties.

Yet, the most extreme example in Mexico of the impact of tourism on archaeological sites has been caused by factors that are very different from those

**Figure 9.5** Teotihuacán. Entrance leading to the Quetzalpapalotl palace, lined with stores selling souvenirs to the tourists. In this case the stores are installed on top of unexplored apartment buildings, the extension of which are seen in the foreground

**Figure 9.6** Entrance to the site of Tulum, lined with stores selling souvenirs to tourists. At the end of the alley can be seen the pre-Hispanic wall surrounding the site

**Figure 9.7** Photo of Tulum taken towards its entrance. Given the small area of the site, and the relatively high flow of tourism it receives, conservation and maintenance problems are growing. To avoid continued deterioration of the site, the Mexican authorities were forced to prohibit entrance to some of the buildings

outlined above. The Xcaret amusement park, located on a late post-classic Maya site on the eastern coast of Yucatán, was built around and between the larger archaeological structures of the site bearing the same name. The site is typical of the region in that it has a series of relatively dispersed civic-religious monumental complexes surrounded by multiple domestic structures. Unfortunately the amusement park has destroyed the physical and visual relationships within and between complexes and this has led to the disappearance of the site as such. It is no longer possible to observe the integration between built and open spaces that reflected both important aspects of social organization and Xcaret ideas about their own community. The site has become a fragmented, incomprehensible reality – one that can only be enjoyed in a limited fashion. The erected – materially invasive – amusement park uses archaeological monuments as a backdrop for pseudo-ecological activities and very profitable night shows which bear no relation whatsoever to the original functions of the archaeological remains.

This destruction has only been possible because of a legal loophole. Under current laws only those places in which archaeological remains are known to exist, or where their existence can be demonstrated, are owned by the state. Mounds produced by the collapse of walls and roofs of pre-Hispanic constructions, or the pyramidal platforms on which the temples were erected, are not questioned by those who own or possess the land on which they are located. But the existence and relevance of remains that cannot be detected on the surface – the spaces between mounds and the underground archaeology – are always in dispute. In a situation where it is already difficult to make a case for buried remains, it is almost impossible to mount a defence for the space between structures. This is tragic since the most important buildings of the site are placed around plazas – as is the case at Xcaret – which logically do not have abundant or sufficiently important archaeological remains to declare them legally an unrestricted federal domain.

Current laws are equally deficient in not conferring protection on the surroundings of an archaeological site. With the single exception of the declared zone of archaeological monuments at Teotihuacán, in Mexico there is not a single instance of an area that has been protected on the basis of a consideration of a visitor's field of vision when standing at the centre of a monumental architecture complex. The importance of this type of protection should be obvious to anyone who stands, for example, on top of the main building at Tula, close to the well known 'atlantes', or on top of the main building at Cuicuilco. The visual pollution produced by modern buildings is harmful and suffocating to an extreme. It obliterates any possibility of understanding the relationships between the site and its immediate environment. Without a doubt, this is the result of an urbanization process out of all control. Incidentally, both examples are the product of relatively recent processes. There are also cases, however, in which the damage could have been restricted to some degree.

It is important to remember that the view from a hotel to, for example, the Caracol of Chichén Itzá is, obviously, the reverse of that from the Caracol to the hotel. Here the agendas of the hotel industry and of conservationists are diametrically opposed: one seeks what the other attempts to avoid. It is especially important, therefore, to create buffering zones around archaeological sites, not only to stop urban expansion but also to avoid visual pollution and to preserve endemic ecological communities. It should be noted that with the intensification of tourism the destruction of flora and fauna can be extreme, not only because of development of the tourist industry, but also due to the illegal trade in and exploitation of all kinds of species. The inhabitants of the communities surrounding Chichén Itzá, for instance, use the roots of the large guanacastes to produce carvings that are sold to tourists and similar sales of jaguar pelts and feathers from exotic birds contribute to the extinction of animal species in the region of Yucatán.

The defence of heritage should run parallel with that of the environment. The best efforts to present, protect and render an archaeological site understandable should go hand in hand with the creation of an ecological reserve around the site. Reserves not only operate as buffer zones but also protect the possibility of future archaeological research into peripheral social groups that are frequently overlooked by archaeologists. Yet without such research, a global understanding of ancient Mexican society (or of any other society) will remain out of reach. Given the dispersed layout typical of a Maya area, reserves of this type are especially important.

All of this, of course, runs contrary to the short- and medium-term interests of those who seek the potential profits that site tourism can offer, both directly and indirectly. It also operates against local communities, given that their ownership or possession of land will be affected, in one way or another, by any decisions taken by a tourism development programme. As in the case of looting, for the purposes of preserving and defending cultural heritage the local community can be the ally and also the principal enemy at the same time. The first question is how can the claims of local inhabitants be changed to favour an endorsement of the creation of parks and buffering zones? How can a convincing case for the preservation of natural resources be made? Second, how can tourism be developed without relegating the community to a marginal role that, far from resolving deficiencies, will deepen existing differences?

Currently, the inhabitants of communities around archaeological sites that double as tourist attractions are hired by archaeological excavation projects and also by developers of the new tourist infrastructure. Perhaps the lucky ones will get menial jobs in the hotels. In relation to the tourist trade and the corresponding economic benefits, the participation of locals is very limited because the best paid positions are not − nor can be under present conditions − filled by them. Similarly, the community − or its members considered as individuals − is not in a position to offer services at a significant scale, nor can it collect visitor fees. The major part of the profits are not reinvested in the region. One of the consequences, a logical one, of this asymmetrical relationship (especially unfair in cases such as the Maya area in which these communities are the descendants of those who built the pre-Hispanic cities that are visited), is that tourism projects fail to produce even the slightest benefit to the site and its protection. Under these conditions, the community operates as a passive element in the majority of cases.

In order to establish an alliance with the community to protect its heritage, it is necessary to change the attitude of the government. Beyond revising current laws to facilitate both an integral protection of archaeological sites and introduce regulations on the development of tourism that will minimize its impacts (which means, among other things, the need to abandon the idea of seeing the archaeological site as part of a hotel facility and instead respect the surrounding environment and the preservation and recuperation of vernacular architecture), it is necessary to reorient objectives and strategies. It is essential to place the well-being of the community at the core of economic development, to encourage the formation of local groups capable of directing and managing this development, to stimulate the active participation of the majority of the community in the larger project, to train local specialists to manage sites in coordination with government proposals and to allow the community to benefit from the collection of a significant portion of visitor fees. In parallel, it will be necessary to work with them to develop the history and to disseminate the material values of the regional culture. The best defence of the past is a community defending its own past. The participation of the community at the level of specialists in research and the work of dissemination is not only desirable but indispensable.

The extreme position of preventing visits to archaeological zones for the sake of conservation minimizes their potential for achieving greater social well-being. This position ignores the fact that they frequently act as foci of development in depressed areas (not uncommon in Mexico). It neglects one of the considerations of the presentation which accompanied the proposal of law put to Congress for the then President of Mexico, a law enacted sixty years ago and which, with minor modifications, continues to regulate the relationship of society to the archaeological heritage of the country (*Exposición de Motivos del Proyecto de Decreto Relativo a la Creación del Instituto Nacional de Antropologia e Historia*). This consideration states:

> That in addition to the important scientific results that are produced by the exploration and research of archaeological and historical monuments, it can also produce significant material results, insofar as it creates flows of tourism that will influence the economy of the country.

It is worth noting that the fundamental preoccupation of this same document is the living conditions of indigenous people.

This need not be taken to imply a subordination of economic development to the tasks of research and conservation. These three activities are fully compatible. Tourism developed under adequate norms, with the vigilance of communities and federal supervision need not distort academic arguments, nor oblige people to conduct undesirable tasks, postpone objectives, or establish time frames that are insufficient for the analysis of materials or for reflection. Posed as a long-term project, centred on regional well-being, with the community as an active agent in global economic and social development, tourism does not enter into conflict with the preservation of the cultural and natural resources of a society or region. Notwithstanding, only when these conditions obtain and this alliance is established, will the archaeological heritage be effectively defended and also assessed as a communal property that lends support and meaning to the national project while obviously serving as an important resource that can support regional development.

From the viewpoint of teaching the ancient history of Mexico, the scheme of isolating archaeological sites to avoid damage is irrational, even when all the problems of tourism discussed above are considered. It ignores the fact that not all visitors to archaeological sites are tourists and that not all tourists who visit archaeological areas are foreigners. In fact, the majority of visitors to 90 per cent of the sites that the Mexican government has opened to the public are Mexican nationals (Panameño, in prep.). In turn, the bulk of these are school children whose teachers believe quite correctly that visits to these sites are an important part of their pupils' civic and historical education. Such a proposition also fails to acknowledge the fact that the archaeological sites have an important didactic potential different in nature from the museum experience. Site visits facilitate conceptualization of pre-Hispanic history. From this perspective, the more people that visit a site, the better.

## CONCLUSION

Mexican archaeologists need to ask themselves what part they will play in the new construct that places the community at the centre of interests and possibilities. This new focus emphasizes the need for researchers to be aware of their own position in a wider context of production and to abandon the idea that they work at the margin of all non-scientific interests. Archaeologists will have to assume that their 'truth' is one of many possible truths, neither more nor less valuable than any other. They will have to learn to listen rather than expect to be heard. They will have to assume the defence of an archaeological site as part of their scientific endeavour and understand that their best ally in that defence is the community which they already know and with which they often maintain strong links. Archaeologists will need to be sensitive to the social and economic problems of these communities, for if they believe that archaeological research includes the archaeology of contemporary society, as all Mexican archaeologists do, then they must consider such problems as their own. If this direction is taken, archaeologists will become a type of old-fashioned developer, producing plans in conjunction with the community which fully respect their values and ideas, integrating and preparing them for shared management without prompting social fragmentation in the name of cultural diversity. Finally, the archaeologists will need to see archaeological sites not so much as scenes which can be enjoyed, but as the best possible means to re-create and develop an awareness of the history of ancient Mexico.

## NOTES

1   The number of archaeological sites in Mexico runs to hundreds of thousands and the Government cannot take them all into federal ownership. Government efforts have been directed towards the slightly over 100 sites that are currently open to visitors, and even this is beyond the financial resources available and in many cases is impractical since many of these sites lie below modern constructions. When an archaeological site is discovered, nothing is done unless it is of great importance from the point of view of scholarship or tourism.

2   *Ejido* lands are owned by the Mexican State. Members of the *ejido* have rights to that land as members of the community and as long as they cultivate the land. They do not own the land; there is a difference between ownership and possession. *Ejidos* were formed by conversion of national land or by expropriation of private land. Rights of *ejidatarios* (members of the *ejido*) can be transferred to their descendants and recently changes to the law were introduced so that *ejidatarios* can now transfer their rights to individuals in the same *ejido* even if they are not members of the same family. The main idea is to concentrate agricultural land so as to improve the efficiency of its exploitation, although in the long term it transforms *ejido* into private land.

3   *Ejidatarios* neither own the land they cultivate nor the archaeological remains in the *ejido*. Both are owned by the Mexican State and this is so before and after an *ejido* is created. The paradox is that if the Government wishes to protect an archaeological site in an *ejido* by regulating land use, they have to compensate members of the *ejido*. Even if the Government issues an expropriation law, they have to pay compensation (to the *ejido* as an entity, not the specific *ejidatario* being affected), and this has to be done at commercial prices. The compensation paid is subject to the *ejido*'s approval, and although the Government has the possibility of expropriating the land they seldom do: they prefer to deal with heritage degradation than with popular discontent.

4   The word 'bought' is introduced here instead of 'compensated', which is a more appropriate term since the Government cannot pay for what it owns; the fact remains that when land containing archaeological remains is withdrawn from the *ejido* lands, the *ejido* expects compensation which the Government, for political reasons, cannot refuse to grant. This compensation is currency and it amounts to the commercial value of the land being expropriated; the transaction, in this manner, is not different from that conducted in the case of privately owned land.

# 10 What's going on around the corner? Illegal trade of art and antiquities in Argentina

DANIEL SCHÁVELZON

This chapter will begin with a review of some recent history. In 1978, a group of people met at Córdoba Cathedral – the most important historical monument in Argentina, dating from the eighteenth century – and resolved to replace its jewellery and original furniture with modern replicas. Their aim was to sell the monstrance – three kilos of gold and silver – the crozier, the jewels, tables, chairs, and everything else valuable. And this is precisely what they did: they sold all the pieces and replaced them with new ones. Then, in 1983, a municipal museum in Buenos Aires held an exhibition of the jewellery and the more valuable pieces and did not hesitate to declare the name of the collector who had purchased them. Meanwhile, in the magnificent cathedral, only simple and cheap copies of tin and coloured glass were left behind. . . .

But these were the dark times of the last military dictatorship, when anyone who dared formally to denounce such events faced the prospect of paying with his or her life. The Bishop of Córdoba, other members of the Church and a group of collectors were found to be responsible for this outrage, which became a national scandal once democracy returned. Yet legal processes ended, after years of stagnation due to the aegis of the church, which protectively cloaked its members. Today, the jewellery and furniture can still be found in the hands of a few well-known Argentinian collectors; many other pieces were sold abroad.

To this example may be added another theft that took place on Christmas Eve in 1980. A group of police and military officers who had acted as a paramilitary unit during the dictatorship (something only learned much later) stole three works by Renoir, a Matisse, two Cézannes, two Degas, two Rodin, a Gauguin, a Daumier and some other impressionists from the Buenos Aires National Museum of Fine Arts. It was a harsh blow for Argentina. However, 'protection' was so effective that the culprits were identified only in 1989, when it was determined that the pieces had been stolen to order. The men who plundered the museum knew so little about art that they had left behind an extraordinary Van Gogh and a large Manet, while taking away some oil paintings by Argentinian artists that commanded only poor market prices!

This same group was responsible for some other major thefts: at the Estévez Museum in Rosario they stole pieces by Murillo, Sánchez Coello, Rivera and El Greco. Taking full advantage of their visit to Rosario, they also stole works by Titian, El Greco, Veronese and two paintings by Goya from the Castagnino Museum. Nine years later, in 1989, one of the thieves, a police officer, was arrested by the FBI in Miami while he was trying to sell one of the Goya oils. The piece was returned to the museum, but the culprits were freed thanks to a judiciary system that even today leaves a great deal to be desired.

FBI inspector Margot Kennedy heard the following numbing words from the arrested police officer: 'I can take out of Argentina whatever painting you want, from whichever museum you fancy; we have an organization that works like a clock and we have complete protection. For us, customs do not exist.' The words were uttered as he offered for sale Goya's oil 'Chicken and Pigeons' to a group of FBI agents. He also showed photographs of a Sánchez Coello stolen from Rosario in 1987. The Goya he offered was priced low ($500,000) because it had suffered some damage through rough handling, and it was proving difficult to find a buyer. Later investigations recovered the Sánchez Coello and demonstrated that senior customs officers were involved in these dealings.

When the person who planned and executed all of these thefts – a fugitive from justice also charged with a number of kidnappings – was caught and questioned, he said that the theft from the National Museum of Fine Arts had been a concession from the Military Government, an allowance in repayment for the kidnapping and disappearance of a few political enemies it wanted removed from the scene.

Such stories, collected from more than 300 cases which have been investigated since 1980, are clear examples of what can happen in a country endowed with a rich cultural heritage that has to suffer from dictatorships, judicial irresponsibility, unmodernized legislation and indifferent and/or corrupt governments. This is the context in which we need to situate such issues in Argentina, where today there is certainly much to be done to protect and defend the national heritage. Unfortunately, it is also a context in which no efforts and initiatives will be sufficient to reverse the irreplaceable losses caused by half a century of plundering.

These phenomena need some explanation, however brief, to enable a foreign reader to understand them. Argentina is a very peculiar country in the context of the South American continent, its society is the result of the extermination of the native indigenous population, massive European immigration and, towards the end of the nineteenth century, the complete disappearance of the Afro-Argentinean population. In 1950, the level of national literacy was among the lowest in the world, at near zero.

By the beginning of the twentieth century, half of the inhabitants of Buenos Aires were foreigners, more precisely Europeans, and they introduced a lifestyle – 'fashions' and tastes – modelled on those of France and England. Vast fortunes were used to bring from Europe complete collections of paintings and sculptures. But the story does not end there: even large palaces were taken apart and transported – with all their furniture – to Argentina; occasionally, the cheaper option was preferred of hiring architects, specialized workers and craftsmen to design and build large public structures and private mansions in the best European style. The national state and some important municipalities sent experts to Europe to buy pieces of art or architecture so often that today it is even possible to see in Buenos Aires zoo a small Byzantine temple. When the heritage of 10,000 years of archaeology is added to this heritage, together with three centuries of colonial art (from the time of Spanish domination), and the rapid assimilation of new international styles during the nineteenth century, the result is a rich context from which works of art can be exported to the large world market.

This eagerness to 'be European', the vision of unlimited progress that modernity instilled in a country where it was easy to accumulate vast fortunes and whose borders were open to everyone – this means everyone who was white – gave way, during the twentieth century, to the development of a dominant mentality for which profit was the most important value. Of course profits were not within reach of the majority of the population, and the richest sectors of society never assumed the full responsibility for their own country. Even today, amid the pragmatism of neo-liberalism, it is difficult to find anybody who will donate a piece to a museum (there are a few exceptions); it is more usual for a family to sell their works of art and to reinvest the profits in some other business. Today – with the exception of very traditional sectors such as land owners and cattle and horse breeders, all of whom can trace back their family histories for many generations – notions of legacy, family tradition, historical heritage mean almost nothing, despite attempts to create a sense of public responsibility. For the vast majority of the population, these notions simply embody a bothersome past hindrance. In this light, it is no coincidence that the upper classes of society oppose both preservationist legislation and control over the indiscriminate export of works of art and antiquities.

Three levels of analysis are necessary to understand Argentina's role in the international illicit market. First, Argentina's own domestic art market. It is a small, generally unstable, diffuse market – with occasional strong moments – whose expansion and contraction parallels the national economy: when dollars are a cheap currency foreign buyers can acquire valuable art at insignificant prices; when dollars are expensive, buyers simply disappear. The State hardly interferes with this market as it is not part of its usual practice to purchase art pieces or antiquities for local museums. Other national institutions and foundations do so only very rarely. Private collections are formed and disappear in a generation; only exceptionally do collectors report or exhibit their collections because of an awesome fear of taxes and theft; a large and hardly dissimulated black market exists, dealing in stolen, falsified and other pieces of dubious origin. Archaeological pieces are sold openly. They are displayed in shop windows of the most popular tourist areas, or in antiquarian shops. Nobody seems to remember that it is all illegal.

Between 1982 and 1994 the size of the legal art market fluctuated between $2.5 million and $50 million per year, while the black market ranged between $2 million and $30 million. Over the same period the average salary of a lower-middle class citizen fluctuated between $50 and $1,000, with real purchasing power being lower than ever because while Argentina is one of the most expensive countries in the world, it is also one in which poverty grows in gigantic leaps. There are large variables involved in this market and it is difficult to discern any clear trends. A painting of the most famous Argentinian artist, Petorutti, for instance, was sold for $250,000 at an auction and two years later resold for a mere $25,000. There are important art galleries dedicated to ancient African art, Oriental art, Latin American archaeology, Russian art and Central European Jewish art; Art Nouveau window frames and antiquities from all over the world abound. These supply many of the large markets of the world.

A second important aspect of the analysis is the very active traffic of, especially, colonial art and archaeological material from Bolivia, Ecuador and Colombia through the Bolivian border, and Peru. Pieces constantly come into Argentina, concealed by the movement of thousands of people crossing the border between Villazón and La Quiaca every day. There are no controls, or they are rudimentary at best.

It is often the peasants who carry out small-scale looting (or *huaqueo*). They bring perhaps less than six pieces to Buenos Aires at any one time, where dozens of dedicated galleries will buy them at prices which reflect their place of origin and then sell them on to local collectors or export them to international markets. For those who take material to Buenos Aires, a five-day trip in a precarious bus, it means selling for $100 and even $200 a piece – a small fortune in Bolivia or Peru – what they have excavated or purchased for a few dollars, no more than $3 or $4 a piece. Once pieces arrive in Buenos Aires it is possible to find a private customer, or to sell them to gallery owners at lower prices. The latter then find it easier to sell them abroad because, in effect, the objects have been laundered: they are exports from Argentina rather than Peru, where it is illegal. It is impossible to calculate the number of objects that have entered and left Argentina in this way over the years, but it has allowed collectors and museums world-wide to assemble complete collections of valuable Andean archaeological material.

Finally, international trade takes on a different character because it reaches a different order of magnitude; no monetary valuation has been produced but figures from some studies are impressive, and the list of works of art that have left the country, legally or otherwise, fills entire books. The system generally involves an object being sent out of Argentina privately, or through a gallery, to be sold by auction in Western Europe or the US. No major customs barriers exist and as there is no system of control for small packages it is easy to take the object out personally in flight luggage. When the operation is more difficult, it is always possible to count on corruption; Rembrandts are known to have been exported by the owner with neither insurance nor customs declarations. But even keeping things within the law is simple: authorization is sought from the national government which cannot legally prohibit the exportation of any work of art unless it decides to purchase it – something it never does. Thus, a permit is usually granted and in the extremely rare instances when one is denied, the alternative option exists of suing the state on the grounds that the denial violates the private interests of the owner and thus infringes the Constitution. It was not until 1993 that attempts made to enshrine in the Constitution the right to a national heritage were successful, albeit in an incomplete and diffuse way.

Another system is to launder material imported into Argentina after illegal export from another country. Pieces which have been stolen, have unclear origins, are fake or possibly fake, or are difficult to sell are brought into the country and exhibited publicly, published in catalogues and even auctioned so that, in effect, the piece is laundered. It acquires a new provenance. They can then be exported to buyer countries, since a legitimate origin can now be established. When the international market passes through an active phase this system can also be used to collect art and archaeological pieces from those Latin American countries which have protectionist legislation. It is not at all difficult to obtain a certificate stating that such an object has been in an Argentinean collection for many years because possession does not infringe any local law and there is no form of control, not even in terms of taxation.

What should be clear after this brief summary is that there are countries that import art and antiquities and countries that export – in other words, countries that buy and countries that sell. Argentina is an exporter, a non-casual reflection of its Third World status. But Argentina's situation is more complex than that of other countries, since it is both the lion's tail of the large US or European markets, and the mouse's head of South America, where collectors of Mexican, Peruvian or Colombian art, among many others, operate. And the important investors in European art of the seventeenth to nineteenth centuries, African art and even Chinese jade and pottery have not even been considered.

Thus, the art business in Argentina is defined not so much by buying or selling works of art, a market in itself, but rather by the country's intermediary role in an international trade. There have been and still are cases where companies triangulate the movement of art pieces between Miami (or other ports in the US), Argentina and Europe. The system is quite simple: a piece is sent to the Miami office of an Argentinean company that deals in works of art. A false document certifying that the piece has just been received from Argentina is given to the purchaser (a US citizen or resident). When difficulties are harder to solve, the piece is illegally brought south and, a few days later, returned north legally, almost always to New York, but occasionally to London, Paris or Zurich. Expenses involved are low: a container with a capacity of 20 cubic feet can cost approximately $2,000.

During the 1970s, while both the domestic market and the external demand for Latin American antiquities boomed, some interesting polemics were voiced in favour of uncontrolled export and against protectionist legislation. The National Secretary for Culture asked both Academies of Law and the Fine Arts about passing a national law to control trade. The Academy of Law advised that export control contravened the basic rights of individual freedom and private property, as enshrined in the Constitution. The National Academy of Fine Arts, by contrast, underscored the contradictions of such a position by suggesting that unrestricted freedom could develop a strong commercial market, similar to the UK or the US, which would favour Argentina by allowing imports of all kinds of works of art. However, the same declaration also included and lamented the list of cultural objects that had previously been taken out of the country. The situation today is exactly like the 1970s – there is a growing awareness that Argentina is an exporter rather than an importer. At present the country is more an intermediary than anything else; all that free transit implies, then as now, is a slow and systematic emptying, rather than an agile market or an enlargement of collections.

This does not mean that art works of great value do not enter the country: over the past few years a single private collector brought in a $10 million Van Gogh, a Monet of the same value, a Warhol, a Turner, a Brueghel, a Gaugin and Picasso's Maternity, for which she spent up to $25 million. A number of similar cases exist, because Argentina continues to be an important economy with large private fortunes by Latin American standards. But works of art leave as easily as they arrive: nothing and nobody can stop this.

At the end of the twentieth century it can be asked whether the total liberalization – or negligence – that characterizes the art and antiquities market in Argentina has had a positive or negative effect? It is a good question, since we could then evaluate the results without considering thornier issues such as cultural heritage, ethics or our responsibility to the future. There is one example which illustrates this nicely. It is a statistic that describes the number of antique or rare books (valued at more than $300 each) that left Argentina between 1980 and 1992. Despite a small sample, with its attendant uncertainties, it shows that at least 55,000 volumes and/or collections of volumes were taken out of the country during this period. By contrast, for the same period, we have no record of any books entering the country. Another interesting figure comes from a quantification of thefts from museums and large collections, and it is no coincidence that trends parallel the boom of the international markets. In 1980 only ten cases were recorded, by 1982 there were twenty, an increasing trend which reached its peak in 1989, with thirty-seven cases. And then, the following year, thefts fell abruptly. By 1992, only twenty cases were recorded and, at present, the decline continues. This decrease was neither the result of good policing nor of enhanced museum and private collection security, but rather reflects a scarcity of interested buyers. Middlemen simply found the business less profitable as international prices dropped and local prices increased. The business lost some of its attraction. It should here

234 DANIEL SCHÁVELZON

be emphasized also that an important proportion of these thefts were made 'to order'.

The argument about art trading is now topical and there are discussions in even the most important national newspapers on the pros and cons of more or less liberalized international trade, on an attempt to avoid the sale of archaeological objects on the open market despite legal prohibition, on the need to enhance the quality and number of museums, or as a drive to work towards a responsible customs system and non-corrupt authorities. The country's responsibility in controlling the territorial borders with its neighbours is also being discussed. Perhaps the most important achievements of the last ten years are, on the one hand, the growth of public concern about the significance of the nation's cultural legacy and the need to conserve it and, on the other, the fact that important sectors of society agree and demand that certain fundamental rights such as the protection of the cultural and natural heritage need to be respected in a democratic society.

The lesson has been hard to accept and it has been learned late, but today it is beginning to be understood that Argentina has an exporting, not importing, role in the international market and that this policy leads to a sad, definite and conclusive emptying of the country's heritage. Perhaps trading of this sort still allows many to amass large fortunes, but policies of the kind described can be summarized in a very Argentinean and pathetic popular expression: 'the last one to leave the country, please don't forget to turn off the lights at the airport.'

## BIBLIOGRAPHY

Berberián, E. 1992. *La protección jurídica del patrimonio arqueológico en la República Argentina.* Córdoba: Comechingonia.

Harvey, E. 1992. *Derecho cultural latinoamericano: Sudamérica y Panamá.* Buenos Aires: Depalma.

Ragendorfer, R. 1992. *Robo y falsificación de obras de arte en Argentina: un negocio floreciente.* Buenos Aires: Ediciones Letrabuena.

Rodríguez, A. 1975. Evasión y protección del patrimonio cultural. *Boletín del Museo Social Argentino.* No. 365: 197–206.

Schávelzon, D. 1993. *El expolio del arte en la Argentina: robo y tráfico ilegal de obras de arte.* Buenos Aires: Sudamericana.

# 11 Looting graves/buying and selling artefacts: facing reality in the US

HESTER A. DAVIS

People in the US have been looting prehistoric graves and buying and selling artefacts from those graves since Europeans first arrived on our shores. In the nineteenth century, it was thought that the large earthen mounds which dotted the landscape in the heartland of America – particularly the Mississippi and Ohio River valleys – must have been built by migrating Mexican Indians or perhaps an unknown 'race' they called 'mound builders'. Most people did not believe that the Native Americans they knew could have made such beautiful artwork as was found buried with the dead. It seems as if the attitude of looters was that these were not graves of 'people' but of an 'extinct race' with no living descendants, so no one cared. (What contemporary looters feel when disturbing skeletons is not known to me, but they are obviously callous about it.) Only in the last fifteen years or so have Native Americans been able to make their voices heard on these matters, and that is changing everything for archaeology and archaeologists, for museum collections, and for dealers and collectors of Native American antiquities.

Congress passed the first national law protecting antiquities in 1906. It protected prehistoric sites on federally owned lands and was prompted by vandalism of the spectacular prehistoric pueblo ruins in Arizona, New Mexico and southern Colorado. The laws and regulations issued based on the law, required permits for scientific excavation (no other excavations were allowed), and levied fines for proscribed activities. Over the next seventy years, however, there was little effort to enforce the law; Congress failed to appropriate money to allow extra personnel for surveillance (particularly for the large land managing federal agencies, the National Park Service, Forest Service and the Bureau of Land Management); personnel were not trained in how to gather evidence; when there was an arrest, judges often dismissed the case on the grounds that collecting a few arrowheads or pots was not a serious crime. In addition, most federally owned land is in the western half of the country, and the 1906 Act did nothing to protect sites in the states east of the Great Plains, where land and its contents are largely owned by private individuals. For the most part, landowners can do with their property as they wish. Even now, in several states, a landowner can bulldoze a mound, plough up a prehistoric cemetery, or lease a site to a commercial digger without recrimination.

Digging prehistoric graves can be a lucrative activity. In Arkansas, during the Great Depression of the 1930s, for example, selling pots and stone tools for cash was sometimes the only way to make enough money to buy food (Harrington 1924). In the major river valleys of the south-eastern US, and the Mississippi and Ohio River valleys in particular, the late prehistoric people produced what are now considered beautiful pieces of art in stone and clay. Some of these bring extremely high prices in today's art market. They were largely made specifically to be placed with the dead; certainly they are normally found in graves, often whole, and not broken in the general village midden. As selling pots became more profitable, so did knowledge of where to find the best objects and how to uncover them to best advantage. Because alluvial valley soil often has no natural stone, those looking for pots developed a probing technique (Figure 11.1) by which they stick a steel rod in the ground. The rod has a small concavity on the end and when they hit bone or pottery, they just dig for the artefacts, although bones were often scattered in the back dirt piles (Figure 11.2). In the 1980s, a 'headpot' (Figure 11.3) from a site in eastern Arkansas was sold for $25,000; in 1994 another similar one passed from a dealer to a wealthy collector for $65,000, perhaps the highest price paid for one of these vessels.

**Figure 11.1**  A 'pothunter' in north-east Arkansas, having been successful in finding pots in graves, uses a metal probe to locate more, 1970

Photograph: Arkansas Archaeological Survey

**Figure 11.2**   A 'pothunter' at work in north-east Arkansas, 1970. A broken pottery vessel is on the left, and the front of a skull has been thrown out on the back dirt
Photograph: Arkansas Archaeological Survey

Since the passage of several state laws in the late 1980s and early 1990s, and the federal law called the Native American Grave Protection and Repatriation Act of 1990 (NAGPRA), this activity seems to be lessening. It is still very difficult, however, to find out how much trade on the international art market is going on in Native American artefacts. Buying and selling of private collections to other collectors or through Sotheby's and Christie's auction houses certainly continues, although how much goes directly overseas for sale is not known. One can easily see that buying and selling artefacts on the internet is increasing, but the increased efforts on the legal front and in public education do seem to be having some effect.

In 1979 the Archaeological Resources Protection Act (ARPA) was passed. This law, while dealing with protection of all archaeological and historic sites on federal land, did not actually amend the 1906 Act, but it did serve to strengthen the hand of federal agencies, and it increased the fines and allowed for jail time for violation of the Act. As a result, and because of other federal and presidential mandates, agencies have been able greatly to increase and publicize prosecutions in the last ten years.

Because the federal government can regulate interstate trade, in a forward-looking section of ARPA, it was made illegal to take artefacts from a site contrary to state laws, carry them across state lines, and sell them. This resulted

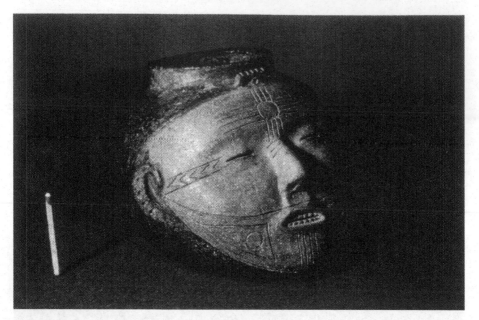

**Figure 11.3** A headpot from the late prehistoric Bradley site in north-east Arkansas
Photograph: University of Arkansas Museum

in an arrest and successful prosecution in a widely publicized case, where an individual dug in a mound in Indiana without permission of the owners of the land, which is an illegal act in Indiana, and took them to Kentucky to sell (Arden 1989). Mr Gerber has served time in jail and is probably still trying to pay off his fine.

There have been a couple of little-known effects of this case that are also hard to document. One of these effects is on one of the major venues for buying and selling artefacts, at least in the eastern US, and that is the 'arte-fact show'. This is not your 'high end' art market (really beautiful and unusual pieces go directly to a collector or dealer). Most of these are local affairs, statewide or regional at best, but this is where artefacts selling for a few thousand dollars or less can be found (Braden 1999). There is a huge trade at these shows in chipped stone tools – the oldest ones or the largest ones going for the highest prices – and this is where a lot of fakes get into circulation. It was at one of these shows that Mr Gerber tried to sell his illegally gotten goods.

Those who organize these shows, and particularly those selling, are now very wary because of the successful prosecutions, and this has brought about the second effect – at least I *think* it has although I do not know this for a fact. It used to be that artefacts identified as coming from a well-known site could bring more money than those without provenience. Now it may be dangerous to have that information, so what little provenience information there may be about an artefact is no longer available; this way it is easier to say it comes from a collection made prior to the passage of the recent laws.

During this same ten-year period, over half the states in the US, perhaps as many as three-quarters now, have passed laws making it illegal to dig in unmarked graves. In a few cases, the state of Arkansas being one, this applies to all land, both publicly and privately owned (Davis 1998). A farmer in Arkansas can no longer dig in an unmarked grave on his own property. It has long been illegal to disturb any marked grave, and one of the arguments for the Arkansas bill during its consideration was 'equal protection under the law'. It is our impression that the amount of looting in Arkansas has dropped. We know for a fact that our most notorious commercial dealer now goes to neighbouring Texas to dig, since the archaeologists and Native Americans combined have not been able to get a protective law passed in that state.

That brings me to the major change in the reality of archaeology in the US today – the empowering of the interests and concerns of the Native Americans about their ancestors' graves. I will not go into the details and background of NAGPRA here, but let me touch on how I believe this law, and particularly the new relationships between Native Americans and archaeology, may be affecting looting and trade in artefacts.

There is a good side and a bad side to what I think is happening now and/or may well happen in the future. With regard to looting graves for fun and profit, it is not only state laws that are giving people pause. The commercial diggers know about NAGPRA and they know that as far as digging graves goes, it applies only to federal land. They also know that Native Americans are vocal about anyone digging in any prehistoric grave. Native American concerns and values about grave robbing always get good press. This makes the looters/dealers very nervous, and probably childhood visions of 'Indians on the War Path' come to mind. But more than this, and perhaps more subtle, is that I think many people have changed their attitude toward digging in graves. It may be that the serious looter in the West has not been affected, although, again, a widely publicized conviction in 1995 may be helping, since the defendant was given six and a half years in prison and a large fine (Tarler and Flanagan 1999: 38–9). However, the vast amount of land which is uninhabited and unprotected must make the good return in the market place worth the risk. However, in the Midwest, I perceive that a combination of rumours about the laws, rumours about strong Native American views, and greatly increased teaching and discussion of these issues in public schools is slowly changing the attitude of the general public. They are realizing that the Native Americans who lived on the land before them had the same feeling about burial and disturbance of the dead as they feel today about their own ancestors. This is all to the good.

Another less propitious consequence of NAGPRA has to be the repatriation of artefacts that come from graves to Native American federally recognized tribes. Private collectors now know enough about the law to realize that if they donate their lifelong collection to a museum, it will undoubtedly be repatriated to one or more tribes. Some think this is appropriate; some people are even contacting tribes themselves for return of pieces. But some collectors, who traditionally would have their collection and their investment recognized by the museum in name and in exhibits, do not want their objects to 'go back to the Indians'. Instead, they will find a dealer and sell the collection, as a whole or piece by piece, which is all perfectly legal. Unless a state law provides for repatriation, repatriation under NAGPRA applies only to institutions or entities which receive federal funds.

I believe, however, that buying and selling of prehistoric artefacts in the US is going to increase, with old collections going newly into circulation. This may, indeed, increase circulation to overseas dealers and collectors as well. Whatever provenience there may have been concerning these pieces is going to be lost. This will mean a loss of a certain level of information which archaeologists have been able to retrieve in the past. Prices are going to go up because the supply of newly dug objects, for the reasons given above, is going to decrease (except perhaps in Texas, where our not-very-friendly Arkansas commercial dealer is still leasing land with known prehistoric cemeteries to dig the graves).

In summary then: we do not have a good handle on the international trade in Native American antiquities, nor do we have a way to document fully how much looting went on before the new laws and therefore how much, if at all, it has decreased. The National Park Service is keeping track of prosecutions under federal and state laws, and these are certainly increasing (Haas 1999: 37). The future for sites with graves and cemeteries looks better, but we must be ever vigilant through prosecutions and through many levels of education – of landowners and of our vast population who receive most of their information about archaeology from watching Indiana Jones movies.

## REFERENCES

Arden, H. 1989. Who owns our past? *National Geographic* 175(3), 376–93.
Braden, M. 1999. Trafficking in treasures. *American Archaeology* 3(4), 18–25.
Davis, H.A. 1998. Facing the crisis of looting in the US. Paper presented at a symposium entitled *The Dead Sea Scrolls: the Future of the Past in the 21st Century*. April, 1998, New York City.
Haas, D. 1999. Preventing looting and vandalism. In *Report to Congress, 1996–1997*, The Federal Archeology Program. Washington DC: National Park Service.
Harrington, M.R. 1924. *A Pot-Hunter's Paradise*. Museum of the American Indian, Heye Foundation, Indian Notes and Monographs No. 1(2).
Tarler, D. and J. Flanagan 1999. Heritage and the law: two landmark decisions. In *Secretary of the Interior's Report to Congress*, D. Haas (ed.), 38–9. Washington DC: US Department of the Interior.

# 12 Reducing incentives for illicit trade in antiquities: the US implementation of the 1970 UNESCO Convention

## Susan Keech McIntosh

In 1972, the US became the first major art-importing country to ratify the 1970 UNESCO Convention on the Means of Prohibiting and Preventing the Illicit Import, Export and Transfer of Ownership of Cultural Property. It did so, however, with the understanding that the Convention was not self-executing and would require implementing legislation. Eleven years later, after exhausting and contentious skirmishes in Congress with the art dealer community, who successfully lobbied to restrict US action under the Convention primarily to Article 9, the US Cultural Property Implementation Act was passed (Bator 1982; Hingston 1989; Coggins 1998).[1] This legislation does the following:

1 It allows the US to impose import restrictions on categories of archaeological or ethnological materials subject to pillage that jeopardizes the national cultural patrimony of a source country which is also a State Party to the convention.

2 It details the conditions under which the President may put such restrictions into effect using the instrument of either a multilateral accord with the source country and other market countries (or, under certain circumstances, a bilateral accord with the source country) or temporary, unilateral emergency restrictions.

3 It creates a Cultural Property Advisory Committee (CPAC), appointed by the President and administered by the US Information Agency, which makes recommendations on requests for protection received by the government from source countries who are also parties to the Convention. Three of the positions on the committee are designated for archaeologists or ethnologists (I have served on the Committee in this capacity since 1996). The other eight members of the committee represent the interests of art dealers, museums, and the general public. Committee members are convened whenever a request is received. Each request is considered separately on a country-by-country basis.

Although the process of devising implementing legislation and of actually setting the procedure designated by that legislation into action has been lengthy, since 1990 implementation of the Convention has gathered momentum and produced some significant results, which will be discussed with particular reference to my own research area – Mali.

First, it is important to mention that States Parties seeking US import controls on certain categories of archaeological or ethnographic material must submit a formal request to the President, who is authorized by the implementing legislation to receive such requests. US protection under the Act is not automatic. The request should include documentation relevant to the following four determinations that the Cultural Property Committee must make, in accordance with the implementing legislation (see Kouroupas 1995):

1  That the cultural patrimony of the State Party is in jeopardy from pillage of its archaeological or ethnological materials.
2  That the country requesting protection has taken measures to protect its cultural property.
3  That import restrictions would be of substantial benefit in deterring the serious pillage described in the first determination and less drastic remedies are not available. It must also be found that other market countries with significant import trade in the materials under consideration are implementing or considering implementing similar restrictions.

   This latter provision reflects directly the success of the art dealer community in the US in convincing Congress that the US should not act alone. However, Congress accorded the President discretion to enter into bilateral agreement under some circumstances.
4  That the application of import restrictions will not impede the exchange of cultural property among nations for scientific and educational purposes.

To date, US import controls on an interim, emergency basis have been granted for specific aspects of the archaeological or ethnological patrimony of El Salvador, Peru, Bolivia, Mali, Guatemala and most recently, Cyprus and Cambodia (Hingston 1989 provides an overview of the CPAC deliberations on the 1987 El Salvador request, which was the first request for emergency assistance to be received by the committee). Bilateral accords to protect cultural property were subsequently signed with El Salvador, Peru, Mali and Guatemala. The US has also signed bilateral agreements with Canada and Nicaragua. (See editors' note.)

The significance of import restrictions as a mechanism of protecting cultural property is of major importance to source countries, because it means that US Customs can, at any time that it has sufficient reason to believe that an object was imported to the US without a proper export permit after the date import controls went into effect, seize the object. The ability of US Customs to act quickly and effectively in determining whether materials are protected by import controls has been facilitated by creation of website (http://exchanges.state.gov/education/culprop/index.html) by the Cultural Property Committee office (formerly part of the US Information Agency, but, since October 1999, part of the State Department's Bureau of Educational and Cultural Affairs), which provides photographic examples of protected categories. Even if the restricted material passes through the port of entry without inspection, it can be seized if a violation of the import restrictions is later found to have occurred (Kouroupas 1995: 86). If the importer cannot produce proof that the object is in compliance with the statute, the object is returned to the country of origin. This procedure, which entails virtually no cost to the source country, can be contrasted with the prohibitively expensive and lengthy process of bringing a legal action under stolen property or other relevant US laws that is the main recourse of source nations whose cultural property is not protected by import controls through the process described above.

Seizures by Customs of protected materials that have occurred to date include two highly publicized cases involving material from the heavily looted Moche royal tombs at Sipán, Peru. In 1994, gold jewellery offered for sale by Sotheby's was seized by Customs after Peruvian officials identified the pieces as originating in Sipán. The seller and Sotheby's had the opportunity to petition to get the objects back by producing evidence of conformity with the law, but did not do so (Cockburn 1996). The jewellery was returned to Peru.

In 1997, a gold backflap weighing 1.3 kg from the royal tombs at Sipán was seized as two individuals attempted to sell it for $1.6 million to an undercover Customs agent (Smith 1997). Lacking an export permit, the two were indicted for fraud, conspiracy and theft, and the backflap was returned to Peru on 15 July 1998.

The benefits of the US implementing legislation extend far beyond seizures and repatriation of protected material, however. Two important aspects of the legislation can be illustrated with reference to Mali, a country whose archaeology has been my research specialty for over 20 years. First, the legislation is proactive and prospective. It is specifically oriented towards the deterrence of pillage and the accompanying destruction of archaeological context rather than towards repatriation of already excavated and exported material (Kouroupas 1995: 85). Second, the legislation explicitly emphasizes the adoption and continuing development of self-help measures by the source country. A bilateral accord is in fact a real partnership between the US and a source country towards a common goal of reducing the looting and site destruction produced by the illicit trade in antiquities.

The effect of these aspects of the legislation in reducing the illicit trade in antiquities and its accompanying pillage can be seen in the case of Mali, whose cultural patrimony from the archaeologically rich Middle Niger region is protected by a bilateral accord signed in 1997, following a four-year period of emergency restrictions. Looting in this region for terracotta statuettes produced between 1,000 and 400 years ago reached crisis proportions in the

**Figure 12.1** At least 200 looters dug at this site near Thial between September 1989 and April 1990

Photograph: copyright Michel Brent, Brussels

late 1980s (McIntosh, R.J. and S.K. 1986; Dembélé and van der Waals 1991; Brent 1994; Sidibé 1995; Sanogo 1999) (Figure 12.1).

At least one object allegedly produced by this looting frenzy made its way into a new exhibit which opened at the Boston Museum of Fine Arts (MFA) in late 1997. The ensuing brouhaha that developed over it and some contested Mayan material from Guatemala in the same exhibit illustrates how protection under the US implementing legislation of the UNESCO Convention can bring both opportunities for action and high visibility that have powerful deterrent effects in and of themselves even if no seizure is actually made by Customs.

One of the deterrent pressures provided by protection under the US implementation is the need it imposes for dealers, collectors and museums who purchase protected material to ensure that they have documents proving that it was either legally exported from the source country or imported prior to the imposition of import controls. This record-keeping of ownership − called provenance − is something that the above-mentioned groups have often been notably lax in observing. Artefacts lacking provenance are usually looted and illegally exported from source nations, as dealers and museum officials have themselves admitted (Robinson 1998). Both professional dealers associations and museum associations such as the International Council of Museums (ICOM) have drawn up codes of ethics and practice that specify that suspicious objects lacking provenance, and thus likely products of illegal activity, should be avoided (ICOM 1987; Palmer 1995: 7).

But just as a child may ignore the repeated admonitions of a parent to cease a bad behaviour and 'be good', the experience of undesirable consequences as a result of persisting in the bad behaviour may be the most efficient way to effect the desired change. The undesirable consequences that the Boston MFA experienced as a result of its exhibit of material from two countries with bilateral accords with the US were of two types: (1) a Customs investigation at the request of the Malian Ambassador to see whether the two statuettes in question entered the US after the establishment of emergency restrictions in 1993 (the MFA refused to divulge the import date of its own volition); (2) much press coverage by the *Boston Globe* (e.g., Robinson 1997; Yemma and Robinson 1997) and *Christian Science Monitor* (Chaddock 1998) newspapers. In reporting Guatemala and Mali's claims that the objects displayed were illegally exported from their countries following clandestine looting, the reporters exposed the MFA's cavalier attitude towards the provenance of the artefacts it was displaying. It appeared to be acting contrary to the codes of museum ethics to which it ostensibly subscribed. The *Boston Globe* quoted a museum donor as saying that the MFA cares little where a piece originates unless the acquisition was 'likely to create a fuss' (Robinson 1998).

One of the principal aspects of the US implementing legislation is that it empowers source countries to 'make a fuss' by requesting that Customs investigate suspicious materials in protected categories that have been recently acquired or offered for sale. Mali has recently done this again with regard to unprovenanced antiquities from the Middle Niger recently offered for sale at public auction. This kind of incentive to museums and dealers to 'be good' and follow principles of good ethics by handling only material with documented provenance will likely have a more immediate effect on their conduct than the admonitions of their parent professional organizations. Collectors aware that protected material lacking documentation of legal export may be subject to summary seizure are likely to demand such documentation and research the provenance with due diligence before purchase. While the long-term goal must be, as Ricardo Elia (1997) has pointed out, to change attitudes and the culture of collecting such that handling, owning and exhibiting unprovenanced material becomes unacceptable, in the short run, changing behaviour through various deterrents both legislative and non-legislative in nature is what we can reasonably aim for.

Of course, deterring illicit trade in the US is only one part of the solution, as the legislation explicitly recognizes. I have emphasized the importance of self-help measures in the implementing legislation and the creation of a partnership with the US to support national efforts in source countries. Four of the eight provisions of the US–Mali accord address this:

> Article II. C. The Government of the United States of America will use its best efforts to facilitate technical assistance to the Republic of Mali in cultural resource management and security, as appropriate under existing programs in the public and/or private sectors;

> Article II. E. The Government of the Republic of Mali will seek to develop and promote professional training programs for archaeologists and museum staff and public institution administrators responsible for cultural patrimony, and to enhance the capabilities of the National Museum of Mali to care for and exhibit aspects of its rich cultural heritage.

> Article II. F. The Government of the United States of America, recognizing the successful public education initiative of the Republic of Mali through the establishment of Cultural Missions that carry out research, site management, and educational programs among local populations at major archaeological sites, encourages the continuation of such measures as part of an overall effort toward sustainable strategies for protecting cultural resources.

> Article II. G. The Government of the Republic of Mali will use its best efforts in restricting the activities of antiquarians within its borders, in making export controls more effective, and in seeking the cooperation of other importing countries in curbing illicit trade in Malian cultural artefacts.
>
>            (from the text of the Memorandum of Understanding
>          between the US and Mali executed 19 September, 1997)

The fact that most accords are subject to continuous review and renewal after five years can be of enormous help to source country archaeologists and heritage managers who may find that archaeology and protection of patrimony sometimes slips off the priority list of their government officials and ministers who are charged with overseeing them along with many other pressing issues. The accord can thus help local archaeologists keep the spotlight on heritage conservation within their own countries. The US can further these efforts in individual cases by USAID assistance with rescue archaeology and inventory, as has occurred in El Salvador, ambassadorial and USIA support, as has just occurred in Mali, support for technical training in the US through Fulbright or other travel programmes, plus a number of other possibilities.

I believe that the legislation has had a very positive effect in Mali. Thanks to the Cultural Mission at Djenné, for example, and its innovative, local

**Figure 12.2** Hired by an antiquities dealer from Mopti, looters hack away at ancient settlements 35 miles north-west of Jenne

Photograph: copyright Michel Brent, Brussels

'sensibilization' (education) efforts, plus its programme of roving 'brigades de surveillance' who keep an eye out for looters, pillage at archaeological sites within a 40-km radius of the town has been virtually halted. Previously, sites in this archaeologically rich area were being demolished wholesale by bands (sometimes whole villages) of looters organized and paid by local antiquarians working for European galleries (Brent 1996) (Figure 12.2). The US and Mali have enjoyed a successful partnership to educate the public about the importance of archaeological heritage and to provide training opportunities for Malians (McIntosh *et al.* 1997). In 1999–2000, this included Fulbright sponsorship of an American archaeologist (R. McIntosh) who collaborated with Malian colleagues at the University of Mali to train students in salvage archaeology techniques and survey methods appropriate to the national site inventory that Mali is undertaking.

But it is clear that these efforts under the implementing legislation are not, in themselves, sufficient, since the legislation calls for the concerted efforts of other market countries as well, where objects formerly destined for the US market may otherwise be redirected. For this reason, France's action in becoming a signatory to the UNESCO Convention in January 1997 is particularly welcome, as it was a major market country for Malian antiquities. But we cannot rest until other major market countries such as Switzerland (which has announced its intention to ratify), Belgium and the UK also join the effort. While one may hope that new, market-country signatories would embrace most, if not all, of the articles of the Convention, the experience of the US shows that implementation of even one article can have a substantial impact that ripples outwards.

## EDITORS' NOTE

On 19 January 2001, a bilateral agreement between the US and Italy was entered into, imposing restrictions on the import into the US of archaeological material originating in Italy dating from approximately the ninth century BC to the fourth century AD. Detailed information is available on the internet at the following addresses:

http://exchanges.state.gov/education/culprop/index.html
http://exchanges.state.gov/education/culprop/overview.html
http://exchanges.state.gov/education/culprop/implemen.html

See also: US-Italy Treaty Against Antiquities Smuggling (*Art Newspaper*, February 2001).

## NOTE

1   The dealer organization responsible for this effort was the National Association of Dealers in Ancient, Oriental and Primitive Art. NADAOPA's website (http://www.artnet.com/orgs/organisations/nada/index.html) states that 'the Association was instrumental in drafting cultural property legislation pursuant to the UNESCO Convention' and posts a membership list with 41 US-based dealers.

## REFERENCES

Bator, P. 1982. *The International Trade in Art*. Chicago: University of Chicago Press.
Brent, M. 1994. The rape of Mali. *Archaeology* 47(3), 26–31; 34–5.
Brent, M. 1996. A view inside the illicit trade in African antiquities. In *Plundering Africa's Past*, P. Schmidt and R. McIntosh (eds), 63–78. Bloomington: Indiana University Press.
Chaddock, G. 1998. Art world wary of new rules. *Christian Science Monitor*, 10 February.
Cockburn, A. 1996. Peruvian antiquities seized as Sipan artifacts. *IFAR Reports* 17(7).
Coggins, C. 1998. US cultural property legislation: Observations of a combatant. *International Journal of Cultural Property* 7(1), 52–8.
Dembélé, M. and J.D. van der Waals 1991. Looting the antiquities of Mali. *Antiquity* 65, 904–5.
Elia, R. 1997. Looting, collecting, and the destruction of archaeological resources. *Nonrenewable Resources* 6(2), 85–98.
Hingston, A.G. 1989. U.S. Implementation of the UNESCO Cultural Property Convention. In *The Ethics of Collecting Cultural Property*, P.M. Messenger (ed.), 129–47. Albuquerque: University of New Mexico Press.

ICOM (International Council of Museums) 1987. ICOM Statutes: Code of Professional Ethics, adopted by 15th General Assembly, Buenos Aires, 4 Nov, 1986. Reprinted in the *International Journal of Cultural Property* 7(1998), 215–22.

Kouroupas, M.P. 1995. United States efforts to protect cultural property: implementation of the 1970 UNESCO Convention. In *Antiquities Trade or Betrayed: Legal, Ethical and Conservation Issues,* K. Tubb (ed.), 83–93. London: Archetype/UKIC.

McIntosh, R.J. and S.K. 1986. Dilettantism and plunder: dimensions of the illicit traffic in ancient Malian art. *UNESCO Museum* 149: 49–57.

McIntosh, R.J., B. Diaby and T. Togola 1997. Mali's many shields of its past. *Nonrenewable Resources* 6(2): 111–29.

Palmer, N. 1995. Recovering stolen art. In *Antiquities Trade or Betrayed: Legal, Ethical and Conservation Issues,* K. Tubb (ed.), 1–37. London: Archetype/UKIC.

Robinson, W. 1997. Mali presses for museum artifacts. *Boston Globe,* 6 December.

Robinson, W. 1998. New MFA link seen to looted artifacts. *Boston Globe,* 27 December.

Sanogo, K. 1999. The looting of cultural material in Mali. *Culture without Context,* No. 4, 21–5.

Sidibé, S. 1995. The pillage of archaeological sites in Mali. *African Arts* XXVIII (4), 52–5.

Smith, J. 1997. FBI: Smugglers had ancient garb. *Philadelphia Daily News,* 7 October.

Yemma, J. and W. Robinson 1997. MFA pre-Columbian exhibit faces acquisition queries. *Boston Globe,* 4 December.

# 13    The rape of Mali's only resource

Téréba Togola

## INTRODUCTION

In November 1997, at a large meeting called by the new Ministry of Culture and Tourism to define a better cultural policy, one participant evoked the economic situation of Mali, which he described as a poor Sahelian country plagued with poor education, chronic rural poverty, diseases and recurring droughts accompanied by famine. He lamented that Mali has no oil, no uranium and no diamonds, and that the country, because of its lack of substantial financial resources and advanced technology, has now to share what small amount of gold it possesses with South African, American, European and Australian companies. 'The only resource we really own is our rich cultural heritage', he said. The participant, who works for a travel agency in Bamako, was apparently not aware of the massive pillaging of Malian antiquities. His remark (an appropriate reference to the multinational companies which are accustomed to helping themselves to the raw materials of developing nations) is applicable as well to the valuable resources of antiquities in many other African nations which have become the target of international smuggling syndicates. In view of this disturbing fact, it is the intention of this chapter to examine some key issues, in particular the importance of cultural heritage and the efforts made thus far by the Malian government to discourage looting and the illicit trade in antiquities.

## THE VALUE OF CULTURAL HERITAGE, OR *FACEN*

In any nation, be it in the north or the south, antiquities constitute a major repository of the people's cultural heritage. To the Bambara (the most important ethnic group in Mali) these cultural artefacts are an integral part of the *facen*. Literally, the *facen* is what we received from a deceased father and, by extension, the ancestors. The *facen* (whose best equivalent in English is 'cultural heritage') comprises a vast array of tangible and intangible elements: land, wealth, ritual objects, art work, knowledge and traditions. To the Bambara and most Mandé groups, the *facen* reinforces the liaison between the living and the dead (who are considered an integral part of the community). It ensures the group's cohesion and maintains its cultural identity. The Bambara strongly believe that, because of these important functions, the *facen,* or cultural heritage, should never disappear. It was transmitted by the ancestors to the current generations who, in their turn, have an obligation to honour it and keep it strong.

Mali's recent history provides an excellent illustration of this strong belief. In 1960, the independence of the country (after a period of seventy years of colonial domination) was associated with an unprecedented interest shown by its citizens in their past and in their cultural heritage. An important manifestation of this interest included the adoption of a new name, Mali, to evoke the ancient medieval empire of Mali and one of the most glorious episodes of the country's history. Schools, streets, public places, cinemas and even musical bands and sport teams were also named after famous historical personages or places. Efforts were made at both national and community levels to revive many aspects of the cultural heritage (traditional songs, myths, traditional costumes) which had been discounted or denigrated during the colonial era. All these elements of the *facen* became, more than ever before, an important source of inspiration for artists. The epics of Sounjata (the founder of the medieval Empire of Mali) and the epic of the Bambara (who founded the Bambara Kingdom of Ségou in the eighteenth century) were reinterpreted by modern bands such as the Super Biton National.

In a recent speech, the president of Mali, Alpha Omar Konaré recalled for his audience the sacrifices made (for future generations) by the ancestors, namely the builders of the great medieval empires of Ghana, Mali and Songhoi as well as by the founders of the now famous cities (like Jenné-jeno) that flourished in the first millennium AD along the Middle Niger. Alpha's allusion to these achievements of the ancestors, it should be pointed out, was an invitation to the younger generations to accept sacrifices (as did the ancestors) and protect the country's new democracy. To Alpha, the best contribution that current generations can make to the nation's cultural heritage, or *facen,* will be the building of a strong democracy after more than two decades of dictatorship.

## THE RAPE OF MALIAN HISTORY

Unfortunately, the archaeological record, in which all these sources of enormous national pride are preserved, is under threat more than ever before from those who – to serve the international art market – are pillaging the highly visible *tells* of the Middle Niger (for the so-called Djenné terracotta or bronze figurines), stripping the sculptural pillars of the Toguna in the Dogon country, profaning sanctuaries in the Dogon and Bambara countries (for ethnographic and ritual objects) or desecrating the modest funerary monuments (tumuli and hypogea) in the southern and central part of the country.

Malian antiquities were first removed during the colonial era, when the French colonial administrators (enlisted to study and document the cultural aspects of their respective districts), scholars (especially ethnologists), and amateur archaeologists started to collect *les belle pièces* recovered either during development projects or through erratic scientific explorations. As one would expect, most of these *belles pièces*, such as the best specimen of the megalithic site of Tondidrou, were exported to France and housed in the Musée Ethnographic du Trocadéro (now Musée de l'Homme) in Paris. Although this removal of Malian antiquities during the colonial era had a negative impact on the country's cultural resources (witness the almost complete destruction of the megalithic site of Tondidrou by Clérisse [a journalist from *L'Intransigent*] and the careless and often unreported excavations in the Méma by the hydrologists of the Office du Niger), its effect on the country's cultural heritage was much less damaging than that of the current pillaging which is devastating thousands of archaeological sites across the country.

This archaeological looting, at first timid and confined to the Dogon country and the Inland Niger Delta, has intensified considerably during the last two decades. The highly visible *tells* located in the barren floodplain of the Inland Niger Delta remain the most vulnerable target. A preliminary statistical evaluation shows that the vast majority of these *tells* (the source of the so-called Djenné figurines) have some evidence of looting (Dembélé *et al.* 1993; Sidibé 1996). Some of these settlements like Natamatao (near the village of Thial), Mounya (approximately 30 km from Djenné), and Hamma Diam (near Sofara) have been more than 90 per cent destroyed by scores of looters who repeatedly return to them (armed with pickaxes, shovels and *daba*), to look for terracotta or bronze figurines, nicely decorated vases or ancient beads. Such is also the case at Gao Saney located near the town of Gao and reported by Arab chroniclers to be part of the dual city of Kaw-Kaw (or Gao), the capital of the Songhoy Empire. This massive mound, with nearly nine metres of archaeological deposits, and central to the understanding of the processes of urbanism and state formation in West Africa, has been nearly totally destroyed for the ancient glass and cornelian beads (highly prized by Touareg and Moorish women) it contains.

The list of notorious cases of devastation and destruction of archaeological sites, historical monuments, and modern sanctuaries across the country is endless. During the last two decades, the looting of the cultural heritage has steadily been extending, reaching new areas or into areas unexplored by archaeologists. In fact, the archaeological potential of many regions was revealed only through intensive looting. This is the case at Baniko, the circles of Bougouni and Kolondièba, all in southern Mali. All these regions were ignored by archaeologists until the 1980s when they became the focus of scores of looters attracted by numerous tumuli where terracotta figurines (similar to the one found by Szumowski in the 1950s at a site called Bankoni and located near Bamako) were extracted.

In the early 1990s, the frontier of the looting extended to the region of Banamba which corresponds to the cradle of the medieval empire of Sosso. It appears that the reason for this intensive looting in the Sosso (where no archaeological research has ever been executed) is the presence of funerary monuments (tumuli and hypogea) with rich grave goods, including nice globular vases and copper and gold artefacts (Sissoko, personal communication, April 1997).

The threat posed by this massive site pillaging to the Malian past is beyond measure. In the absence of substantial written documents, archaeological remains are the most important source of information about the country's history, as well as for the reconstruction of the way of life of the ancient societies. While economies, diet and technologies are relatively easy to document, the religions, social organizations and belief systems of these ancient societies are hidden, or often expressed in symbols. One of these symbols is ancient art. As the McIntoshes put it, ancient art is 'the clearest window' to ancient ritual acts and belief systems (McIntosh R.J. and S.K. 1986). But, to retrieve this kind of information, archaeologists must find and record the art pieces in their archaeological context, in other words, with all the other associated elements that have survived. Without the archaeological context, the art objects are scientifically irrelevant and their cultural value is limited to their stylistic and aesthetic qualities.

## WHO IS TO BLAME?

These criminal activities are sustained by a chain of actors, which includes, at one end, the poor illiterate Sahelian peasants who deface numerous archaeological sites (with long and deep trenches) and receive about US$30 for the best find, and, at the other end – in Europe and the US – the international art smuggler who can sell the same piece for US$175,000 to US$250,000. Between these two are the wealthy merchants who generally live in urban centres like Bamako and Mopti, have international connections and serve as middlemen.

Besides this chain of actors, there are other circumstances which currently favour the removal of Malian antiquities through looting and illegal traffic. The first, and probably not the least, of these circumstances is the massive Islamization that the country has been witnessing since the 1960s. Following this Islamization (which has affected many regions known to have resisted Islam for centuries, like the Dogon and the Bambara countries), Malian sculptural forms have become objects of disdain and sometimes even worse humiliation at the hand of Islamic iconoclasts. All *boly* (fetish) and figurines – seen as an important obstacle to the spread of Islam – were destroyed through burning or breaking in public. To give just one example, in 1996, the Kamablon (an important sanctuary in Kangaba in the cradle of the ancient Empire of Mali) was set on fire by a fundamentalist Muslim.

The second of these circumstances is caused by the attitude of people in the West toward art. In this part of the world, there has been, for several centuries, an increasing secularization of art. Because of this secularization, the context in which the art pieces were originally used appears to be irrelevant. Therefore, there is no scruple in collecting the so-called 'primitive art' for its aesthetic qualities rather than for its original purpose. As we know, these 'primitive art' objects are displayed in private galleries and often living rooms with only a minimal reference to their sources. This is, for instance, the case of the terra-cottas from the Inland Niger Delta, all labelled as Djenné figurines.

The third and last of these circumstances is the lack of substantial archaeo-logical research, including the total absence of a proper inventory of sites and historical monuments in the country. Although the contribution of archaeology to our understanding of cultural change in some areas has been impressive (note the precocious and autochthonous urban civilization along the Middle Niger), there are still large areas of the country that remain completely unexplored by archaeologists. This situation, due to the extremely limited resources both for research and preservation of archaeological remains and historical monuments, seems to leave many areas of the country at the mercy of looters.

## LIGHT OF HOPE

Most Malians, like the participant from the travel agency, increasingly believe that the richness and diversity of their cultural heritage can help ameliorate, by means of tourism, the current economic difficulties. This attitude, together with their pride in a glorious past, makes it easy to mobilize the population for the protection of the endangered cultural heritage. Although the archaeo-logical potential of the country has yet to be brought to the knowledge of the common citizen, there is an increasing awareness at the decision-making level (and sometimes outside the professional arena), that the current haemor-rhage of archaeological materials can only result in the loss of the people's cultural identity and the erosion of their pride. This increasing awareness of the importance of cultural material has prompted several legislative and educa-tional measures aimed at eliminating the root causes of the looting plague.

The first efforts towards the protection and preservation of cultural heritage in Mali date back to the 1950s, when the colonial administration promul-gated the Arrêté no. 4179 in December 1954, in which twenty-three archaeological sites and historical monuments were identified and clear instruc-tions were provided for their protection (McIntosh et al. 1997).

Not much was done during the decades immediately following the country's independence in 1960. Then, in the 1980s, with the explosion in looting and smuggling, the government established the Commission Nationale pour la Sauvegarde du Patrimoine Culturel, with representatives in nearly fifty good-sized cities. A body of legislation banning unauthorized digging as well as the export of archaeological materials (except for scientific studies), and regulating archaeological research, was also implemented. It should, however, be pointed out that these legal instruments quickly proved not to be the answer to the problem of looting which, as noted earlier, was extending inexorably to new areas.

In the 1990s, efforts to protect the cultural heritage were directed towards improving the level of cultural awareness among local communities. In 1993, this policy of sensibilization moved into a higher gear with the creation of cultural missions on each of the three world heritage sites: one in Djenné, one in Bandiagara and one in Timbuktu. These cultural missions allow trained people to live for an extended period of time in the target towns, and in so doing become part of the community. As part of this campaign to raise public awareness, the issues of establishing local museums and bringing cultural arte-facts closer to their roots and point of origin are being addressed. Gao and Fambori, (near Douentza) both now have local museums. In May 1998, Madame Adam Ba Konaré (the current first lady of the country) laid down the foundation stone of the museum of Djenné.

This strategy of improving public awareness has successfully established and consolidated the people's pride in their past and their cultural heritage. Now, the citizens of Djenné consider Jenné-jeno and the site in the immediate vicinity of the town as an enormous source of pride. Partly because of this pride, the looting of archaeological sites has been pushed into the interior. In Joforogo, a small village near Ségou, the villagers are keeping relics of Bakary Jan (war hero of the Bambara Kingdom of Ségou) in a wooden cabinet, awaiting the village museum that they are planning to build. At the beginning of 1999, an old man from a small village near Kangaba visited the National Museum. He had been sent by the village elders who had discov-ered that some of their cultural artefacts linked to *komo* society were disappear-ing. Associations for the preservation and the promotion of cultural heritage are springing up all over the country.

It should also be stressed that, on the international level, Mali has ratified the 1970 UNESCO Convention on the Means of Prohibiting and Preventing the Illicit Import, Export and Transfer of Ownership of Cultural Property. This important instrument can contribute a great deal to the reduction of the illegal trafficking of cultural heritage, as shown by the recent bilateral accord between Mali and the US. Unfortunately, many wealthy countries – consumers of African antiquities – have yet to ratify this convention.

## CONCLUSION

Archaeological remains are one of the most reliable sources of information about the past, but this chapter has also demonstrated the more subtle rele-vance of the conservation of Malian cultural heritage. This heritage has, during the last decades, been subjected to unprecedented pillage to supply antiquities to the illicit trade. It is imperative for Mali (as well as for other African countries who suffer from the same plague) to keep on its agenda substantial programmes for research and protection of cultural heritage. The value of the past is beyond measure.

# REFERENCES

Dembélé, M., A.M. Schmidt and J.D. van der Waals 1993. Prospections archéologiques dans le delta intérieur du Niger. In *Vallées du Niger*, 218–32. Paris: Éditions de la Reúnion des Musées Nationaux.
McIntosh, R.J., B. Diaby and T. Togola 1997. Mali's many shields of its past. *Nonrenewable Resources* 6(2), 111–29.
McIntosh, R.J and S.K. 1986. Dilettantism and plunder: dimensions of the illicit traffic in ancient Malian art. *UNESCO Museum* 149: 49–57.
Sidibé, S. 1996. The fight against the plundering of Malian cultural heritage and illicit exportation. In *Plundering Africa's Past*, P.R. Schmidt and R.J. McIntosh (eds), 79–86. Bloomington: Indiana University Press.

# 14 Dealing with the dealers and tomb robbers: the realities of the archaeology of the Ghor es-Safi in Jordan

KONSTANTINOS D. POLITIS

The recent pillaging by tomb robbers of sites on the south-eastern shores of the Dead Sea in Jordan is typical of many archaeological sites in the Near East. However, it is ironic that while these clandestine activities obliterate the remnants of history, they simultaneously provide a source of income for one of the world's poorest communities.

After the 1967 Arab–Israeli war and the political upheavals of the early 1970s in Jordan, the area south-east of the Dead Sea, modern Ghor es-Safi which was ancient Zoar, became enclosed in a military zone. Many years passed before civilians could safely return and even then economic development came slowly to this geographically isolated area. Agricultural lands were laid to waste and the only resource which could be extracted from the shores of the Dead Sea was salt, which had a relatively low value and so contributed little to the local economy.

In the early 1970s, the Jordanian government relocated the village of Safi to the north of the Wadi al Hasa in order to free the land on which the old town was built to make available the rich alluvial soils for agriculture. The Jordan Valley Authority (JVA) was given the responsibility to develop these lands efficiently into agricultural fields. They awarded contracts to an Italian construction company, which was contracted to install a state-of-the-art irrigation system in an effort to revitalise the land. Building such a system meant excavating large tracks of land to make huge leaching trenches and to lay down many kilometres of underground water pipes in the areas of old Safi called Khirbet Sheik 'Isa, Tawahin es-Sukkar, al Ameri, Oneza and an-Naq' (Politis 1998). Unfortunately these sites were also the location of bronze age, Roman-Byzantine and medieval Islamic settlements. Inevitably, the employees of the Italian company discovered unknown ancient remains and what they did not destroy, they collected. Pottery and glass vessels, carved and inscribed stones, metal work, jewellery and even mosaic pavements were allegedly found. Soon the poverty-stricken inhabitants of Safi realized that they could sell to the Italian engineers the artefacts which lay below the very ground on which they lived. Many families were officially allocated plots of

land on the ancient sites by the JVA with little or no objection from the
local representative of the Jordanian Department of Antiquities. And so, men,
women and children took to robbing the earth of its unknown ancient treasures and selling them for any small price they could obtain. The ancient site
which the villagers were ruthlessly digging up was the biblical city of Zoar,
obliterating forever much of its archaeological record.

The ancient topography of the Ghor es-Safi is accurately depicted on the
unique sixth–seventh-century AD mosaic floor map in the Greek Orthodox
church of St George's at Madaba in Jordan. This southern part of the Dead
Sea portrays the Sanctuary of Lot on a mountain above a city which had
three towers, a gate and two red-roofed buildings surrounded by six palm
trees indicating an oasis. A Greek inscription labels the city as 'Balak, also
Segor, now Zoora'. This city is known as Zoar in the Old Testament of the
Bible and has been described by numerous ancient writers. In the Roman
period a cavalry unit was based there. In the early Byzantine period (fourth–
seventh centuries AD) it was an important administrative centre and the seat
of a bishop. During the medieval 'Islamic' period (twelfth–fifteenth centuries
AD) it was a major commercial and industrial centre, particularly for the
production of sugar and indigo. There is no doubt that throughout its long
history it was a relatively wealthy city.

The historic identification of Safi as biblical Zoar is of considerable importance. It not only helps clarify the geography of the Holy Land in the
sixth–seventh centuries AD (on the basis of the Madaba map), but also lends
credence to the Old Testament episode of the five 'Cities of the Plain' and
the destruction of two of them, Sodom and Gomorrah. Although the exact
date of this Old Testament story is debatable, it could be placed between the
Early Bronze Age I (c. 3000 BC), the period to which most of the large
cemetery at an-Naq' belongs, and the Iron Age (c. 1000 BC), which has only
recently been identified as the era of the large agricultural settlement of
Teleilat Qasr Musa Hamid (Politis 1999).

Since little archaeological work has taken place in the Ghor es-Safi, any
undisturbed remains still in situ would be extremely valuable evidence for
reconstructing the sequence of events in the ancient city of Zoar. If the an-
Naq' cemetery was scientifically studied, it might provide critical information
regarding the population of Zoar in the Early Bronze Age and Byzantine
periods. Who were these people and where did they come from? Did they
die out during the Great Plague of AD 541–570, which was the worst outbreak
in the Mediterranean until the Black Death of AD 1348? If so, would this
account for the large number of tombstones of children and adolescents?
Once tombstones are removed from the graves they originally marked their
context is lost, preventing any further study.

Since the discovery and excavation of the Sanctuary of Lot in the late
1980s and throughout the 1990s, much attention has been focused on the
rich archaeological remains in the Ghor es-Safi, particularly at Khirbet Sheik
'Isa, the ancient city of Zoar, and at an-Naq' its adjacent cemetery.

**Figure 14.1** Bulldozed remains of the medieval and Byzantine buildings of the ancient city of Zoar

In 1992, a bulldozed heap of architectural stones at Khirbet Sheik 'Isa was all that remained of the buildings of medieval and Byzantine Zoar (Figure 14.1). The most informative pieces, capitals and inscribed or decorated blocks, had been illegally carried away during the 1970s when new agricultural fields were being established by the JVA and an Italian construction company was installing an underground irrigation system. Some of these stones had been seen at the company's local headquarters until the project finished and the Italian employees returned to Italy. There are now reliable reports that some of these artefacts from the Ghor es-Safi can be found in or near Milan in northern Italy where the company is based and where many of its employees live.

The vast cemetery at an-Naq' with its tens of thousands of graves has taken longer to pillage (Figure 14.2). Its sheer size and wealth of valuable grave goods has incited increasing numbers of illicit excavations which continue to this day. The unemployed local population has, over the years, taught itself the skill of tomb robbing to survive (Figures 14.3, 14.4 and 14.5). They have even learned to distinguish between Byzantine and bronze age period antiquities and refer to the former as 'Christian' and the latter as 'Jewish'. Since the local tomb robbers are Muslim they feel no guilt in disrupting these graves, and now their looting has extended into the Islamic part of the cemetery. There too, most seem prepared to disregard the sanctity of their deceased ancestors in a frenzy to collect saleable *objets d'art*. The situation became so alarming to the archaeologists working at the nearby Sanctuary of Lot, that they decided to publicize this destruction (Politis 1994).

**Figure 14.2** The cemetery of an-Naq' showing looted graves

**Figure 14.3** Villagers looting an-Naq'

**Figure 14.4** Bracelets and glass vessels cushioned in a shell-suit jacket during looting

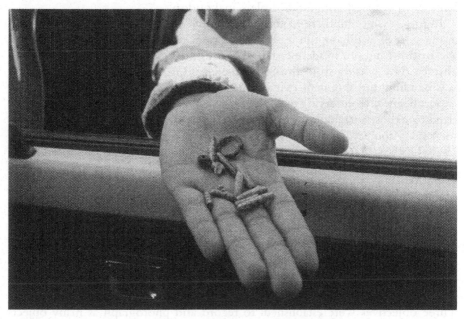

**Figure 14.5** Looted small finds offered for sale through the author's car window

In February 1994, a CNN report on the tomb robbing at Safi was broadcast around the world. It placed much of the blame on high unemployment in this impoverished area and the government for neglecting to protect archaeological sites adequately. This was immediately followed by the Australian Broadcasting Corporation in a similar programme. Embarrassed by the international coverage, the Jordanian government sent out the army to seal off the area. Days later, French journalists were arrested attempting to film the looting scenes at the an-Naq' cemetery. Initially, the destitute tomb robbers seemed to be protected by the army who sympathized with their plight. And indeed, both journalists and archaeologists also had difficulty in condemning the villagers of Safi for looting the ancient sites in a desperate effort to feed their families.

In March, a series of newspaper articles appeared in the Jordanian local press scrutinizing the situation and alluding to a cover-up. Although buying and selling antiquities is illegal in Jordan, wealthy Jordanians as well as foreign diplomats and expatriate business people collect them quite openly. There is hardly a stylish home in the capital city, 'Amman, that does not have some ancient pot or stone decorating it. The characteristic Early Bronze Age I pottery from the Safi cemetery has been particularly popular. Evidence now shows that this fashion is not restricted to Jordan. The tourist shops of Jerusalem, where dealing in antiquities is not illegal and prices are much higher, can easily provide customers with artefacts from this region. They have even reached antiquities dealers in London.

In July, a large shipment of antiquities bound for New York was intercepted at the port of Southampton by British customs officers. Experts called in from the British Museum to identify the objects confirmed that they included some characteristic pottery from the Safi cemetery. The London-based dealer who was handling the shipment (Mr J) claimed to have obtained a valid Jordanian export licence. Considering that only bona fide academic institutions are authorized to export antiquities legally for study purposes, it is certain that this permit was a forgery. But since the UK is not a signatory to the international 1970 UNESCO Convention prohibiting the transportation of unregistered antiquities, the shipment was allowed to continue on to the US. The only action that could be taken, was to alert American customs authorities. The US has signed the Convention and could stop such illegal trade. Apparently though, the antiquities in question were allowed into the US since they now had dubiously acquired an export licence from Lebanon.

In the light of the events of 1994 and the inadequate response of the Jordanian authorities to stop the tomb robbing, an independent campaign was mounted by archaeologists at the Sanctuary of Lot, headed by the author of this article, to counter the looting and subsequent dealing in antiquities. Three objectives were established: to record and photograph as many objects coming from the robbed-out sites as possible; to collect as many of these objects as possible for the Jordanian Department of Antiquities (particularly important objects such as inscribed stones); and to interact with the tomb robbers and intermediary antiquities dealers in order to ascertain the provenance of the objects and identify the network of buyers and sellers. A strategy was developed to achieve these goals (Khouri 1999; Shanks 1999a).

First, several notorious tomb robbers were discreetly approached in order to gain their confidence. Once this was established, a series of interviews were conducted in private and on the ancient sites. Some of these interviews were taped with the consent of the tomb robbers. A large amount of valuable information was gathered and transcribed by this method (Politis 1998a).

This information led us to several intermediary dealers in the Jordanian cities of Kerak and 'Amman. Most notable was the former head of the Italian hospital in Kerak, Dr N, who with the support of the Muslim Brotherhood Party, had been elected mayor of Kerak. During one undercover meeting at a petrol station near Kerak on 5 June 1995, Dr N offered to sell us two inscribed tombstones from Safi for 1,000 Jordanian Dinars each (roughly £1,000), and boasted of having many more in his possession. After photographing and recording the two stones we declined his proposition and left him furious for, in his own words, 'having wasted his time'. The encounter was reported to the Director-General of Antiquities who admitted that he knew of Dr N's antiquities collection but he felt that he could not accuse him because of his political and tribal affiliations. On another occasion, we were introduced to a cousin of Dr N who specialized in the sale of Roman and Byzantine glass vessels. In 1999, Dr N was offering to sell all his antiquities to the Jordanian Government for $3 million.

On 5 May 1997, we visited the house of Mr D, a retired police officer, living in Marka near 'Amman and recorded seven Safi tombstones which he wanted to sell. Politely declining his offers we left, but not before he had shown us a video tape of other antiquities which were for sale. Since then, several of the tombstones have appeared on the antiquities market in London (see Mr I encounter below).

Other information which we gathered included names of employees of the Arab Potash Company and Jordan Valley Authority who, unknown to their employers, were buying antiquities from the locals in Safi and selling them on to dealers in Kerak who in turn sold them to dealers in 'Amman. Their contacts in 'Amman included diplomats in the US, Saudi Arabian and Italian embassies. One report claimed that Bedouins drove overland with pick-up trucks from Petra to buy antiquities for the tourists visiting that site (a shipment of antiquities from the Ghor es-Safi which included pottery and an inscribed tombstone was confiscated by the Department of Antiquities in Petra and is now in the Petra museum storeroom). Another account alleged that antiquities were illegally exported to Israel in barrels of oil along the Potash company's roads that cross over the Dead Sea.

With the approval of the Minister of Tourism and Antiquities and the Director-General of Antiquities, we began purchasing some of the more important antiquities directly from the tomb robbers. This had a double effect. It helped gain the confidence of the poor tomb robbers and disrupted the dealing network. Meanwhile we explained to the tomb robbers that unlike the dealers we were buying these antiquities in order to keep them in Jordan. Ultimately, we explained, we planned to build a museum in Safi to exhibit them. A building plan for the museum has now been approved by the Ministry of Tourism and Antiquities which will sponsor the construction of the project together with the Arab Potash Company and other private sources.

A public relations campaign was an integral part of our battle against the antiquities trade. In conjunction with this, we put pressure on the Department of Antiquities to fence as many sites as possible and generally to improve security. The most effective method of protecting archaeological sites under threat from looters though, is to excavate them. Thus, as soon as the excavation project at the Sanctuary of Lot drew to a close, plans were made to survey and excavate other sites in the Ghor es-Safi.

In 1996 and 1997, I led a rescue excavation sponsored by the British Museum and the Department of Antiquities at Khirbet Qazone (Politis 1998b: 611–14). The site, which has exceptionally well-preserved textile and leather shrouds, consists of some 3,500 robbed-out shaft tombs belonging to the second–third centuries AD. The best parallel to Khirbet Qazone is Qumran and this association is now considered of major significance to scholars of the Dead Sea scrolls (Shanks 1999b: 49–53). Had we not undertaken these urgent excavations, this important new information would certainly have been lost.

In 1999, a topographic and resistivity survey was conducted of Khirbet Sheik 'Isa and Tawahin es-Sukkar (Jones et al. 2000) and a previously unknown iron age site of Teleilat Qasr Musa Hamid was discovered (Politis 1999: 543–4). In the following year, excavations were begun there and in the an-Naq' cemetery (Papadopoulos and Politis, forthcoming).

Meanwhile, the inscribed tombstones which were recovered from the tomb robbers have been fully recorded and studied, and are now in the final stages of publication by the National Hellenic Research Foundation in Athens (Meimaris et al. forthcoming). The new information from this work is already proving to be invaluable to scholars of the early Christian Byzantine period. The fact that the tombstones were recorded and/or collected directly from the tomb robbers in the Ghor es-Safi (thereby preventing them from being sold to antiquities dealers) not only established a provenance for the stones, but also facilitates the return of those that did leave the Ghor es-Safi area as well as Jordan.

The objects which were sold to antiquities dealers (who, in turn, sold them to collectors abroad) were sometimes traced since some pieces had been photographed and marked. Two such cases were tracked down to a major collector in London (Mr K) (Shanks 1999b: 51). Mr K has a particular interest in ancient Zoar and has managed to acquire the best-known private collection of antiquities from the Ghor es-Safi, which includes inscribed tombstones and papyri, pottery and glass vessels.

Mr I is a leading Jordanian antiquities dealer. From several undercover encounters with Mr I, I was able to establish the extent of his illegal antiquities dealing. He and his family had been involved with the illegal trade of antiquities for many decades. They had been buying illicit antiquities from various sources in Jordan and transporting them via United Nations aid trucks travelling from Jordan into the Israeli-occupied West Bank. Once in Israeli jurisdiction, which permits trading in antiquities, the objects found their way to local and international markets. Such methods were not without precedent.

In the late 1940s, the Dead Sea scrolls, which were supposed to be a chance find by a wandering Bedouin, first came up on the Israeli antiquities market. In 1961, Sheriff Nasser, King Hussein's uncle offered one such scroll to the US Ambassador to Jordan. The offer was politely declined but a report was filed in the State Department about the incident (*Art Newspaper* 1997). The scroll in question was apparently sold to a dealer and eventually found its way into the collections of the Israel Museum in Jerusalem.

**Figure 14.6** Aerial photograph showing the cemetery of an-Naq' in 1992 before the onset of large-scale looting. The arrow indicates the precise location of the subsequent looting activities recorded in Figures 14.3–5

Photograph: Department of Antiquities, Jordan

**Figure 14.7** Aerial photograph showing the cemetery of an-Naqʻ in 1999. The largely undisturbed surface of 1992 is pockmarked by looted graves. Again, the arrow indicates the precise location of the looting activities recorded in Figures 14.3–5

More recently, London-based dealer Mr J (mentioned above) has been a well-known supplier of antiquities from Jordan, and from the Ghor es-Safi in particular. During the 1990s, Mr J had a steady source of antiquities coming from Jordanian dealers such as Mr I and although the sale of antiquities is allowed in the UK, it does not sanction Mr J's dealings with the illegal activities of Mr I and the like. After a visit to Mr J's north London warehouse/shop in 1994, I was able to see for myself the quantity of antiquities he was distributing. So many Jordanian antiquities were available that J's policy was to encourage average people to buy them by selling them at a very low price via a mail-order catalogue.

The intensive, uncontrolled tomb robbing, illegal dealing and mass exporting of Ghor es-Safi antiquities resulted in a temporary glut on the international market, which was relieved by discount sales in order to liquidate the stocks. The consequence has been the devastation of the ancient sites in the Ghor es-Safi and a depletion in the supply of antiquities which at one time seemed infinite (Figures 14.6 and 14.7). Today several very important cemeteries belonging to Bronze Age, Roman, Byzantine Christian, Jewish and Islamic periods have been virtually erased. Invaluable information about these populations has gone for ever. Even if some objects could be recovered, their specific context would never be known, diminishing their archaeological value. The few short rescue excavations that have been conducted will be the only source of data on which to base reconstructions of the ancient societies which once flourished in the Ghor es-Safi. Indeed, it is a sad fact that by the year 2000 so little was left of the ancient cemeteries that the tomb robbers resorted to unearthing modern burials. It was reported in the *Jordan Times* (3 September 2000) that the bodies recovered were 3,700 years old and marvellously preserved. The grave robbers had tried to sell them for US$100,000. In actual fact, the bodies had been excavated from graves lined with cement blocks and were obviously modern.

The tragic fate of biblical Zoar is common to many important archaeological and historic sites in the Near East. It is a typical example of a developing country unofficially subsidizing its economy by selling off its cultural heritage. Much of this problem could be alleviated by educating and informing local governments, as well as poor villagers, that caring for and developing their archaeological sites as cultural resources for tourism can provide them with a long-term viable future, unlike tomb robbing which meanwhile continues to provide a new, though finite, supply of antiquities for the international art market.

## NOTE

For legal reasons false initials have been used throughout rather than real names.

## REFERENCES

*Art Newspaper* 1997. The Temple Scroll. Uncle of King Hussein offered Dead Sea scroll to US. *Art Newspaper*, April, no. 69, 1–2.

Jones, R.E., G. Tompsett, K.D. Politis and E. Photos-Jones 2000. The Tawahin es-Sukkar and Khirbet Sheik 'Isa Project. Phase I: the Surveys. *Annual of the Department of Antiquities of Jordan* 44, 523–34.

Khouri, Rami G. 1999. Robbed ancient cemeteries at Ghor es-Safi include collection of inscribed gravestones in Greek and Aramaic. *Jordan Times*, 22 February.

Meimaris, Y.E., K.I. Kritikakou, S. Brock and K.D. Politis (forthcoming). *Catalogue of 4th–6th century A.D. Funerary Stelae from Zoara (Ghor es-Safi, Jordan)*. Athens: National Hellenic Research Foundation.

Papadopoulos, T. and K.D. Politis (forthcoming) Teleilat Qasr Musa Hamid and an Naq' Survey and Excavation 2000. *Annual of the Department of Antiquities of Jordan*.

Politis, K.D. 1994. Biblical Zoar: the looting of an ancient site. *Minerva* 5(6), 12–15.

Politis, K.D. 1998a. Survey and Rescue Collections in the Ghawr As-Safi. *Annual of the Department of Antiquities of Jordan* 42: 627–34.

Politis, K.D. 1998b. Rescue Excavations in the Nabataean Cemetery at Khirbat Qazone. *Annual of the Department of Antiquities of Jordan* 42, 611–14.

Politis, K.D. 1999. Telaylat Qasr Musa Hamid. *Annual of the Department of Antiquities of Jordan* 43, 543–4.

Shanks, H. 1999a. How to stop looting. A modest proposal. *Archaeology Odyssey*. Sept./Oct., 4, 8 and 56–7.

Shanks, H. 1999b. Who Lies here? Jordan Tombs Match Those at Qumran. *Biblical Archaeology Review*. 25(5), 49–51.

# 15  Plunder of cultural and art treasures – the Indian experience

S.K. Pachauri

## INTRODUCTION

The Convention on the Means of Prohibiting and Preventing the Illicit Import, Export and Transfer of Ownership of Cultural Property was adopted on 14 November 1970 by the General Conference of UNESCO. In this convention the term 'cultural property' is broadly defined to mean property specifically designated by a state to be of importance for archaeology, prehistory, history, literature, art or science, and belonging to certain named categories such as rare collections of fauna, flora, minerals and anatomy; products of archaeological excavations; elements of artistic or historical monuments; antiquities more than 100 years old such as coins with inscriptions and engraved seals; paintings, engravings, and sculptures; and rare books and manuscripts. Much of the Convention is admirable, with formulations such that cultural property found within the national territory 'forms part of the cultural heritage of each state'. Unfortunately, however, the crucial operative part is woefully inadequate.

Under Article 7 of the Convention, States Parties undertake to 'take the necessary measures, consistent with national legislation, to prevent museums and similar institutions within their territories from acquiring cultural property originating in another State Party which has been illegally exported after entry into force of this Convention, in the States concerned'. Clearly, this Article hinges on the effectiveness of 'national legislation'. There is also an obligation in Article 7 to take steps to recover and return stolen cultural property at the request of the country of origin, provided it has been imported after the entry into force of the Convention and that the requesting state pays 'just compensation to an innocent purchaser or to a person who has valid title to that property'.

The Indian Constitution has made clear provision regarding the protection of monuments and the export of cultural material. Article 49 of the Constitution of India reads: 'It shall be the obligation of the state to protect every monument or place or object of artistic or historic interest, declared by or under law made by Parliament, to be of national importance from spoliation, disfigurement, destruction, removal, disposal or export, as the case may be'. In accordance with the UNESCO Convention of 1970, the Indian Government in 1972 enacted a Bill in Parliament to regulate the export of antiquities, after first repealing the Antiquities (Export Control) Act of 1947. In the 1947 Act, for the first time, an antiquity had been defined as an object/article of historical significance made of stone, metal, terracotta, etc., which was not less than 100 years old. The new Act is more stringent as it prescribes new punishments and takes cognizance of a variety of offences.

The 1972 Act regulates internal and external trade in antiquities, and provides for compulsory registration of certain notified categories of antiquities, identification and declaration of art treasures from among the notable human works of art and compulsory acquisition of antiquities and art treasures. All these measures have been taken so that the cultural wealth of the country can be preserved for posterity. The main objective of this Act is to prevent permanent export of antiquities and art treasures out of the country. However, the Government of India has the discretion to allow temporary export of antiquities and art treasures which are intended to be taken out of the country for various exhibitions abroad and for a specified period. The approval for such temporary exports is given by the Director-General, Archaeological Survey of India (ASI). In order to prevent the export of antiquities and art treasures, officers of the ASI are posted at important sea and air customs points to help the concerned authorities in identifying and detaining antiquities and art treasures that might be taken out of the country.

The officers for registration of antiquities (Registering Officers), and for the issue of licences for dealers in antiquities (Licensing Officers), are spread over the country. The Registering Officers work under the Directors of Archaeology and Museums in each State, who are coordinators for the purpose of the Act and are responsible to the Director-General, ASI. Officers of the ASI of the rank of Superintending Archaeologist are declared as Licensing Officers for the purpose of this act. The various law enforcement agencies like the Central Bureau of Investigation (CBI), Directorate of Revenue Investigation (DRI), Customs and the Police also help the Director-General, ASI within India and Interpol abroad.

The Antiquities and Art Treasures Act 1972, along with rules which came into force with effect from 5 April 1976, deals exclusively with moveable cultural property of two broad categories: Antiquities and Art Treasures. The Act provides for (i) compulsory registration of notified categories of antiquities; (ii) regulation of the export trade in antiquities and art treasures; (iii) prevention of smuggling of, and fraudulent dealings in, antiquities; (iv) compulsory acquisition of antiquities and art treasures for preservation in public places; and (v) certain other matters connected therewith or incidental or ancillary thereto.

*Salient provisions of the 1972 Antiquities and Art Treasures Act*
Section 2(a) gives an elaborate definition of an antiquity:

1  (i)    any coin, sculpture, painting, epigraph or other work of art or craftsmanship;
   (ii)   any article, object or thing detached from a building or cave;
   (iii)  any article, object or thing illustrative of science, art, crafts, literature, religion, customs, morals or politics in bygone ages;
   (iv)   any article, object or thing of historical interest;
   (v)    any article, object or thing declared by the Central Government by notification in the Official Gazette to be an antiquity for the purpose of this Act, which has been in existence for not less than one hundred years; and

2  any manuscript, record or other document which is of scientific, historical, literary or aesthetic value and which has been in existence for not less than seventy-five years.

Section 2(b) defines art treasures as:

> 'Art treasure' means any human work of art, not being an antiquity, declared by the Central Government, by notification in the Official Gazette, to be an art treasure for the purposes of this Act having regard to its artistic value;

> Provided that no declaration under this clause shall be made in respect of any such work of art so long as the author thereof is alive.

Section 3 lays down that the export of an antiquity or art treasure without a permit issued by the Central Government shall be unlawful.

Section 5 lays down that no person shall carry on the business of selling or offering to sell any antiquity without a licence granted by ASI.

Registration of antiquities has been given priority in the Act. Section 14 (sub-section 3(a)) emphasizes that certain classes of antiquities, as notified in the official Gazette, will be required to be registered with the ASI within 15 days of acquisition. Every person, including any foreign national residing in India, has to register any notified antiquities in his or her possession.

Section 24 defines the power to determine whether or not an article is an antiquity or an art treasure. According to this Section, if any question arises as to whether any article, object or thing, manuscript, record or other document is or is not an antiquity, or an art treasure, for the purposes of this Act, it shall be referred to the Director-General, ASI, or to an officer not below the rank of a Director in the ASI and authorized by the Director-General, ASI, or such officer, as the case may be, whose decision is final.

Section 25 deals with penalties. The punishment provided under Section 25(1) for export or attempt to export any antiquity or art treasure in contravention of Section 3 is a mandatory minimum sentence of six months which may be extended to three years with fine. The punishment for all other offences under this act is a maximum of six months or fine.

It shall not be lawful for any person to export any antiquity or art treasure except under and in accordance with the terms and conditions of a permit issued for the purpose by such authority as may be prescribed. Antiquities and art treasures, however, in certain cases are allowed to be taken abroad for short and specific periods under Temporary Export Permits issued by Director-General, ASI.

To facilitate the Customs authorities in allowing non-antiquities to be exported, the ASI has set up Expert Advisory Committees to issue Non-Antiquity Certificates. These are located in Bangalore, Mumbai, Calcutta, Cochin, Madras, New Delhi, Srinagar and Varanasi. The local ASI officers act as conveners of these committees.

In addition, all important international exit points for sea and air transportation (i.e. Mumbai, Delhi, Calcutta, Madras and Cochin) have been provided with ASI officers to help and assist the Customs Authorities in distinguishing antiquities from non-antiquities before the latter are exported. In case of any dispute arising as to whether any object is an antiquity or not, the decision of the Director-General, ASI under Section 24 is final.

The UNIDROIT Convention on Stolen or Illegally Exported Cultural Objects was adopted at a diplomatic conference in Rome on 23 June 1995. Its efficacy has yet to be properly substantiated and will be decided world-wide. Among the important countries to have signed this Convention are France, Italy and the Netherlands, although so far only Italy has ratified. The Convention demands the return of any stolen cultural object – the definition of which relies on the same categories of cultural property as those set out in the 1970 UNESCO Convention. The return of unlawfully exported cultural objects is mandatory only in specified circumstances. A court of the requested state must establish that the removal of the object from its territory significantly impairs one or more of the following interests:

(a)   the physical preservation of the object or of its context;
(b)   the integrity of a complex object;
(c)   the preservation of information of, for example, a scientific or historical character;
(d)   the traditional or ritual use of the object by a tribal or indigenous community;

or establishes that the object is of significant cultural importance for the requesting state.

Antiquities taken from a monument would fall under (b). Some other categories will fall under (c) or (d) or be considered of significant cultural importance to the requesting state so as to come within the general provision. What may be called ordinary antiquities would fall under (a) if their removal had significantly impaired the context.

It is appropriate to give a brief description of the nature of threats posed to India's historical monuments, magnificent temples, and works of art by human hand during the formative years of the ASI. Some quotes from the famous address of Curzon, delivered at the Asiatic Society, Calcutta on 20 December, 1900, are revealing:

> In the days of William Bentick, the Taj was on the point of being destroyed for the value of its marbles. The same Governor General sold by auction the marble bath in Shah Jehan's Palace at Agra, which had been torn up by Lord Hastings for a gift to George IV, but had somehow never been despatched. In the same regime a proposal was made to lease the gardens at Sikandra to the Executive Engineer at Agra for the purpose of speculative cultivation.
>
> At an earlier date when picnic-parties were held in the garden of Taj, it was not an uncommon thing for the revellers to arm themselves with hammer and chisel, with which they whiled away the afternoon by chipping out fragments of agate and a cornelian from the cenotaphs of the Emperor and his lamented Queen.
>
> When the Prince of Wales was at Agra in 1876, and the various pavilions of Shah Jehan's palace were connected together for the purposes of an evening party and ball, local talent was called in to reproduce the faded paintings on marble and plaster of the Moghul artists two and a half centuries before. The result of their labours is still an eyesore and a regret.
>
> In 1857, after the Mutiny, it was solemnly proposed to raze to the ground the Jumma Masjid at Delhi, the noblest ceremonial mosque in the world, and it was only spared at the instance of Sir John Lawrence. As late as 1868 the destruction of the great gateways of the Sanchi Tope was successfully prevented by the same statesman.
>
> When the Prince of Wales came to India in 1876, and held a Durbar in this building (the Red Fort), the opportunity was too good to be lost; and a fresh coat of whitewash was plentifully bespattered over the red sandstone pillars and plinths of the Durbar hall of Aurangzeb.
>
> Some of the sculptured columns of the exquisite Hindu-Mussulman mosque at Ajmere were pulled down by a zealous officer to construct a triumphal arch under which the Viceroy of the day was to pass.

This type of vandalism, which took place in the nineteenth century at the hands of the rulers that Curzon so candidly mentioned, is of course no longer there. However, monuments are still allowed to be misused and encroached upon, or simply left alone to deteriorate and decay.

## MODUS OPERANDI ADOPTED IN ANTIQUITIES THEFT AND SMUGGLING CASES

1   Local thieves keep watch on objects in temples and historical monuments, and even in museums, they strike when an opportunity presents itself.

2   After the theft, the thieves wait until the hue and cry over the crime dies down.

3   They then dispatch their contact man to Delhi or another big city with photographs of the stolen material, where they establish contacts with prospective foreign buyers or with dealers. In some cases, photographs are taken before the crime is committed.

4   These dealers study the photographs, date the object and agree on a price.

5   Only after the price is settled does the stolen object pass from one hand to another.

6   Sometimes replicas of originals are prepared. A certificate for 'Non-Antiquity' is obtained from the ASI by producing a replica instead of the original. With a certificate in hand, the original, not the replica, can be exported illegally.

7   In a few cases, the smuggler prepares two similar packets, one containing the original object and the other containing a fake. The packet containing the replica is inspected and checked by Customs. It is then replaced with the original object with the connivance of the Customs staff.

## CASES (AT A MACRO-LEVEL)

Examples are provided here of major cases detected at the macro or national level which have an international significance.

*Bronze Nataraja image and other objects from Viswanathaswamy temple. Pathur village, Tanjavur district, Tamil Nadu (twelfth century AD)*

In October 1976, one Ramamurthy was digging for sand in Pathur village when this Nataraja image was discovered. Nothing further was heard about it for nine months until July 1977 when it surfaced mysteriously in England and was widely reported. The Tamil Nadu Government alerted Interpol but it was not until 1982 that the police confiscated the image from the British Museum where it had been sent for cleaning by the Bumper Development Corporation. A court case was filed by the Tamil Nadu Government in London. The Bumper Development Corporation protested innocent purchase and claimed that its Nataraja was not the stolen object from Pathur village. Ramamurthy was apprehended in India and, along with the other witnesses, he identified the statue in London; forensic experts provided evidence of its authenticity and documentary evidence was also produced by the Tamil Nadu Government.

On 17 February 1988, in London, the High Court delivered judgment in favour of India. An appeal by the Bumper Development Corporation was dismissed on 13 February 1991. The object was brought by the Indian High Commissioner, London and handed over to the Tamil Nadu Government on 9 August 1991 at Madras.

*Dancing Siva (Nataraja) from Sivapuram, Tamil Nadu. Early Chola period (tenth century AD)*

This famous bronze image of Nataraja was one of six idols found in 1951 while a field was being dug in the village of Sivapuram, in Tanjavur district, Tamil Nadu. Under the Indian Treasure Trove Act of 1878, the find was handed over to the temple authorities of Sivagurunathaswamy temple of Sivapuram in 1953. The condition of the Nataraja, after being under the earth for several centuries, had badly deteriorated, and therefore it was given to one Ramaswamy Sthapati of Devi Silpasala in 1954 for repair, and it remained with him until 1956. During this period a replica was prepared and sent to the temple, while the genuine one was sold for only Rs 5,000/-. When it changed hands again, it was bought for Rs 17,000/- by an executive of a foreign company in Madras. It remained in the possession of the executive until 1964 when it was exchanged for fifty-nine miniature bronze images plus Rs 500,000/-. Thereafter, in 1969, it was bought by a buyer at a price of Rs 575,000/- through a middleman.

Douglas Barret of the British Museum, when he visited India in 1964, had seen the original Nataraja in the possession of a Mr Lance Dane, an executive of a company in Mumbai. In his book *Early Chola Bronzes* Barret mentioned that the Nataraja idol formerly in the Sivapuram temple, was in the private collection of Mr Dane. On the basis of this publication the Tamil Nadu Government ordered an inquiry in 1969 and when it was finished the Director of the Government Museum in Madras declared the Nataraja idol in the Sivapuram temple to be fake, and that the original was missing.

It was learnt in 1970 that the Sivapuram Nataraja had reached the US. It had been despatched from India in 1969 from Palam Airport, Delhi on a foreign airliner. The Nataraja idol reached New York via London and came into possession of one Mr Ben Heller, who sold it to Mr Norton Simon of Norton Simon Foundation, Los Angeles for $1,000,000 in 1973. After some time, Norton Simon sent the idol to the British Museum, London for repairs and Scotland Yard impounded it as stolen property.

The Government of India filed court cases in the UK in 1974 and shortly after in the US for the restitution of this property. Documentary evidence, photographs and the publication of Dr Barret were produced as evidence of ownership, which was established in court, despite Norton Simon's plea of innocent purchase. After protracted litigation in 1976 the matter was settled. An agreement was reached with the Norton Simon Foundation whereby the idol of Nataraja would remain with the Foundation on loan from the Government of India for a period of ten years, after which time it would be returned.

In 1986, the Director-General, ASI went to the US to recover the image and on 5 May it was thoroughly examined by him and by experts such as Dr Stella Kramrisch and Elizabeth Rosen, before being taken over on the same day in the presence of officials of the Indian Embassy and representatives of the Norton Simon Foundation. The Nataraja idol reached India on 8 May 1986 and on 15 May 1986 it was handed over to the representatives of the Tamil Nadu Government at Madras.

*Dancing Siva (Nataraja) in Bronze. Chola, late tenth–early eleventh century AD, stolen from Tiruvilakkudi district Tanjore (Tamil Nadu). Returned by Kimbell Art Museum*

This image of 105 cm height and weighing 100 kg was stolen from Easvaran temple in Tiruvilakkudi village, in Tanjavur district, Tamil Nadu, on or about 20 February 1978. It was traced with the help of Interpol.

It was reported to the Government of Tamil Nadu that Bina Khulasi and Albert Ainran of Everest Art Gallery London had deliberately given a false declaration and sold the Nataraja to the Kimbell Art Museum in August 1979. The Tamil Nadu Government requested the Government of India to take action to ensure its retrieval. The Indian Embassy in Washington took up the case with the US Department of State.

The Director of the Kimbell Art Museum suspected that the bronze might have been stolen and contacted the Indian Embassy in Washington, whereupon its return was requested by the Government of India. The Kimbell Art Museum asked to keep the Nataraja on exhibition for ten years after which time it would be returned to India at the Museum's own expense. The Tamil Nadu Government, however, did not agree to this request.

The Museum then suggested an exchange whereby it would return the Nataraja but receive an equivalently valued antiquity from Tamil Nadu as compensation. Again, the Tamil Nadu Government did not agree to this suggestion, although it was ready to give all assistance if the Kimbell Museum proceeded to recover the amount paid for the purchase of the stolen idol.

Ultimately the Museum agreed to return the idol after an indemnity agreement was signed by the Government of India on 12 August 1985. The idol was then returned to the Indian Embassy at Washington. It was brought back to India by the Director-General, ASI in May 1986. The Government of India conveyed its gratification and thanks to Kimbell Art Museum for their cooperation and return of the Nataraja idol.

## CASES (AT MICRO-LEVEL)

Examples are provided here of cases at the micro or state level which have a regional significance.

Andhra Pradesh is one of the major states in South India and is characterized by its rich temple heritage and archaeological wealth. Some of the
typical instances of thefts which were detected by the Andhra Pradesh State
Archaeological Department in recent years are:

1  3 December 1997: Task force officials of Hyderabad raided the Hotel
   Regal, in Secunderabad, and seized three idols of Lord Rama, Laxmana
   and Sita Devi. Suspects admitted to finding the idols when they dug
   the temple ruins at Peddammapet, Karim Nagar District.
2  At the Singoor Dam Site two sculptures of Anjaneya and Hanuman
   were taken. A criminal complaint was lodged with the local Police
   Station in Medak District.
3  On 4 May 1998 some idols were stolen from the Ramdayan temple
   of Narsapur village in Adilabad District. On 12 July 1998 the thieves
   were arrested and the idols recovered. They were found to include
   copper items of Lord Rama, Laxmana and Sita Devi etc.

These are three examples of theft of temple idols or other temple property.
There may be many other such thefts in other states of India which escape
detection and never come to light. In this way a large portion of the cultural
heritage is lost forever.

The smuggling of works of art and antiquities is essentially a white-collar
crime as it involves a certain amount of sophistication and expertise in assessing
the value of the object to be illegally transported and sold. Although the
Indian Government enacted the Antiquities and Art Treasures Act of 1972,
after taking into consideration the UNESCO Convention of 1970, there are
still inadequacies and loopholes which allow the illicit trafficking of antiquities. The most glaring omission seems to be that the punishment prescribed
under section 25 of the Act is very mild. It ranges from a minimum of six
months to a maximum of three years imprisonment with fine. A second flaw
is that, although the export of antiquities without a valid permit from the
competent authority is not permissible under this Act, there is no ban on
the export of handicraft items. The smuggler can exploit this loophole by
mixing handicrafts in with export consignments. Under the provisions of the
Customs Act, when a consignment contains more than five objects only 10
per cent are required to be checked. Such checks are done on a random
basis and experience has shown that they are rarely taken seriously. Official
connivance at this level has become a serious matter. There should, in fact,
be a very thorough check by both Customs and ASI officers so that any
antiquity suspected of illegal export is immediately recognized. Another weakness of the 1972 Act is that there is no provision to stop the manufacture
of handicrafts which imitate antique originals. This encourages the production of fakes. Many original antiquities have been exported out of India under
the cover of this non-provision. The exporter confuses the authorities at time
of inspection by showing only the fake items and then replacing them with
originals at the time of export.

It is relevant here to mention that non-governmental organizations and voluntary agencies engaged in the field of archaeological research can play a major and worthwhile role in disseminating information about the illicit trafficking of antiquities. They can also monitor such activities and bring them to the notice of the law enforcement agencies who can then take appropriate action. One such organization is the McDonald Institute for Archaeological Research in Cambridge, England, which publishes the newsletter *Culture Without Context*. In India, the Indian National Trust for Art and Cultural Heritage (INTACH) also plays a significant role in this field. Hence, voluntary agencies and non-governmental organizations should receive support of the Government so that they may facilitate the task of checking illicit trafficking of cultural items.

## CONCLUSION

The greatest deterrent to the vandalism of cultural property is public awareness, and thus there is a need to encourage in people a sense of love and pride for their cultural heritage so that they may understand the importance of the law in preserving the heritage for posterity. Poor and innocent villagers are often enticed to help white-collar criminals in their illicit operations without realizing the irreparable loss that they cause. People do not come forward to register antiquities they possess because of the apprehension that the Government will acquire them. Again, this can only be tackled by education at grass roots level.

India is one of the world's largest repositories of cultural material which is to be seen spread all over the country. Except for monuments under the protection and control of the central and state Governments, however, no serious attempts have so far been made to document and prepare an inventory of these relics of the past. They are lying uncared for in remote villages, thick forests and hilly tracts – all of which are gold mines for thieves and smugglers. The time has come to photograph and prepare inventories of this wealth of loose and scattered sculptures and other objects which lie in dilapidated monuments and structures. Such inventories will be of immense help in establishing titles to lost cultural properties and their retrieval. The incentives and rewards for persons giving information concerning cultural heritage offences should be high and attractive so that people will come forward with information. In the event of theft of a cultural object, the lookout notices should be circulated globally, instead of being restricted to India, so that museums, purchasers and other observers outside India are aware of the object and can desist from acquiring it.

The retrieval of cultural property is yet another serious problem, it has several constraints and deserves a global response. Article 7(b)(ii) of the UNESCO Convention of 1970 has provision for repatriation of cultural property exported illegally, but for some governments, however, it has certain drawbacks, such as the need to pay compensation to the innocent purchaser of a stolen object. Added to this, non-ratification by some countries, absence of restrictions on the import of cultural property of other countries, lack of uniformity in the definition of antiquity and cultural heritage weaken its effect. Moreover, litigation is too expensive and time-consuming. In view of the above constraints, bilateral agreements under the auspices of the Convention appear to be more viable for the protection of cultural heritage. These bilateral agreements impose legally binding obligations on the nations and must therefore be encouraged.

However, disputes may still arise while negotiating either through the bilateral agreements or other arrangements such as Article 7(b)(ii) of UNESCO Convention, 1970. In such circumstances, the retrieval cases might be taken care of by an International Court of Justice, preferably by a Special Bench to be constituted for the purpose, instead of knocking on the doors of the Honourable Courts in the respective countries.

The definition of the term 'antiquity' has been found lacking in precision and varies from country to country. A widely acceptable definition should be worked out by member States. Where this is not possible, the definition of the country of origin should be honoured by the other member State while negotiating the retrieval.

UNESCO has a major role to play in coordinating state actions on these matters. In many cases UNESCO has initiated action and international conventions or recommendations have emerged in due course. More may do so in the future. UNESCO member states themselves will have to act and take on the fight against international smuggling and theft and be prepared to take substantial initiatives. UNESCO could: act as a resource centre; commission investigative reporting on the unlawful trade in antiquities; collect evidence on price differentials in the trade of antiquities; take an active role in disseminating information on codes of ethics and practice affecting trade in antiquities and collect information on lapses from the recommended standards; support the development of existing electronic databases carrying information on the trade in antiquities; and encourage a dialogue between dealers, auction houses, archaeologists and government officials to formulate a common approach to implementation of policy.

The UNESCO Intergovernmental Committee for Promoting the Return of Cultural Property to its Countries of Origin or its Restitution in Case of Illicit Appropriation, set up in 1978, has both an active and watchdog role. It should monitor how States are selecting members of the committee to establish whether there are collections of antiquities which could be released onto the market and whether the development of a policy to this effect is desirable. It adopted Object ID, an international standard for the description of objects, in January 1999, a decision endorsed by UNESCO General Council in November 1999, which is being actively promoted.

There is ample opportunity in India for both legal creativity and diplomatic skills when working with UNESCO. Indifference constitutes treason to our cultural heritage. It is well known how priceless antiquities continued to be smuggled from India when an international campaign was launched and much more has to be done – as suggested in this article – to review the law and plug the loopholes. As we stand at the dawn of a new century what we must understand is that the world has truly shrunk and become a Global Village, and so a new consciousness has to be built, step by step, and developed so that people will understand the importance of art objects, and not resort to plunder. This also requires the breaking down of cultural barriers and the spread of knowledge of each others' cultures. It is also necessary to develop a new consciousness which is secular, rational and humanistic so that people can share and respect each others' cultures alike, and not suffer from bigotry and prejudice. I can do no better than quote the immortal verse *Geetainjili* from the renowned Indian poet Rabindranath Tagore:

> Where the mind is without fear and the head is held high;
>> Where the knowledge is free;
> Where the world has not been broken up into fragments by
>> narrow domestic walls;
>> Where words come out from the depth of truth;
> Where tireless striving stretches its arms towards perfection;
>> Where the clear stream of reason has not lost its way into
>> the dreary desert sand of dead habit;
> Where the mind is led forward by Thee into ever widening
>> thought and action . . .
> Into that heaven of freedom, my Father, let my country awake.

## BIBLIOGRAPHY

*Antiquities and Art Treasures Act* 1972.
*Economist.* 1997. 'Misplaced Treasures: Unplundering Art.' 29 December.
Barrett, D. 1965. *Early Chola Bronzes.* Bombay: Bhulabhai Memorial Institute.
The Indian Constitution, 1949. http://alfa.nic.in/const/a1.html
Joshi, M.C. and K.S. Ramchandran 1980. *The Problem of Imitations of Antiquities.* Delhi: Agam Kala Prakashan.
Meyer, K.E. 1974. *The Plundered Past: The Traffic in Art Treasures.* London: Readers Union.
O'Keefe, P.J. 1997. *Trade in Antiquities – Reducing Destruction and Theft.* London: Archetype and UNESCO.
Sarkar, H. 1981. *Museums and Protection of Monuments and Antiquities in India.* Delhi: Sundeep Prakashan.
Singh, B.P. 1998. *India's Culture – the State, the Arts and Beyond.* Delhi: Oxford University Press.
UNESCO 1970. Convention on the Means of Prohibiting and Preventing the Illicit Import, Export and Transfer of Ownership of Cultural Property.
UNIDROIT 1995. Convention on Stolen or Illegally Exported Cultural Objects.
Watson, P. 1997. *Sotheby's: Inside Story.* London: Bloomsbury.
www.object-id.com

# 16  Point, counterpoint

KATHRYN WALKER TUBB

## THE NEED FOR ACTION

The theories of moral philosophy or ethics which have been proposed from
the fifth century BC Sophists of Ancient Greece to the present share, with
all human thought, reflections and refractions of what has preceded them and
of their present. Critical analysis of such theories examines them by applying
unavoidably the biases and perspectives of the here and now. Moral philosophy is not fixed nor should it be. No single overarching theory survives
universal and indefinite application. Indeed, in endeavouring to identify and
stipulate all the ramifications of a single theory, the germ of a common sense
notion tends to be lost, to be replaced by elegant argument divorced uneasily
from life.

The chapters in this volume are very much in the here and now. Discussion
of legislation and its failure to protect cultural heritage in general, and archaeological sites in particular, is engaged in of necessity. Ethical codes which have
been drafted and adopted by dealers' associations and by various heritage
groups, such as archaeologists, conservators, museum personnel etc., are scru-
tinized. Recognition of human nature − greed, survival, power, control, custodianship, social responsibility − features in debates over the survival of the
past and which part of the past. For many engaged in debating as to how to
effect the preservation of the archaeological record, an awareness of the rate
of loss caused by agricultural and industrial/urban development and the looting of sites to provide antiquities for the market, makes it clear that steps need
to be taken now if humanity is to salvage something from the spiralling and
accelerating destruction. In many areas, little is recoverable. This fact, coupled
with the awful knowledge that the changing of opinions and circumstances is
a long-term undertaking, opposed − more often than not − by indifference and
outright hostility, makes it an excruciatingly slow process, and leads to a sense
of hopelessness; yet, for those who perceive the loss, and grieve over it, yield-
ing to defeat ensures succumbing to it.

To do nothing is to embrace such a counsel of despair. In the face of the devastation of the sites and monuments of the past, a fact gaining recognition but failing to attract the requisite preventive response, it is understandable that the ethical issues need to be addressed substantively, focusing on identifying moral actions at a practical level. The outcome is one from which academics tend to shy. The rather uncomfortable truth is that the discourse begins to smack of preachiness; a certain intolerance resonates in it. Liberal modesty would tend to argue the impropriety of such a standpoint, criticizing it for its lack of impartiality or objectivity and scientific detachment. Reflexive thinking would caution against its authoritarian tenor. However, notwithstanding such reservations, there is surely a duty to participate in decrying the destruction of the archaeological heritage and in trying to engage and alert the widest possible audience to the hazard. This is even more imperative since the deprivation of information is final and irretrievable. Sadly, a moratorium on destructive activities is a fanciful proposition. Enlarging the debate must proceed in tandem with the destruction, but the destruction is outstripping consciousness-raising. Those who confront the destruction of the archaeological record, and who recognize the lost information which it entails, may be accused of idealism, even foolishness, when they rail against it, but they are impelled to resist it.

## RECENT DEVELOPMENTS IN THE UK

The turn of the century has seen rather schizophrenic developments in the UK. On the one hand, the government announced in the beginning of 2000 that the UK would accede to neither the 1970 UNESCO Convention nor the 1995 UNIDROIT Convention. On the other hand, despite this, a Department of Culture, Media and Sport Parliamentary Select Committee on Cultural Property: Return and Illicit Trade was set up, under the chairmanship of Gerald Kaufman, to investigate the evidence surrounding these issues and to consider possible remedies for identified problems. Written evidence was submitted by the Standing Conference on Portable Antiquities,[1] United Kingdom Institute for Conservation of Historic and Artistic Works (UKIC), the Metropolitan Police, HMS Customs and Excise, the Antiquities Dealers Association, the British Art Market Federation, Sotheby's, Christie's, the Art Loss Register and so on. Hearings were conducted at which oral evidence was heard. The proceedings of this undertaking and the recommendations reached by the Select Committee were published in July 2000. Perhaps somewhat unusually, Alan Howarth, Minister for the Arts, set up an Advisory Panel in May 2000, before the Select Committee had finished hearing evidence, under the chairmanship of Norman Palmer, with, ostensibly, at least a partially identical remit. The Panel's brief was firstly 'to consider the nature and extent of the illicit international trade in art and antiquities, and the extent to which the UK is involved in this' and, second, 'to consider how most effectively, both through legislative and non-legislative means, the UK can play its part in preventing and prohibiting the illicit trade, and to advise the Government accordingly' (DCMS 2000b: 5). The Select Committee's report contains a wealth of information incorporating the extensive written and verbal evidence submitted to it and is an invaluable reference document in consequence. The Advisory Panel's report is pithy, brief and a model of clarity.

Both the Select Committee and the Advisory Panel clearly accepted that there is a substantial trade in stolen and illegally exported cultural material. It was also clear that Select Committee discussions investigating possible mechanisms which might serve to facilitate better controls focused on two areas: the creation of a national database and the setting of a threshold value for items requiring the imposition of controls, such as import and export licensing. It must be borne in mind that artefacts derived from clandestine excavation cannot benefit from either system. First, unexcavated antiquities are unknown and unknowable. Visiting the hole in the site left by the looter is unlikely to give very much of an idea of the absolute identity of the material which might have been removed. This type of theft, either from a private landowner, or from the state in those countries which claim state ownership of archaeological remains, cannot be entered on a database. Only artefacts which have been inventoried and catalogued, and which have formed part of a collection of some description, can be logged into a database, referral to which may assist in demonstrating ownership. At the risk of labouring the point, previously unexcavated antiquities are inherently and uniquely vulnerable to theft in consequence, since claims for recovery involving questions of title are unlikely to be successful. The likelihood of escaping detection is high; the prospect of prosecution is remote. The establishment of a national database is an obvious objective which should be realized, but its inability to protect antiquities still in their archaeological contexts must also be acknowledged. It is the particular difficulty posed by such material that has led to the inclusion of Article 3.2 in the 1995 UNIDROIT Convention on Stolen and Illegally Exported Cultural Objects. The significance of this article is spelled out in Article 2.3 of the *Policy Statement of the Institute of Archaeology, London, Regarding the Illicit Trade in Antiquities* (Appendix 2).

The argument for treating antiquities as a distinct category has been developed further elsewhere (Tubb 1997b). Dealers often respond to suggestions that all unprovenanced archaeological material be regarded as suspect by invoking the concept of habeas corpus, a presumption of innocence until guilt is proved, and ascribing it to this material. For example, in a recent radio interview conducted by Jolyon Jenkins, James Ede replied to a question concerning the issue of unprovenanced materials by stating:

> Am I not to buy these things because I can't have a piece of paper with it? I think that would be nonsense. As far as I'm concerned this is turning our normal burden of proof on its head. I don't regard something as being guilty until proven innocent.
>
> (Jenkins 2000)

Prott has pointed out the inappropriateness of such a stance, with reference to the 1995 UNIDROIT Convention, by explaining that the principle
of habeas corpus applies to criminal law and not to civil law. UNIDROIT
is the International Institute for the Unification of Private Law and concerns
itself with private law issues. Actions for recovery of disputed cultural material
normally take place in civil courts. She states:

> The principle 'innocent till proven guilty' is a principle of crim-
> inal law which is not affected by the Convention. The test in
> civil claims is the same under the Convention as it is now – i.e.
> the balance of probabilities. In some countries judges already
> require evidence of reasonable enquiries before allowing a defence
> of 'good faith'.
>
> (Prott 1997)

Indeed, habeas corpus (literally 'you have the body' in Latin) applies to a
person ('the body') being held in police custody and exists to protect people
from random arrest and incarceration. It does not apply to things.

Second, the imposition of threshold values, below which the issuing of
licences covering import and export, or suggested logbooks/passports for
cultural material, or entry on a database would be deemed to be unworth-
while, always features large in such debates, in efforts to create a practical system
with a reasonable capacity for delivering results within restricted parameters of
resourcing. The suggested figures range from £500 to £10,000. According to
the Art Loss Register, a London–based organization founded in 1990 with the
support of insurance companies and the art trade which operates a database of
stolen and looted cultural objects, the International Association of Dealers in
Ancient Art (IADAA) agreed in November 1999 that their members would
access the Register whenever transactions involving antiquities valued above
£10,000 were concerned. Searching for evidence that an object at a lower
value has been stolen is reckoned to be uneconomical, although the Art Loss
Register itself, in its promotional literature, sets a minimum value of £1,000
per object for registration with it of a theft by a victim.

It is here that the dialectical differences discussed by Brodie in the introduction to this volume are forcefully in evidence. Any archaeologist knows
that what is being decried by looting is loss of information, loss of context.
One only needs to watch a single episode of Channel 4's 'Meet the Ancestors'
to appreciate how much information can be gleaned from even the most
unpromising remains. Therefore, discussions which centre on recovery already
spell defeat for the archaeological record. That notwithstanding, the critical
defining criterion is price. Resolute and repeated assertions that the destruction to archaeological sites is unaffected by the monetary value of the retrieved
artefacts seem to have no validity in this forum and are met by incomprehension or dismissal as idealistic and unworkable.

The definition of cultural 'property' (an apt term in this context in particular, although not necessarily a happy one) in the 1970 UNESCO Convention

on the Means of Prohibiting and Preventing the Illicit Import, Export and Transfer of Ownership of Cultural Property is often criticized for being too wide. The market claims to be awash with modest artefacts of little value which are virtually indistinguishable from one another. Attempts at identifying them are portrayed as unachievable. What is often left unsaid is that identification is unachievable because of a lack of willingness and resources. The fallaciousness of this stance is easily accessed by examining the research led by Robin Thornes for the Getty Information Institute, and widely circulated in two publications entitled *Protecting Cultural Objects: a preliminary survey* (1995) and *Protecting Cultural Objects in the Global Information Society: the making of Object ID* (1997). A short video (eight minutes) has also been produced to publicize the work. Following a process of extended consultation and collaboration, Thornes has created a new standard which he describes as 'a minimum standard created for a specific purpose – that of describing objects to enable them to be identified' (1997: 1–2). Equally, a new industry is emerging which is conducting research into effective means of tagging or marking cultural material (Radcliffe 1995). Ideas in development include the use of smart water, laser ablation and microchips. The difficulties here turn on the need for a workable and practical system to emerge that would make scanning objects achievable by using a single machine for the purpose of reading the 'tag'. Also, the permanence and safety of such schemes will need to be assessed by conservation-restoration professionals. Were such a scheme to be inexpensive, it need not be reserved solely for items of high monetary value. Furthermore, it is worth bearing in mind that an item ascribed a low price today is likely to be traded in future at hugely inflated and inflating prices, as fashion, with its usual fickleness, shifts from one type of artefact to another, and as values are hyped by clever marketing, inflation and investment collecting. As despoliation of archaeological sites continues at an ever-accelerating pace, as more and more remote areas are exploited and as this non-renewable resource is exhausted, scarcity can also be predicted to have an impact on monetary value. If any serious attempts are to be made to protect that diminishing and threatened resource, antiquities of dubious origin must be identified and rendered unmarketable. Such a prospect is doomed if the majority of artefacts are to be excluded at the inception of their entry into the market on the basis of monetary value. Sadly, optimism is not warranted. In Jolyon Jenkins' radio programme cited earlier, Jerome Eisenberg, a noted dealer in antiquities and the publisher of *Minerva* magazine, stated 'The provenance on small pieces of little value, it's not necessary to check the provenance', and 'If I tried to check every piece that I sell, and I have over 3,000 pieces in stock, I'd have to employ two or three scholars full time to check provenances, and it is seriously not necessary'. (Jenkins 2000).

However, efforts to increase awareness of the general public, and to break through the incomprehension with which the archaeological monologue is greeted, are being made. Most significant among them recently was the production in June of a report entitled *Stealing History: the Illicit Trade in*

*Cultural Material*, commissioned by the Museums Association and the International Council of Museums UK (ICOM UK) from the Illicit Antiquities Research Centre of the McDonald Institute, University of Cambridge (Brodie, Doole and Watson 2000). At the press launch of the publication, four speakers spoke briefly, picking up various strands concerning the looting of sites and the illicit trade of cultural material more generally.

Tony Robinson, presenter of Channel 4's 'Time Team', and a prolific and versatile actor, spoke feelingly of looting as an attack on all of society, and on children in particular, via the medium of loss of heritage. He expressed concern that the UK's legislation is weak and bureaucratic, expressed dismay that the police and the judiciary in this country do not take looting seriously, and concluded by stating that he was outraged by the present, but not pessimistic about the future.

Manus Brinkman, Secretary General of ICOM since 1998, spoke with less optimism, detailing steps taken by ICOM to try to raise awareness generally of the problem of the illicit trade. He stated quite categorically that the theft of a people's history effectively kills them. This theme is relevant to two other papers in this volume. Patrick Boylan's review of the development of international agreements designed to protect cultural material in times of conflict, culminates with the Second Protocol to the 1954 Hague Convention for the Protection of Cultural Property in the Event of Armed Conflict. Part of the impetus for the drafting of the Second Protocol derived from the intentional targeting of cultural remains by vying ethnic groups to obliterate all traces of the presence of their rivals from contested territory during the violent dissolution of the former Yugoslavia (Chapter 3 this volume). This served the dual purpose of demoralizing people by destroying symbols of identity and by rendering any realignment of borders and claims to land more difficult. Téréba Togola presents another situation (referred to further below) in which the present population of Mali actively participates in the obliteration of its past for short-term gain and minimal profit, to stock markets in the developed world (Chapter 13 this volume). Such losses are brutal; they contribute to societal psychic disturbance consequent upon the loss of a sense of belonging, of connectedness to place in space and time, and of identity.

The third speaker at the launch was Colin Renfrew, Director of the McDonald Institute for Archaeological Research, Cambridge, and ardent campaigner for preservation of the archaeological record. He expressed his advocacy for the UK adoption of both the 1970 UNESCO and 1995 UNIDROIT Conventions and spoke of the human past as a shared heritage. Finally, Patrick Greene, President of the Museums Association, addressed the duty to educate, advocating it as a matter of urgency.

*Stealing History* contains recommendations not only to the UK Government but also to museums and UK museum organizations (2000: 6–7) and contains advice on the exercise of due diligence by museums (49–52), a notion brought to prominence in this sphere by its inclusion in the 1995 UNIDROIT Convention on Stolen and Illegally Exported Cultural Objects under Article 4.

The formation of the International Standing Committee on the Traffic in Illicit Antiquities in October 1999 (Brodie and Watson 1999: 23–4), and the holding of major conferences in New Jersey, New York and Cambridge,[2] are all encouraging signs of increasing engagement with the problem. Many organizations, such as the World Archaeological Congress, the European Association of Archaeologists, and the Standing Conference on Portable Antiquities, have passed resolutions committing their members to support the endorsement of the 1970 UNESCO and 1995 UNIDROIT Conventions. They urge their respective governments to adopt these conventions where they have not already done so (Brodie 1999: 27). Unaffiliated declarations, such as the Rutgers Resolution, also form part of this movement (Scarre 1998: 18–19).

It is a curious fact that the Select Committee recommended 'that the UK sign the UNIDROIT Convention' (DCMS 2000a: li) and not the 1970 UNESCO Convention, whereas the Advisory Panel advised 'against accession to the UNIDROIT Convention under the present circumstances' (DCMS 2000b: 7) but supported accession to the 1970 UNESCO Convention.

## CAUTIONARY TALES

The relevance of such actions, and the inadvisability of dismissing out of hand the potential for becoming involved, can be demonstrated by two case histories.

The first concerns the Oxford University Research Laboratory for Archaeology and the History of Art. In 1990, an interview with its Director was broadcast on Channel 4 as part of a documentary entitled 'The African King'. This documentary concerned the looting, on a massive scale, of Mali's archaeological sites to retrieve terracotta figures of great beauty for sale in Europe and North America (van Beek 1990). Demand for these figures has also led to the production of a flood of fakes.

Authentification by thermoluminescence dating of pieces smuggled out of Mali (smuggled since their export is banned under the legislation of that country) results in the provision of that piece of paper – the certificate of authenticity – which is a passport to a high-value price tag in galleries and auction houses the world over. Such test results are always cited in sales catalogues where provenance is conspicuous by its absence.

The interviewer asked the Director whether he recognized that a genuine Malian terracotta would be contraband, and this was acknowledged. It was then ascertained that TL dating was undertaken on a no-questions-asked basis. When challenged to explain this policy, the answer was that you had to earn money in Thatcherite Britain, that this was a business. The reply to the charge, that the name of the university, which should stand for disinterested science, was being sold to run a commercial operation compromising the moral status of the researchers, was rejected as being too simplistic.

The film was powerful. In an editorial in *Antiquity*, Chippindale deemed it 'as sad an archaeological story as may be told' (1991: 6). Not surprisingly, it provoked widespread censure, most particularly from specialists in African archaeology, and led to a change of policy prohibiting TL dating of unprovenanced ceramic materials.

Sadly, the destruction of Mali's archaeological past has proceeded unchecked during the intervening eight years as attested to by Manus Brinkman, Secretary General of ICOM, who reported to the Museums Association Conference in the UK that 'If the pillaging continues on the same scale, all sites in the Niger valley will have been destroyed by the year 2005' (1998: 6).

The second case concerns the Institute of Archaeology, University College London, the largest archaeology faculty in the UK. The Institute was founded in 1934 by Mortimer Wheeler with the express intention of providing 'training in fieldwork techniques and the ancillary skills needed for the proper recording and publication of the results of fieldwork' (Evans 1987: 3). However, by the 1980s, these commendable ideals were under pressure from less laudable considerations.

In the 1980s, it need hardly be said that money was king. Business was the sole model for universal application. This was an era in which some might suggest that Oscar Wilde's 'man who knows the price of everything and the value of nothing' had come into his own (1892: Act 3, Lord Darlington). Universities were operating under severe financial constraint. It seemed obvious to the powers that be, that what was clearly needed were entrepreneurial academics who would set up commercial ventures designed to bring in some of the revenue so desperately needed. To that end, a pump-priming fund was created to support the setting up of such fledgling companies.

The antiquities trade was awash with money and required services that the Institute was ostensibly well placed to provide. Needless to say, the process of investigation into the feasibility and advisability of pursuing such a venture was protracted and debated furiously, with those for and against adopting ever more polarized positions.

During this time laboratory space was rented to an individual trained in both conservation and archaeometallurgy whose personal private company was used as a test case. To the outside world, this was often mistakenly perceived to be the Institute's own company. Pre-Colombian gold alloy artefacts arrived in neat wooden crates from Switzerland for authentification, as did Khmer sculptures, Luristan bronzes and so forth. The Sevso Treasure, a notorious collection of late Roman silver consisting of fourteen pieces valued at anything between £40 million and £100 million, became associated with the Institute under the auspices of the private company.[3] In light of the association of this material with the Institute, the students christened the proto-company 'Shady Deals Inc.' (Old Fox 1991).

During a committee meeting in the Institute of Archaeology where the advisability of setting up a commercial Institute company which would offer analytical and conservation services to the trade was being deliberated, it had actually been suggested that there was no such thing as bad publicity. While these deliberations were going on at the Institute, the storm broke in Oxford over the commercial activities of the Oxford Research Laboratory and the outcry that followed the screening of 'The African King' put paid to that notion.

By 1990, the prospect of establishing an Institute Company to serve collectors and dealers was abandoned in light of the fact that a decision to screen out potentially illicit material would make it commercially unviable. The pilot private company moved to accommodation in Birkbeck College. It was replaced by the 'Services Division', whose policy document on acceptance of objects and materials proved to be unacceptable to the trade (Appendix 1). So far as the author knows, no work was ever undertaken by it. The Institute, as a collective entity, then ceased actively to address issues relating to the illicit trade in antiquities until, in the summer of 1998, the new Director instigated renewed discussions on the development of 'future policy and practice regarding the trading of antiquities'.

In the intervening years between 1990 and 1998, consumption of the archaeological heritage, this non-renewable resource, for the purposes of feeding a voracious market, had continued unabated. At a Staff Meeting in December 1998, it was agreed that the Institute should urge the government to sign and ratify the 1970 UNESCO Convention and the 1995 UNIDROIT Convention. This was duly done, and the preparation of a document to spell out the consequences of such a stance was prepared for debate. A long, hard look ensued, taking into account resultant restrictions on individual staff members. The strictures listed in section 4 caused the most disquiet, since it was felt that they encroached on both individual and academic freedom – clearly, ideals no-one would wish to see jeopardized. Ultimately, the view that such self-limitation and self-censorship was warranted prevailed in the light of the threat to the archaeological heritage, and the *Policy Statement of the Institute of Archaeology, London, Regarding the Illicit Trade in Antiquities* was duly adopted by the Staff on 8 December 1999 (Appendix 2). Its content is self-explanatory.

Perhaps not so amazingly, in the light of those discussions, it transpires after some preliminary investigation that the Institute is unique in the UK, and possibly the US also, in being an academic department of archaeology (as opposed to a university museum) possessing such a policy adopting an ethical stance concerning illicit antiquities. This is no mean achievement. It is a public statement which refutes the contention of dealers and collectors that archaeologists and associated heritage professionals are only motivated by self-aggrandizement and self-interest, and that they will undertake work on any material regardless of provenance if it happens to be in furtherance of their own careers and renown. The thoroughness of the debate and the depth of engagement signal the gravity accorded by the Institute to the destruction of archaeological sites and to the illicit trade in antiquities.

Furthermore, this awareness has been transferred into action by its incorporation across the board into the teaching curriculum. Both Institute undergraduate students and graduate students, enrolled in taught Master's degree programmes, are introduced to the issues concerning the trade in antiquities, to cultural heritage laws and ethical codes, to marketing strategies and to the essential divergent views of the opposing camps (Section 2.1, Article 5f, Appendix 2). In addition, the course information leaflets carry the following statement: 'The Institute of Archaeology supports the principles of the 1970 UNESCO Convention and the 1995 UNIDROIT Convention and is unique as a UK academic department in having an ethics policy concerning the illicit trade in antiquities.' The Ethics Panel (Section 5, Appendix 2) investigates particular situations on an individual basis and offers guidance where appropriate action is not immediately evident.

Herein, then, with the introduction of the policy document, lie both a cautionary tale and a moment of self-congratulation for the Institute. Ideally, other university departments will feel a need to address such issues for themselves and hopefully follow suit. Individuals throughout the global academic community obviously subscribe to organizations such as the Institute of Field Archaeology, the Archaeological Institute of America, the Museums Association and the International Council of Museums, and abide by their ethical codes. However, a similar undertaking, department by department, and university by university, will broadcast a powerful message, one in need of constant reinforcement and reiteration.


## CONCLUSION

Such an agenda will not be easy. Birkbeck College's advertisement for a new MSc degree in the Scientific Examination of Works of Art, which was scheduled to accept its first intake of students in the autumn of 2000, is alarming, particularly since Chinese artefacts are being shown on the market (Grovesnor House Antiques Fair, 14–20 June 2000) with labels attached citing Birkbeck College as their source of authentication (Betts personal communication). Article 8.5 in the ICOM *Code of Professional Ethics*, which places restraints on authentication and identification of objects where there is 'reason to believe or suspect that these have been illegally or illicitly acquired, transferred, imported or exported', needs to be more widely applied. Objects found in context do not require a certificate attesting that they are genuine.

Moreover, the Royal College of Art's willingness to host the London and Provincial Antique Dealers Association (LAPADA) Show (which it does annually in October) is deeply disturbing. Certainly, in October 1999, antiquities were being exhibited and sold; antiquities from countries such as China, Cambodia and Peru, known to be haemorrhaging looted artefacts at a desperate cost to the archaeological record. The exhibitors were predominantly dealers in fine art, antiques and jewellery. However, three dealers were selling items such as Chinese Han and Tang tomb figures, Khmer ceramics, Apulian vessels and early bronze age pottery of the type referred to by Politis

in his chapter in this volume. The antiquities all appeared to be being offered
for sale with certificates of authenticity that seemed to the casual observer to
be unsupported, in the main, by scientific testing. Perhaps then, such unsupported certificates should be regarded as constituting nothing more than a
guarantee that a price refund would be forthcoming should the object prove
to be a fake or pastiche in the future. One of the dealers has defined provenance on the company's website as 'All artifacts have been established as
genuine and are guaranteed to be as described'. It is unclear whether this
misleading (for an archaeologist, at any rate) definition is what is meant on
the flyer, which refers to 'Provenanced collections of Greek, Roman and
Egyptian Antiquities South East Asian and Chinese Ceramics' (Oxford Forum
of Ancient Art). Also featured at the show was a loan exhibition entitled
'2,000 Years of Andean Art', which featured feathered tunics, pre-Inca gold
masks, and a '1.9 meter tall standing bronze figure of a Shaman, the High
priest of Andean culture' (anonymous promotional blurb on ticket pamphlet).
At a lecture in Cambridge in January 2000, Bourget spoke of the ease with
which textiles are smuggled out of Peru by simply rolling them up in a newspaper and where large pieces are often cut up to maximize profits. Clearly,
the author has no proof of impropriety concerning any of the material that
was exhibited at the LAPADA Show. However, looted archaeological sites
throughout the world bear witness to the fact that an enormous number of
artefacts have been wrenched from their contexts and, frustratingly, will be
unable to be identified categorically as such because of the severing of their
connection with the particularity of their pasts. Certainly, provenances were
not displayed; only assurances that the objects were genuine were evident.
Considering the furore caused by the exhibition of unprovenanced antiquities on two occasions recently by the Royal Academy of Art,[4] simple ignorance
of the issues by the Royal College perhaps should not be assumed, although
ignorance might be preferable to indifference.

The failure of the heritage community to deliver its message was perhaps
most clearly demonstrated by the partnership of Fortnum and Mason, an
exclusive and highly regarded department store in the heart of London –
situated on the south side of Piccadilly, virtually across from the Royal
Academy of Art, with Ancient Art, a dealership which began life as a supplier
of artefacts by mail order but which has profited and expanded to include a
shop in Windsor (Tubb and Brodie 2001). For a period of five weeks in the
Spring of 2000, the Gift Department of Fortnum and Mason hosted the
'Millennia Collections' where customers were invited 'to celebrate and
acknowledge the year 2000 with something from a millennium ago'.[5] The
goods on display were rearranged each week to showcase different eras, 'to
take you through different millennia, different cultures and different civilisa-
tions – giving you an opportunity to own something unique and special'.[6]
The invitation was to use, wear and love antiquities 'as they were in ancient
times'.[7] The sale was advertised in *RA*, the Royal Academy magazine (2000:

57) and in *Where*, a free magazine distributed in good hotels aimed at tourists and other visitors to London. The idea was clever and the marketing was judiciously targeted. Prices ranged from somewhere in the region of £30 to about £30,000 for a small bronze figure of an enthroned Zeus installed on an inscribed base. The salesman remarked that anything above the £30,000 limit would be a museum piece and that the Zeus bronze could not now be exported from Greece. An 'Apulian-Corinthian Helmet Type B with nose guard' was described as being from Greece rather than Italy as the Apulian reference might indicate. It was suggested that damage to the crown of the helmet might have resulted from a blow causing the death of the original owner. Certainly, although the helmet had not been cleaned mechanically to remove any of the bulky copper corrosion products, incised decoration could be discerned on the piece. The asking price was £19,750. Spearheads from Mesopotamia were there for the taking at £495 each. Alternatively, for the same amount, an Early Han 'cocoon' painted pot could be purchased. Oil lamps, much maligned by the trade (see below) were available, two of which were on offer for £245 and £395 respectively. The final week coincided with Easter and featured Byzantine crosses, fossilized dinosaur eggs and Biblical artefacts presenting again that distinctive regional early bronze age pottery associated with ancient Zoar which had also been on sale at the LAPADA Show. Here the asking prices ranged from £145 to £245. Interestingly, the last page of the booklet was devoted in the main to answering hypothetical questions such as 'Shouldn't they be in museums?' and 'Why is there so much?'.[8] The answers make interesting reading. To the first the reply is that:

> Antiquities and ancient art are not only about priceless Greek vases and marble friezes, they include items that were used as part of everyday life by these ancient civilisations. What happened to a Roman oil lamp – a disposable item used in its millions and as insignificant as today's light bulb? These 'everyday items' often lack the polish needed by collectors of more refined antiquities and are surplus to the already overstretched museums.
>
> The vast majority of items are not rarities. Everyone should have the opportunity to own a small piece of history, provided that the artefacts are sufficiently common and are neither of any national heritage nor should be legitimately in a museum environment.[9]

To the second the reply is that:

> There are hundreds of thousands of domestic antiquities already in circulation. Museum basements are often choking with pieces and it is an open question as to how well they are being cared for or whether they will ever be displayed. With industrialisation and urbanisation the antiquities in the ground are, in some countries,

worth more as hardcore, and coins worth much more melted down
for their gold and silver content.

Complacency is obviously not an option. These two answers make it
perfectly plain that the price tag approach is grossly flawed and fails utterly
to communicate the fact that the damage to an archaeological site is the same
regardless of which artefactual remains are recovered. Context becomes a
setting in a living room or in the gift department of an elegant shop. Objects
in these surroundings epitomize decontextualization and, divested of the information they could have imparted with which the knowledge of the past
could have been so enriched, are truly mere gewgaws. There is no mistaking
the fact that, despite some encouraging signs, heritage professionals must
continue to hector for positive action in an effort to protect the archaeological heritage for future generations. This brings us full circle. It is difficult
to be optimistic about the chances of success when faced with the rapacity
which prevails at present, but giving up on trying to save archaeological sites
for posterity ensures failure and consigns those sites which survive today, to
the same fate suffered by so many yesterday, of destruction tomorrow.


## NOTES

1   The Members of the Standing Conference on Portable Antiquities are: Association
    of Local Government Archaeologists; British Archaeological Association; Council
    for British Archaeology; Council for Scottish Archaeology; Finds Research Group;
    Joint Nautical Archaeology Policy Committee; McDonald Institute for Archaeo-
    logical Research; Museums Association; Museums and Galleries Commission;
    National Monuments Record for England (English Heritage, formerly RCHME);
    National Trust; National Trust for Scotland; Prehistoric Society; Rescue; Roman
    Finds Group; Royal Archaeological Institute; Royal Commission on the Ancient
    and Historical Monuments of Scotland; Royal Commission on the Ancient and
    Historical Monuments of Wales; Scottish Museums Council; Society for Medieval
    Archaeology; Society of Museum Archaeologists; Society for Nautical
    Archaeology; Society for Post-Medieval Archaeology; Society for Promotion of
    Roman Studies; Standing Conference of Archaeological Unit Managers; Surrey
    Archaeological Society; Ulster Museum; United Kingdom Institute for Conserva-
    tion; University College London; Wessex Archaeology.
    The Observers are: CADW: Welsh Historic monuments; Department of Culture,
    Media and Sport; English Heritage; Environment and Heritage Service for
    Northern Ireland; Historic Scotland.
2   The conference in New Jersey was organized by and held at Rutgers University
    from 30 October to 1 November 1998 and was entitled 'Art, Antiquity and the
    Law: Preserving Our Global Cultural Heritage'. The conference in New York
    was organized by the National Arts Journalism Program and the Italian Academy
    for Advanced Studies in America and held at Columbia University from 15 to
    17 April 1999 and was entitled 'Who Owns Culture? International Conference
    on Cultural Property and Patrimony'. The conference in Cambridge was organ-
    ized by the Illicit Antiquities Research Centre and held at the McDonald Institute
    for Archaeological Research from 22 to 25 October 1999 and was entitled 'Illicit
    Antiquities: the Destruction of the World's Archaeological Heritage'.

3   For the academic report on the Sevso Treasure, see Bennett and Mango 1994.
    For an insight into the nature of the notoriety of this material see, for example,
    Norman and Keys 1990a and b; Watson 1992; Norman 1993; D'Arcy 1993;
    Boylan 1993; Fenton 1994; Renfrew 1999: 31–7; Watson 2000.
4   The two exhibitions referred to are 'In Pursuit of the Absolute', which ran from
    20 January to 6 April 1994 and featured a large selection of objects from the
    George Ortiz collection (see, for example, Alberge 1994; Renfrew 1994; Sylvester
    1994), and 'Africa: The Art of a Continent', which ran from 4 October 1995 to
    21 January 1996 (Bailey 1995; Varadarajan 1995; MacDonald and Shaw 1995).
5   From 'The Millennia Collections', an anonymous sales booklet.
6   Ibid.
7   Ibid.
8   Ibid.
9   Ibid.
10  Ibid.

# REFERENCES

Alberge, Dalya 1994. Master of Antiquities, Master of Ceremonies. *Independent*,
    (London), 19 January.
Anon. 2000. 'The Millennia Collection' (20 March–22 April 2000). Sales promotion
    booklet by Fortnum and Mason with Ancient Art.
Art Loss Register. Undated pamphlet. Helping the Victims of Art Theft. London
    and New York.
Bailey, Martin 1995. Out of Africa but Not Out of Egypt. *Art Newspaper* 53, (London),
    November.
Beek, W. van 1990. The African King: An Investigation. *Rear Window*. Channel 4
    Television.
Bennett, A. and M.M. Mango 1994. *The Sevso Treasure, Part 1*. Journal of Roman
    Archaeology, Supplementary Series 12. Ann Arbor: Journal of Roman Archaeology.
Birkbeck College. Centre for the Scientific Examination of Works of Art. Online.
    URL: http://www.cryst.bbk.ac.uk/~ubcg01d/CSEWA/index.html
Boylan, Patrick 1993. Treasure Trove with Strings Attached. *Independent* (London),
    9 November.
Brinkman, Manus 1998. Quoted in Shock Tactics Used to Prompt Action, anony-
    mous contribution to MA Conference Section, *Museums Journal*: 6.
Brodie, Neil 1999. Conference Reports: World Archaeological Congress 4. *Culture
    without Context* 4: 27.
Brodie, Neil, Jenny Doole and Peter Watson 2000. *Stealing History: the Illicit Trade
    in Cultural Material*. Cambridge: McDonald Institute for Archaeological Research.
Brodie, Neil and Peter Watson 1999. Conference Reports. *Culture without Context*
    5: 23–4.
Chippindale, C. 1991. Editorial. *Antiquity* 65: 6–8.
D'Arcy, David 1993. Shadow of the Sevso Treasure. *Vanity Fair*, (New York), October:
    150–68.
DCMS 2000a. *Cultural Property: Return and Illicit Trade*. House of Commons paper
    No. 371-I-III. London: Stationery Office.
DCMS 2000b. *Ministerial Advisory Panel on Illicit Trade*. London: DCMS.
Evans, John D. 1987. The First Half-Century – and After. *Bulletin of the Institute of
    Archaeology* 24: 1–25.
Fenton, James 1994. A Collection Robbed of Its True History. *Independent*, (London),
    31 January.

Jenkins, Jolyon 2000. *File on Four*. BBC Radio 4. 27 June.
MacDonald Kevin and Thurston Shaw 1995. Out of Africa and Out of Context. *Antiquity* 69: 1036–9.
Norman, Geraldine 1993. Battle Over Origin of £40m Roman Silver Collection. *Independent* (London), 22 September.
Norman, Geraldine and David Keys 1990a. Sale of Roman Treasure Could Fetch £100m. *Independent* (London), 9 February.
Norman, Geraldine and David Keys 1990b. Sotheby's Sale of Silver 'A Daring Move'. *Independent* (London), 9 February.
Old Fox 1991. View from the Trenches. *Who Dares Wins* (Quarterly Journal of the Society of Archaeology Students) 5: 3.
Prott, Lyndel 1997. Personal Communication. 3 November.
Radcliffe, Julian 1995. Recording and Identifying Systems. Unpublished paper presented at *Art Theft and Its Control Conference*, organized by the Conference Division, Lloyd's of London Press. London. 14–15 November.
Renfrew, Colin 1994. Justifying an Interest in the Past. *Guardian* (London), 26 January.
Renfrew, Colin 1999. *Loot, Legitimacy and Ownership: The Ethical Crisis in Archaeology*. Amsterdam: Eenentwintigste Kroon-Voordracht.
*Royal Academy Magazine* 2000. No. 66 Spring: 57.
Scarre, Chris 1998. Conference Reports. *Culture without Context* 3: 18–19.
Sylvester, David 1994. A Fruitful Loss of Virginity. *Guardian* (London), 26 January.
Thornes, Robin 1997. *Protecting Cultural Objects in the Global Information Society*. Los Angeles: Getty Information Institute.
Thornes, Robin 1995. *Protecting Cultural Objects Through International Documentation Standards: A Preliminary Standard*. Los Angeles: Getty Art History Information Program.
Tubb, K.W. 1996. Thoughts in Response to the Draft Principles to Govern a Licit International Traffic in Cultural Property. In *Legal Aspects of International Trade in Art*. Vol.V, *International Sales of Works of Art*, M. Briat and J.A. Freedberg (eds), 113–16. Paris, The Hague: ICC Publishing S.A. and Kluwer Law International.
Tubb, K.W. and N.J. Brodie 2001. The Antiquities Trade in the United Kingdom. In *Destruction and Conservation of Cultural Property*. R.L. Layton, P.G. Stone and J. Thomas (eds), 102–16. London: Routledge.
Varadarajan, Tunku 1995. Who Holds the Rights to Africa's Heritage? *Times* (London), 2 October.
Watson, Peter 1992. The Case of the Silver Treasure. *New York Times* (New York), 28 June.
Watson, Peter 2000. Ancient Curse. *Sunday Times*, News Review Section (London), 20 February.
Wilde, Oscar 1892. *Lady Windermere's Fan*.

# APPENDIX 1

*Institute of Archaeology Services Division*

The Institute of Archaeology was founded in 1937 by Sir Mortimer Wheeler, and it has always maintained his emphasis on the practical aspects of archaeology – both in the field and in post-excavation studies. The examination and analysis of excavated material is an integral part of archaeological study, and an ever-increasing amount of information can be obtained by means of modern scientific techniques.

The Services Division offers an extensive range of analytical facilities supported by expertise in conservation, materials science, environmental archaeology, computer science, and world archaeology of all periods.

*Policy on the acceptance of objects and materials*

Over the past few decades, there has been an enormous increase in the looting and illegal trafficking of antiquities. Looting destroys vital archaeological information: the site itself may be lost, the context of the objects is not recorded, and vital information may be lost through inappropriate handling and treatment. Many looted antiquities find their way into private collections, where they remain unknown to the wider community. The Institute of Archaeology is totally opposed to the looting and illegal export of antiquities and adheres to the *ICOM Code of Professional Ethics* which opposes acting 'in any way that could be regarded as benefiting such illicit trade, directly or indirectly.' Accordingly, the Services Division will accept objects only of known, documented origin.

To ensure adherence to this policy, a prospective client must demonstrate the history of any object tendered for examination or treatment by the Services Division. Documentary evidence of ownership for a considerable number of years will be of assistance in indicating that an object does not derive from the recent outburst of illicit activity. The information provided may be checked with specialists in the archaeology or ethnology of the area of origin, with police authorities, departments of antiquities and with international agencies combating the illegal trade of antiquities.

Authenticity studies will not be among the services offered by the Division unless initiated by police authorities, government departments of antiquity or, in exceptional circumstances, public museums. The Division reserves the right to refuse to undertake any project without giving reasons.

The results of examinations undertaken by the Division will be available to anyone with a demonstrable scholarly interest. The Division reserves the right to publish the results of any work undertaken, usually after an agreed period of time. In this way, the Division will contribute to the corpus of accessible archaeological data, and will demonstrate what can be learned through informed examination.

27/9/90

# APPENDIX 2

*Policy Statement of the Institute of Archaeology, London, regarding the illicit trade in antiquities*

INTRODUCTION

As archaeological and heritage professionals, staff of the Institute deplore the looting of archaeological sites, the removal of material from context and the illicit trade in antiquities. This document presents the Institute of Archaeology's policy on the implications of an ethical position against illicit excavation and the illicit trade in antiquities.

It should be noted that the document has been formulated with 1970 as the benchmark before which the principles of the conventions are not applied since neither the 1970 UNESCO Convention on the Means of Prohibiting and Preventing the Illicit Import, Export and Transfer of Ownership of Cultural Property nor the 1995 UNIDROIT Convention on Stolen or Illegally Exported Cultural Objects are retroactive. Indeed, the entry into force of the 1970 UNESCO Convention is regarded as having formally alerted the international community to the problems that the Convention addresses. From this time onwards, ignorance of these issues can no longer be put forward as an excuse for trafficking in illicit cultural property. An allowance is thus made for the ways in which such material has been collected in the past while making it plain that continuation along these lines is unacceptable.

## LEGAL INSTRUMENTS

At the Staff Meeting of 9 December 1998, the following decision was taken:

It was agreed that the Institute should be seen to be amongst those urging the Government to: (a) sign and then ratify the UNESCO 'Convention on the Means of Prohibiting and Preventing the Illicit Import, Export and Transfer of Ownership of Cultural Property' (1970) and (b) sign and then ratify the UNIDROIT Convention on Stolen and Illegally Exported Cultural Objects 1995.

The following implications for the Institute of Archaeology as a body, and for individual staff members, of supporting the UNESCO and UNIDROIT conventions were agreed as policy at the Staff Meeting of 8 December 1999.

*Implications for Staff of the 1970 UNESCO Convention*   In supporting the ratification of the Convention, staff by implication support its principles and can lend support to it in the following ways:

Article 5 requires that States Parties to the Convention establish a series of services to protect the cultural heritage, including the following:

Article 5b covers the establishment of national inventories of protected property. Many States find this commitment is beyond their resources and struggle to meet it. This is probably the most commonly voiced lament expressed when the convention is discussed. Staff could collaborate with those experiencing such difficulties and offer assistance.

Article 5f covers the duty to educate and make known the provisions of the Convention, and this should be reflected, both implicitly and explicitly, in our teaching and in our involvement with the wider community. In particular, it should be Institute policy that all students are taught about the dangers of looting and of the illicit trade in antiquities as part of their courses. Article 10 also advocates educating the public. To that end, staff should strive to make clear the importance and significance of the concept of context especially to collectors and dealers.

Article 5g requires that States see that 'appropriate publicity is given to the disappearance of any items of cultural property'. This implies that staff members should document, report to the authorities and urge appropriate public exposure of damage to sites caused by clandestine excavation, theft of artefacts and architectural elements when/if they are privy to such information.

Article 6 requires States to provide certification of legal exportation of cultural property. The Standing Conference on Portable Antiquities is currently urging the government to re-evaluate the system in the UK, since it has been alleged that the system is being used to establish false provenances for illicit material and that the legislation does not adequately protect the heritage. Staff should support such a re-examination of the status quo (see Brodie 1999 and Cook 1995).

Article 7 concerns taking steps to prevent the import of illicitly exported material and its acquisition by museums and similar institutions. By extension, although not specifically stated, such material has also often been stolen. The implication is that, if staff are shown material which they suspect to be illicit, they should alert the relevant authorities such as the Art and Antiques Squad of the Metropolitan Police, Interpol, Customs and Excise, the Cultural Property Unit of the Department of Culture, Media and Sport and the original owner (see Prott and O'Keefe 1988).

*Implications of the 1970 UNESCO Convention for the Institute Collections*   The Convention has another series of implications for the Institute as a body that curates archaeological material as part of UCL's collections. The following two paragraphs were adopted by staff as policy to cover all of the Institute's collections (including the Petrie Museum of Egyptian Archaeology and the collections of the former Museum of Classical Archaeology):

The Institute must not acquire by purchase, loan, gift, bequest or exchange any object or specimen unless the Director and curatorial staff are satisfied that valid title to the item in question can be acquired, and that in particular it has not been acquired in, or exported from, its country of origin (or any intermediate country in which it may have been legally owned) since 1970, in violation of that country's laws (including the UK). This also applies to any objects that may be temporarily borrowed for exhibition in-house.

In addition, the Institute will not acquire objects in any case where the Director and curatorial staff have reasonable cause to believe that the circumstances of their recovery involved the recent (since 1970) unscientific or intentional destruction or damage of ancient monuments or other known archaeological sites, or involved a failure to disclose the finds to the owner or occupier of the land, or to the proper legal or governmental authorities.

*Implications for Staff of the 1995 UNIDROIT Convention*   It should be noted that, unlike the UNESCO Convention, under the UNIDROIT Convention individuals do have a statutory right of action. However, as UNIDROIT relates to the recovery of stolen cultural property rather than its study, it has no direct legal implications for staff unless they are involved in transactions themselves, or on behalf of the Institute for its collections (see below). Nevertheless, as with the UNESCO Convention, urging the UK to ratify the Convention assumes that staff support the principles of the Convention, which is to assist individuals and groups who have lost cultural property through illegal means, to recover their material.

Of particular relevance is Article 3.2, which states that unlawfully excavated objects or those which have been lawfully excavated but unlawfully retained 'shall be considered stolen' provided such a definition of the material is consistent with the law of the country in which the excavation took place.

This is significant because the size of the market in antiquities and the large turnover of artefacts is inconsistent with suggestions that material on the market all comes from long-standing collections made prior to 1970. A clear indication that an object has been looted and/or illegally exported from its country of origin is the lack of a provenance (and here a provenance would also include clear documentation that it had been in a collection before 1970). Recent research suggests that between 80–90 per cent of the objects being traded have no clearly established provenance. Such unprovenanced material must be regarded with deep suspicion and, in the absence of evidence to the contrary, is deemed to have been unlawfully excavated or lawfully excavated but unlawfully retained.

Staff Members must think of such material as stolen, treat it as such and alert the relevant authorities as stated above under Article 7 of the 1970 UNESCO Convention.

## RELEVANT ETHICAL CODES

Opposition to looting and to the illicit antiquities trade is enshrined in the ethical codes of many museum and archaeological professional bodies.

The ICOM Code of Professional Ethics, for example, opposes acting 'in any way that could be regarded as benefiting such illicit trade, directly or indirectly', and this was included in the (then) Institute of Archaeology Services Division Policy on the Acceptance of Objects and Materials (1990) which stated that 'The Institute of Archaeology is totally opposed to the looting and illegal export of antiquities and adheres to the ICOM Code of Professional Ethics'.

Article 1.6 of the Institute of Field Archaeologists' Code of Conduct states that 'an archaeologist shall know and comply with all laws applicable to his or her archaeological activities whether as employer or employee, and with national and international agreements relating to the illicit import, export or transfer of ownership of archaeological material. An archaeologist shall not engage in, and shall seek to discourage, illicit or unethical dealings in antiquities.'

The Archaeological Institute of America's Code of Ethics advises archaeologists to refuse to participate in the trade in 'undocumented antiquities' by refraining from activities that enhance the commercial value of such objects.

This Code identifies undocumented antiquities as 'those which are not documented as belonging to a public or private collection before December 30, 1970 . . . or which have not been excavated and exported from their country of origin in accordance with the laws of that country'.

## ETHICAL IMPLICATIONS FOR STAFF OF A STANCE AGAINST THE ILLICIT TRADE IN ANTIQUITIES

The following ethical implications arise from a stance against looting and the illicit trade:

Work must not be undertaken (except on behalf of the police, courts or government of origin) on objects where there is insufficient information to establish a licit provenance or where the material is known to be illicit. Before agreeing to study, analyse or conserve material, staff must exercise due diligence in establishing that the material has not been illegally excavated, acquired, transferred and/or exported from its country of origin since 1970. (N.B. Metal-detecting on unscheduled sites is not illegal in England and Wales and artefacts recovered by this means are not subject to the above. However, Staff must attempt to ensure that finders have valid title to their objects.)

Staff must not undertake scholarly publication of unprovenanced material unless it can be demonstrated clearly that the artefact or specimen has been in a collection since before 1970 or was legally exported from its country of origin. This is in line with the publishing policy of the *American Journal of Archaeology*, which states that it 'will not serve for the announcement or initial scholarly presentation of any object in a private or public collection acquired after 30 December 1973, unless the object was part of a previously existing collection or has been legally exported from the country of origin'. This applies also to unpublished reports, including condition reports, given to the possessor of an object, which have also been used to enhance the value of such pieces on the market and should therefore not be undertaken on unprovenanced material.

Staff must not undertake valuations of material, unless for insurance purposes for public bodies or to assist the authorities.

The formation by Staff of personal teaching collections is permissible provided that the material has been acquired in compliance with all the above conditions. Any personal collections should be declared to the Institute's Ethics Panel. Staff must not buy or sell such material.

Staff must not buy or sell antiquities nor act as an intermediary for profit in any such transactions. Staff must not accept gifts or emoluments from dealers and collectors for professional services, in support of excavations or for research projects.

Staff need to protect themselves at all times from situations of conflict of interest and must consult the Institute's Ethics Panel in such situations. There is most danger of being compromised in the area of sponsorship and funding.

Notwithstanding the above, Staff should strive to increase the dialogue between themselves and dealers, collectors, the government and the public to ensure archaeological concerns are heard and clearly understood and to ensure that staff understand and have considered opposing viewpoints. In particular, staff should campaign for transparency in the dealings of the antiquities market.

## ETHICS PANEL

In some cases, it may not be immediately clear to Staff what the appropriate ethical course of action should be. The Institute has therefore established an Ethics Panel which will meet on an ad hoc basis to consider individual cases and provide advice.

## REFERENCES

Brodie, Neil 1999. Statistics, damned statistics, and the antiquities trade. *Antiquity* 73(280), 447–51.

Cook, Brian 1995. 'The Antiquities Trade: a curator's view' in K.W. Tubb (ed.), *Antiquities Trade or Betrayed: Legal, Ethical and Conservation Issues*, London: Archetype/ UKIC, 186–9.

Prott, Lyndel V. and Patrick J. O'Keefe 1988. *Handbook of national regulations concerning the export of cultural property*. Paris: UNESCO.

# Index

Abandoned Shipwreck Act 1987 113,
  131–245
abandonment 111, 112, 128, 148
academia 38–9, 206–7, 286–9
acquisitions policy 35
Additional Protocols to the 1949
  Geneva Conventions (1977) 70, 79,
  84
Addyman, Peter V. 179–84
Adler, G.J. Hague Convention 1954
  68
Afghanistan, National Museum 6
*Akerendam* wreckage 148–9
*Alabama* wreckage 113, 114
an-Naq' cemetery, Jordan 258, 259–62,
  265–6
Antiquities and Art Treasures Act 1972,
  India 269–70, 276
antiquities market 229–30, 269
Arab Potash Company 263, 264
Archaeological Resources Protection Act
  (ARPA) 1979, US 237
Archaeological Survey of India (ASI)
  269, 270–2, 275, 276
archaeology; *see also* marine archaeology;
  cultural influence 38–42; extinction
  3–4; heritage 156, 205–27; landscapes
  179; standards 138–9, 149;
  sustainability 38; value 151–2
archives 160, 206, 254, 277;
  conservation 168, 172–3; legislation
  152–3; marine artefacts 164; metal
  detection 181–2
Argentina 228–34
armed conflict *see* cultural protection

ARPA *see* Archaeological Resources
  Protection Act
art markets 228–9, 232–4, 269; museum
  collections 23–4; Native Americana
  237; pillage 251; tomb robbing 186
Ashmolean Museum collection 32–4
ASI *see* Archaeological Survey of India
assemblage, The Waverley Report 189,
  190
auctions 25–9, 192, 195–7, 201–2, 237
authenticity, Malian terracottas 3, 286

Baedeker Raids 58
Balkan states 7–8, 79–80
Banner of Peace, Roerich Pact 52–3
Banteay Chmar bas-reliefs 7
Batheaston Hoard 180
Bator, P.M. 187
Beazley, Sir J. and Lady 34
*belles pièces* 252
Birkbeck College, ethics 288, 289
*Birkenhead* wreckage 113, 114
Black Death AD 1348 258
black markets 187; Argentina 230–1
Blue Shield *see* International Committee
  of the Blue Shield
*boly* 253
Boston Museum of Fine Arts (MFA)
  2–3, 244–5
Boylan, Patrick J. 43–108
Brodie, Neil J. 1–22, 179–84,
  185–204
Buenos Aires Draft Convention 139–55;
  commercial salvage 149; ICOMOS
  Charter 140, 150–1, 152–4, 156–61;

international waters 142; jurisdiction 143–5; LOS Convention 142–5; Sovereign immunity 145–7
Buenos Aires National Museum of Fine Arts 228
buffer zones 224
Byzantine period, Jordan 258–9

Cambodia 6–7
catalogues *see* auctions
*Central America* wreckage 5, 111, 137, 138–9
chemical stability, marine artefacts 162–3, 168, 169–73
Chichén Itzá, Mexico 207, 221, 224
Chola bronzes 274–5
civil disturbance *see* protection
coins; export licensing 194; metal detectors 180–2
collateral damage *see* damage, collateral
collections; Argentina 230–4; Greek vases 23, 24; Native Americana 237, 239–40
commercial salvage 110, 111, 113, 119–21, 130; *see also* salvage; conservation 162–3; licensing 123
commercialization 220–3
common heritage 45
communality 210
community involvement 12–13, 15, 39, 161, 210–13; pre-Hispanic monuments 224–5, 226–7
conservation; *see also in situ* preservation; chemical stability 162–3, 168, 169–73; first-aid 170–3; methodology 168–73; pre-Hispanic monuments 207, 212, 219–20; shipwrecks 5, 162–78; tourism 14–15, 219–26
contiguous zone 143
Cook, Brian 191
Corinth Museum 2
corrosion, post-excavation 171
CPAC *see* Cultural Property Advisory Committee
criminal responsibility 98
crusades, the 43–4
cultural cleansing 6–8
cultural genocide 63
cultural heritage *see* heritage; property
cultural identity 208–10, 211–12, 251, 254

cultural property *see* heritage; property
Cultural Property Advisory Committee (CPAC) 241, 242
cultural protection *see* protection
cultural resources 38–40
cultural symbols; looting 43, 70–1, 95, 98; vandalism 44, 74, 80, 95, 285; war trophies 43, 71
cultural war crimes 80, 84–5
curatorial influence 32, 34–5
Curzon address 1900 272
customs (trade), Argentina 229, 233

damage 43, 71, 74, 77, 163, 229; agricultural/urban development 16–17; collateral 6–7, 47–53, 58, 69, 94; conservation 168, 169; looting 40–1, 214–19; natural processes 165; post-excavation 171; pre-Hispanic monuments 214–19; wartime 43, 70–1, 74, 95
Davis, Hester A. 235–40
DCMS *see* Department of Culture, Media and Sport
*De Braak* wreckage 5
Dead Sea Scrolls 264, 265
decentralization 209
Declaration of Brussels 1874 47
Declaration of Santo Domingo 146
Deep Ocean Expeditions (DOE) 138
deep sea technologies 137, 142, 162–3
defacement 44, 47–53; *see also* vandalism
deforestation 215–16, 220
'demand' countries 1–2
Department of Culture, Media and Sport (DCMS) 186, 198–9; Export Licensing Unit 191–2, 193, 195–6; Ministerial Advisory Panel 281–2; *see also* Palmer enquiry
Department of Trade and Industry (DTI) 198–9
Djenné figurines 252, 254
DOALOS *see* United Nations Division of Ocean Affairs and Law of the Sea
DOE *see* Deep Ocean Expeditions
Dromgoole, Sarah 109–36
DTI *see* Department of Trade and Industry

Early Bronze Age, Jordan 258, 259
Easvaran temple, India 275

ecological damage, tourism 215–16, 220, 224
education 11–12, 226, 239, 240, 246–7, 255; *see also* public awareness
EEZ *see* exclusive economic zone
Eisenhower, Gen. Dwight D. 60, 68
Ejército Zapatista de Liberación Nacional (EZLN) 211
*ejido* system, Mexico 210, 215, 217, 227
El Cayo, Mexico 213
English Heritage 164, 166, 180
enhanced protection, Hague Conventions 1954 55, 69, 72, 75, 95–8
Estévez Museum, Argentina 229
ethics 4, 5, 17–19, 24, 280–300;
    Institute of Archaeology 294–6;
    International Council of Museums 35;
    marine archaeology 167–9, 173;
    public awareness 288–9, 296, 298–300
Euphronios krater 23–4
European Commission Regulation No. 3911/92 190–3, 194–8, 202
European Conventions 139, 147
excavation 206, 235, 264–6, 268; *see also* salvage; conservation 164–5, 166; Draft Conventions 147–8; legislation 149, 150–1; marine 116–17, 129, 158, 163–5, 166
exclusive economic zone (EEZ) 142, 143–5
Exeter, bombing of 58, 59–60
exploitation 42
export licensing 185–204, 262; EC Regulation No. 3911/92 190–3; United Kingdom 185–204, 282, 283; Waverley criteria 192, 195; Waverley Report 187–90, 202
Export Licensing Unit 191–2, 193, 195–6
extinction, archaeological 3–4
extradition, Hague Convention 1954 99–100
EZLN *see* Ejército Zapatista de Liberación Nacional

*facen*, cultural heritage 250–1
fakes *see* authenticity
Falk, R.A. 68–9
fetishes, Malian 253
field laboratories, conservation 170

First Protocol to the 1954 Hague Convention 75–6, 80, 82, 84
first-aid, conservation 170–3
forgeries 3, 29, 262, 286
free trade 15–17
Frontera Chols, Mexico 212–13

Gao Saney, Mali 252
*Geetainjili* 279
*Geldermalson* wreckage 4–5
Geneva Conventions 1925 51
Geneva Conventions 1949 61–4, 67, 73; Additional Protocols 1977 70, 79, 84
Geneva Conventions 1980 79
Getty Information Institute 284
Getty rules 35
Ghor es-Safi, Jordan 257–67
global patrimony 38
grave robbing 235–40; *see also* tomb robbing
Great Plague AD 541–570 258
Greek vases 23–37, 197
Green, J. 165, 166
Gulf Wars 69, 77–8

*habeas corpus* 282–3
Hague Convention 1899, 1907 47–9, 63, 65, 75; breaches 54; military necessity 67, 68, 83–4
Hague Convention, Rules of Air Warfare 1923, 1925 51, 56, 69
Hague Convention 1954 7–8, 10, 54, 64–76, 77–8; breaches 80, 98; First Protocol 75–6, 80, 82, 84; Second Protocol 1999 82–6, 91–108, 285; special protection 55, 69, 72, 75, 95–8
Hague Convention 1970 78
Harris, Sir Arthur 58–9
Hattatt, R. 34
headpots, Native American 236
heritage 9–10; *see also* underwater cultural heritage; *facen* 250–1; shipwrecks 109–36; treaties 46–53; zones 144
historical prerogative 112–13
Hitler, Adolf 56
Hitler art squads 44
HMS *Birkenhead* wreckage 113, 114
Horses of St Mark's, Venice 43–4
*huaqueros* 1, 12

*I-52* wreckage 5, 137
IADAA *see* International Association of Dealers in Ancient Art
ICA *see* International Council on Archives
ICBS *see* International Committee of the Blue Shield
ICCROM *see* International Centre for Conservation, Rome
ICOM *see* International Council of Museums
ICOMOS *see* International Council on Monuments and Sites
ICRC *see* International Committee of the Red Cross
identity 208–10, 211–12, 251, 254
IFLA *see* International Federation of Library Associations and Institutions
ILA *see* Buenos Aires Draft Convention; International Law Association
IMO *see* International Maritime Organization; International Museums Office
Import, Export and Customs Powers (Defence) Act (1939) 188
*in situ* preservation 150–1, 158, 165, 166; shipwrecks 109, 116–18, 121–2, 126–8, 130–1
INAH *see* Instituto Nacional de Antropología e Historia
India 268–79
Indian National Trust for Art and Cultural Heritage (INTACH) 277
indigenous populations 208–10, 211–12, 229, 235
Institute of Archaeology Services Division 294–6
Instituto Nacional de Antropología e Historia (INAH), Mexico 212
INTACH *see* Indian National Trust for Art and Cultural Heritage
intellectual property 152
International Association of Dealers in Ancient Art (IADAA) 283
International Centre for Conservation, Rome (ICCROM) 81–2, 85
International Committee of the Blue Shield (ICBS) 81–2, 83, 85, 95
International Committee of the Red Cross (ICRC) 77, 79, 82–3, 86

International Council on Archives (ICA) 81, 83, 85
International Council on Monuments and Sites (ICOMOS) 80–3, 85, 117, 127; Charter 1996 140, 150–4, 156–61, 166, 169
International Council of Museums (ICOM) 7, 35, 80–3, 85, 245; Code of Professional Ethics 18, 289, 295, 298; public awareness 284–5, 287, 298–9
International Federation of Library Associations and Institutions (IFLA) 81, 83, 85
International Law Association (ILA) 139–40; *see also* Buenos Aires Draft Convention
International Maritime Organization (IMO) 141
International Museums Office (IMO) 54, 56–8, 64
international treaties 47–53
international waters 127, 137, 138, 149
investment collecting 23, 24
'invisible' market 30, 31

Jenkins, Jolyon 282, 284
JNAPC *see* Joint Nautical Archaeology Policy Committee
Joint Nautical Archaeology Policy Committee (JNAPC) 164, 166
Jordan Valley Authority (JVA) 257–8, 263, 264
jurisdiction 98–9, 114, 138, 139–40, 143–5; *see also* law
JVA *see* Jordan Valley Authority

Khirbet Qazone, Jordan 264
Khmer ceramics 289
Khmer Rouge 6–7
Kuntur Wasi, Peru 12–13, 14

LAPADA *see* London and Provincial Antique Dealers Association
laundering 2, 3, 186, 202, 231–2
law 40, 282, 283–4, 297–8; *see also* jurisdiction; Argentinian 232–3; civil 8, 121–4, 128; common 1, 8, 121–4, 128; customary international 48, 59, 63; domestic 109, 114, 121–4, 128; finds 109–36, 120, 150; Hague

Conventions 66–7, 78, 80, 83, 92, 94; heritage protection 120, 122; Indian 269–72; international 3, 124–33, 140–1; international humanitarian 44–6, 61, 63; international waters 127, 137; Malian 242, 245–8; marine insurance 111; Mexican 205, 223, 225; national patrimony 2–3; private 283; salvage 122, 129–30, 149–50; United Kingdom 282–4, 297–8; United States 237–8, 237–9, 240

Lazrus, Paula 38–42

League of Nations 54, 55, 64

licensing *see* export licensing

Lieber Code 46–7, 67

London and Provincial Antique Dealers Association (LAPADA) Show 289–91

looting 23–4, 43, 187, 206, 244, 259–62; *see also* grave robbing; pillage; tomb robbing; art 44, 62; export licensing 199–200; free trade 16–17; graves 235–40; India 268–79; Mali 245–7, 250–6, 285, 286–7; marine sites 163, 165; Mesoamerica 206, 212, 231; metal detectors 181; pre-Hispanic monuments 214–19, 231; provenance 185, 200–1; South Italian vases 197–8; State-ordered 44, 49, 60, 62; to order 214–15, 246–7; treaties 46–53, 95, 98; wartime 6–8, 45

LOS Convention; Buenos Aires Convention 142–6; international waters 137–8, 142; jurisdiction 143–4; sovereign immunity 145–7

Lübeck, British bombing 58–9

*Lusitania* wreckage 117

McDonald Institute for Archaeological Research 277, 285

McIntosh, Susan Keech 241–9

Mali 3, 242, 245–8, 250–6, 285, 286–7

marine archaeology 115–18, 120, 153, 158–61; *see also* shipwrecks; underwater cultural heritage; conservation 162–78

*Mary Rose* museum 40, 115, 163–4

'Meet the Ancestors' Channel Four documentary 283

Merchant Shipping Act 1995 122, 123

Merryman, J.H. 8–9, 10, 65

*mestizo* (mixed-race) cultures 208–10

metal detection 179–84, 193, 299

Mexican Revolution 1910 208, 210

Mexico 205–27; cultural identity 208–10; tourism 211, 213, 219–26

MFA *see* Boston Museum of Fine Arts

MFAA *see* Monuments, Fine Arts and Archives units

military necessity 49, 67–70, 83–4, 93

military sites, shielding 95

MNA *see* Museo Nacional de Antropología

monolithic states 209, 210

Monuments, Fine Arts and Archives (MFAA) units 60–1, 64

moral philosophy 280

mound builders 235

Musée de l'Homme, Paris 252

Museo del Templo Mayor, Mexico 208–9

Museo Nacional de Antropología (MNA), Mexico 211–12

museums 23–4, 31–5, 180, 211–12, 239–40, 244–5; cultural identity 208–9; looting 45, 235; protection 52–3, 55–6, 63–4, 66

NAGPRA *see* Native American Grave Protection and Repatriation Act

Nalda, Enrique 205–27

*Nataraja* bronze images 273–5

National Academy of Fine Arts, Argentina 233

National Hellenic Research Foundation, Athens 264

National Museum of Fine Arts, Argentina 229

national treasures 188, 190

Native American Grave Protection and Repatriation Act (NAGPRA) 1990, US 237, 239

Native Americana 235–40

neozapatism 209, 212

neutral institutions, Roerich Pact 53

nighthawks 1, 181, 183

Nohmul, Belize 206

Nørskov, Vinnie 23–37

*Nuestra Señora de Atocha* wreckage 4–5

numismatics *see* coins

Nuremberg trials 62–3

Oaxaca, Mexico 212
O'Keefe, Patrick J. 137–61
One-Million-Dollar-Vase 23–4
ownership 8, 110–22, 128, 210–13, 282
Oxford Code 1880 47

Pachauri, S.K. 268–79
Palenque, Mexico 212, 213
Palmer enquiry 2000 189, 201; see also
  DCMS Ministry Advisory Panel
Palmer, Norman 281–2
patrimony, global 38
perfidy, cultural property 51, 59–60, 79,
  95
pillage 43–4, 70–1, 98, 241, 244–7,
  250–67; see also looting
Politis, Konstantinos D. 257–67
pothunters 236–7
pottery, Bronze Age 257, 259, 262, 289,
  291
poverty, looting 259–62
pre-Hispanic cultures, Mexico 200,
  205–27, 231
pre-Hispanic monuments 214–19, 231;
  Chichén Itzá 207, 221, 224; Oaxaca
  212; Palenque 212, 213; Quitovac
  211; Sipán 243–4; Teotihuacán 211,
  215, 220–1, 223; Tulum 221–2;
  Xcaret 221–3; Yaxchilán 212–13
preservation see conservation; in situ
  preservation
professional ethics 5, 17–19
Professional Shipwreck Explorers
  Association, Inc. (ProSEA) 151–2
project management 153, 158–61
property 8, 9–10, 43–108, 121–2,
  282
ProSEA see Professional Shipwreck
  Explorers Association, Inc.
prosecution, Hague Convention 1954
  99
protection 43–108; armed conflict 77–8,
  83, 91–108; civil disturbance 54;
  Geneva Conventions 1949 63–4;
  Hague Conventions 47–9, 51, 64–76;
  Protocols 76–87, 91–108; Roerich
  Pact 1935 47, 52–3; World War II
  54–61
Protection of Antiquities Act 1951,
  Norway 148–9
Protection of Wrecks Act 1973 114, 123

provenance; certificates 290, 297;
  conservation 173–4; ethics 299;
  Euphronios krater 24; export licensing
  185–6, 191, 192, 197, 200–2; Greek
  vases 24, 26–8, 35, 36; looting 3, 185,
  200–1, 244–5; Native Americana
  238–9, 240; Roman coins 182; UK
  legislation 282, 284, 297–8; Waverley
  Report 189
public awareness 11–13, 38–42, 85, 161,
  277, 284–5; see also education; ethics
  287, 288–9, 296, 298–300
pueblo ruins 235

Quitovac, Mexico 211

reburial, in situ preservation 165, 166
reconstruction 206–7
Red Cross see International Committee
  of the Red Cross
religious symbols see cultural symbols
relocation 94
repatriation see restitution
replication 10–11, 273
respect, Hague Convention 1954 66–7,
  70–1, 93–4
restitution 49–50, 61, 239–40, 244, 274,
  278
restoration 168, 169–70, 206, 207
RMS Titanic see Titanic
RMS Titanic Inc. 138, 152
Roerich, N.K. 52
Roerich Pact 1935 47, 52–3, 70, 75
Roman sites 180–2
Rules of Air Warfare, Hague
  Convention 1923, 1925 56

safeguarding, Hague Convention 1954
  66–7, 71–2, 93
Safi tombstones 263, 264
St Mark's horses, Venice 43–4
Salisbury Hoard 180, 193
salvage 5, 109–10, 119–21, 138–9, 153,
  158–61; see also commercial salvage;
  excavation; conservation issues
  119–20, 162–3, 164–6
Salvage Association 111
San Andrés Larrainzar agreements 211
Sanctuary of Lot, Jordan 258, 262, 264
Schávelzon, Daniel 228–34
Schneider, J.T. 52–3

SCOPA *see* Standing Conference on
  Portable Antiquities
screening regulations 187
Second Protocol to the 1954 Hague
  Convention (1999) 82–6, 91–108,
  285
Sevso treasure 287
Shah Jehan's Palace, Agra 272
shipwrecks 4–5, 109–36; *see also* marine
  archaeology; underwater cultural
  heritage; access 127, 162; coastal 109,
  113, 142; conservation 5, 162–78;
  deep sea 110, 121, 137–8, 142,
  162–3; *in situ* preservation 109,
  116–18, 121–2, 126–8, 130–1;
  international waters 114, 121, 127;
  law of finds 120; legislation 137–61;
  ownership 110–21; salvage 5, 109–10,
  119–21, 130, 153, 158–61; tourism
  14
Sipán royal tombs, Peru 243–4
SITC *see* Standard International Trade
  Classification
Sivagurunathaswamy temple, India
  274–5
slash-and-burning 215–16
smuggling 78, 95, 250, 278
Sodom and Gomorrah 258
Sophism 280
source countries 1–2
sourcing *see* provenance
South Italian vases 28–30, 34, 197–8,
  200
sovereign immunity 145–7
Spanish Civil War 54, 55, 58
Spanish galleons 113–14, 119–20,
  146–7
special protection, Hague Convention
  1954 55, 69, 72, 75, 95–8
Spencer-Churchill, Captain E.G. 32–4
spiritual heritage 79
sport diving 109–10, 118, 123
SS *Central America see Central America*
Standard International Trade
  Classification (SITC) 198–9
Standing Conference on Portable
  Antiquities (SCOPA) 181
'Stealing History: the Illicit Trade in
  Cultural Material' report 284–5
Strati, A. 122
succession, ownership 112–13

sustainability 4, 15, 40
Sutherland, Amanda J. 162–78

Tagore, Rabindranath 279
Taj gardens, India 272
Taliban 6
*tells*, Mali 252
temple fragments 194
temple idols 273–5, 276
Teotihuacán, Mexico 211, 215, 220–1,
  223
terracotta figures, Mali 3, 286
theft to order 165, 228–9, 233 4
thermoluminescence dating 286–7
Thornes, Robin 284
'Time Team' Channel Four
  Documentary 285
*Titanic* 5, 117, 137, 138, 139
'to order' looting 214–15, 246–7
Togola, Téréba 250–6, 285
Toman, Jiri 64
tomb robbing 29, 30, 40–1, 186,
  257–67; *see also* grave robbing;
  looting
*tombaroli* 1, 24, 30, 39, 41
tombstones, Safi 263, 264
Tondidrou megaliths, Mali 252
total embargo regulations 187
tourism 13–15, 118, 157, 206, 267;
  conservation 219–26; ecological
  damage 215–16, 220, 224; Mexico
  211, 213, 219–26
trafficking 78, 200, 219, 295, 296
Treasure Act 1996 179, 181
treasure hunting 115–16, 118, 119–21,
  179–84; *see also* looting
treasure troves 179, 181, 190
treaties, cultural property 45–53, 59
Treaty of Versailles 1919 49–50
Treaty of Westphalia 1648 45
Tubb, Kathryn Walker 280–300
Tulum, Mexico 221–2

UKIC *see* United Kingdom Institute for
  Conservation of Historic and Artistic
  Works
UNCLOS *see* LOS Convention
underwater cultural heritage 114–15,
  122, 137–61, 158; *see also* cultural
  heritage; shipwrecks; legislation
  109–36

UNESCO 61–2, 74, 78, 80, 101–6,
    278–9; *see also* Hague Conventions;
    UNESCO Conventions; underwater
    cultural heritage 110, 140–2;
    World Heritage Convention 1972
    78
UNESCO Convention 1970, cultural
    property 1, 185, 241–9, 255, 262;
    Indian implementation 268–9, 271,
    276; international 17–18, 19, 247;
    provenance 24; United Kingdom
    281–6, 288–9, 296–8; US
    implementation 241–9
UNESCO Convention 1972, cultural
    heritage 10
UNESCO Convention 1998,
    underwater cultural heritage 166
UNESCO Convention 1999 Draft,
    underwater cultural heritage 5, 10, 19,
    126–33, 140–2
UNIDROIT Convention 1995 10, 19,
    185, 271; Indian implementation 271;
    United Kingdom 281–6, 288–9, 296,
    297–8
United Kingdom Institute for
    Conservation of Historic and Artistic
    Works (UKIC) 281
United Nations Convention on the
    Law of the Sea 1982 *see* LOS
    Convention
United Nations Division of Ocean
    Affairs and Law of the Sea
    (DOALOS) 141
universalization 209

vandalism 60, 70–1, 77, 80, 163, 235;
    cultural symbols 44, 74, 80, 285; pre-
    Hispanic monuments 214–19; treaties
    47–53, 70–1, 95, 98
*Vasa* museum 115
vases; Greek 23–37; South Italian 28–30,
    34
Vatican City special protection zone 69
Villehardouin, G. de 44
visual pollution 220, 223–4
Viswanathaswamy temple, India 273–4
Vitelli, K.D. 9

war *see* protection
war crimes 62–3, 70, 80, 84–5
war trophies 43
warships, sovereign immunity 145–6
wartime looting 6–8, 45
*Wasa* wreckage 163–4
Waverley criteria 192, 195
Waverley Report, the (1952) 187–90,
    202
Weary Herakles statue 2
wet-storage 172
World Heritage Convention 1972 78,
    83–4

X-radiography 167, 172
Xcaret, Mexico, amusement park 221–3

Yaxchilán, Mexico 212–13

Zapatista movement, Mexico 211
Zoar, Jordan 258–9, 267, 291